D1520393

RESEARCH IN PHILOSOPHY & TECHNOLOGY

Volume 10 • 1990

TECHNOLOGY AND RELIGION

Research in Philosophy & Technology

General Editor
Frederick Ferré
Department of Philosophy
The University of Georgia

<table>
<tr><td>

European Editor
Walter Ch. Zimmerli
Lehrstuhl für Philosphie II
Otto-Friedrich Universität, Bamberg

</td><td>

Review Editor
Leonard J. Waks
Science, Technology and Society Program
The Pennsylvania State University

</td></tr>
</table>

Editor Assistants
Helene Brittain and Lora McDonald-Lanier
The University of Georgia

Editorial Board

RESEARCH IN PHILOSOPHY & TECHNOLOGY

A Research Annual

TECHNOLOGY AND RELIGION

Editor: FREDERICK FERRÉ
Department of Philosophy
The University of Georgia

VOLUME 10 • 1990

 JAI PRESS INC.

Greenwich, Connecticut   *London, England*

Copyright © 1990 JAI PRESS INC.
55 Old Post Road, No. 2
Greenwich, Connecticut 06830

JAI PRESS LTD.
118 Pentonville Road
London N1 9JN
England

ISBN: 1-55938-062-4

Manufactured in the United States of America

CONTENTS

COLLOQUIUM SECTION

CONTEMPORARY DISCUSSION SECTION

REVIEW SECTION

BOOK REVIEWS

LIST OF CONTRIBUTORS

Waldo Beach

The Divinity School
Duke University

Albert Borgmann

Department of Philosophy
University of Montana

Michael J. Carella

Department of Philosophy
San Diego State University

Charles Dyke

Department of Philosophy
Temple University

Darrell J. Fasching

Department of Religious Studies
University of South Florida

Frederick Ferré

Department of Philosophy
University of Georgia

Robert C. Good

Department of Philosophy
Rider College

Jim Grote

St. Vincent de Paul Society

Frank R. Harrison, III

Department of Philosophy
University of Georgia

David A. Hoekema

American Philosophical Assoc.
University of Delaware

William B. Jones

Department of Philosophy
Old Dominion University

Martin H. Krieger

School of Urban & Regional Planning
University of Southern California

Steven Lee   Department of Philosophy
                                          Hobart and William Smith
                                          Colleges

Charles Mabee   Department of Religious Studies
                                          Marshall University

A. Warren Matthews   Department of Philosophy
                                          Old Dominion University

Carl Mitcham   Philosophy & Technology Studies
                                          Polytechnic University

Robert C. Neville   School of Theology
                                          Boston University

David Novak   Department of Religious Studies
                                          University of Virginia

John F. Post   Department of Philosophy
                                          Vanderbilt University

Friedrich Rapp   Philosophie und Technologie
                                          University of Dortmund

Larry Rasmussen   Union Theological Seminary

Thomas Rogers   Department of Philosophy
                                          California Polytechnic State University

James F. Salmon   Society of Jesus
                                          Maryland Province

David E. Schrader   Department of Philosophy
                                          Washington and Jefferson College

David C. Snyder   Department of Philosophy
                                          Calvin College

J. Mark Thomas   Au Sable Institute of
                                          Environmental Studies

Jane Mary Trau

Department of Philosophy &
Religious Studies
Barry University

Gabriel Vahanian

Faculté de Théologie
Protestante
Université de Strasbourg

A. Arnold Wettstein

Department of Religion
Rollins College

GENERAL EDITOR'S INTRODUCTION

This is the second in our series of theme issues. Volume 9 began the series with "Technology and Ethics." The call for papers on "Technology and Religion" for Volume 10, in turn, was productive of an impressive outpouring of manuscripts. It is worth reflecting on what they reveal about the current state of philosophical thinking on the relationships between these great phenomena of human life.

The taxonomy with which this volume opens (Jones and Matthews), might be used by readers to give some broad perspective on what was and was not done by our contributors. Conversely, reflecting on the proposed taxonomy, after reading these articles, might give a basis for evaluating the categories themselves for applicability and completeness. This interesting dual task is what an early version of this Editor's Introduction began by attempting, but it soon became clear that this was too much to try in such a brief context. I leave it for readers to do for themselves. Doing it might suggest a number of areas in which new essays for future volumes might usefully be written.

The contributions to the Theme Section of this volume are a varied lot, carrying out our announced aim at providing a forum for the widest possible spectrum of philosophical approaches and interests. Topics are varied, as well, including, after the aforementioned proposed taxonomy, an analysis of theology and "Star Wars" (Wettstein), a Jewish meditation on nuclear weapons (Novak), two studies of television evangelism (Beach and Good), an examination of technology as a religion (Thomas), a confrontation with Lynn White's accusations against the Judeo-Christian tradition (Harrison), an evocation of biblical resources for technological social problems (Rasmussen), critiques and appreciations of Jacques Ellul (Mabee and Fasching), a probe into Christianity and Artificial Intelligence (Vahanian), a high metaphysical perspective on technology (Neville), and two examinations of technology as source of temptations (Schrader and Krieger). Unity amid all this diversity comes from the common attempt of all these authors to draw together what is often left unrelated. For the most part, as well, their articles are similar in resisting any simple "pro" or "con" stance toward the technological phenomenon. All recognize that we have a deep issue before us, and most write with the awareness that any serious engagement of religion with technology is likely to leave both—and with them our social and natural environments— significantly altered.

Our Colloquium Section, containing the proceedings of a program of the Society of Christian Philosophers, held in conjunction with the Eastern Division of the American Philosophical Association in New York, December, 1987, continues the theme of technology, particularly human reproductive biotechnology and religion (Trau), with an explicit opening, as well, into philosophy of science and religious language (Post). Colloquium sections like these are not planned as a regular feature of *Research in Philosophy and Technology,* but if suitable programs of this sort are submitted, particularly if arrangements can be made in advance, they will be considered for future volumes.

Our Contemporary Discussion Section, in which we plan to publish articles of current interest, regardless of topic, this time contains two articles which might, by stretching, have appeared in the Theme Section. One is on myths and the "medicalization" of contemporary culture (Carella); the other is on technology and communities of celebration (Borgmann). Since the bane of theme sections is dilution, however, we present them, despite their obvious pertinence to technology and religion, without forcing them in any special direction.

Finally, we introduce an innovation in the history of this Annual: a book review section. Our Editorial Board agreed that despite the infrequent appearance of our publication, it would be unfortunate not to provide notices and evaluations of the books appearing in our growing field. Therefore, with the able energies of Leonard Waks enlisted as Book Review Editor, we now add this function to our others. It was Waks's idea to provide symposia of reviews with replies by the authors. We hope that this innovation will be both helpful and pleasing to our readers.

Our next volume will have "Technology and Politics" as its theme. We shall hope also to have fuller transatlantic representation of authors in Volume 11, thanks to another innovation, the addition of a European Editor in the person of Walther Ch. Zimmerli. Readers in Europe are encouraged to submit article proposals and papers directly to the European Editor for more expeditious handling of queries and refereeing. There are thoughts currently of adding other editors from other parts of the world, particularly a Latin American Editor and an Asian Editor. Volunteers and nominations are welcome.

It would be wrong to end without a heartfelt word of thanks to Helene Brittain, Assistant to the Editor, and to her successor, Lora McDonald-Lanier, who labored well over the many details required in receiving, refereeing, and revising the articles that went into this volume. Technological changes at JAI Press, Inc., our publisher, have added to the excitement for Brittain and McDonald-Lanier, whose expertise with word processing software and multiformatted diskettes has been important for all concerned. Thanks also are due to Deans W. Jackson Payne and John J. Kozak, of the College of Arts and Sciences at the University of Georgia, for providing office space, equipment, and salary for this sine qua non assistance.

—Frederick Ferré
General Editor

THEME SECTION

TOWARD A TAXONOMY OF TECHNOLOGY AND RELIGION

William B. Jones and A. Warren Matthews

Recent studies of technology have demonstrated that technology is not simply "applied science" (Volti, 1988, pp. 54-66). It follows that the relationship of technology and religion can (and must) be considered a separate issue from the relationship between science and religion. Thus, not only can one *not* assume that the same patterns of conflicts and alliances hold between technology and religion as hold between science and religion, one cannot even assume that the *categories* developed in discussions of relationships of one pair are appropriate for discussions of the other.

Would-be students of the relationship between technology and religion thus find themselves in a situation not unlike that faced by pre-Linnean botanists and zoologists who possessed neither a satisfactory system for organizing the vast array of information confronting them, nor a reliable criterion for distinguishing crucial data from inessential facts. Of course, solutions to these problems came only with Darwin's theory and the advent of evolutionary taxonomy (Ruse, 1973, pp. 122f). Viewing the matter retrospectively, one can

Research in Philosophy and Technology, Volume 10, pages 3-23.
Copyright © 1990 by JAI Press Inc.
All rights of reproduction in any form reserved.
ISBN: 1-55938-062-4

see that the early biologists faced a dilemma: they needed the yet-to-be-developed theoretical structure in order to know which data to collect and how to put it in meaningful order; on the other hand, a significant amount of data had to be collected and organized before the theory could emerge. A particularly troublesome aspect of situations like this is the danger of (prematurely) fastening upon an inadequate theory, with the result that vital data remains uncollected and crucial connections unexplored, while insignificant facts are amassed and unilluminating relationships studied.

Two aspects of this episode in the history of biology are worthy of note in the present context: (1) meaningful empirical investigation of phenomena did take place prior to the availability of a truly satisfactory theory to guide it; and (2) both overall schemes and individual classifications, worked out at one time, subsequently were altered as more facts were assembled, and more powerful theoretical structures developed. While there is no guarantee that things will work out as well in the long run with the present topic as they did in case of biology, there would appear to be no alternative to following a course paralleling that followed by the biologists; students of technology and religion must make as systematic a study of the relationships between these two as is possible without the benefit of a unified viewpoint like that which guided post-Darwinian taxonomists. In doing so, they must at all times stand ready to reevaluate the results of their efforts, both with respect to completeness and with respect to systematic adequacy, and, in particular, they must beware of becoming too rigidly attached too soon to a given scheme.

Implicit in the above discussion is the view that the very *nature* of the study being embarked upon [i.e., the study of the relation(s) between technology and religion] is not fixed and determinant, but may evolve into something quite unintended and even unimagined by those helping to launch it. Scholars familiar with the work of Thomas Kuhn (1970) will not find the suggestion of such an eventuality surprising. To make this point is not, however, to assert that the enterprise being undertaken will or should become a science, but to call attention to a common property of all such intellectual endeavors, including the sciences. Certainly, humanists will have no trouble with the suggestion that it may, on occasion, be worthwhile to undertake an investigation of a question for which there is no agreed-upon methodology and no clear notion of the nature of the likely result. Indeed, it is characteristic of the humanities that such should be the case. Students of philosophy, in particular, are accustomed to disagreement concerning fundamentals, and to the emergence not only of unexpected answers but of unanticipated issues and questions leading to new lines of inquiry. The open character of the present enterprise is further guaranteed by its evident need to draw upon the resources of a variety of disciplines: philosophy, history, anthropology, sociology, religious studies, etc., with their differing methodologies, commitments, and goals.

It might seem that the obvious first step toward developing a taxonomy would be to try to draw up an exhaustive list of possible relationships between technology and religion, and to look for examples of these among present and past religious traditions and technological activities. Subsequent analyses of the results of such a study would, one would hope, reveal patterns suggesting further lines of inquiry. Those familiar with the extensive discussion which has taken place during the last two or three decades under the general rubric "science, technology, and society" will realize right away that the matter has already advanced beyond such a simple, initial approach—not because a sophisticated taxonomy of technology and religion has already been worked out, but because the relationships between technology, on the one hand, and social institutions, values, and human affairs generally, on the other, have been examined sufficiently to make clear that the really crucial issues in the area have to do with technological *innovation,* whether it be outright invention, or the transfer of technology from one culture to another. Clearly, every device or process ever put to use had to be developed sometime, somewhere, and had to be brought into those societies which utilized but did not invent it. Again and again, technological innovations have made a major impact upon human societies and have played a central role in the overall process of sociocultural evolution (Lenski and Lenski, 1974, p. 79).

Consequently, it appears likely that the most interesting and important relationships between technology and religion pertain to technological innovation, and thus that the most fruitful and illuminating classificatory scheme(s) will reflect the central role of innovation. Indeed, most examples of relationships elicited by the phrase "technology and religion" are likely to be cases of a religious tradition reacting to a technological innovation, a religious tradition contributing to a social climate fostering (or inhibiting) technological innovation, or some technological innovation having an impact upon a religious institution or value. Any classificatory scheme that aspires to comprehensiveness must provide for the possibility of significant relationships between technology and religion which did not involve innovation. Accordingly, the first main category in the classificatory system put forward here encompasses relationships that hold under conditions of technological stability. The second and third main categories encompass, respectively, cases in which a religious tradition takes some action toward, or has some effect upon, technological innovation(s), and cases in which technological innovation affects a religious institution, practice, or value.

TECHNOLOGY AND RELIGION IN THE ABSENCE OF TECHNOLOGICAL INNOVATION

The question of just which types of relationships, holding between technology and religion in the absence of technological innovation, are worthy of attention and study is more subtle than it might first appear. The exclusion of technological innovation implies that the technology being considered must have been established in the relevant society for quite some time—else one would be dealing with a case of technological innovation, and so must the religion—or one would be dealing with a case of religious tradition confronting a technology that is *novel to it,* which occurs, for example, when a religion spreads into a region in which the technology is present. This possibility is discussed below along with the related case of a novel technology being brought into a region in which a religion is established.

A possible, but uninteresting, kind of relationship that may exist between a technology and a religious tradition in such a static situation is mutual noninteraction, neither having any discernible effect on the other. In the most extreme case (Appendix, I-0-1), the religious tradition shows no awareness of or ignores the technology. In a less extreme case (I-0-2), the religious tradition shows an awareness of the technology, e.g., by referring to an object or activity in its sacred writings, but takes no stance with regard to it, and has no discernible effect upon it and vice versa. Instances of the first type (I-0-1) may exist, but it would be difficult to demonstrate that they do. Reference to a technological practice in a sacred writing may be the only available evidence of its existence at a certain time and in a given culture. Such cases are, by definition, excluded from category I-0-1. Furthermore, noninteraction is very difficult to prove, especially in the absence of even a rudimentary theory of sociotechnological phenomena. No attempt is made here to establish either the existence or the significance of members of these two classes (I-0-1 and I-0-2).

A more interesting cagetory (I-0-3) involves the acceptance of an established technology by a religious tradition. For example, writing has been practiced in many cultures for so long that the question of its origins either is not raised, or is addressed on a mythological level. Indeed, writing has been around for so long that some may be reluctant to classify it as a technology at all. If one reflects, however, upon the practical significance of record keeping in ancient Babylonian society (Childe, 1951, pp. 122f) and upon the impression which "papers that talk" made upon native Americans at the dawn of the colonial period, and then compares these to the significance of computerized data processing and "wireless" (radio, TV, microwave) transmissions in contemporary America, such reservations will vanish. Nearly all major world religions have availed themselves of this technology, as is evidenced by the importance to each of them of sacred writings.

Another example of the acceptance of a technology by a religious tradition is provided by the Japanese sword, the making of which is a religious ritual. In his widely acclaimed *The Ascent of Man,* Jacob Bronowski depicts the making of such a sword in the temple workshop at Nara (Bronowski, 1973, pp. 131f). Wielding these swords, the fiercesome samurai were the sinews of

Japanese society during the feudal period, a society in which the religious order presiding over the making of the swords had a special place. Instances of such mutual involvement and support by a technology and a religion fall into the overlap region of the category under discussion (I-0-3) and another (I-0-4), which encompasses cases in which an established technology supports some religious institution or value.

A religious tradition may also reject or oppose the utilization of an established technology or its products (I-0-5). John Wesley's rejection of the use of the products of fermentation and distillation seems to qualify for this category. Knowledge of some of these processes is, of course, quite ancient and, by Wesley's time, had been exploited in England for centuries. Observing the destructive power of what would now be called "alcoholism," Wesley concluded that, while there was a place for the proper use of alcohol, the effects of its abuse were so ruinous that it was best avoided. In a sermon entitled "The Use of Money," he addresses the question of which kinds of work a Christian may engage in:

> Neither may we gain by hurting our neighbor *in his body*. Therefore we may not sell anything which tends to impair health. Such is, eminently, all that liquid fire, commonly called drams, or spirituous liquors. It is true, these may have a place in medicine . . . . But all who sell them in the common way, to any that will buy, are poisoners general.

Arguing that the destructiveness of alcohol far outweighs its benefits, Wesley concluded that mankind would be better off without it: "Distilled liquors have their use, but are infinitely overbalanced by the abuse of them; therefore, were it in my power, I would banish them out of the world." (Harmon, 1974, p. 2321). Eventually, a significant fraction of American Protestants embraced this conclusion.

It is also to be noted that if Wesley's argument is valid, then wine-making, ale-brewing, liquor-distilling, etc., are examples of category I-0-6, technologies that are destructive of religious institutions and values. Whether Wesley is correct on this point is not a question that we address in this chapter. Obviously, similar questions could be raised with respect to any technology cited as an example of I-0-6.

ACTIONS AND INFLUENCES OF RELIGION UPON TECHNOLOGICAL INNOVATION

A religion may encounter new technology through (a) geographical migration (either the new technology is brought into a society in which the religion is established, or the religion spreads into an area in which the technology is present), or (b) the invention of genuinely novel technologies in a society in which the religion is established. When a religious tradition encounters a technology that is genuinely novel or previously unknown in the culture of which it is a part, there are a number of stances it may assume. These possibilities are considered below, first with respect to genuinely novel technologies. It is also important to consider the effects which religious traditions may have upon technological innovation which are not direct, and not the result of overt or intentional actions taken by a religious group. These are considered in a third part of this section.

Stances Taken by Religious Traditions Toward Novel Technologies, Either Imported or Encountered Externally

First of all (II-A-1) the religious tradition may simply show no awareness of, or ignore, technologies which are different from those employed in the culture to which the religion is indigenous. The situation with regard to this category closely parallels that of the first category previously discussed; instances of it may exist, but it would be difficult to demonstrate that they do. Pretty much the same is true of category II-A-2. It is certainly possible for members of a religious tradition to be aware of unfamiliar technologies being utilized in other societies, but not to consider the possibility of their utilization in their own society. It would be difficult, however, to establish that a person or group was aware of some exotic technology, but did not even consider that it might be utilized in their own society. A possible instance of II-A-2 is provided by the Egyptian practice of embalming their dead leaders. The children of Israel who resided in Egypt knew of the Egyptian practice of embalming. Their patriarch Joseph died in Egypt and was embalmed by the Egyptians. When the Israelites left Egypt under the leadership of Moses they carried the coffin of Joseph with them. (Genesis 50:26 and Exodus 13:19). Nothing is said in these accounts concerning the possibility of the Israelites adopting this practice. Perhaps it did not occur to them to do so. Perhaps they lacked the required materials and skills. In any case, they did not make a practice of embalming their leaders in Biblical times. Eventually, at least, Judaism assumed a negative stance (category II-A-5, below) toward embalming. According to contemporary Judaism "The departed is to be laid to rest as quickly as possible. Embalming is to be avoided, unless the law requires it." (Tripp, 1982, p. 329).

If a technology is brought into a society and in time becomes widely used, the religious leaders of the society must inevitably become aware of it at some point, even if they take no stance regarding it. Obviously, such cases (which fall under category II-A-3) will be difficult to establish, not only because it is so hard to prove any negative existence claim but also because of the complexity of the matter in many cases: one might conclude after a major research effort that no identifiable position on a certain technology ever emerged in a particular religious tradition, even though various members of that tradition did assume stances on issues relating to it. For example, gunpowder, which was invented by the ancient Chinese, came into general use in warfare in Europe beginning in the fifteenth century. Gradually, after a number of refinements, it revolutionized warfare. Given its enormous destructive power, one might wonder whether the Church ever took a stand on its use. Clearly, one should not expect a simple answer to this question.

Finding instances in which a religious group or religious leader approves or promotes the utilization of a technology from another place (II-A-4) is not too difficult. A fascinating example is provided by Cotton Mather's championing of inoculation as a method of combating smallpox. A clergyman more often remembered for his unfortunate role in the Salem witch trials, Mather took a heroic stand against the overwhelming majority of Boston's physicians, led by Dr. William Douglass, during the spring and summer of 1721 (Harris, 1971, pp. 9-26; Boas and Boas, 1956, pp. 1-17; Morison, 1956, pp. 271-272). A member of the Royal Society, Mather had read in its *Philosophical Transactions* of the successful use of the technique in China and in Turkey. Earlier, one of his Negro slaves had related to him that the method was practiced in Africa and that he himself had undergone the procedure, having thus incurred a mild case of smallpox along with future immunity. Alarmed by the smallpox epidemic raging in Boston that summer, and spurned by nearly all of the city's physicians, Mather prevailed upon Dr. Zabdiel Boylston to try inoculation, which involved the gruesome procedure of transferring infectious matter from the open, running sores of a smallpox victim to an open cut in the flesh of the person being inoculated. Boylston inoculated his own son and two slaves. Subsequently, Mather had his ten-year-old son, Samuel, inoculated. All survived the epidemic.

The other physicians attacked the procedure in the newspapers and before the city magistrates, using both scientific and religious arguments. Five other clergymen joined Mather in a reply to the latter, but they were unable to stem the tide of public abuse that was directed at Boylston and Mather. Boylston was assaulted on the streets more than once. Arsonists attempted to burn his house, into which a bomb was thrown on one occasion, almost killing his wife. Mather was also the victim of public rancor. A bomb was thrown into his bedroom but did not explode.

Boylston continued to inoculate the increasing numbers of persons who sought the treatment as the epidemic continued. When it was over, 15% of the noninoculated who contracted the disease had died. And six of the 242 persons who had been inoculated, or 2.5%, had died. Boylston believed that some of these had probably become infected with the disease before being inoculated and that others of them, being quite elderly, had possibly died of unrelated causes. For his efforts, Boylston was invited to visit and to join the Royal Society, and to write an account of his struggle. Mather also prepared a written treatment of the matter for his friends in the Royal Society. In it, he advanced the view that the disease stemmed from tiny organisms, which entered the body through the respiratory system. Basically correct, Mather's hypothesis could not be vindicated until much later because the organisms in question are viruses, which are so extremely tiny they defied positive detection until much later.

Instances of the rejection of an alien technology by a religious tradition (II-A-5) are fairly common. Some are as old as Genesis. The ancestors of the ancient Israelites apparently were herdsmen. Their wanderings brought them into contact with settled, agricultural societies, but the possibility of adopting this mode of existence did not receive the approval of their religious tradition. In the story of Cain, who tilled the soil, and Abel, who herded sheep (Genesis 4:1-16), Jehovah approves of Abel's offering from his flocks but rejects Cain's offering of crops. Scholars, for example, Speiser, in *The Anchor Bible* (Speiser, 1964, p. 31), and Robinson, in *The Abingdon Bible Commentary* (Robinson, 1929, p. 224), generally interpret this story in terms of the conflict between the pastoral and agricultural ways of life. When the children of Israel settled in the Promised Land following the Exodus from Egypt, they faced the problem in an acute form because the practice of agricultural technology, which they learned from the Canaanites living there, was interwoven with religious rituals, just as was the making of the Japanese sword. Unable to disentangle material technology from religious observances, the Israelite settlers had little choice but to adopt the entire package. Thus, writes Theodore H. Robinson, in his *A History of Israel,* "Along with the material side of Palestinian civilization, the tribes have taken over the religious views and practices of their predecessors, practically *en block* " (Robinson, 1932, p. 167). How could they have known which elements of this package were essential to growing crops—no matter which god's blessing was invoked—and which could be replaced by some corresponding element of their own religion (assuming there was one)? Participating in Baal worship, however, was a threat to Yahweh worship, and to the very fabric of their society. This conflict shows itself in the story of Gideon (Judges 6:25-32), who, for religious motives, destroyed his father's altar to Baal and the nearby Asherah pole, a Canaanite device which his father and the other men of the village had employed in the practice of agriculture-cum-Baal-worship.

The experience of the children of Israel with agricultural technology is especially interesting for present purposes in that while there is no question that it constitutes an instance of a society confronting a new but preexisting technology, its status in other respects is not so clear. It is not a case of technology being transferred into an established society and there having an impact upon its religious institutions and values, as happened with Western technology in Japan. On the other hand, it is not really a case of a religion spreading into new geographical regions and confronting the institutions and values associated with technologies utilized there, as happened with Buddhism,

Christianity, and Islam. The issues here have not to do with the spread of Yahweh worship among the Canaanites. Rather, the Yahweh-worshipping Israelites migrated into a region in which was practiced a technology novel to them. The question is, are the differences between these three kinds of situations significant? Should there be separate categories for them in the taxonomic scheme? These questions illustrate the point made at the outset that the structure of a taxonomy depends upon the content of the relevant field. Only detailed scholarly endeavors can provide the answers. In the initial, tentative scheme put forward herein, the three are simply grouped together as II-A.

Not only is the rejection of alien technologies by religious traditions as old as Genesis, it is a major theme in modern history. As Western industrial technology has spread around the globe, it has frequently aroused the opposition of established religious traditions and their leaders. Such opposition is, perhaps, best exemplified by Mahatma Gandhi (at once holy man and political leader), his spinning wheel, and his goats. And, unless human society becomes completely homogenized globally, it is likely to remain an important theme in the future.

Stances Taken by Religious Traditions Toward Inventions, Technologies Newly Devised in Societies in Which the Religion is Indigenous or Established

Overall, most technological innovations that human societies have to deal with undoubtedly involve technological transfer, in which a society is confronted with a preexisting technology that is novel to it. After all, a device or process only has to be invented once in order to be available for use. But it does have to be invented at some time and place and may be invented repeatedly at different times and places. Thus, invention lies at the very heart of the entire technological process, and that of sociocultural evolution, as Lenski terms it (Lenski and Lenski, 1974, p. 79). The stances which religious traditions may assume toward genuinely novel technologies or inventions parallel closely those which may be assumed with respect to alien technologies. First of all, there simply may be no awareness of a particular invention or of invention generally (II-B-1). Instances of this category may exist, but demonstrating that they do would, again, be very difficult. In contrast, given the fevered pace at which novel materials, processes, and devices are produced concurrenty, many must surely come to the attention of religious leaders and groups in one context or another without any position being taken regarding them (II-B-2). Here, the key issue evidently is which of these categories is significant.

A religious leader or tradition may (a) be aware of a specific invention or of the possibility of a certain kind of invention, and (b) promote or mention favorably its use or development, (II-B-3). Indeed, a religious tradition may provide both the intellectual framework and the sense of mission that leads to a new product or process. An example is provided by the wandering Chinese sage, Ko Hung (AD 253-333), of the Taoist tradition, whose chief article of faith seems to have been that one could attain health, longevity, and even immortality by virtuous living and a very special diet (Ware, 1966). Accordingly, he collected information about roots and plants, their dietary and medicinal uses, and the derivation or healing and health-insuring drugs from them. He compiled an enormous amount of material but accepted others' reports too uncritically and did not seem to appreciate the need for controlled experimentation. Thus, while some of his recommendations were harmless and some were truly beneficial, others were lethal!

Fascinated, as many have been, by the incorruptibility of gold, its immunity to corrosion and decay, Ko Hung was convinced that a proper combination of it with mercury would insure immortality, emnabling one to fly off to heaven. Not surprisingly, he engaged in alchemy, using its techniques to produce a poor man's substitute for gold, a combination of reconverted cinnabar and gold fluid. He left a recipe for producing a purple powder that would, supposedly, turn molten lead into gold. Just as their counterparts in the West, Chinese alchemists and allied investigators and workers developed a number of processes and procedures for preparing and purifying various substances. For example, in Ko Hung's time, they were using saltpeter (potassium nitrate) to dissolve cinnabar (mercuric sulfide) into a watery solution (Temple, 1986, p. 226). By Ko Hung's time, charcoal was being used in heating to purify various substances. By the second century AD, the Chinese were obtaining pure sulfur from"fool's gold" (iron pyrites) by roasting. For present purposes, the significant thing about Ko Hung's quest is that it combines the practical, the ethical, and the religious in such a way that a religious sanction is given to the search for new chemical techniques.

Another invention which seems to have been prompted by the needs of a religious tradition is printing. While most Westerners will think immediately of Gutenberg and his famous Bibles, the reference here is to the sacred texts of the Buddhists which began to be printed in China early in the eighth century AD. Proto-printing techniques such as ink rubbings from stone carvings seem to have created a tide of rising expectations, as more and more of the faithful aspired to have copies of the scriptures in their homes. The Buddhists simply had to have more copies of their sacred texts than could be produced by proto-printing and hand-copying. The technique which emerged was block-printing, done with hand-carved wooden blocks, one for each page of text. The earliest extant printed text in the world is a Buddhist charm scroll printed in China between 704 and 752 AD. It was found at Kyongju, Korea, in 1966 (Temple, 1986, pp. 110-111). The first complete printed book is also a Buddhist text, the *Diamond Sutra,* translated into Chinese. It bears the date of its printing, corresponding to May 11, 868 AD. The perfectly preserved scroll was found in "The Caves of the Thousand Buddhas" near Tun-Huang in 1907 by Sir Aurel Stein (Temple, 1986, p. 112). Movable type was tried in China during the eleventh century, but because of the large number of Chinese characters, it did not enjoy the success it met when introduced in Europe in the fifteenth century (Silverberg, 1969, pp. 83-86).

Rejection of, or opposition to, a new technological device or process by a religious tradition, organization, or leader (II-B-4) has been so common in the West since the industrial revolution that it seems a natural part of the landscape, not unlike the on-going conflict between science and religion, to which it is related, and with which it is often confused. In North America, the religious groups best known for their rejection of new technologies are the Mennonites, the Amish, and related groups. The Amish are the most strict. They seek to separate themselves from the world and to lead a simple life, freed of its enticements. In Pennsylvania, they are called "the plain people" because of their simple unadorned style of dress and mode of life. Typically, they are farmers, tilling the soil with horses, which also provide their only transportation. The use of electricity and telephones is forbidden. Education is permitted only through the eighth grade (Sweet, 1950, pp. 102-103; Clark, 1949, pp. 146-147, 349). Crudely put, their rejection of technological innovations made since their religious community became established seems to involve three elements: (1) a desire to avoid contact and involvement with human society at large; (2) a desire to lead a simple, austere life without luxury or ostentation; and (3) a mind-set or psychological stance characterized by a reluctance to change established patterns and habits—illustrated by the Amish of Iowa who, despite having lived there for a long time, maintain the clothing of German peasants (Clark, 1949, pp. 146-147).

Other religious traditions which are widely known for their opposition to the utilization of new technologies are much more selective in what they oppose or reject. Members of certain Pentecostal, Holiness, or Church of God groups refuse modern drugs and medical treatment, but generally make full use of modern means of transportation and communication. The opposition of the Roman Catholic Church to the fertility and birth-control technologies developed in recent decades is well known. However, it avails itself fully of modern transportation and communication technologies, and generally gives its blessings to medicine's attempts to heal and to alleviate suffering.

The U.S. Catholic Bishops have also taken a stand against nuclear weapons in a "Pastoral Letter on War and Peace" (Murnion, 1983, p. 290). In it they oppose: any "first use" of nuclear weapons, any "limited exchange" (because of the likelihood of escalation), and any use of nuclear weapons on population centers or civilian targets. They declare that deterrence policies are acceptable only on a strictly conditioned basis, and call for a negotiated halt of testing, production, and deployment of new nuclear weapons and deep cuts in existing nuclear arsenals. Much earlier (1957), the World Council of Churches, which includes as members Protestant, Anglican, and Eastern Orthodox churches, had taken a stand against nuclear warfare and weapons testing, and for the abolition of war and disarmament (Hiebert, 1961, p. 245). These two church groups faced the question of what would constitute an acceptable *use* of a nuclear weapon, could not give a positive answer, and concluded that efforts should be made to reduce or eliminate them.

Indirect or Unintended Influences of Religion Upon Technology

The indirect influences of religion upon technology are much more difficult to identify than the more-or-less direct effects considered thus far. Once suggested, they are much harder to confirm, especially in the absence of a comprehensive theory of sociotechnological phenomena. Even so, some interesting theses have been put forward which should be noted here, not because they constitute the final truth on some matter, but because they illustrate both the type of interaction that falls under the rubric and the kind of tentative grouping which is both necessary and all that is possible at this stage.

Perhaps the really surprising thing is that there is not available a more fully developed account of the relationships between technology and social institutions. Certainly, the idea of such a study is not new. William F. Ogburn included a sociological treatment of technology in his *Social Change* (Ogburn, 1950), published in 1922, and later (1957) joined Francis R. Allen, Hornell Hart, and others in writing a book completely devoted to the topic, *Technology and Social Change* (Allen et al., 1957). Another early (1935), but somewhat more specialized work, is S.C. Gilfillan's *The Sociology of Invention* (1935). More recently (1970), Gerhard and Jean Lenski made the sociotechnological dimension a central element of their "ecological-evolutionary" approach to sociology (Lenski and Lenski, 1974). In contrast to the sociology of science, which has become institutionalized as a research specialty in sociology, the "sociology of technology" is still relatively undeveloped. There is no identifiable group of sociologists primarily concerned with it, no focused set of research problems, no coherent research program, and no body of significant results (Gaston, 1984, pp. 465, 471). One wonders why no more came of that early work which seemed so promising. Perhaps sociologists just got interested in other things. Perhaps their research methods do not lend themselves readily to this subject area. Perhaps, as suggested earlier with regard to the present topic, many disciplines will have to be involved to obtain significant results. In any case, the present analysis has to proceed with only fragmented and piecemeal assistance from sociological studies of technology.

One of the best known claims that a religious tradition created or enhanced conditions favorable to technological development (II-C-1) is the thesis that the Judeo-Christian view of creation made possible in the West both the scientific study and the technological manipulation of the natural order. More specifically, the argument is that the Judeo-Christian view, according to which the natural world was created by God and put at man's disposal (rather than being itself "filled" with gods or spirits which must be respected and, perhaps, feared), frees man to study and to use plants, animals, and other natural objects for whatever purpose he chooses. Well-known advocates of this view include Harvey Cox (1966, pp. 19-21), Lynn White, Jr. (1972, 259-265), and Carl Amery (discussed in Cerézuelle, 1983). While Cox gives the matter a positive interpretation, White and Amery find it in the roots of the ecological crisis. The complexity of such issues and the difficulty of arriving at anything like a defensible conclusion regarding them is shown by the fact that Cox renounced, in the revised edition of his work (Cox, 1966, p. xi), any claim to "scholarly balance or universal thoroughness," and that he subsequently modified his views more than once. (For a discussion, see Ferré, 1986, pp. 99-107).

Another widely discussed thesis linking a religious development or tradition to technological advancement is Max Weber's claim that the Protestant work ethic was a key causative factor in the industrial revolution and the rise of capitalism (Weber, 1930). Weber's thesis has been attacked from many directions (Green, 1959). Eventually, he modified his views at least to the extent of recognizing the roots of what he termed the "Protestant ethic" in pre-Reformation Christianity and ancient Judaism (Lenski and Lenski, 1974, p. 306). That is, he moved toward the position of Cox and White, of which his view may be regarded as a predecessor. In the early 1950s new life was given to the earlier, more restricted Weber thesis by a statistical study carried out by Isidor Thorner (1952), who found a higher incidence of inventions and discoveries (i.e., more per millions of population) in Protestant countries than in Catholic countries (except for France, in which, he argued, scientists tend not to be Catholics). Thorner's work does seem to address one of the great obstacles to progress in this whole area: it is so hard to make a reliable assessment of the truth of the claims being made. Thus, Gaston complains of perhaps the best known commentator on technology, Jacques Ellul, who terms his work "sociological," that his ideas "are virtually impossible to test empirically," that he "does not present a systematic framework for studying sociological questions about technology," and that "his basic thesis . . . is merely postulated" (Gaston, 1984, p. 492). This charge, leveled at so prominent a writer, underlines once again the lack of a paradigm in the field, to use Kuhnian terminology.

A third example of how a religious tradition may have fostered technological development is provided by the traditional account of the beginnings of China (Speiser, 1964, pp. 16-17). According to these stories, China was founded by three legendary figures, the Three August Ones, who were the originators of everything that separated civilized man from the savage. They taught the people to hunt, fish, raise crops, use fire, and build homes. They devised the first calendars and set down the Chinese system of writing. Thus far, the story seems to parallel Greek mythology; Prometheus stole fire from heaven and brought it down to humanity; Demeter taught people to farm; and so on. Up to this point, the two traditions follow a common pattern: the marvelous arts and skills that make civilization possible must have been gifts from the gods, or something rather like gods; surely, no one should suppose that mere mortals should have invented or discovered them. Indeed, the suggestion that mere human beings might, through their inventions, better their lot by making significant changes in the arrangement of things is folly and can be expected to reap the rewards thereof. Such seems to be the moral of the story of Icarus, who, in his exuberance at being able to fly, soared so high the sun melted the wax holding the feathers in his wings so that he plunged to his death.

The second chapter of the Chinese account goes rather differently. Following the Three August Ones came the Five Sovereigns, the first of whom supposedly introduced the practice of medicine, road building, and the oxcart. His empress taught the people how to spin silk from the cocoons of moths. During the reign of the fifth sovereign, the Yellow River repeatedly overflowed its banks, causing great devastation and suffering. A clever engineer, named Yu, devised systems of dams and ditches to check the floods. So impressed was the old emperor that he announced that Yu should be his successor on the throne, since his own son had no such talents. Thus began the legendary Hsia dynasty, which, according to the traditional accounts, lasted until the rise of the Shang dynasty (about 1500 BC).

Thus, while the Chinese story begins with superhuman figures teaching the people to hunt, fish, farm, etc., it makes the transition, first to an emperor who did similarly wondrous things, and then, in stages, to an emperor whose own son is less fit to rule than a clever engineer. Clearly, the story affirms that the human situation can be improved significantly by clever inventions, and that those who make them should be rewarded, honored, and put in positions where their cleverness will be of maximum benefit. It is not surprising that this story should be one of the legends of a people who were to make so many inventions during a period of over 3000 years. It would be folly to claim that the Chinese technological prowess was simply the result of having these mythical legends. It would be equally absurd to suggest that things would have been no different if the Chinese had had a religion featuring the metaphysical musing of detached sages, or stories of the pranks of a cosmic trickster. A more precise statement of the effect of the Chinese myths upon their technological achievements will have to await further scholarship.

It is also possible that a religion could reinforce or promote conditions that inhibit invention and technological innovation in general (II-C-2). Establishing that such is the case in an individual instance will not be easy, however, for the reasons discussed above. The lack of even a rudimentary set of principles governing sociotechnological phenomena is, again, a severe handicap. There are, however, at least two factors identified as affecting technological innovation which seem quite plausible and which seem to be gaining acceptance among social scientists. One factor is the magnitude of the existing store of technological resources (roughly "information"); the other is the extent of intersocietal contact (Ogburn, 1950, chapter 6; Lenski and Lenski, 1974, pp. 62-69; Richter, 1982, pp. 78-81). That is, roughly speaking, the more technology one is surrounded by, and the more opportunities one has to learn of materials, devices, processes, etc., being used in other societies, the more likely one is to think of or try something new. Conversely, the narrower one's technological base and the more restricted one's contacts with others, the less likely one is to become involved in innovation. It follows that any religious tradition that tends to minimize either the technological base of a society, or its contact with other groups, is a candidate for inclusion in category II-C-2. Quite clearly, the Amish fit this pattern. Not only do they explicitly reject various technologies (electricity, telephones, automobiles, etc.), they deliberately limit the technological base of their communities, and their opportunity for contact with society at large. Thus, one would not expect them to make even modest inventions or innovations which do not conflict in any obvious way with their religious principles.

THE IMPACT OF TECHNOLOGICAL INNOVATION UPON RELIGION

The most readily identifiable class of effects that new technologies have upon religion are those which are direct and obvious. One needs no sophisticated social theory to identify them. These are considered in the first part of this section. Indirect or derivative effects of technological innovation are considered in the next two parts of this section, first in cases in which the impact upon religion results from technologically engendered *alternatives* to religious institutions, beliefs, and values. This subclass of the indirect effects of technology upon religion has been singled out because it seems to include the most important of these effects. An additional category is provided for other derivative effects of technological innovation.

Direct Effects of the Utilization of New Technologies Upon Religion

As just noted, identifying a direct effect of some technological innovation upon religion is a fairly straightforward affair. Deciding just which categories should be marked off under this heading is not. One might think it possible, in rough parallel to the pattern followed earlier, to divide the direct effects of new technologies into those which tend to promote religious ends and those which are destructive of them (leaving aside those which seem to have no direct effect upon religion). Such a classification would, of course, require that one be able to identify reliably which effects are "good" and which "bad." Any illusions one might have on this score will be removed if one reflects, for example, upon the effects of the introduction of printing with movable type into Western Europe. This invention made it possible for ordinary Christians to have copies of the Bible to read. Without this development, there would, almost certainly, not have been a Protestant Reformation. Nor would there now be fundamentalist ministers debating the "inerrancy" of the Bible. Surely, not everyone would agree that these developments are good (or that they are bad). Similar remarks could be made about the advent of radio broadcasting, or television. Each of these had easily identifiable direct effects upon religion, but not everyone would agree that they are good (or that they are bad).

There would appear to be three ways to approach the problem of classifying the direct effects of technological innovation upon religion: on the basis of differences among the causes (the technological innovations), on the basis of differences among the effects upon religion, and upon the basis of correlations between members of the first two groups. Utilizing any of these methods will require a complete canvassing of these classes unless scholarly endeavors in the meantime lead to insights that make such unnecessary. In any case, further progress on the matter must await the results of these hoped-for efforts.

Detrimental Effects of Technologically Engendered Alternatives Upon Religious Institutions, Beliefs, and Values

One of the most important ways that technological innovations affect religion indirectly is that they provide, or help to provide, alternative and, often, competitive values, social institutions, and belief systems. To the extent that these alternatives compete successfully with or replace those associated with a religious tradition, to that extent the religious tradition suffers.

Technology affects values or ends (III-B-1) because it, among other things, makes available completely new options, or changes significantly the relative cost of realizing some goal, so that, for example, something becomes a live option when it previously was not (Mesthene, 1970, pp. 45-62). To the extent that the new or newly available activity or goal competes successfully for people's time and resources, to that extent will preexisting goals and values suffer. For example, before the advent of radio and television, local churches, especially those in small towns or rural areas, did not have to compete with listening or viewing as an alternative to church programs, especially in the evenings. Similarly, the development of modern transportation systems—at first railroads, then automobiles and highways, and then airlines—and the higher level of affluence brought by industrialization opened up a whole range of activities not possible or even imagined before: sightseeing and vacation trips covering hundreds and even thousands of miles, trips to special sites for sports activities such as skiing, major league athletic competition with teams traveling between cities separated by great distances, etc.

None of the preceding is intended to suggest that people did not travel, take vacations, participate in or watch sports activities, etc., before the technological developments mentioned took place. The point is simply that a whole range of possibilities opened up and that, even though people have come to have more time and more money at their disposal, the old goals and activities have to face competiton not previously known to them. And not only do people have choices they did not have before, they are forced to make some of these choices, by default if not by conscious choice. Such forced decisions are especially common in the medical area; for example, should life-saving surgery (now an option) be performed upon a severely deformed neonate who, if she survives, is highly likely to be mentally retarded? Any systematic attempt to deal with such dilemmas requires that fundamental questions of values and ends be addressed, questions which a given religious tradition may not be prepared to answer. It is thus faced with a new challenge for which there is no guarantee it can meet.

The second way that technological advancement affects religion is that it fosters the development of social institutions which assume some of the social functions previously served by the church (III-B-2). The Christian church was once the last (and often the only) resort of the infirm and the destitute. It was the primary (if not the only) source of relief for victims of natural disasters. It took a major responsibility for education, and it was the center of the social life, especially outside urban centers, which accounted for only a small fraction of the population. As Western nations have become more affluent, following industrialization, other institutions, especially government, have assumed more and more of these responsibilities. Thus, argues R.A. Buchanan, religious institutions have been deprived of "the social 'ambulance' function which had hitherto been one of their most valued contributions to society." (Buchanan, 1972, p. 240).

The situation is similar to the field of education, with the pattern manifesting itself most recently in the United States at the college and university level. The churches had a major role in higher education in early U.S. history. Many, if not most, of the leading private universities had church beginnings. Then came a wave, first of state universities and land-grant institutions, and then, somewhat later, of community colleges and urban universities. Furthermore, many of the institutions that were founded by churches ceased to have ties to them. Thus, while enrollments in higher education have soared, the church's role in it has shrunk incredibly.

Finally, as suggested earlier, affluence and industrialization have made it possible for a great variety of activities to flourish, with the result that the church has ceased to be the center of social life (except perhaps for a small percentage of the population, mostly in rural areas).

A third way that technology indirectly affects religion is by contributing to the development of alternative sources of authority (III-B-3). It was noted above that printing with movable type made it possible for ordinary Christians to have their own copies of the Bible. A secondary effect was that the Bible itself became a source of authority in competition with the priest's reading and interpretation of it. Technology has also played a crucial role in the development of science, which has become an authority, separate from and in competition with the church. An absolutely crucial element in modern science has been and continues to be the technological resources it brings to bear on its problems. What would Galileo have been without the telescope? Van Leeuwenhoek without the microscope? Rutherford without ion sources? Lawrence without the cyclotron? Consequently, the entire science-and-religion debate feeds into this category of this taxonomy.

Other Derivative Effects of Technologically Induced Social Changes

Perhaps the first major effect of technological innovation to be noticed was changes in social organization. Karl Marx made this insight a central theme. Almost certainly, there are more types of these effects that bear upon religion than have been identified thus far. But until scholarship is further advanced and/or at least a rudimentary theory of sociotechnological phenomena is available, a complete and satisfactory classification of the effects of technological innovation upon religion cannot even be contemplated. It is hoped that the scheme set forth herein will be helpful in the interim as a way of organizing what is now known and as a source of suggestions for further work.

APPENDIX: TAXONOMIC SCHEME

I. Relations Between Technology and Religion in the Absence of Technological Innovation

    I-O-1.   Mutual noninteraction: Disregard or lack of awareness of a technology by religious tradition

    I-O-2.   Mutual interaction: Awareness exhibited by religious tradition, but no stance taken

    I-O-3.   Acceptance of a technology by religious tradition

    I-O-4.   Support, by established technology, of religious institutions and values

I-O-5. Rejection of, or opposition to, an established technology by religious tradition

I-O-6. Established technology destructive of religious institutions and values

II. Actions and Influences of Religion Upon Technological Innovations

A. Stances taken by religious traditions toward novel technologies, either imported or encountered externally

II-A-1. No awareness of alien or novel technologies

II-A-2. Awareness of the existence of such technologies, but no contemplation of the possibility, nor of the implications, of their utilization in the society with which the religion is associated

II-A-3. Awareness of the possibility or actuality of the utilization of alien or novel technologies, but no stance assumed regarding it

II-A-4. Approbation or promotion of utilization of alien or novel technologies by a religion or religious leader

II-A-5. Disapproval or opposition to alien or novel technologies by a religion or religious leader

B. Stances taken by religious traditions toward inventions, technologies newly devised in societies in which the religion is indigenous or established

II-B-1. No awareness of an invention, or of invention generally

II-B-2. Awareness of, but no stance assumed regarding invention(s)

II-B-3. Approbation or promotion of invention(s)

II-B-4. Disapproval of, or opposition to, invention(s)

C. Indirect or unintended influences of religion upon technology

II-C-1. Religious tradition reinforces or promotes conditions that favor an invention or innovation generally

II-C-2. Religious tradition reinforces or promotes conditions that preclude or hinder invention or innovation

III.   The Impact of Technological Innovation Upon Religion

   A.   Direct effects of the utilization of new technologies upon religion

   B.   Detrimental effects of technologically engendered alternatives upon religious institutions, beliefs, and values

   III-B-1.   Effects upon values

   III-B-2.   Loss of social function

   III-B-3.   Contributions to alternative sources of authority

   C.   Other derivative effects of technologically induced social changes

REFERENCES

Allen, Francis R. et al. *Technology and Social Change* (New York: Appleton-Century-Crofts, 1957).

Amery, Carl. *Das Ende der Vorsehung* (Hamburg: C. Rowolt, 1972).

Boas, Ralph, and Boas, Louise. *Cotton Mather: Keeper of the Puritan Conscience* (New York: NYU Press, 1956).

Bronowski, Jacob. *The Ascent of Man* (Boston: Little, Brown & Co., 1973).

Buchanan, R.A. "The Churches in a Changing World." In C. Mitcham and R. Mackey, eds., *Philosophy and Technology: Readings in the Philosophical Problems of Technology* (New York: The Free Press, 1972).

Cérézuelle, Daniel. "Concerning the Religious Origins of Technological Civilization." In P.T. Durbin, ed., *Research in Philosophy and Technology,* vol. 6 (Greenwich, CT: JAI Press, 1983).

Childe, V. Gordon. *Man Makes Himself* (New York: Mentor, 1951).

Clark, Elmer T. *The Small Sects in America* (New York: Abingdon, 1949).

Cox, Harvey. *The Secular City: Secularization and Urbanization in Theological Perspective,* rev. ed. (New York: Macmillan, 1966).

Durbin, Paul T., ed. *Research in Philosophy and Technology,* vol. 6 (Greenwich, CT: JAI Press, 1983).

Durbin, Paul T., ed. *A Guide to the Culture of Science, Technology, and Medicine* (New York: The Free Press, 1984).

Ferré, Frederick. *Philosophy of Technology* (Englewood Cliffs, NJ: Prentice-Hall, 1988).

Gaston, Jerry. "Sociology of Science and Technology." In P.T. Durbin, ed., *A Guide to the Culture of Science, Technology, and Medicine* (New York: The Free Press, 1984).

Gilfillan, S.C. *The Sociology of Invention* (Chicago: Follett, 1935).

Green, Robert W., ed. *Protestantism and Capitalism: The Weber Thesis and Its Critics* (Boston: Heath, 1959).

Harmon, Nolan B., ed. *The Encyclopedia of World Methodism* (Nashville, TN: The United Methodist Publishing House, 1974).

Harris, Jonathan. *Scientists in the Shaping of America* (Menlo Park, CA: Addison-Wesley, 1971).

Hiebert, Edwin N. *The Impact of Atomic Energy* (Newton, KS: Faith and Life Press, 1961).

Kuhn, Thomas S. *The Structure of Scientific Revolutions,* 2nd ed. (Chicago: University of Chicago Press, 1970).

Lenski, Gerhard, and Lenski, Jean. *Human Societies: An Introduction to Macrosociology,* 2nd ed. (New York: McGraw-Hill, 1974).

Light, Donald, Jr., and Keller, Suzanne. *Sociology* (New York: Alfred A. Knopf, 1975).

Mesthene, Emmanuel G. *Technological Change: Its Impact on Man and Society* (New York: Mentor, 1970).

Mitcham, Carl, and Mackey, Robert, eds. *Philosophy and Technology: Readings in the Philosophical Problems of Technology* (New York: The Free Press, 1972).

Morison, Samuel Eliot. *The Intellectual Life of Colonial New England* (New York: NYU Press, 1956).

Murnion, Philip J., ed. *Catholics and Nuclear War* (New York: The Crossroad Publishing Co., 1983).

Nordenskiöld, Erik. *The History of Biology: A Survey* (New York: Tudor Publishing Co., 1928).

Ogburn, William F. *Social Change,* rev. ed. (New York: Viking, 1950).

Richter, Maurice N., Jr. *Technology and Social Complexity* (Albany: State University of New York Press, 1982).

Robinson, Theodore H. "Genesis." In *The Abingdon Bible Commentary* (New York: Abingdon-Cokesbury Press, 1929).

Robinson, Theodore H. *A History of Israel,* vol. 1 (Oxford: The Clarendon Press, 1932).

Ruse, Michael. *The Philosophy of Biology* (London: Hutchinson University Library, 1973).

Silverberg, Robert. *Wonders of Ancient Chinese Science* (New York: Hawthorn Books, 1969).

Speiser, E.A. "Genesis." In *The Anchor Bible* (Garden City, NY: Doubleday, 1964).

Sweet, William Warren. *The Story of Religion in America* (New York: Harper & Row, 1950).

Temple, Robert. *The Genius of China: 3,000 Years of Science, Discovery, and Invention* (New York: Simon and Schuster, 1986).

Thorner, Isidor. "Ascetic Protestantism and the Development of Science and Technology," *American Journal of Sociology* 58:25-33 (1952).

Trepp, Leo. *Judaism,* 3rd ed. (Belmont, CA: Wadsworth Publishing Co., 1982).

Volti, Rudi. *Society and Technological Change* (New York: St. Martin's Press, 1988).

Ware, James R. *Alchemy, Medicine, Religion in the China of A.D. 320: The Nei P'ien of Ko Hung* (Cambridge, MA: MIT Press, 1966).

Weber, Max. *The Protestant Ethic and the Spirit of Capitalism* (London: George Allen and Unwin, 1930).

White, Lynn, Jr. "The Historical Roots of Our Ecological Crisis." In C. Mitcham and R. Mackey, eds. *Philosophy and Technology: Readings in the Philosophical Problems of Technology* (New York: The Free Press, 1972).

ULTIMATE WEAPONS IN A PENULTIMATE AGE:

A THEOLOGICAL ASSESSMENT OF SDI TECHNOLOGY

A. Arnold Wettstein

Addressing the nation on March 23, 1983, Ronald Reagan proposed a Strategic Defense Initiative, to embark on a program which would "intercept and destroy strategic ballistic missiles before they reached our own soil or that of our allies." He observed that our reliance on the threat of mutual retaliation to avoid nuclear war "is a sad commentary on the human condition," and asked, "Wouldn't it be better to save lives rather than to avenge them?" The opportunity to develop a morally preferable policy is made possible, he asserted, by the sophistication of current technology. His challenge to the scientific community, which had given us nuclear weapons, was "to turn their great talents now to the cause of mankind and world peace, to give us the means of rendering these nuclear weapons impotent and obsolete."[1] The SDI continues as a major component of administration policy, and a source of continuing controversy in Congress and the nation.

Research in Philosophy and Technology, Volume 10, pages 25-41.
Copyright © 1990 by JAI Press Inc.
All rights of reproduction in any form reserved.
ISBN: 1-55938-062-4

All sides agree that we are in the grip of nuclear crisis, that the U.S.S.R. and the United States have enough warheads to destroy each other many times over. Most concur that the policy of Mutually Assured Destruction is inherently unstable, with the balance of terror always a moving target, encouraging each side to build more weapons and their delivery systems. Former National Security Adviser Zbigniew Brzezinski asserts that "A strategic posture that safeguards peace by the threat of annihilation . . . is ethically troubling, morally corrosive, and dehumanizing."[2] Critics of the policy of deterrence question its moral viability because "our security as a nation rests on the threat of genocide."[3]

An intriguing aspect of the arguments offered in the Star Wars debate is that appeals to morality appear to make use of quite different definitions of the term. Those who insist that defense is preferable find moral value implicit in an intention or activity, while those who deny moral superiority to defense see the matter consequentially—whether or not some good end will actually be served. Another curious characteristic of the reasoning processes is the continual mixture of moral (M), technical (T), and political (P—the art of the possible) considerations. The support of SDI may slide from

1(a)   it is better to protect than avenge (M); to

1(b)   we must be prepared to defend against tactical nuclear engagements (P); all the while assuming that

1(c)   substantial homeland protection is possible (T).

A contrary position may move from the assertion that

2(a)   nuclear defense is infeasible (T); to

2(b)   the costs are intolerable (M); adding that

2(c)   the result would be a worsening of superpower relations (P).

The discussion is more susceptible than most to categorical confusion. The situation is exacerbated by the interinfluence of the types of consideration. Examine the connection in the argument that if

3(a)   anti-missile defense is inevitably imperfect (T); then

3(b)   a defensive system will escalate the arms race through series of countermeasures, worsening superpower relations (P); and, therefore,

3(c)   the proposal is not only unwise but wrong (M).

Or consider a course of thought in which technological possibilities open up new moral options: if

4(a) adequate accuracy of low-yield tactical nuclear weapons is achievable (T); and

4(b) the exchange of tactical weapons could be limited to the battlefield because neither superpower would initiate a strategic exchange on account of its suicidal character (P): then

4(c) it would be right to develop a defensive system which would reduce the number of non-combatant casualties from fall-out or non-intended collateral effects (M).

When arguments from differing categories intrude on one another, finding a way of sorting them out is imperative. A highly favored thought-terminating cliché in philosophical discussion is that the debater is comparing apples and oranges. The fact is that in the great subjects of public decision, apples, oranges, bananas, technical, political (pragmatic), and moral concerns are all involved. One tempting philosophical treatment could be to establish an order of priority: first establish what is morally preferable, then determine whether it is politically possible, and finally examine whether it is technically feasible. We see in the nuclear dilemma, however, that the political realities of post-World War II confrontations have led many who otherwise eschew violence to support a nuclear deterrent (P determining M) as well as particular technological accomplishments redefining moral options (M following T). Ultimately, the moral must have a kind of precedential character, in value if not in time, to be pursued whether or not it is immediately rewarding or moral concerns are reduced to the status of one set of manipulatible political factors among others. Suppose a system of relative weights would be devised. For example, let us award reasons of each type what we determine to be appropriate numerical values:

5(a) effective defense and improved warhead accuracy make limited nuclear exchanges possible (T, 20 pts.);

5(b) tactical weapons are more likely to be used than strategic (P, 30 pts.);

5(c) but casualties among noncombatants are morally unwarrantable, whether direct or indirect (M, -10, -20, -100?).

Must not a single substantial moral consideration counteract any amount of countervailing valuation? In this case, statements 5(a) and 5(b) both become irrelevant when an action is judged intrinsically immoral.

The elaborate interconnections among the moral, political and, technological considerations in the debates about SDI require a multifaceted if complex decision-making method. What follows is a proposal of such a method from a theological perspective.

I

A theological appraisal of even such a practical question as whether or not we ought to support SDI implicitly (if not explicitly) begins with the most comprehensive scheme possible—a story of origins in the creation and a destiny in the eschaton. A theological position finds its origins in awe and gratitude before the given universe and a sense of responsibility toward its end. Theological methods may become oriented too rigidly to a conception of creation and its orders in terms of natural law, subject to the danger of missing genuine novelty in the creative process or projecting ethnocentric notions of human individuality, gender role differentiation, etc., on everyone's human condition. The opposite distraction in theological method would be in adhering too closely to a model of an expected end of the historical process. Utopias are notoriously susceptible to use as vehicles for projected values or tools of oppression.

More productively, the theologian may begin with the task of discernment in the present in the light of the faith's perceptions about the primal past and the ultimate future: "What can we affirm . . . about God's purposes for life in the world?"[4] The first characteristic of a theological method will be its language peculiar to religious discourse, proclaiming the biblical saga or story and our place between its times of creation, redemption, and fulfillment. The vision described here is one of God's purpose as *shalom*, a peace far more than the mere absence of conflict, but as the statements of churches will declare, a "*shalom* in which all people enjoy peace, security and well-being."[5] In the biblical understanding, God's mercy is ever conjoined with justice and the end-time will not only be one when swords are beaten into plowshares (Micah 4:3), but "like the days of a tree shall the days of my people be, and my chosen shall long enjoy the work of their hands" (Isaiah 65:22). In the proclamation of Jesus, the peacemakers are blessed and the disciples told not even to hate their enemies, much less kill them. "Love your enemies and pray for those who persecute you" (Matthew 5:44). Thus is affirmed "God's will for the world . . . ; we are called to be makers of *shalom* and agents of reconciliation."[6] The Biblical expectation is of a time when

Steadfast love and faithfulness will meet; righteousness and peace will kiss each other. (Psalm 85:11)

The theologian, informed and inspired by such a vision and called to its service, is nevertheless under no illusion about the actualities of the present. A second characteristic of the theological method is the recognition of the dialectical quality of a time understood as *kairos* rather than *chronos,* a time qualitatively unique, with dreadful dangers as well as extraordinary possibilities, rather than a moment like any other. In the *Heilsgeschichte,* the divine drama of human salvation, Christian theology presents us living in the penultimate age, in a fallen world in which we must deal with the power struggles fueled by human pride, greed, and lust for power, while never losing sight of the nonultimacy of the moment in which we live and act. A great "Nevertheless" empowers the dialectic in each direction, away from the illusory naiveté of simplistic faith, on the one hand, and from cynicism bred of despair, on the other. Wolfhart Pannenberg rightly insists that it is of value to hear from the purists

> while also sobering their enthusiasm by means of Christian realism. For that realism—concerning the power of sin in human societies and in their political conflicts—has characterized the Christian outlook on the world of politics from the beginning.[7]

The Christian theologian's talk of realism is soon tempered with the faith that "God was in Christ reconciling the world to himself" (2 Corinthians 5:19), that in Christ the ultimate battles are already won and the final victories proleptically realized.

Persons of faith will then live, think, and act dialectically, fully though not exclusively present to the actual world, appreciative of the opportunities of the *kairos* yet not misguided in thinking of these as their own constructs. Edward Schillibeeckx is unquestionably correct in asserting that the kingdom of God, the eschaton, is never brought about by warfare or coercion: "It works through *metanoia,* repentance. It is a victory over evil through obedience to God, and not through human force."[8] Yet it is through human agency that the kingdom comes; human activity can provide the conditions in which it may be known: "God . . . gave us the ministry of reconciliation" (2 Corinthians 5:18).

The theological dialectic in a penultimate age will then derive its moral absolutes from the eschatological vision, while recognizing the political (art of the possible) necessities of life in a fallen world. Moral decisions are entangled with political necessities. Nevertheless, political decisions will make further moral realizations possible. Margaret A. Farley writes, for example, that the mutuality and equal regard between persons promised in Christ's resurrection "does not merely beckon from the future; it continually impinges upon the present, demanding that every relationship . . . be at least turned in the direction of equality and opened to the possibility of communion."[9] Theological method thus seeks to generate middle axioms by which to open political decisions toward the ultimate moral ends. Alan Geyer says "the question . . . is: how shall we try to tilt the ambiguities?"[10]

A third characteristic of the theological method in social ethics is that however transcendent may be the source of norms in the purposes of God, the point of impact is the human nexus, the arena of responsible decision and action. Some will be tempted to view the political, and particularly the technological, in opposition to the contemplative vocation central to the life of faith. Technology seems diametrically opposed to that "waiting on the Lord" which is the key to contemplative renewal. Ascetics will wonder if "technology is simply the false hope of the false self."[11] But if with Milton "they also serve who only stand and wait," they serve in support of a broader human enterprise in which the waiting is as much an action as the doing. Meanwhile, others are tempted to view the technological as the domestic, the beast of the Apocalypse with whom any compromise involves entrapment.[12] For some, nuclear weapons are the ultimate example: "With nuclear weapons we had technology that was evil in itself, not merely how it might be used but arguably in its very existence."[13] The invidious character of the demonic, however, is not its intrinsic evil but its nature as distorted good: the demonic is the potentially angelic twisted to wrong ends. Psychoanalysts quite correctly advise that we come to terms with our demons. Societally, the demonic character of technology is always ambiguous because it is originally or ontologically rooted in our very humanity. Paul Tillich has pointed out that in the Garden of Eden the human task was twofold: to name the animals (cognitive) and to till the soil (technological).[14] The human agent may not represent the goal of the cosmic process, but stands, nonetheless, at the center of ethical deliberation and decision. Believers stand there aware of obligations for action grounded in a covenantal relationship with God.

Such implicit activism must not distract us from a fourth characteristic of theological method: concern for the spiritual. The theologian is concerned about value-formation and the cultivation of those sensibilities which can shape a viable moral life. Global problems, national policies, and the way we talk about them may foster debilitating attitudes within people. Along with psychologists such as Robert Lifton, the theologian will be troubled by the "nuclear absurdities," our inability "to imagine the real," the absence of security, the possible "nuclear numbing" which may have emptied us of human feeling through the terror of our very existence under the shadow of the Bomb. Debates on moral, political, and technical issues reflect or may influence those deeper attitudes of anxiety or hopefulness which may finally be the determining factors in what we will do in a penultimate age.

II

Theology must develop a strategy for moral decision-making in a world not only subject to political constraints, but limited by the human condition. Whether or not to research and/or deploy SDI becomes a question of preference over other available alternatives. For when *shalom* is understood as God's central purpose for the human community, maintaining purity of personal intention or conscience is secondary to determining those actions more likely, in a penultimate age, to promote the conditions in which that purpose would be more realizable. Theologically-informed moral assessments will not then see a defensive system as ethically preferable merely because it disavows massive destruction; they will rather examine the political factors: will SDI be less or more likely to serve the causes and conditions of peace?

The alternatives are easily plotted:

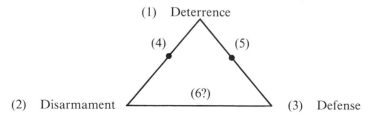

In addition to possible support of a program of (1) deterrence, (2) disarmament, or (3) defense, further options surface in the debate: (4) maintaining a level of deterrence while seeking reductions in armaments through negotiation, and (5) promoting an "enhanced deterrence" through defensive systems until offensive weapons might be safey reduced. An option (6) is more problematic if confined to the defense-disarmament axis, because the development of defensive systems is founded on a distrust of the adversary seemingly incompatible with genuine negotiations toward arms reductions. The distrust endemic to option (4), combining deterrence with initiatives toward disarmament, is at least tempered by the realization that each power is in a mutually intolerable situation which they both find in their interest to relieve. Talk of using SDI as a "bargaining chip" actually does not follow from option (6) but from (4)—being clear about deterrent capabilities while negotiating gradual reductions, with verification systems, intermediate rewards, etc.

Assuming that the five listed alternatives are all technologically possible, their evaluation from a moral point of view requires some functional "middle axioms." Three may be deduced directly from commitment to *shalom*:

(1)   prevention of nuclear war;
(2)   reduction of casualties in the event of such a war;
(3)   avoidance of socially intolerable costs.

While the call to the peace of *shalom* ideally involves the prevention of all war, the axiom is stated in particular relation to the issue. That the prevention of nuclear war has a special moral urgency is the result not only of its greater destructive potential, but its involvement of noncombatants and consequent violation of the justice implicit in *shalom*. It could be argued that the risks of conventional war are actually acceptable if they serve the greater purpose of preventing nuclear war. The reduction of casualties if a nuclear war would be waged derives from the care about persons implicit in the biblical vision of *shalom*, and the avoidance of entanglement in intolerable costs becomes an axiom, not only by virtue of the compassion in this kind of peace, but through its structure as a peace of human fulfillment and satisfaction. Actually, all three axioms may be offered as philosophically "self-evident" in that they may be derived from either a de-ontological or consequentialist system.[15]

To these, however, the theologian must add another, derived from a role of responsibility in a created world and a vocation based on God's intention of *shalom* for humankind:

(4)   developing those conditions which are conducive to progress toward just and fulfilling relationships between people and nations.

While realistic about the limitations on life in a penultimate age, theology refuses to take on the cynicism of compliance in power struggles which envision no ends beyond themselves. George F. Kennan stated the task and the tension:

> Our main concern must be to see that man, whose own folly once drove him from the Garden of Eden, does not now commit the blasphemous act of destroying, whether in fear or in anger or in greed, the great and lovely world in which, even in his fallen state, he has been permitted by the grace of God to lived.[16]

While functioning as operational guides, middle axioms are not themselves absolute. Under particular conditions, one may be overruled in deference to a stronger claim by another: it could be that weapons systems, in spite of their excessive costs, could claim moral priority over social and economic programs if they are indeed necessary to maintain the peace without which any such programs would be meaningless.

In view of these axioms, however, the policy options are immediately narrowed. The theologian will have little interest in supporting (1) simple deterrence, exclusively, for if Mutually Assured Destruction is the only policy, one would be complying with an assessment without hope. A unilateral commitment to a policy of (3) defense, would raise serious questions about the responsibility of creating a climate conducive to peace while a simple devotion to (2) disarmament, might be premature, risking subjection to factors over which one's own nation has little or no control, because one wrongly applies the principles of the ultimate age to the penultimate. The debate concentrates, then, on whether a policy compounded of deterrence with disarmament initiatives or deterrence with defensive systems is more likely to lead toward a more just and stable world.

That deterrence of any sort is an acceptable moral policy is no longer unambiguously clear, if it ever was. In its Pastoral Letter on Peace, the National

Conference of Catholic Bishops reflects on the destructive potentials of nuclear power which "force us to undertake a completely fresh appraisal of war."[17] The bishops carefully reexamine traditional just war theory which had been used to give warrant to any use of force, reassessing each criterion in the light of the nuclear potential. The cause must be deemed just, to be sure, but whether it can be of such seriousness as to justify the possibly massive destruction of a nuclear attack is questionable. Of course, it must be an action declared by a "competent authority," with the "right intention" and be the "last resort" after all other options for adjudicating the dispute have been exhausted. While these *Jus ad Bellum* criteria might conceivably be met in deliberating a nuclear response, the bishops seriously question whether two others can: the "probability of success" and "proportionality." How could a nuclear war be judged successful? How could it be won? And how could the damage to be inflicted possibly be considered reasonably proportional to the "good" of its cause? Their reservations about *Jus in Bello* criteria, that is, concerning the manner in which a war would be fought, are even more intense: standards of "proportionality" of nuclear weapons systems would be very difficult to meet and "discrimination" would be virtually impossible to apply. In a nuclear exchange, the direct or indirect destruction effected on noncombatants is in their view unavoidable; these are always to be condemned.[18] The Peace Pastoral is, however, pragmatic enough to find a way to ameliorate the obvious conclusion of this appraisal, that any action likely, if not certainly, to destroy noncombatants would be wrong because it is an abrogation of the victims' natural right to survive as innocent bystanders. Instead, the Peace Pastoral admits a consequentialist evaluation: "A narrow adherence exclusively to the principle of non-combatant immunity as a criterion for policy is an inadequate moral posture for it ignores some evil and unacceptable consequences."[19] On the verge of concluding with an exclusive commitment to alternative (2) for disarmament, the bishops shift to support a compound policy (4), deterrence and "steps toward progressive disarmament."

The United Methodist Council of Bishops issued a briefer Pastoral Letter in 1986, accompanied by an extensive "Foundation Document" for study by the church. In their review of the just war criteria, the Methodist bishops also question the applicability of the "reasonable hope of success," "discrimination," and "proportionality" criteria but they conclude:

> These considerations posed by the still-valuable just war tradition require us to say *No*, a clear and unconditional *No*, to nuclear war and to any use of nuclear weapons.[20]

The document goes on to criticize "the idolatry of deterrence" on further grounds: a position is wrong which "presumes the power of ultimate judgment in the destruction of other nations"; a policy is wrong which blinds its supporters to the multidimensional needs of real security while offering in actuality a pseudosecurity based on fear.[21] Further, the view of Pope John Paul II in his 1982 United Nations statement that deterrence "may still be judged morally acceptable" as a step toward "progressive disarmament" has been contradicted by recent experience, as the development of more sophisticated weapons of deterrence has in reality raised the level of mutual suspicion.[22] What is more, the policy of deterrence perpetuates distorted and inhuman images of an "enemy," obstructing the nurture of a climate more conducive to peace. Alan Geyer extends this point claiming that "deterrent dogmas" reinforce "political absolutism" along with isolationist and reactionist styles of diplomatic behavior, with "civilians . . . held hostage . . . to the decisions of political elites."[23]

The last series of arguments focus largely on the "deterrent dogmas" and their obstructionist application. Any position becomes idolatrous when it foregoes the ability to accept criticism and adapt to change. The MX missile was opposed as well as supported by proponents of deterrence. A pragmatic deterrence policy can well operate devoid of the dogmas, without commitment to its own elaboration. Further, the precision of just war theory is obscured at several key points: it is notoriously inadequate in establishing standards by which proper proportionality can be determined, and it assumes a distinction between noncombatants and combatants which no longer applies. Not only are military targets located in centers of civilian population, but persons responsible for any given weapon live and work on a broad spectrum of technological planning, design, construction, deployment, and use activities in which the "combatant" is but one frequently minor member of a team.

The relinquishing of dogmas of deterrence does not necessarily produce a more effective policy position. Some claim that although any use of nuclear weapons is morally wrong, deterrence is required under current conditions, proposing something of a "bluff deterrence." The declaratory policy differs from the operational; there would be no retaliation.

The difficulty with such posturing is that only a credible deterrent can credibly deter. Michael Novak rightly insists that "a deterrent system must be reasoned and thorough; it must cover every major contingency . . .; it must be intentional; it must be the product of intelligence, foresight and will."[24] A nation must have the will as well as the ability to strike: a credible deterrent requires efficient weapons operationally deployed, the likelihood that such weapons would be used, and survivability in ensuring exchanges. For some years now, both superpowers have realized that each has moved away operationally from the declaratory policy of MAD to policies involving more selected, flexible responses, from the triad of land, sea, and air-based weapons to assure retaliatory capacity. Former Secretary of Defense Harold Brown articulated the "countervailing strategy" which would make clear that "the Soviet leadership knows that if they chose some intermediate form of aggression, we could, by a selection of large but still less than maximum nuclear attacks, exact an unacceptably high price."[25] Technological improvements in weapons systems, especially in computer-controlled mechanisms, have made selective targeting possible. The "mental image of nuclear war as a spasm of city-busting is some twenty years out of date."[26]

A deterrent policy of counter-force rather than counter-value, neutralizing the adversary's ability, rather than will, to fight, undergirds the credibility of deterrence, because massive weapons are unlikely to be used, either to avoid moral compromise or national suicide; the limited weapons entail much lesser risks. Selective attacks "carried on to deter a continuation . . . of attacks by the aggressor" could be morally justifiable.[27] Such a limited deterrence is selected not only to serve the first of the middle axioms, preventing nuclear war, but is also directed toward the second, limiting casualties in the event counterattack is necessary.

The reluctance of the Methodist bishops, among others, to embrace this deterrence by flexible response is accountable to several considerations. First, they worry about the effect of incessant cost overruns on the economy as well as social programs. Second, they see more technically effective weapons systems as provocative, with MX, Pershing, and Cruise missiles matched by Soviet SS-18s, SS-19s, and SSX-25s, escalating the arms race. But most decisively, their overriding concern seems to be that such a strategy encourages the erroneous belief that a limited nuclear war is possible and winnable. In their pastoral sensitivity to matters of the human spirit, both episcopal groups are deeply concerned about any exchange which would cross "the nuclear threshold," believing that rapid escalation to full-scale exchanges would be inevitable. Even such cold warriors as McGeorge Bundy, George F. Kennan, Robert S. McNamara, and Gerard Smith have claimed that

> No one has ever succeeded in advancing any persuasive reason to believe that any use of nuclear weapons, even on the smallest scale, could reliably be expected to remain limited.[28]

The concern is serious. The danger of learning comfortably to "live with the bomb," regarding it as just another weapon, is enormous. On the one hand, people become desensitized, with one generation accepting collateral destruction of nonmilitary population centers as inevitable, while the next plays its war games ready to "nuke" the enemy. On the other, strategists may not adequately prepare for the extraordinarily complex command systems required if tactical weapons are to be used in battlefield engagements: with widespread authority to fire, who would apply the restraints?

Once all of that is acknowledged, however, we must affirm what is clear at least up until now: the reluctance of nations to instigate nuclear suicide. If there is a nuclear threshold, there is also a strategic nuclear threshold. While "reliable reasons" could only be confirmed retrospectively in these matters, it is conceivable that a limited exchange could issue in such a stand-off that once each superpower saw the resolve of the other, neither would continue.

Such a highly problematic state of affairs is so unstable that it cannot be allowed to stand as continuing policy. In view of the fourth middle axiom, both sets of bishops are charged to call for movement toward a more secure set of international relationships. A deterrent, flexible or not, is no end in itself. One initiative which would couple it with progress toward disarmament would be a repudiation of first-use of nuclear weapons followed by further negotiation on banning of tests. The justification for the U.S. government's refusal to commit itself to a no-first-use policy has, of course, been the superiority of the Warsaw Pact conventional forces in Europe and the threat they pose. Although the supposed superiority has been seriously questioned, an emphasis on increasing conventional weaponry could accompany the declaration of a no-first-strike policy. Freeman Dyson claims that the development of precision-guided nonnuclear munitions "offers a reasonable substitute for tactical nuclear weapons."[29] When the costs of such research and deployment are compared with those of the Star Wars systems, they will seem managable.

III

After the original rhetoric announcing SDI, it soon became clear that talk of a complete umbrella or fully protective shield was exaggerated, and that the actual purpose of the new defensive systems would be to enhance deterrence. Critics point out that the objective is not actually to protect populations but to shield weapons. SDI is thus to be evaluated, in terms of our operative middle axioms, not simply as a defensive system but in conjunction with deterrent programs. Proponents contend that SDI would provide a transition to a nuclear free world, a permanently effective way of dealing with the nuclear terror.

A review of the technological viability of what we have come to call "Star Wars" discloses an extraordinarily complex set of technical systems, many of which have yet to be invented. Beyond the hardening of our own ballistic missile silos, making our weapons less vulnerable to attack, the comprehensive system would have four phases. The first, covering the boost phase in an enemy launch, includes *Surveillance, Acquisition, Tracking,* and *Kill Assessment* (SATKA). The aim is to intercept the rocket in the relatively brief period of the rocket's launch.[30] Interception in the next phase, *Separation,* is complicated by the fact that the enemy may take certain measures, passive but difficult to detect, such as deploying decoys along with active warheads. The third stage, *Space Trajectory,* presents the same difficulty of detection complicated further by enormous distances, while the fourth, *Terminal,* phase of reentry and delivery of payloads carries the dangers of exploding defensive weapons in our own territory. Even with systems in place to intercept missiles at each of the four stages, the widely agreed probability is that some would get through; even a system 90% effective would allow "unacceptable damage." Weapons proposed in the technical planning include space and ground-based chemical lasers, space-based particle beams, nuclear-driven energy weapons, kinetic energy weapons, interceptor missiles, and hypervelocity gun systems. Finally, the program would include a *Battle Management/Command/Control and Communications Technology Project,* to develop a survivable and effective command system.

Experts differ in assessing the technological feasibility of SDI. Edward Teller speaks of the incalculable increases in technological capacities in computers, at least multiplying their powers ten-fold every decade since 1945, as a case suggesting that in technology, everything is possible.[31] Former NASA Director James C. Fletcher, reporting after chairing the administration's Defense Technology Study, claimed that the technologies reviewed "make . . . an effective defense conceivable." In 1984 he recommended research, though not deployment. Robert Bowman, retired from Air Force service in which he directed space research programs, is so convinced of the technological impossibility of SDI that he has organized an Institute for Space and Security Studies to inform the public.[32] Others, like Richard DeLauer, former Undersecretary of Defense for Research and Engineering, worry about countermeasures, believing that with unrestrained development of offensive systems, "no defensive system will work."[33] Robert Jastrow attempts to counter such concerns by citing Department of Defense experts who estimate the cost to the Soviets of overwhelming our defense as three times the cost of the defense itself. He does not, however, mention the ease with which attacks might make space platforms or the laser directional mirrors inoperative; Freeman Dyson points out that a single pebble colliding at orbital velocity with a large, delicate death-ray machine in space would take it out.[34] Often, technologists contend that military research carries serendipitous value through spin-offs accruing to the civilian sector, but analysts make the cogent assertion that the Star Wars technology is so exotic that the industrial/high tech sectors will more likely experience a "crowding out."[35] The Congressional Office of Technology Assessment concluded that "a comprehensive antiballistic missile system should not serve as the basis of public expectation or national policy."[36] The fact is that in no way can SDI be tested as a complete weapons system: "We will not be able to judge it technically until it fails strategically."[37]

With anything but a ringing endorsement for the feasibility of the SDI technologies in the scientific community, it is difficult to be assured on a technical basis that SDI would significantly contribute to the first moral middle axiom, the objective of preventing nuclear war. Possibly, it could contribute to other moral objectives: in the absence of ultimate effectiveness against the ultimate weapon, defense systems would most probably reduce casualties in a nuclear exchange.[38] How significant such a reduction might be depends on other, political factors. If a sufficient level of mutuality is established so that the exchange would be concluded at a limited or tactical level, the reduction could be major; if the exchange is elevated to a series of retaliatory strategic strikes, it would be negligible or irrelevent. On the other hand, this relative good could be compromised by other factors, that is, if its costs should be crippling, or if its development would undermine more stable relations between the superpowers.

The argument that concerted development of SDI would be destablizing is a strong one. Regardless of technological assessments, here we must deal with directly political issues. The nuclear stand-off between the superpowers, delicate as it is, would be disrupted by an American ability to make Soviet missiles inoperable. The political dangers of such a prospect of an unequal balance of terror, with only one of the superpowers having a credible retaliatory capacity, could be either a temptation to the Soviets to launch a preemptive strike while they retain the ability to do so, or the entry of both superpowers into a new phase of the arms race, developing countervailing weapons and defensive systems, countermeasures and counter-countermeasures. Some insist that the Soviets have already begun the buildup of defensive systems in violation of the ABM Treaty by construction of a radar installation at Kosnoyarsk in Siberia.[39] Although this has now been admitted, a massive program of SDI research and deployment would have a far more extensive impact on the nuclear balance.

Some SDI proponents will acknowledge the destabilization but claim it would be limited to a transitional phase, until a stable defense is in place. When they tell, however, of how they intend to manage the transitional period, they begin with the project of hardening American missile silos, exacerbating the very effect they should wish to avoid. A Presbyterian background paper argues against SDI on both ethical and political grounds: "the pursuit of a policy that seeks the security of one society at the expense of the security of its primary opponent is of questionable morality and . . . improbable value since the opponent will always seek to redress the balance."[40] The targeted nation would have no alternative but to escalate its own weapon system research and deployment.

Further, the jeopardy into which SDI would continue to lead the ABM Treaty is destabilizing in another way. Written and ratified agreements between the superpowers have dubious value when one claims a privilege of unilateral reinterpretation.

A weapons system of any kind is, of course, but one item among others to be supported by a nation's resources. Another middle axiom insists that budgetary expenditures become moral issues when they preempt funds which are designated to serve important social goods. In an industry notorious for cost overruns, Star Wars defensive systems would require phenomenal expenditures. Programs of human service, education, and scientific probes into space would most likely find their funding in serious danger. Paul Nitze attempted to estabish the criterion of cost-effectiveness, that a given defense system must cost less to deploy than to counter, but the principle has been abandoned. Eugeny Velikhov of the Soviet Academy of Sciences claims that the cost of countering a space-based system would require but 1 to 2% of the cost of establishing one. The two groups of bishops are deeply concerned about what they take to be the staggering costs of SDI research, let alone deployment, calling the enormous expenses an act of aggression against the poor.

Beyond the economic concerns, the fourth middle axiom derived from the goal of *shalom* raises the question of the effect SDI programs would have on the international climate and the human spirit. Will it contribute to that kind of human condition which makes a reduction of arms and an increase of mutual trust possible, or is it more likely to deepen mistrust and extend alienation? The driving motive behind the defense initiative seems to be a desire for self-sufficiency. The initial announcement appeared without prior consultation with European and other allies, whose survival is as much at stake as our own. The SDI possibility appears to be an expression of a new isolationism, an attempt to be in complete control. President Reagan has said "We will trust in American technology and not in agreements with the Soviet Union."[41] The program fixes on a military solution to difficulties with the Soviets that are basically political in character, and would reinforce an entrenched rigidity and inflexible stereotypes in relation to our major adversary. Psychologically speaking, the defensive way of thinking is obsessive; spiritually, it is idolatrous. Signers of the "New Abolitionist Covenant" refuse to believe that "our own technological creations can save us."[42]

While idolatry is always destructive, on the contemporary international scene it could be disastrous. Adherence to outdated notions of national sovereignty will obstruct a nation's full and vital participation in what we see more evidently every day as an interdependent world. National sovereignty can no longer be confined to the terms of a fortress mentality or self-sufficiency, but needs rethinking in terms of networking rather than isolation.

SDI, then, fails to be convincing in its moral seriousness in view of the four axioms derived from *shalom* as God's intention for humankind. The alternative of deterrence with initiatives toward disarmament we have found to be more likely to prevent nuclear war. The provocative character of the deployment of SDI components counteracts whatever it might have contributed toward saving lives in the event of nuclear conflict. The staggering cost estimates indicate serious social and economic repercussions. Finally, the option of deterrence combined with defense demonstrates little interest in fostering those conditions which would make the peace of *shalom* possible; rather, it seems to promote suspicion rather than trust, alienation rather than interdependence. The most direct way SDI could have a positive effect on the nuclear stalemate would be through its abandonment.

IV

In a society in which pluralism is a principle, not merely a pragmatic adjustment, a theological analysis will not pretend to produce apodictic solutions to highly contingent problems. The theologian speaks to and for those for whom the saga of creation and redemption provides the meaning of their lives, whose vocation is *shalom*. Theology will seek alliances with those who come to the debates with quite different premises, arranging the apples and oranges in their fruit baskets according to quite different principles. What the theologian hopes to bring to the deliberations is not only a particular answer, but a method suggestive enough to facilitate in others the clarification of their own priorities.

NOTES AND REFERENCES

1.   Ronald Reagan, "Launching the SDI," in Z. Brzezinski, ed. *Promise or Peril: the Strategic Defense Initiative* (Washington, DC: Ethics and Public Policy Center, 1986), 48-49.

2.   Ibid., p. x.

3.   Sharon D. Welch, "A Geneology of the Logic of Deterrence: Habermas, Foucault and a Feminist Ethic of Risk," in *Union Seminary Quarterly Review, 41*(2):23 (1987).

4.   James M. Gustafson, *Ethics from a Theocentric Perspective*, vol. I (Chicago: University of Chicago Press, 1981). p. 24.

5.   Resolution of the Fifteenth General Synod of the United Church of Christ, 1986.

6.   Ibid.

7.   Wolfhart Pannenberg, in Ernst W. Lefever and E. Stephen Hunt, eds., *The Apocalyptic Premise: Nuclear Arms Debated* (Washington, DC: Ethics and Public Policy Center), p. 359.

8.   Edward Schillibeeckx, *Christ: the Experience of Jesus as Lord* (New York: Crossroad, 1980), pp. 695-696.

9.   Margaret A. Farley, "New Patterns of Relationship: Beginnings of a Moral Revolution", in *Theological Studies,* 36, 1975, p. 646.

10.   Alan Geyer, *The Idea of Disarmament: Rethinking the Unthinkable* (Elgin, IL: Brethren Press, 1982), p. 200.

11.   P. Hans Sun, "Notes on How to Begin to Think about Technology in a Theological Way," in Carl Mitcham and Jim Grote, eds., *Theology and Technology: Essays in Christian Analysis and Exegesis* (Lanham, MD, and London: University Press of America, 1984), p. 191.

12.   See Jacques Ellul's essays in the Mitcham and Grote volume, or his commentary on the Book of Revelation.

13.   Danny Collum and Jim Rice, "To Tell the Truth," in *Sojourners,* 16(5):18.

14.   For a more extensive discussion of Tillich's analysis of technology, see A. Arnold Wettstein, "Reviewing Tillich in a Technological Culture," in John J. Carey, ed., *Theonomy and Autonomy* (Macon, Ga.: Mercer University Press, 1984), pp. 113-133.

15.   Kavka suggests these moral goods without finding it necessary to defend them. Gregory S. Kavka, "Space War Ethics," in *Ethics,* 95:674 (April 1985).

16.   George F. Kennan, in *The Atlantic Monthly,* May 1959, cited in Alan Geyer, *The Idea of Disarmament: Rethinking the Unthinkable,* (Elgin, IL: Brethren Press, 1982).

17.   National Conference of Catholic Bishops, *The Challenge of Peace: God's Promise and Our Response,* May 3, 1983, p. 37.

18. Cf., pp. 28-34.

19. Ibid., p. 57.

20. The United Methodist Council of Bishops, *In Defense of Creation: the Nuclear Crisis and a Just Peace* (Nashville, TN: Graded Press, 1986), p. 34.

21. Remember Winston Churchill's phrase, "Safety will be the sturdy child of terror, and survival the twin brother of annihilation."

22. *In Defense of Creation . . .*, pp. 46-47.

23. Alan Geyer, p. 46.

24. Michael Novak, "Nuclear Morality," in *America,* July 3, 1982, 7.

25. Harold Brown, "Excerpts from Address on War Policy," *New York Times,* Aug. 21, 1980, Sec. A, p. 9.

26. Jospeh P. Martino, "Star Wars—Technology's New Challenge to Moralists," in *This World,* No. 9 (Fall 1985), 24.

27. William V. O'Brien, *The Conduct of Just and Limited War* (New York: Praeger, 1981), pp. 39-40.

28. McGeorge Bundy et. al., "Nuclear Weapons and the Atlantic Alliance," in *Foreign Affairs,* 60(2):751.

29. Freeman Dyson, "Bombs and Poetry," in *Values at War* (Salt Lake City: University of Utah Press, 1986).

30. Lt. Gen. James A. Abrahamson, Statement to Congress, in *Strategic Defense Initiative: Folly or Future?* (Boulder, CO: Westview Press, 1986).

31. Edward Teller, cited in George A. Kenworth II, "The Case for Strategic Defense: An Option for a World Disarmed," in *SDI: Folly or Future,* p. 130.

32. Among his publications is *Star Wars: A Defense Insider's Case Against the Strategic Defense Initiative,* (New York: St. Martin's Press, 1986).

33. Cited by David Holloway, "The Strategic Defense Initiative and the Soviet Union," in *SDI: Folly or Future,* p. 149.

34. Freeman Dyson, *Weapons and Hope* (New York: Harper and Row, 1984).

35. Walter Zegvald and Christian Enzing, *SDI and Industrial Technology Policy: Threat or Opportunity?* (London: Frances Pinter, 1987), p. 177.

36. See *Ballistic Missile Defense Technologies* (Washington, DC: U.S. Government Printing Office, 1985).

37. Adam M. Garfinkle, "The Politics of Space Defense," in *Orbis,* 28(2):243 (1984).

38. For this reason, Gregory Kavka supports limited SDI research (cf. Kavka).

39. Max M. Kampelman, "SDI and the Arms Control Process," in *Atlantic Community Quarterly,* 23(3).

40. Background Paper on Militarization of Space, 198th General Assembly (1986) of the Presbyterian Church (USA).

41. Cited in *Soujourners,* 16(3):21.

42. The Covenant was published in *Sojourners,* August, 1981, 18-19. The citation is from Danny Collum and Jim Rice, p. 20.

TECHNOLOGY AND
ITS ULTIMATE THREAT:
A JEWISH MEDITATION

David Novak

INTRODUCTION

During the all day service of Yom Kippur, the Day of Atonement, a significant section of the liturgy consists of a vivid reenactment of the rites of atonement which took place in the Second Temple in Jerusalem. In one of the most prominently practiced Jewish rites, that of the Ashkenazim (Jews of German and East European origin), a concluding prayer is ascribed to the High Priest: "For the people of Sharon he would say, 'May it be Thy will O' Lord our God and God of our ancestors that their homes shall not become their graves.'"[1] (According to scholars, Sharon was a valley subject to devastating flash floods, against which its residents were helpless.[2]) The source of this liturgical piece is the Palestinian Talmud, which elaborates on an earlier statement in the Mishnah that the High Priest prayed a short prayer just after leaving the

Research in Philosophy and Technology, Volume 10, pages 43-70.
ISBN: 1-55938-062-4

Holy-of-Holies, he being the only person allowed entrance into it, and only once, annually, on Yom Kippur.

The prayer was to be kept short lest the people assembled in the Temple fear that the High Priest had died in the mysterious chamber.[3] In the original version of the prayer, according to the politically sophisticated rabbis of the Roman city of Caesaria, the High Priest said, "And concerning Thy people Israel, may they not dominate one another (*yigbahu serarah*),"[4] in addition to his prayer for the hapless people of Sharon who were constantly in such jeopardy. The prayer, then, consists of two distinct parts: (1) a call for deliverance from political tyranny, (2) a call for deliverance from physical cataclysm. The High Priest, as both spiritual and political leader of his people,[5] at a moment of his own immediate relief from anxiety (lest he die in the Holy-of-Holies, or lest his atonement rites for Israel be rejected by God), was thus in a position to truly sympathize with those whose vicar he was.

In that far off time, anxiety about the political realm and anxiety about the physical realm, although generically connected, could still be specifically separated. In our day, however, the nuclear threat has specifically connected these two sources of anxiety. This closer connection between the political realm and the physical realm results from the predominance of technology in the modern world, a predominance epitomized by the nuclear threat. As such, radical thought is demanded of all who care about humankind and its earthly dwelling.[6]

Since such care can certainly be expected from the theologians in the various religious traditions, nothing less than a radical reexamination of their respective traditions is called for. Now this reexamination, this *re-search,* can be of two kinds: (1) It can have a more specifically normative thrust; that is, it can suggest a definite course of action to be taken in the interest of lessening or eliminating the nuclear threat for the sake of world peace; or (2) it can have a more reflective thrust; that is, it can meditate on the more general issues of life and death, the human relationship with the earth, and the human relationship with the works of its hands, the essential question of technology itself.

This essay relates to the second kind. It does not presume to offer any specific suggestions of a normative kind. That would require a knowledge of the scientific, technological, and political issues involved in the nuclear threat, knowledge which is not within my own range of expertise or direct interest, although I by no means minimize the importance of these issues because of my own limitations. Rather, this essay is an attempt by a Jewish theologian to meditate on the essential question of technology itself. My view, thus, is theoretical, not practical, although it could, I hope, *inform* practical discussions on the very pressing normative issues of deterence, disarmament, etc. That *information* of practical discussion, however, could only be implied *from* the essay; it can not be found explicitly *within* it. Therefore, this essay is about technology epitomized by the nuclear threat, not about the nuclear threat per se. Indeed, it seems to me that more reflection on the general question of technology might lead to new ways of thinking about and acting on the nuclear threat, but, at this point in time, I am as yet unable to do that.

The ancient prayer presented at the beginning, like all significant petitionary prayers, deals with three essential relationships: (1) that between God and humans, (2) that between humans themselves, and (3) that between humans and their world. Now, one could make a convincing argument that the nuclear threat has radically changed all three of these essential relationships. If so, each of them must be reconstituted in order that a meditation in this area might be truly relevant in the present and for the future, that it might address what is before us, and what lies ahead of us. This process of reconstitution involves a radical reexamination of our past. It must be a process of reinterpretation, a contemporary hermeneutic. The question is where the process is to begin. Where does the apodictic sequence start? This is the crucial methodological question, because if Jewish theology is to say something to the world—in our case, the world dominated by technology—then it must understand that technology itself can be intelligently approached only on a level where it is most immediately experienced by all of humankind. That level is neither the relationship between humans themselves, nor the relationship between humans and God.

Intelligent approach is not immediately on the level of the interhuman relationship because the nuclear threat as the epitomy of technology is not human destructiveness of other humans per se, but rather the threat of humankind being destroyed by the technical environment of its own making. Human destructiveness of other humans has been with us since Cain and Abel; being literally destroyed by the works of our hands is the *novum*. Moreover, the level of intelligent approach is not the relationship between humans and God for two reasons: (1) A large and significant segment of humankind is either indifferent to this relationship as it is understood in the West, or willfully denies its existence altogether. (2) Even for those of us who are neither indifferent nor denying, the nuclear threat seems to vividly confirm the Psalmist's utterance, "the heavens, the heavens are the Lord's, but the earth He has given to humankind" (Psalms 115:16). It would seem that the level of intelligent approach for a contemporary theologian is to examine how the nuclear threat has changed the relationship between humans and their environment, and then what traditional resources are available to us for rethinking that relationship. In the light of this project, the traditional understandings of the interhuman relationship and the God/human relationship must be reexamined and choices made from among them.[7]

For a Jewish theologian, especially (although Christian theologians are not exempt in that the Hebrew Bible is their "Old Testament"), the charge must be faced that the Hebraic doctrine of the all-powerful and authoritative God, and the human created in the image of this God, is itself largely responsible for the stance towards the environment which has led to the threat of the annihilation of humankind and its earthly dwelling. If this charge is true, then it is hard to see how anyone can still affirm the moral relevance (however generally understood) of a book and its tradition, whose doctrine of the essence of humanness is now judged to be the source of death rather than its own proclamation that "it is a tree of life (*etz hayyim*) to those who hold fast to it" (Proverbs 3:18).[8]

MODERN TECHNOLOGY

Modern technology is concerned with the relationship between humans and the works of their hands. Nuclear bombs are such works, and their meaning in terms of human self-understanding can be determined only within this overall context. And, although ancient technology and its role in antiquity are very different from modern technology and its role in our world, nevertheless, a fundamental distinction made by Aristotle is indispensable at the very outset of any reflection on any technology at any time.

At the very beginning of the *Nichomachean Ethics,* when positing that the meaning of all human action is determined by its purpose, Aristotle makes the following point:

> Sometimes the activities (*energeiai*) are themselves the ends; other times the ends are certain products (*erga tina*) apart from the activities themselves . . . In the latter situation, the products are inherently (*pephyke*) superior to the activities which produced them.[9]

Now, for Aristotle, the only truly fulfilling human life of *eudaimonia* (inadequately translated "happiness": better translated "doing and being well") clearly involves those activities which are ends-in-themselves and which are co-equal with human nature in the most serious sense. *Techné,* that is, human making of tangible things, conversely, is not an eudaimonic activity precisely because there is a gap between the producer and the product.[10] As such, although techné is necessary for human life, it is not co-equal with it because the nonliving, nonconscious thing would become more valuable than the living, conscious human agent who made it. Essentially, they are disparate in that once production is complete they are no longer related. In other words, for Aristotle—and here he is the quintessential ancient philosopher—techné is fundamentally paradoxical if elevated to an end-in-itself; namely, what is inherently inferior would be valued as superior. In this sense, Aristotle's designation of the paradoxical valuation of things over persons is somewhat comparable to the Scriptural designation of the paradox of idolatry. "Their idols are silver and gold, the works of human hands . . . their makers will become like them, all who trust in them" (Psalms 115:4,8). One can and should today be even more emphatic about the nuclear weapons we have made. Are not silver and gold rather benign compared to plutonium?

With the growing modern emphasis of the human person as *homo faber*— what might be called "technical man"—the gap between the producer and his or her products was viewed in a new way. The transcendence of the product was now regarded as only temporary. Thus, Hegel, almost paraphrasing Aristotle, describes the product of human work first as an "object" (*Gegenstand*) belonging to consciousness as a "purpose" (*Zweck*) and, then, as something *external* and *other*.[11] He does not stop here, nor does he abruptly eliminate *techné* from essentially human activity, as Aristotle did. Rather, Hegel—and here he is the quintessential modern philosopher—sees techné as but one movement included in and transcended by (*aufgehoben*) the ongoing historical development of spirit/consciousness.

> Consciousness (*das Bewusstsein*) stepping back from its product (*Werk*) is in fact the universal . . . against its product, which is that which is determined (*das Bestimmte*), transcends itself qua product and is itself the undetermined space, which does not find itself fulfilled by its product.[12]

Humankind as emerging consciousness at this moment is homo faber, capable of creating much more than things and, hence, only subordinate to them for a moment in its history as consciousness. After the dialectical transcendence of this technical historical moment, consciousness is now free to deal with the higher, nontangible realms of morality, politics, religion, and, ultimately, philosophy.

Following in Hegel's footsteps, Marx stops the dialectic, however, at this productive economic point, and he sees the subsequent realms of morality, politics, religion, and philosophy as being reducible to the realm of production, and basically illusions if regarded as truly transcending them.[13] Nevertheless, even for Marx, the human person is not subordinate to the works of human hands, and, whereas Hegel employs a dialectic of transcendence to affirm human autonomy over things, Marx employs what I would call a dialectic of infinity; namely, the human person qua uniquely human life makes itself through the works of its hands. Yet the capacity for production is limitless. The maker, the human species-being (*Gattungs-leben*), conscious of its own creative power, values itself over any finite product it happens to produce at any one time. In the human individual's identification with the total human collective, that individual is no longer subordinate to the alienation (*Entfremdung*) of domination by the surplus value of his or her own labor in the hands of someone else.[14] For that "someone else" has also been totally identified with the full human collective and, thus, ceases to be alienating. The master-slave dialectic has been at last overcome, in Marx's eyes. For Marx, then, techné returns to the rightful role of being a subordinate effect when homo faber becomes fully collectivized and is conscious of this collectivization as the prima causa of human life in its fabricated, social, environment. The fundamental human problem here is not the works of human hands, but that they are not controlled by the whole human collective in and for itself alone.

What we see in Hegel, and even more so in Marx, is a radical change of the four Aristotelian causal principles. For Aristotle, in making (*poiésis*)—which includes human techné—the purpose (*telos*) is a preexistent entity which determines how it is viewed as an intelligible form (*eidos*) by a maker (*poioun*), who molds what is physically given.[15] For Hegel, and especially Marx, on the other hand, the maker him or herself creates an intelligible form and then molds what is given into a finished product (*der Werk/das Bestimmte*), to which he or she is essentially superior.[16]

One of these causal principles does not seem to have changed at all from Aristotle to Marx: the material principle. Although Aristotle had a specific term for it, $hvl\bar{e}$,[17] when presenting his concise theory of all four principles in concert, he basically describes it as "that from which something becomes" (*to ex hou ginetai*),[18] and it is precisely here that the nuclear threat belies Hegel's confidence in human transcendence and Marx's confidence in human infinity.[19] The nuclear threat shows that humankind is neither transcendent nor infinite, and even belies Kant's moral confidence in the human person as "an end-in-itself" (*Zweck an sich selbst*) because, as Hannah Arendt insightfully pointed out, the end which the human person is, is itself what it becomes through homo faber, its maker.[20] Thus, how is "self-creation" any better or any safer than the self's creation of things? For Kant, the autonomous human person can only be constituted as superior to the human person as a sensuous being, who is still part of the phenomenal order. The antinomies between the collective and the individual, between the present and the future—which most directly concern homo faber—these are left as unsolved "casuistical questions" by Kant. Is the human person an end-in-itself as an individual or as a species-being? The history of philosophy shows what Hegel and Marx and others did with Kant's unfinished philosophical agenda, and this seems to show that Kant stands with them, not above them. The same problem confronts them all.[21]

The nuclear threat shows itself to us as the transcendence of the work of our hands over and against us. That is why there is no "technical solution" to it, no simply "getting a handle on it," as Heidegger convincingly stated.[22] Our works, through the military persons or technicians who serve them, and not through the scientists who made them, these *things* are the threat, a threat that could very well be realized by human mistake, not human intent. This situation exists universally, irrespective of the ideologies (capitalistic, socialistic, or whatever) of the societies involved in them. Our works now directly threaten the full human collective, and seem to be possessed by more and more members of that collective—that collective in which Marx and many other modern Utopians placed such absolute faith. They have transcended us, rather than the other way around. Moreover, that transcendence is not intelligible per se and, thus, it is not benignly attractive, like Aristotle's telos.

Modern technology asks for no justification, and gives none.[23] Rather, we seem to be returning to the pre-Aristotelian (and, thus, pre-philosophical) notion of *telos* as blind fate, an unintelligible, malignant, temporal end to human life.[24] Whereas, for the pre-Aristotelians, that unintelligible and unpredictable temporal end presented itself only as the terminus of the life of the human individual, it now shows itself as the terminus of the entire human species, if not even beyond that. The late Hans J. Morgenthau, not as the expert on the specifics of the nuclear threat that he surely was, but rather as a philosopher presenting the essence of the issue, wrote over twenty-five years ago:

> It is a distinctive characteristic of our secular age that it has replaced the belief in the immortality of the human person with the attempt to assure the immorality of the world he leaves behind. . . . The significance of the possibility of nuclear death . . . destroys the meaning of immortality by making both society and history impossible.[25]

Finally, we cannot invoke a better technology to overcome our dilemma inasmuch as all technology, from Aristotle, who minimized it, to Marx, who maximized it, has assumed that the material principle, which for humans can only be the earth, is a perpetual datum—something always there for whatever we want to do with it. Yet the nuclear threat has destroyed our conscious relationship with the very matter of our planet. The earth no longer shows itself to us as the irreducible substratum upon which we forever stand. Could anyone after 1945 simply write, "and the earth stands forever (*l'ad*)," as did the author of Ecclesiastes (1:4)? It seems that a nuclear holocaust will not only destroy human civilization, but that it will also destroy the very possibility of even a "saved remnant" of human civilization ever regenerating itself again.[26]

RETURN TO NATURE: MODERN PROPOSALS

Even before the actual emergence of the nuclear threat to both civilization and the biosphere (to use Teilhard de Chardin's felicitous phrase[27]), there have been modern attempts to challenge the supremacy of technology by calling for a return to nature. This attempted return to nature has taken three main forms.

The first attempted return to nature, and the one which seems to have the most in common with the classical idea of nature, is modern *natural rights* theory. This theory can be characterized by its minimal claims, a characterization consistent with modern science's assumption of the methodological primacy of Ockham's Razor. Modern natural rights theory has been concerned with what is minimally indispensable for human society to persist, namely, with such rights as the protection of human life, dignity, and property. Here the "nature" in "natural" (contrary to classical natural law theory, as we shall soon see) is not a substantial transcendent whole of which human social nature is a part. In the modern theory, nature is not a ground but only a limit, something human inventiveness must take into account, but which is not, or cannot be, its source of norms.[28] It is only a *conditio sine qua non*. Because of this minimal view of nature, this type of natural rights theory has been endorsed by some recent philosophers who would be the first to deny that they are part of the classical tradition of natural law at all.[29]

The weakness of this theory is that it presupposes more of the *status quo ante* than can be taken for granted today, certainly after the rise of the nuclear threat, and even after the purposeless destruction seen in the two world wars. Much of it never deals with the human capacity for nihilistic destruction, so manifestly evidenced in this century's first half alone. Along with the medievals (but, significantly, without their theological and metaphysical grounds), it seems to assume that there is an immanent *inclinatio naturalis* in human life to preserve itself both individually and collectively.[30] As Émile Durkheim showed, however, loss of social cohesion and purpose can often be the antecedent rather than the consequence of human self-destructiveness.[31] As such, even the immanent will to live is contingent on something which transcends it. Thus, our postnuclear question is not what the social and political order is to be, but more radically, what can inspire us to preserve society and human life at all. This more radical question presupposes the very transcendence that modern natural rights theory either denies altogether or prudently brackets. Without this transcendence, however, it is hard to see how technology can be limited in any cogent way.

The second attempted return to nature I call (for want of a better term) "naturism." Naturism, by affirming the ecological dangers of technology, the dangers technology poses to the integrity and viability of the earth, thereby recognizes the unique gravity of the nucler threat and that the technology which brought it about must be limited. Its practical program has been to simply reject technology as much as is humanly possible today, and with whatever political and even physical means at its disposal. Theoretically, it seems to be based on the notion that humans are essentially sentient beings, and they should be reintegrated back into sentient nature, back to the earth.[32] The means to this return have, of course, been quite varied. Thus, naturism has taken such diverse forms as pacifism, conservationism, vegetarianism, nudism, etc.

Nevertheless, the weakness of this approach is that it fails to realize that the violence it so abhors is not a technical invention, that it too is part of the sentient realm, that "the wolf shall dwell with the lamb" (Isaiah 11:6) is a prophetic hope, not a description of nature as it is here and now to be imitated. Indeed, sentient nature itself is morally neutral, offering no intelligible criterion for emphasizing peace and rejecting aggression. It is simply no normative standard. Today's "naturists" would be very hard pressed to argue why their peaceful view of nature is any truer than the aggressive view of nature advocated by the so-called "Social Darwinists," whose ideology they no doubt abhor.[33] Further, the romantic rather than rational outlook of naturism has led some of its proponents to employ the very violence, which they see coming from technology, against technology—a vicious circle indeed! As Plato astutely pointed out, the sentient realm cannot be normative, precisely because it shows itself in paradoxes.[34]

Finally, the greatest philosophical attempt in modern times to reintegrate the human person back into a transcendent natural realm (similar to the project, if not the actual systems, of Aristotle and Spinoza) is that of A. N. Whitehead. For Whitehead, nature is conceived of as a developing process towards higher and higher levels of consciousness and freedom. This process is, moreover, open-ended and, therefore, infinitely progressive. Within this system of nature, God functions as the "lure" for all lesser entities; that is, God, by virtue of having knowledge of all possibilities, provides tempting opportunities for each creative entity to further develop into higher and higher levels of actualization.[35] This God functions neither as first sufficient cause like Spinoza's causa sui, nor as the wholly determined ideal like Aristotle's telos,[36] nor does this God function like the God of Scripture, who directly commands His people.

It is hard to see what this God could possibly forbid. He seems incapable of saying "no" in any radical sense, that is, a "no" not just for the sake of a "yes" coming quickly on its heels. There seems to be no limit to the creative thrust into the future by either God or man. Indeed, creativity seems to be God's only imitable attribute, or, more accurately, God seems to be part of a creativity whose name is *progress*. As he writes, "The novel hybrid feelings derived from God with the derivative sympathetic valuations are the foundations of progress".[37] Yet has not an uncritical, that is, unlimited, acceptance of the value of progress led to our present crisis of technology, not only with the nuclear threat but, also, with the whole ecological dilemma? Hence, technology must be limited by humans, and it can be so limited only when humans accept an intelligible moral standard which transcends their own inventiveness. The containment of technology surely requires such a transcendent "no".[38] In the moral sphere, such a "no" manifests itself as a prohibition, a "thou shalt not." For example, the first Scriptural commandment, according to the rabbinic tradition, is a negative commandment, namely, "And the Lord God commanded humans (*'al ha' adam*) . . . from the tree of the knowledge of Good and Evil you shall not eat" (Genesis 2:16).[39]

RETURN TO NATURE: THE CLASSICAL APPROACH

The classical idea of nature regarded it as a transcendent realm in which humans could intelligently participate by looking to it as a normative standard. This realm, especially as constituted by Aristotle, was regarded as both intelligible and intelligent.[40] The apex of this intelligible/intelligent nature is God, who is thinking (*noésis*) who thinks (*noéseós*) thinking (*noésis*).[41] Being intelligible, human intelligence can know it; being intelligent, human intelligence can imitate it. In other words, it transcends human consciousness as both object and as subject, but human consciousness cannot transcend it. That is why it is *the* normative standard, and this idea has had an enormous influence on subsequent thought, indeed on theology most of all. For example, Maimonides, who interpreted numerous Scriptural passages figuratively when they conflicted with what he accepted as philosophically proven truth, interprets literally the Psalmist's words, "The heavens declare (*mesapprim*) the glory of God" (Psalms 19:2).[42]

This idea of nature was based on the assumption that the heavens are of a different and more perfectly indestructible matter than the earth, and that the circular motion of heavenly bodies is more perfectly perpetual than the linear, terminable motion found on earth. For this latter motion seems to involve constant exertion (*bia*) and eventual exhaustion, being weighted down as it is with the inertia of earthly matter.[43] In terms of the human relation to this higher realm, Aristotle saw truly human active well-being (*eudaimonia*) as being the theoretical life, whose object is the eternal heavens as they orbit around God as the prime Attractive Mover. The theoretical life is preeminently eudaimonic precisely because it seems to remove the human agent from the physical exertion and exhaustion associated with techné, which is the constant battle with nonhuman forces on earth. The theoretical life, rather than the technical life, is seen as the only antidote to the violence and alienation that is so regressive and opposed to intellectual progress, progress determined by how much of the preexistent norm is discovered and understood. For Aristotle, it is the only opportunity for the human soul to become at least functionally divine.[44] The practical corollary regarding our nuclear threat, as I have outlined it, can be quickly drawn. In this view, nature humbles technology by showing itself as the ultimate attraction to the human intellect.

How much of this is plausible, let alone applicable today? Since Galileo, we no longer regard heavenly matter and heavenly motion as different from or superior to earthly matter and earthly motion.[45] Since Newton, we regard the laws of gravity as applying universally. The resulting mechanization of physics led to the rejection of the idea of a cosmic organism both intelligible and intelligent.[46] Even if teleology is still a useful concept in describing certain phenomena of the biosphere, it is nonetheless difficult to ascribe an intelligence to these phenomena, let alone one which transcends human intelligence and can thus be normative for it.[47] Hence, the late Leo Strauss, one of the most vigorous, insightful and learned opponents of mechanistic explanations of human affairs, was honest enough to admit at the very beginning of his now classic study of the idea of natural law and the historical shift to the idea of natural right, that people were forced to accept a fundamental, typically modern, dualism of a non-teleological natural science and a teleological science of man. . . . An adequate solution to the problem of natural right cannot be found before this basic problem has been solved. Needless to say, the present lectures cannot deal with this problem.[48]

In other words, we are left, for the time being at least, with Kant's humanly limited teleology, namely, man as an end-in-itself,[49] and all the problems his "formalism" entails in terms of being integrated with the rest of human social life, as well as with the nonhuman realm. Indeed, as we have seen, Kantianism is particularly weak in providing limits for homo faber.

Strauss saw the problem as being the reconciliation of modern natural science with the idea of human virtue. Even were this not the issue, there is a much more ancient moral problem facing classical teleology. For the culture which a life according to nature (*kata physin*), as opposed to a life contrary to nature (*para physin*), presupposes, is itself a culture that is fundamentally morally suspect. Thus, a moral critique of classical culture long predates a scientific critique of the cosmic teleology, as its greatest philosopher proclaimed.

The moral problem concerns the essential character of such a culture, a culture so profoundly committed to leisure (*scholé*). Here again we return to Aristotle. For he, to a large extent following his teacher Plato, saw leisure not as indolence, but rather as a climate where the technical response to bodily needs and their management is handled by one type of person, who is thus subordinate to another type of person. This latter type alone enjoys leisure, and by so doing, is alone freed by this service to engage in theoretical activity.

It seems that human active well-being is to be within the context of leisure (*en ta scholé*). We exert ourselves (*ascholoumetha*) in order that we might be leisurely, just as we wage war in order that we might bring about peace.[50]

Moreover, this peaceful leisure requires slavery.[51] Now it is true that in principle Aristotle is not defending slavery as an historical institution. For him, slavery is justified only when it is a case of those who are naturally (that is, intellectually) superior ruling those who are naturally inferior. Clearly, the historical accident of being captured in war, which is how most slaves became slaves in the ancient world, does not ipso facto mean that such hapless victims are naturally inferior to their captors.[52] When this was indeed the case, however, Aristotle regarded the slave as one whose very raison d'être lies in someone else, and that is not only necessary but desirable as well.[53]

Against all of this, it was Hegel—knowing Aristotelian philosophy so well—who insightfully showed that the master is just as alienated from himself as is the slave, in fact more so, for the master winds up being more dependent on the slave than the slave is on him. The whole system of slavery entails the negation of "independent consciousness" (*selbstaendiges Bewusstsein*).[54] Thus, whereas historical slavery does not necessarily have Aristotle's philosophical justification for it, the principle of absolute dominance does and, as such, there is a justification for an interalienation within society itself even without the legal institution of slavery per se. Finally, slavery is based on the metaphysical dualism of the dominance of matter by consciousness, or of the body by the mind.[55] As Descartes and others have asserted, our mental relationship with our own bodies is the beginning of our extensive relationship with physical nature.[56]

The nuclear threat involves a fundamental interalienation among humans, namely, the belief that one human group knows what is best for itself and everyone else, so that everyone else must be subordinate to it. The nuclear threat results from a fundamental alienation of the human person from earthly nature, the belief that this nature is essentially there as a human resource.[57] Therefore, it seems rather unlikely that the cultural matrix of beliefs which posits the dominance of one human group by another, and the dominance of earthly nature by humans, that such a cultural matrix is going to be able to provide us with the radical guidance we need to contain technology, which in essence is the issue of dominating and being dominated. It seems we should look elsewhere for the radical guidance we so desperately need to overcome this vicious and mortally threatening syndrome.

THE SABBATH AND ITS LAW

It was the first century Hellenistic Jewish theologian, Philo of Alexandria, who presented Judaism as transcending Greek philosophy, that is, both containing its truth superlatively and surpassing its defects. In Philo's treatment of the Jewish Sabbath as an institution and an idea, he presents it in a way clearly designed to show that it surpasses the Platonic-Aristotelian idea of leisure (scholé) and the inherent social alienation it necessarily and willingly entails. In this treatment we begin to see how the Jewish idea of the Sabbath is a fundamentally different way of constituting the relationship with God, with other humans, and with the nonhuman environment. It suggests a different role for technology in theologically constituting full human personhood.

No doubt, in opposition to the idea Plato and Aristotle presented, which was, in fact, a conceptualization of the social reality of their own culture, Philo writes as follows about the Sabbath:

> Furthermore when He forbids bodily labour on the seventh day, He permits the exercise of the highest activities, namely, those employed in the study of virtue's lore. . . But since we consist of body and soul, he (*Moses*) assigned to the body its proper tasks (*ta oikeia erga*) and similarly to the soul what falls to its share, and his earnest desire was, that the two should be waiting to relieve each other. Thus while the body is working, the soul enjoys a respite, but when the body takes its rest, the soul resumes its work, and thus the best

forms of life (*hoi aristoi tón bión*), the theoretical and the practical, take their turn (*ameibosin*) in replacing each other.[58]

Although he is using vocabulary formulated by Aristotle (*energeia, theórétikos, praktikos*), Philo is constituting their interrelations in a Jewish way. The highest actions (*tas ameinous praxeis*) are connected with the study and the teaching of the Torah. Moreover, like Josephus, Philo emphasizes the weekly reading and exposition of the Torah in the synagogue as a communal act involving the entire community.[59] He especially mentions servants, both male and female, as participants in the activities of the Sabbath, that is, both the positive involvement in Torah learning and the negative restraint from ordinary weekday labor. In fact, he even mentions that since the servants are not serving their masters on the Sabbath, the masters themselves have to do more menial tasks for themselves on that day than on weekdays.[60] In his most specific rejection of Plato and Aristotle, he justifies this mutuality in the entire community, including slaves, because "no human (*anthrópos*) is a slave from nature (*ek physeós doulos oudeis*)".[61] Finally, he places both the active life and the theoretical life ultimately on the same level; that is, they are both constituents in a revolving cycle, neither being superior to the other. Thus, the Sabbath limits the dominance of each one by the other because it is lived by all.

In a much later rabbinic text, this concept of the Sabbath being a mixture of the theoretical and the bodily, and the resultant blending of socioeconomic differences in the community, comes out in an even more vivid way. There, we find a dispute between two rabbis as to whether the Sabbath was given for pleasure (*ta 'anog*) or for the study of the Torah.[62] The subsequent discussion resolves the dispute by concluding that the Sabbath was given for pleasure (and there is no doubt that "pleasure" here means sexual pleasure) to the scholars who "weary themselves" in the study of the Torah all week long, and that it was given for the study of the Torah to the laborers who, "being engaged in their labor," can only engage in Torah study on the Sabbath. Thus the Sabbath is no less "physical" than it is "spiritual," but it regularly overcomes these distinctions and the socioeconomic forms of dominance they entail.[63] The basic social activity eliminated on the Sabbath is economic production and interchange, where human intercourse is determined by things,[64] an idea most explicitly typified in the prohibition of making fire on the Sabbath.[65] Finally, concerning the relationship between men and women (of which there is so much discussion these days, especially in religious communities), the rabbis saw the "thou" (*attah*) addressed in the Decalogue to remember and keep the Sabbath, as being both male and female. In the rabbinic specification of Sabbath activity, not only are women freed from the usual "womanly" chores like cooking, sewing, and washing, but they are also entitled to be full participants in the very act of sanctification (*qiddush*) whereby the holiness of the day is initially proclaimed.[66]

The overcoming of socioeocnomic dominance on a regular cyclical basis through the Sabbath does more than involve members of the covenanted community per se. Thus, not only was one not to have a slave who was a member of the covenanted community (that is, one who had been circumcised and immersed, and who was responsible for many of the commandments of the Torah) do his or her labor, but one was to extend this privilege even to an uncircumcised slave.[67] In other words, even a nonparticipant in the Covenant was not to be used for the sake of someone else in his or her observance and enjoyment of the Sabbath. For the same reason, gentiles, whether formally part of the Jewish polity (*ger toshab*) or not (*nokri*), were also protected from exploitation by Jews on the Sabbath.[68] In rabbinic law, one is not allowed to so much as suggest to a gentile to do any work for a Jew on the Sabbath, nor may a Jew force Sabbath observance on a gentile in the gentile's domain.[69] The gentile, then, is neither forced *to be for Judaism,* nor is he or she forced *to be part of Judaism.* There is neither the dominance of the egoistic conquerer nor the dominance of the altruistic missionary.[70]

Coming closer to the question of the environment, the technological-ecological problem with which we have been concerned, already in the Decalogue one is prohibited from using animals on the Sabbath. In rabbinic law this extends to riding on them, not just "working" them in the strict agricultural sense.[71] Animals are also not to be slaughtered for food on this day.[72] Nevertheless, since a Jew is responsible for the well-being of his or her animals, they are to be fed on the Sabbath and, in the case of milking animals, they are to be milked on the Sabbath lest they suffer pain. To indicate that this is for their sake and not our own, the milk taken from them is not to be used by us.[73] In terms of the nonsentient realm, there is to be no planting or reaping, nor any of the attendant activities on the Sabbath.[74] There is also not to be any hoarding or similar preparation on the Sabbath for any other day.[75] The prohibition of both production and commerce on the Sabbath is the final extension of Sabbath limitations from our relationship with the natural environment to our relationship with the technical environment of our own making. The rabbis extended this prohibition to even touching things which may not be used on the Sabbath or serve no aesthetically pleasing function for the Sabbath (*muqtzeh*).[76] The Sabbath is, then, a limit on our construction of the purposes whereby we technically order both time and space. It is not difficult to understand, therefore, why the imperial Romans, for whom ordering was an end in itself (and not just a means to an end as it was for the more intellectual Greeks), found the Sabbath so odious and were particularly contemptuous of the attraction it had for some of their own people.[77] Pax Romana and Shabbat Shalom are clearly and fundamentally different.

THE SABBATH OF CREATION

The great bulk of the legal treatment of the Sabbath in the Halakhah concerns prohibitions as, indeed, the majority (365) of the 613 commandments of the Torah are negative precepts.[78] Concerning this, my late revered teacher, Professor Abraham Joshua Heschel, wrote,

> Indeed, the splendor of the day is expressed in terms of abstentions, just as the mystery of God is more adequately conceived *via negationis,* in the categories of negative theology which claims that we can never say what He is, we can only say what He is not.[79]

Nevertheless, even negative theology does not end up with *Nothing,* but is a dialectic which begins with distinctions in order to reach some hard-won affirmations.[80] Returning to the Sabbath, what we have seen so far in terms of the Sabbath prohibitions is the outer gate of a palace, an outer gate designed to protect the treasures within.[81] One must begin with *Halakhah* because it is the most evident manifestation of Judaism. One does not end there, however. The inner treasures are expressed in *Aggadah,* which might be designated as Judaism's theological imagination.[82] Let us now look at some of the *Aggadah* of the Sabbath, in terms of the relationship between God and the human person, for it is the relationship which grounds the subsequent interhuman relationship and the relationship between humans and their environment, both technical and natural. Here we will find some even more profound thoughts which speak to our technological-nuclear crisis.

It has been noted by some perceptive observers that there is no idea of nature in the classical Scriptural and rabbinic texts.[83] Now this is an overstatement if nature is understood as a formal order immanent within creation itself. In both Scripture and rabbinic literature, there is clearly an idea of a formal order within creation, which even God has promised to maintain and respect.[84] Indeed, it is often invoked as a demonstration of God's constancy and consistency; He has given "righteous" commandments to His human creatures and, by analogy, righteous directions to nature itself.[85] Nevertheless, if nature is understood, conversely, as an eternal realm, *always there,* to which both God and creation are answerable because they are both contained within it, then Judaism clearly places a much higher value on both divine creativity and human creativity, and sees them directly related without any such tertium quid as nature *coming-in-between.*[86] In rabbinic conceptuality an entity is either "made by divine hands" or "by human hands."[87] Human creativity is, then, imitatio Dei.

Unfortunately, too many readers of the book of Genesis have assumed that the creative imitatio Dei is as follows: "In the beginning God created heaven and earth" (Genesis 1:1), then, "And God blessed them . . . fill the earth and conquer it (*ve-khibshuha*)[88] and dominate (*u-redu*) the fish of the sea, the birds of the heavens and all living things which swarm on the earth" (1:28). Just as God conquers and dominates His universe (the macrocosm), so man "created in His image" (*be-tzalmo*) conquers and dominates the earth and its environment (the microcosm). Creativity on both levels is, thus, essentially characterized as conquest and dominance. There is a hierarchy of power which entails a parallel hierarchy of authority.

Nevertheless, Scripture itself in the next chapter presents a different view of the world in which the human person is placed by God. Here we find that the microcosm is a garden whose human occupants are "to tend it (*le 'obdah*) and to guard it (*le-shomrah*)" (Genesis 2:15). In this version of creation, the human person is uniquely human in being the subject of both a commandment (about eating from the tree of the knowledge of Good and Evil) and a warning about the future ("you shall surely die"—2:17). Here both a task and a destiny are presented. The human person is clearly limited. In this version of creation, man is portrayed as being united with woman with whom alone he shares the reciprocal intimacy of flesh and word (2:23-24).[89] Most students of Scripture have noted the disparity between these two respective anthropologies. The critical question of separate Biblical sources aside, since post-Biblical Judaism's adherents experience Scripture—certainly the Pentateuch—as a unitary document and doctrine, the question arises: Which version of creation is theologically primary and which secondary to it, and thus to be interpreted through it? Furthermore, in which version do we see the essential relationship between God and the human person affirmed by subsequent Jewish tradition?.[90]

In the Decalogue the following analogy is made between divine creativity and human creativity:

> Remember the Sabbath day to hallow it. . . . For the Lord made the heavens and the earth, the sea and everything in it and He rested on the seventh day; therefore, He blessed the Sabbath day and hallowed it (*va-yiqadeshehu*). (Exodus 20:8, 11)

The human person's creaturely uniqueness is to be directly related to God, not as creator but in transcendence of creation. Both man and God on the Sabbath transcend their respective techné. For what the Sabbath does for creation, both divine and human, is to provide a limiting purpose—a telos—for both of them simultaneously.[91]

The mistake of many is to assume that the human person per se is the *telos* of creation, an "end-in-itself," to use Kant's reconstituted anthropocentric teleology.[92] Modern natural science, however, has taught us how the ever-expanding and ever-complex universe shows less and less evidence of such anthropocentrism being true, and that to celebrate "creative man" as the purpose of creation is to celebrate homo faber as the essence of humanness. Yet, have we not seen that homo faber, like Cain, finds his "responsibility (*avoni*) too great to bear?" (Genesis 4:13). Scientific knowledge and moral experience both reject such an arrogant conclusion.[93] Indeed, the Talmud notes that one of the reasons that the human person was created on the eve of the Sabbath, *after* everything else, is that if humans become arrogant, exalting themselves *over-and-above* the rest of creation, even the mosquito can always remind them, "you were created last."[94]

The climax of creation is not the human person but the Sabbath, and the Sabbath is the intimate symbol of the Covenant, "an everlasting covenant (*brit 'olam*) between Me and the children of Israel, an everlasting symbol (*'ot hi l 'olam*)" (Exodus 31:16-17).[95] Creation is not complete on the sixth day when the human person is created, but only on the hallowed seventh day. In other words, God created the universe in order to have a relationship with the human person, and the human person creates his or her own microcosmic environment in order to have a relationship with God. That relationship is epitomized by the Sabbath.[96] The Covenant is that relational reality. Unlike a conquerer and a tyrant whose power is its own justification, the Sabbath is commanded to a tender and a guardian of a garden, in imitation of God who tends and guards the universe.[97]

The role of the Sabbath as the telos of creation is brought out in this *aggadah:*

> Genibah said that it is like a king who made a bridal chamber (*huppah*): plastering it, tiling it, painting it. But, what was the bridal chamber still lacking?—a bride to enter it. So what was the world lacking?—the Sabbath.[98]

This is a common leitmotif in rabbinic theology, that the Torah is the purpose of creation, that without it the world would revert to primordial chaos.[99] Since the Sabbath is considered the equivalent of all the commandments of the Torah, no doubt because it along out of all of them is presented in the creation narrative, profanation of the Sabbath is considered to be a denial of God the creator.[100] Just as the Torah is the content of a mutual relationship so that God Himself is portrayed as keeping it, so is God Himself portrayed as keeping the Sabbath.[101]

Just as divine making is ordered and limited for the sake of the Sabbath, so is human making. That is why the building of the Sanctuary, which symbolizes the cosmos itself, does not override the Sabbath.[102] The building of the Sanctuary stopped in time for the Sabbath. Indeed, the building of the Sanctuary is considered to be the height of intelligent human work (*mel'ekhet mahshebet*), and the thirty-nine types of work it entailed are the same thirty-nine specifications of the prohibition of work on the Sabbath.[103] If the height of human creative work is prohibited on the Sabbath, all the more so is ordinary human labor prohibited.

In terms of work as preparation for the Sabbath, note the following:

They said about Shammai the Elder that all his days he ate in honor of the Sabbath. If
he found a fair animal, he would say, "this is for the Sabbath." If he found one which
was fairer, he would set aside the second one and eat the first. . . . The School of Shammai
say that on the first day of the week one should already start thinking about the coming
Sabbath (me-had shabyekha le-shabbteykha).[104]

Now the Talmud contrasts this with the view of Hillel the Elder, that one should
take each day as it comes and trust that God will provide for the Sabbath
ahead. Although in strictly legal disputes the law follows the Hillelites,[105] it
is worth noting that this dispute is not seen as strictly legal by later authorities;
indeed, a number of them follow the moral example of Shammai and his
school.[106] Along these lines, an earlier rabbinic text admonishes one to regard
all of one's work as if all of it had been completed (ke' ilu . . . 'asuyah)[107] by
each and every Sabbath. Hence, the rabbis forbade any talk or even thought
of business on the Sabbath.[108]

It should be emphasized, however, that all of this teleology is only intelligible
in a covenantal context, and can only be seen in the context of the relationship
between God and the human person. Nevertheless, as the author of Job
especially pointed out, God's relationship with creation is not limited to the
relationship with His human creation.[109] It is not a symbiosis. In terms of the
relationship with the natural order per se, creation is an ongoing process, a
point also made by contemporary cosmological physics in its view of an ever
expanding universe.[110] This comes out in the following dispute between the
Hillelites and the Shammaites concerning the precise wording of the
benediction said when fire is kindled to demarcate the end of the Sabbath and
the beginning of the ordinary week (habdalah). The Shammaites say that one
is to praise God who "has created (she-bar'a) the light of the fire." For the
Hillelites, on the other hand, the wording is "who creates (bor'e) the lights of
the fire."[111] The Talmud sees the theology behind this legal dispute as follows:

Rava said that no one disputes that God has created (de-bar'a mashm'a) it; what is disputed
is future creation (d'atid le-mibr'a) implied in the term "who creates (bor'e)." The
Shammaites deny future creation, the Hillelites affirm it.[112]

The Talmud then brings a number of Scriptural citations which refute the
concept of creation being a fait accompli. Rashi, the great medieval
commentator, points out that the Hillelite affirmation of future creation means
that creation is perpetual (bor'e tamid),[113] an idea also reflected in the liturgy.
Even on the Sabbath, as on weekdays, one praises God for being "the beneficent
renewer of creation continually (be-khol yom tamid)."[114]

What emerges from this is that the essentially covenantal character of the
Sabbath is not an anthropomorphic projection of a human experience onto the
cosmos per se. Indeed, any physical evidence for the Sabbath being different from
weekdays—like the cessation of the falling of the Manna during the Israelite

sojourn in the Wilderness—was considered miraculous and not repeatable.[115] Thus, the holiness of the Sabbath is known only when one is *before* God *with* the world; not *through* the world *unto* God. Time and space, the ways we experience and initially order the world, are constituted differently by the Sabbath.[116] Thus, Sabbath space-time is of a different world than ordinary space-time.

On the human side of the Sabbath, we see a similar approach. It will be recalled that the world as macrocosm is the making of God, and the world as microcosm is the making of man. Just as the macrocosm has a life of its own outside the Covenant, so does the microcosm, which comes out in another dispute between the Hillelites and the Shammaites. This dispute concerns whether or not one's vessels—that is, manufactured things, including machines—must cease working on the Sabbath (*shebitat kelim*). The Shammaites say yes; the Hillelites say no.[117] The reasoning employed by each group is explained as follows: the Shammaites hold that the prohibition of labor extends from the producer of a thing to the thing itself; the Hillelites hold that the prohibition is limited to the producer him or herself.[118] Thus, automatic technology need not be stopped for the Sabbath as long as it does not require human attention on the Sabbath, as long as it permits its makers and even its attendants to transcend it.[119] It will be recalled that the law is according to the opinion of the Hillelites.[120]

We can see that not only does Judaism not demand the renunciation of technology per se, neither does it require that technology rest with us on the Sabbath. What Judaism does require is that technology serve humans on the Sabbath and not disturb their rest by requiring their attention. Limiting technology does not mean crippling it. For us, today, the Sabbath does not mean an impossible Utopianism.

Indeed, techné, epitomized by the human person making fire, is considered a result of the Sabbath. A rabbinic legend indicates that the first human was terrified when the first Sabbath ended and the light of the sun was being taken away, terrified that he would be overcome by the unknown darkness of nature. At that point, God provides him with two stones with which to make fire. Thereupon, he praised God for the fire. The text concludes that this is the reason why God is praised for fire and its light at the conclusion of every Sabbath.[121] Fire is thus not stolen from God, but, rather is given by God. Adam is not Prometheus. Also, the last act of work before the onset of the Sabbath is to kindle lights for the Sabbath, lights whose illumination is to be enjoyed aesthetically, but not used in any technical way.[122] The very transcendence of the Sabbath limits techné, but it limits nature, too, and teaches humans that they are not simply subject to nature and its darkness, but that they can clear a dwelling out of nature and light their own portion in the darkness. Homo faber qua homo faber, too, is sanctified when the fire warms and illuminates, rather than when it burns and destroys—sanctification can happen only when techné is preceded and succeeded by the peace of the Sabbath.

THE SABBATH AND ESCHATOLOGY

Because the Sabbath so radically changes the human relationship with the environment, basically altering the uses of time and space, early in the history of Judaism it was seen as an eschatological symbol. As early as the noncanonical Hellenistic work, *Life of Adam and Eve,* it is stated that "the seventh day is the sign of the resurrection and the world-to-come."[123] This motif has regularly been repeated. In fact, the motif is so commonplace that the Grace after Meals, to be recited regularly by every Jew, has the following petition to be recited after each of the three Sabbath meals: "May the All-Merciful bequeath to us a day which is wholly Sabbath and everlasting rest."[124] If the Sabbath is an eschatological symbol—or, better, *the* eschatological symbol— then we have an example for the well-known theory of the late Mircea Eliade, a theory which asserts that the innovation of the Hebrew Bible was to present a linear idea of time as opposed to the idea of time as "eternal return," that sacred time is experienced in ever recurring cycles.[125] In the linear idea of time, conversely, time is understood as having an ultimate climax when God and humankind will finally and irrevocably be reconciled. The telos qua purpose and the eschaton qua temporal terminus become one and the same. As an eschatological symbol, the cyclical character of the Sabbath is removed from its essence and confined to its pre-eschatological manifestation. If this is the case, however, then the essence of the Sabbath pertains to the end of time, not to the time here and now which we are trying so desparately to save from being destroyed by the works of our hands. Then, the Sabbath—even affirming all its holiness, to be sure—would not in truth speak to the nuclear dilemma directly facing us in the present world. Our concern now is with life before death much more than with life after death.

There is another way of looking at the symbolism of the Sabbath.[126] At the very end of his presentation of all the laws of the Sabbath, Maimonides writes,

> Whoever keeps the Sabbath according to its law and honors it and makes it delightful (*u-me'angah*) to the best of his ability, it has already been explicated in prophetic tradition (*be-qabbalah*) that his reward in this world is greater than the reward stored up in the world-to-come. It is written, "Then you will delight (*tit'anag*) with the Lord, and He will make you ride on the high-places of the earth, and He will feed you from the heritage of Jacob your father, for the mouth of the Lord has spoken it." (Isaiah 58:14).[127]

Now Maimonides was probably the greatest critic of eschatology in the history of Judaism.[128] For him, the world-to-come is not the future eschaton of history, but it is a transcendent dimension, parallel to history and open to participation by those here and now capable and prepared to apprehend its reality.[129] For this reason, he radically disconnected the Messianic Age from any identification with this transcendent realm. For him, the Messianic Age will be a political realm within ordinary human history.[130] Even though this transcendent realm is timeless per se, the full human experience of it comes only after death, after the separation of the soul from the body. Here, Maimonides's debt to Plato and the whole Platonic tradition is obvious. Nevertheless, when it comes to the Sabbath, he just as obviously departed from his Platonism and was stressing a more uniquely Jewish idea: that the Sabbath, finite in time and kept and experienced by mortals, better intends our relationship with the transcendent God than does an image of our own eternity.[131]

Finally, if the Sabbath is essentially an eschatological symbol, a symbol of a spiritual age subsequent to our own time, then it ought to clearly take precedence over bodily human existence. No threat to bodily life, if this theory is true and carried to its logical conclusion, could possibly justify profaning the Sabbath in any way. Yet, in the *Halakah*—which no subsequent theology can contradict—"the Sabbath is made for man, not man for the Sabbath."[132] The Sabbath must be profaned when human life is threatened. This stance, no doubt, arose when the entire Jewish nation who had remained faithful to the Covenant, was threatened with extermination by the Seleucid forces of Antiochus Epiphanes during the Maccabean revolution. If the Jews would not defend themselves on the Sabbath, the enemy would slaughter all of them.[133] This could not be allowed to happen because the Sabbath as the epitomy of the Covenant requires human life as much as it requires divine life, and human life, unlike divine life, requires external actions to maintain its duration on earth. The Covenant, then, through the Sabbath, protects the human person from being destroyed by homo faber; through the six days of mandated labor, it protects the human person from being the helpless victim of the forces of nature; and through the affirmation of the covenantal relationship between God and the human person, it protects the human person from being subordinate to the Sabbath rather than to the God who gave it.[134]

CONCLUSION

In his great work on the Sabbath and its meaning for moderns, my late revered teacher, Professor Heschel, wrote over thirty years ago,

> To set aside one day a week for freedom, a day on which we would not use the instruments which have been so easily turned into weapons of destruction . . a day on which we stop worshipping the idols of technical civilization . . . a day of armistice in the economic struggle with our fellow men and the forces of nature—is there any institution that holds out a greater hope for men's progress than the Sabbath?.[135]

Surely, "man's progress" includes progress in rethinking the nuclear threat. Heretofore, we have assumed that human progress is measured by what we have made.[136] Now, the works of our hands have taken our souls away from us. Henceforth, we can only experience progress in the return of our souls.[137]

According to ancient Jewish lore, the epitomy of that homecoming is that Sabbath and all that it brings.[138]

NOTES AND REFERENCES

All translations, unless otherwise noted, are by the author.

1.   *High Holyday Prayerbook,* P. Birnbaum, ed. (New York, 1960), p. 541.

2.   See R. Mosheh Margolis, *Penay Mosheh,* on Y. Yoma, 5.3/42c.

3.   M. Yoma, 5.1. See Maimonides's comment there re: Lev. 16:2; T. Kippurim, 2.13; Y. Yoma, loc. cit.; B. Yoma, 53b.

4.   Y. Yoma, loc. cit.

5.   For rabbinic disapproval of this concentration of political and ecclesiastical authority in one person during the Second Temple period, see B. Kidd, 66a; Y. Hor., 3.2/47c.

6.   See Karl Jaspers, *The Future of Mankind,* trans. E.B. Ashton (Chicago, 1961), p. 6.

7.   See Hans-Georg Gadamer, *Truth and Method,* trans. G. Burden and J. Cumming (New York, 1982), pp. 275ff.

8.   Even some prominent contemporary theologians have made this charge. Note Gordon D. Kaufman, *Theology for A Nuclear Age* (Manchester and Philadelphia, 1985), p. 31: "In all of this our western religious symbolism has been more a hindrance than a help for our ecological blindness, and it too easily lends itself to the enforcement of legitimation of our parochial political objectives." Cf. J. Cohen, "The Bible, Man, and Nature in the History of Western Thought: A Call for Reassessment," *The Journal of Religion,* 65:(2):155ff. (April, 1985).

9.   *Nichomachean Ethics,* 1094a1. Greek text from Loeb Classical Library (Cambridge, MA, 1926).

10.   See ibid., 1040a10-20.

11.   *Phaenomenologie des Geistes,* Hoffmeister, ed. (Hamburg, 1952), p. 286. For Hegel's admiration of Aristotelian teleology, see ibid., p. 22.

12.   Ibid., p. 291. See A. Kojève, *Introduction to the Reading of Hegel,* trans. J.H. Nichols, Jr. (Ithaca, NY, 1980), p. 25; also, L. Dupré, *The Philosophical Foundations of Marxism* (New York, 1966), pp. 25ff.

13.   See *Karl Marx on Society and Social Change,* ed. N.J. Smelser (Chicago, 1973), 3ff.; 86ff.

14.   See "Economic and Philosophic Manuscripts" (1844) in *Writings of the Young Marx,* trans. L. D. Easton and K. H. Gaddat (Garden City, NY, 1967), pp. 294-295. See also, A. Schaff, *Marxism and the Human Individual,* trans. O. Wojtasiewicz (Garden City, NY, 1959), p. 77.

15.   *Physics,* 194b25. Greek text from Loeb Classical Library (Cambridge, MA, 1929. Thus, in human practice, the ends are primordial; only the changeable means are under human control. Clearly, the former qua *physis* are superior to the latter qua *techné* See *Nichomachean Ethics,* 1112a20ff.

16.   *Phaenomonolgie,* p. 291.

17.   See *Physics,* 192a30.

18.   *Physics,* 194b25.

19.   For Marx, "Death seems to be a harsh victory of the species over the particular individual and to contradict the species' unity, but the particular individual is only a particular generic being and as such mortal." ("Economic and Philosophic Manuscripts," op. cit., p. 307). Cf. Franz Rosenzweig, *The Star of Redemption,* trans. W. W. Hallo (New York, 1970), pp. 3-5.

20.   *The Human Condition* (Garden City, NY, 1959), p. 137.

21.   The vagueness of Kant's position was severely criticized by Hegel. See *Grundlinien der Philosophie des Rechts,* sec. 150; also, A. Donagan, *The Theory of Morality* (Chicago, 1977), pp. 9-14.

22. See "The Question Concerning Technology," trans. W. Lovitt in *Heidegger: Basic Writings,* D. F. Krell, ed. (New York, 1977), pp. 288-289.

23. See Jacques Ellul, *The Technological System,* trans. J. Neugroschel (New York, 1980), pp. 129, 256-257.

24. See *Nichomachean Ethics,* 1100a10ff.; also, Martin Heidegger, *An Introduction to Metaphysics,* trans. R. Manheim (Garden City, NY, 1961), pp. 49-50.

25. "Death in the Nuclear Age," in *Jewish Reflections on Death,* J. Riemer, ed. (New York, 1974), pp. 41, 44. See the author's review of this anthology, with particular attention to Morgenthau's essay, in *Judaism,* 24(4):503-504 (Fall, 1975).

26. For current scientific opinion on this subject, see R. P. Turco *et al.,* "Nuclear Winter," *Science* (Dec. 23, 1983), passim. There is much in Jewish tradition to support the view that the duration of the universe is by no means necessary. See, e.g., Gen. 9:11-17 and Is. 40:6-8, 54:9, and 65:16ff.; Ezek. 37:1-14; R. Saadyah Gaon, *The Book of Beliefs and Opinions,* trans. S. Rosenblatt (New Haven, CT, 1948), 6.3; D. Novak, *Halakhah in a Theological Dimension* (Chicago, CA, 1985), pp. 103ff. Thus, Ecclesiastes's philosophical assumption of the earth's inherent permanence, which is the ontological basis of his general pessimism about the ultimate significance of any human action (1:2; 12:8), is one of the reasons why the very religious character of this book was questioned in Jewish tradition. See *Vayiqra Rabbah* 28.1 and R. Gordis, *Kohelet The Man and His World* (New York, 1951), pp. 39-42.

27. See his *The Phenomenon of Man,* trans. B. Wall (New York, 1959), pp. 77f.

28. See Leo Strauss, *Natural Right and History* (Chicago, 1953), pp. 166ff. For the difference between a ground (*archē*) and a limit (*peras*), see Aristotle, *Metaphysics,* 1022a10. For the most extreme rejection of any kind of natural limit, see Jean-Paul Sartre, *Being and Nothingness,* trans. H. Barnes (New York, 1956), esp. pp. 617ff.

29. See, e.g., Giorgio del Vecchio, *Justice,* trans. Lady Guthrie (Edinburgh, 1952), p. 87, n. 3; H. L. A. Hart, *The Concept of Law* (Oxford, 1961), pp. 188-189; John Rawls, *A Theory of Justice* (Cambridge, MA, 1971), passim.

30. Although Thomas Aquinas speaks of the *inclinatio naturalis* of self preservation (*Summa Theologiae,* 2-2, q. 64, a. 5), it is the weakest moral ground and must be combined with grounds theologically and metaphysically constituted. See D. Novak, *Suicide and Morality* (New York, 1975), pp. 44ff.

31. See *Suicide,* trans. J. A. Spaulding and G. Simpson (Glencoe, IL, 1951), chaps. 3 and 5. For a critique of the constitution of society as transcendent (as God is transcendent), see D. Novak, *Law and Theology in Judaism* (New York, 1976), Vol. 2, pp. 19-20.

32. For a theological version of this widely held point of view, see Kaufman, *Theology for A Nuclear Age,* pp. 44ff. This book is heavily influenced by the vastly popular book by Jonathan Schell, *The Fate of the Earth* (New York, 1982). Perhaps the most vivid expression of this point of view is still to be found in the fiction of D. H. Lawrence, esp., *The Rainbow* (New York, 1916), p. 2. For ancient precedents, see Novak, *The Image of the Non-Jew in Judaism,* pp. 244ff.

33. See, e.g., W. G. Sumner, "The Challenge of Facts," in *The People Shall Judge* (Chicago, 1949), Vol. 2, pp. 83-85.

34. *Republic,* 439Bff, 523Bff. For a naturist attempt to counter the view of Plato et al., see Mary Midgley, *Beast and Man: The Roots of Human Nature* (Ithaca, NY, 1978), pp. 75-82.

35. See L. S. Ford, *The Lure of God: A Biblical Basis for Process Theism* (Philadelphia, 1978), 1-44.

36. See Spinoza, *Ethics,* pt. 2, props. 1, 5; Aristotle, *Metaphysics,* 1073a25ff.

37. *Process and Reality* (New York, 1929), pp. 288-289. See ibid., pp. 131, 263.

38. See G. E. Moore, *Principia Ethica* (Cambridge, 1903), pp. 44-45.

39. See B. San. 56b and 58b-59a; also, Novak, *The Image of the Non-Jew in Judaism,* chaps. 2-8.

40. Cf. Plato, *Timaeus,* 29E-30C.

41. *Metaphysics,* 1074b35. Greek text from Loeb Classical Library (Cambridge, MA, 1935).

42. *Guide for the Perplexed,* 2.5. For Maimonides's view of nature, see Novak, *The Image of the Non-Jew in Judaism,* pp. 292-294.

43. See Aristotle, *Physics,* 215a1. See Midgely, *Beast and Man,* 199-200, as an example of the error of mixing the metaphors of heavenly nature and earthly nature.

44. See *Nichomachean Ethics,* 1177a10-15.

45. See *Discoveries and Opinions of Galileo,* trans. S. Drake (Garden City, NY, 1957), pp. 262-263; also, R. G. Collingwood, *The Idea of Nature* (New York, 1960), pp. 102-103.

46. Intelligence and intelligibility become located in the human observer/orderer. See Kant, *Critique of Pure Reason,* Bxiii; also, Martin Heidegger, "Modern Science, Metaphysics and Mathematics," in *Heidegger: Basic Writings,* pp. 265ff.; L. Gilkey, *Maker of Heaven and Earth* (Garden City, NY, 1959), pp. 123ff.

47. See S. Toulmin, "Nature and Nature's God," *The Journal of Religious Ethics,* 13(1):44ff (Spring, 1985). Cf. Aristotle, *Physics,* 198b10ff.

48. *Natural Right and History,* 8. See, also, Juergen Habermas, *Communication and the Evolution of Society* (Boston, 1979), p. 201; Alasdair MacIntyre, *After Virtue* (Notre Dame, 1981), p. 152.

49. See Kant, *Fundamental Principles of the Metaphysic of Morals,* trans. T. K. Abbott (New York, 1949), pp. 45ff.; also, Novak, *Suicide and Morality,* pp. 94-97. For attempts to avoid the problem of ethical teleology without cosmic teleology and still be considered natural law (e.g., non-Kantian) theories of normative ethics, see H. B. Veatch, *Rational Man: A Modern Interpretation of Aristotle's Ethics* (Bloomington, IN, 1962), pp. 76 and passim; J. Finnis, *Natural Law and Natural Rights* (Oxford, 1980), pp. 52-53.

50. *Nichomachean Ethics,* 1177b1. See Plato, *Republic,* 370C, 374E; *Theaetetus,* 175E. In modern capitalism and socialism the relation is exactly inverted, as Max Weber noted, "one does not work to live, one lives to work." (Quoted in Josef Pieper, *Leisure the Basis of Culture,* trans. A. Dru (New York, 1952), p. 20). Pieper rightly shows that, for Plato and Aristotle, and for Aquinas after them, *scholē* is essentially different from *decidia* (sloth) [ibid., 40].

51. See *Politics,* 1278a1, 1325a25, 1328b35-1329a5. In assuming the indispensability of slavery, Aristotle follows Plato. See *Republic,* 469B-C. For the dispensability of slavery in Classical Judaism, conversely, see Novak, *Law and Theology in Judaism,* Vol. 2, pp. 87ff. Furthermore, the Torah scholar (*talmid hakham*) is to live off of his own labor and not be supported by the labor of others because he is a scholar. See Bekh. 29a, re: Deut. 4:5 (cf. Tos., s.v. "mah") and Maim., *Hilkhot Talmud Torah,* 1. 7 and 9; also, B. Shabb. 118a and parallels. Cf. *Responsa Tashbatz,* nos. 142-148; R. Obadiah Bertinoro on M. Abot, 4.5; Beresheet Rabbah, 72.5, 98.12.

52. Cf. Plato, *Republic,* 286Bff.

53. *Politics,* 1254a15. For some qualification, see, *Nichomachean Ethics,* 1161b5-10.

54. *Phaenomenologie,* 147. See Pliny, *Naturalis Historia,* 29.19.

55. *Politics,* 1254b5-10. In this passage, *psychē* and *nous* are synonyms.

56. See *Meditations,* 6; also, Spinoza, *Ethics,* prop. 12ff.; Locke, *Second Treatise of Government,* 5. Cf. Maurice Merleau-Ponty, *Phenomenology of Perception,* trans. C. Smith (London, 1962), pp. 148ff.

57. See Heidegger, "The Question Concerning Technology," pp. 296ff.

58. *De Specialus Legibus,* 2.61, 64, trans. F. H. Colson, *Philo* (Cambridge, MA, 1937), Vol. 7, pp. 344-347. Philo characterizes this study (*hai dia logon kai dogmaton ton kat' aretēn*) as *philosophein* prescribed by the Torah. See, also, *De Decalogo,* pp. 97-101. The Roman Catholic philosopher, Josef Pieper, attempts to synthesize the idea of the Sabbath and *scholē.* See, *Leisure the Basis of Culture,* pp. 42-43. His attempt is questionable, however, because the unity of the community of the faithful he sees in Sunday (his Sabbath) worship is based on all of them being related to the transcendent God in a communal activity ordained by revelation. (See, ibid., pp. 51-52, and, esp., p. 54, for his critique of Proudhon's failure to see the sacred foundation of the

equality he noticed in the Christian celebration of Sunday; also, pp. 56-57, 60.) *Scholē*, on the other hand, is based on the immanent intellectual excellence of a few being permanently supported by the unceasing labor of many. Finally, his limitation of the Sabbath to the Christian celebration of Sunday (ibid., p. 63) is myopic. For the essential difference between the Jewish Sabbath and the Christian Sunday, see Hermann Cohen, *Religion of Reason Out of the Sources of Judaism,* trans. S. Kaplan (New York, 1972), p. 367. Earlier, however, Cohen saw no harm in changing the Jewish observance of the Sabbath from Saturday to Sunday. See his "Der Sabbat in seiner kultur-geschichtlichen Bedeutung—Nachwort," *Juedische Schriften* (Berlin, 1924), vol. II, pp. 45ff.; also, E.G. Hirsch, "Sabbath," in *Jewish Encyclopedia,* Vol. 10, pp. 604-605.

59. *De Specialus Legibus,* 2.62. See Josephus, *Contra Apionem,* 2.175 and *Antiquities,* 16.43.

60. *De Specialus Legibus,* 2.66-68. See B. Shabb., 119a and Maim., *Hilkhot Shabbat,* 30.6.

61. *De Specialus Legibus,* 2.69. For a reiteration of this social significance of the Sabbath, see Cohen, *Religion of Reason Out of the Sources of Judaism,* pp. 155ff.

62. *Pesiqta Rabbati: Decalogue,* 3, Friedmann, ed., 121a. See B. Ket, 62a-b. Cf. B. Shabb., 119a-b, re: Is. 58-13 and Rashi, s.v. "mehader."

63. For the community-creating character of the Sabbath, see, e.g., Y. Erub., 3.2/20d and M. Buber, *Moses* (New York, 1958), pp. 83-85.

64. See Is. 58:13; Jer. 17:27; Neh. 10:32.

65. See B. Shabb., 70a re: Ex. 35:3.

66. B. Ber. 20b re: Ex. 20:8 and Deut. 5:12; also, ibid., 5lb re T. Ber. 5.25.

67. See *Mekhilta: Yitro* re Ex. 20:8-10, Horovitz-Rabin, ed., 230; also, see 331. For the obligation of a circumcised slave to keep the Sabbath as well as many other commandments, see B. Hag. 4a and parallels.

68. See B. A. Z. 64b; Y. Yeb. 8.1/8d.

69. See M. Shabb., 16.6, 8; B. Shabb., 150a; Maim., *Hilkhot Shabbat,* 6.1. As for non-Jews observing the Sabbath, this is forbidden by the 2nd century C. E. Palestinian authority, R. Simon ben Laquish (B. San. 58b, re: Gen. 8:22; see *Debarim Rabbah* 1,8). Maimonides (*Hilkhot Melakhim,* 10.9) sees this prohibition as being directed against religious syncretism (cf. prohibitions against "judaizing" by the Church fathers, e.g., Ignatius, *To the Magnesians,* chap 10). Nevertheless, later European authorities permitted it, undoubtedly because of their experience with Christian sabbatarian sects. See Novak, *The Image of the Non-Jew in Judaism,* pp. 27-28, 48, 357, 366.

70. See, e.g., B. Yeb., 47a.

71. M. Bet., 5.2 and B. Bet, 36b.

72. M. Shabb., 7.1.

73. For the usual prohibition, see B. Shabb., 95a; Maim., *Hilkhot Shabbat,* 8.7; *Maharam me-Rothenburg: Responsa,* nos. 82-83, ed. Kahana, 93-94. For permission to milk when the animal's pain is involved, see *Rosh: Shabbat,* 18.3 (re: B. Shabb., 128b and 140b) and R. Jehiel M. Epstein, *Arokh Ha-Shulhan: Orah Hayyim,* 305.20.

74. M. Shabb., 7.1.

75. Ex. 16:27; B. Pes., 46b; also, *Encyclopedia Talmudit,* 9:116ff.

76. B. Pes., 47b re: Ex. 16:5.

77. See, e.g., Tacitus, *Historiae,* 4.3; Juvenal, *Satires,* 14.105-106; Augustine, *De Civitate Dei,* 6.11; also, *Greek and Latin Authors on Jews and Judaism,* I-II, ed. M. Stern (Jerusalem, 1974-1980), passim. See the Roman-like argument of the apostate rabbi, Elisha ben Abuyah, on Y. Hag., 2.1/77b (cf. Philo, *De Specilaus Legibus,* 2.60). For Jewish recognition of the attraction of the Sabbath to non-Jews, see Josephus, *Contra Apionem,* 22.282.

78. For detailed treatment of the Sabbath laws, see I. Grunfeld, *The Sabbath: A Guide to Understanding and Observance* (New York, 1959).

79. *The Sabbath: Its Meaning for Modern Man,* 2nd.-abb. ed. (New York, 1963), p. 15.

80.   Re: *via negativa* (*negationis*), see Novak, *Law and Theology in Judaism,* Vol. 2, pp. 36-37.

81.   See Maimonides, *Guide for the Perplexed,* 3.51.

82.   See A. J. Heschel, *God in Search of Man* (New York, 1955), pp. 324ff.; also, D. Novak, *Law and Theology in Judaism* (New York, 1974), Vol. 1, pp. 1ff.; D. Tracy, *The Analogical Imagination* (New York, 1981), pp. 128 and 149, n. 96.

83.   See Strauss, *Natural Right and History,* p. 81, and José Faur, "Understanding the Covenant," *Tradition,* 9(4):41 (Spring, 1968).

84.   See, e.g., Jer. 8:7; Amos 3:3ff.; Job 28:23-28 and 38:1ff.; M. Gitt., 4.4, and B. Yeb., 61b.

85.   See, e.g., Deut. 4:6-8; Ps. 104:1ff, re: the analogy between God's macrocosmic responsibility and the human soul's microcosmic responsibility, see B. Ber., 10a.

86.   See Martin Buber, *I and Thou,* trans. W. Kaufmann (New York, 1970), pp. 64-65.

87.   See, e.g., M. Kel. 17.12; M. Neg. 11.3; Hull. 55b; Maim., *Hilkhot Hobel u-Maziq,* 6.4 re: B. Makk., 7b; also Heschel, *The Sabbath,* pp. 110-111. Both divine and human making (*ma'aseh*) are the result of conscious intention (*kavvanah*). See, e.g., B. Ber. re: Gen. 1:28 and M. Kel. 25.9.

88.   See B. Yeb. 65b; also, *Sifre:Debarim,* no. 268 re: Deut. 24:1, ed. Finkelstein, 287. These texts and their parallels deal with dominance (*kebishah/be'ilah*) as in the male initiation of sexual intercourse with the female. It is important to note, however, that in the second creation account, the woman is *brought to* the man (2:22) and that the man *cleaves* (2:24) to her. "Cleaving" (*ve-dabaq*) means to be dependent. See Deut. 4:4; also, *Beresheet Rabbah,* 17.8.

89.   See B. Yeb. 63a.

90.   For a profound response to the two creation accounts in Genesis, based on this traditional assumption, see Joseph B. Soloveitchik, "The Lonely Man of Faith," *Tradition,* 7(2):2ff (Summer, 1965). For an example of primary (literal) versus secondary (figurative) exegesis, based on theological-philosophical criteria, see Maim., *Hilkhot Yesoday Ha-Torah,* 1.8-9.

91.   For *telos* as limit (*peras*), see Aristotle, *Metaphysics,* 994b15.

92.   See *Critique of Judgment,* sec. 84.

93.   For a sustained critique of this anthropocentrism in modern theology, see James M. Gustafson, *Ethics from a Theocentric Perspective* (Chicago, 1981), Vol. 1, pp. 88ff.

94.   B. San. 38a.

95.   For the concept of the Sabbath as intimacy between God and His people, see B. Bet. 16a, re: Ex. 31:17. For the concept of the Sabbath as mutuality between God and the human person, see B. Shabb. 119b, re: Gen. 2:1; also, Nahmanides on Deut. 5:15.

96.   See R. Obadiah Sforno on Ex. 31:17. Furthermore, the Talmud states that "the human person (*adam*) was created on the eve of the Sabbath . . . that he might enter the realm of God's commandments (*mitzvah*) immediately" (B. San., 38a). The statement in the Mishnah with which this statement is associated, viz., that God's creation of each human individual sui generis requires each one of them to say, "The world was created for my sake" (M. San. 4. 5), was interpreted to mean that each person must regard his or her sin as having cosmic signficance (see Rashi on B. San. 37a, s.v. "bi-shebili"; also, T. Kidd. 1.13-14 and B. Kidd. 40b, re: Eccl. 9:18). All of this, then, emphasizes that the human person is to be obedient to God and caring for the rest of creation.

97.   See, esp., Ps. 104:1ff.

98.   *Beresheet Rabbah* 10.9, p. 85. Cf. B. San., 38a, re: Prov. 9:1-3.

99.   See B. Pes. 68b, re: Jer. 33:25 and *Rashba* and *Ran* thereon; also, R. Jacob ibn Habib, *Ayn Ya'aqob,* intro., s.v. "Shib'ah."

100.   Re: the Sabbath as the equivalent of the whole Torah, see *Shemot Rabbah* 25.16. Re: the Sabbath as primoridal, see *Sofrim* 13.14 (cf. B. R. H. 22a, re: Ex. 12:2). Re: denial of the Sabbath as denial of divine creation, see *Mekhilta Yitro,* 234, re: Is. 43:12.

101.   See *Tanhuma: Ki Tiss'a,* no. 33, printed ed. Re: divine observance of the Torah in general, see Y. R. H., 1.3/57b, re: Lev. 22:9; D. Novak, *Halakhah in a Theological Dimension,* 122ff.

102. B. Shabb., 97b, re: Ex. 35:1; Y. Shabb., 7, 2/9b; *Mekhilta: Va-yaqehel*, 345. See Jon D. Levenson, "The Temple and the World," *Journal of Religion*, 64(3):282ff (July, 1984).

103. M. Shabb., 7.2; B. Shabb., 49b; B. Hag., 10b and Rashi, s.v. "mel'ekhet mahshebet;" also, *Responsa Radbaz*, 5, no. 1522, re: B. Shabb., 41b and parallels; Maim., *Hilkhot Shabbat*, 1.5.

104. B. Bet., 16a. See *Mekhilta: Yitro*, 229.

105. B. Erub., 13b.

106. See *Pesiqta Rabbati: Decalogue*, 3, p. 115b.

107. *Mekhilta: Yitro*, 230.

108. B. Shabb., 150a, re: Is. 58:13; Maim., *Hilkhot Shabbat*, 24.1ff. For the difference between the norm and the ordinary practice,however, cf. the note of R. Moses Isserles on *Shulhan Arukh: Orah Hayyim*,128.44.

109. See Job 38:1ff.

110. See Steven Weinberg, *The First Three Minutes: A Modern View of the Origin of the Universe* (New York, 1977), pp. 11-43.

111. M. Ber., 8. 5. See ibid., 9.2

112. B. Ber., 52b. See Heschel, *The Sabbath*, p. 134, n. 9.

113. B. Ber., 52b, s.v. "de-bar'a mashm'a."

114. *The Traditional Prayer Book for Sabbath and Festivals*, David de Sola Pool, ed. (New York, 1960), p. 185.

115. See *Shemot Rabbah* 25.15. The account of the river *sabbation*, which did not flow on the Sabbath, is clearly folklore. See B. San., 65b; Josephus, *Bellum Judaicum*, 7.79-99; Pliny, *Naturalis Historia*, 31.24.

116. For this reason the Sabbath is considered to be the transcendent source of the other days of the week. See *Zohar: Noah*, 1:75a-b. Cf. Plato, *Timaeus*, 37D.

117. M. Shabb., 1.8; B. Shabb., 18a and Tos., s.v. "ve-laym'a." See Maim., *Hilkhot Shabbat*, 3.1. The founder of the Karaites, Anan ben David, in his *Book of Precepts*, extends the reasoning behind the Shammaite ban of *shebitat kelim* on the Sabbath to the enjoyment of a fire, even if kindled before the Sabbath and continuing to burn by itself on the Sabbath—something even the Shammaites themselves did not forbid—based on an analogy between Ex. 35:3 and 20:10. See *Karaite Antholoqy*, ed. and trans. by L. Nemoy (New Haven, 1952), pp. 17-18.

118. T. Shabb., 1.21 and Y. Shabb., 1.5/3d, re: Ex. 20:9.

119. See B. Erub., 104a and Maim., *Hilkhot Shabbat*, 23.4.

120. Cf. *Mekhilta: Mishpatim*, 332.

121. *Midrash Tehillim*, sec. 92, ed. Buber, 202b-203a. See Y. Ber., 8.6/12b; A. J. Heschel, *Who is Man?* (Stanford, 1965), p. 83.

122. See B. Shabb., 23b and 25b, re: Lam. 3:17 and Tos., s.v. "hadlaqat ner."

123. *Vita Adae et Evae*, 41.1, in *Apochrypha and Pseudepigrapha of the Old Testament*, R. H. Charles, ed. (Oxford, 1913), Vol. 2, p. 151. See M. Tam., 7.4 and *Mekhilta: Ki Tiss'a*. 343.

124. *The Traditional Prayer Book*, p. 623. See *Midrash Tehillim*, sec. 92, p. 201a. Also, see Gershom Scholem, *On the Kabbalah and Its Symbolism*, trans. R. Manheim (New York, 1969), pp. 145-146. The statement that "the Sabbath is one sixtieth of the world-to-come" (B. Ber. 57b) indicates the gap between the earthly Sabbath and the heavenly Sabbath. For the rabbis, one sixtieth was a negligible quantity. See Hull, 97b and B. Ned, 39b. For the Sabbath in Christian eschatology, see Augustine, *De Civitate Dei*, 22.30.

125. See *The Myth of the Eternal Return* (New York, 1954), 102ff.; *The Sacred and the Profane* (New York, 1961), pp. 106-107, 110-111. Cf. Rosenzweig, *The Star of Redemption*, pp. 310-315.

126. Re: symbolism, see Paul Tillich, *Systematic Theology* (Chicago, 1951), Vol. 1, p. 239; also, Novak, *The Image of the Non-Jew in Judaism*, pp. 128-130.

127. *Hilkhot Shabbat*, 30.15.

128. See D. Novak, "Maimonides' Concept of the Messiah," *Journal of Religious Studies,* 9(2):42ff. (Summer, 1982); "Does Maimonides Have A Philosophy of History?" *Proceedings of the Academy for Jewish Philosophy,* 4:56ff (1983).

129. See *Hilkhot Teshubah,* 8.8. Note the critique of R. Abraham ben David of Posquières thereon, re: B. San. 97a, interpreting Is. 2:11.

130. See *Hilkhot Melakhim,* 11.1ff.

131. See *Qohelet Rabbah* 1.3 re: Zeph. 1:3.

132. See B. Yoma, 85b and parallels. Cf. Mark 2:27 and parallels.

133. See I Macc. 2:32-42; Josephus, *Contra Apionem,* 2.2, and *Antiquities,* 12.6. Cf. Jub. 50:12 and Louis Finkelstein, "The Book of Jubilees and the Rabbinic Halakah," *Harvard Theological Review,* 16(1):51 (Jan., 1923).

134. See B. Yeb., 6a-b, re: Lev. 19:3; also, *Midrash Tehillim,* sec. 92, p. 202b; Maim., *Hilkhot Shehitah,* 14.16.

135. *The Sabbath,* p. 28. See Maimonides, *Guide for the Perplexed,* 2.31/end.

136. For a Jewish critique of the modern idea of progress, see Leo Strauss, "Progress or Return?—The Contemporary Crisis in Western Civilization," *Modern Judaism,* 1(1):29 (May, 1981).

137. See Ps. 19:8. For loss of soul as the state of being under the control of *alien* forces, see Lam. 1:11, 16, 19.

138. See B. Bet., 16a, re: Ex. 31:17 and parallels; also, Louis Ginzberg, *Legends of the Jews* (Philadelphia, 1925), Vol. 5, pp. 112-113, n. 104.

ABBREVIATIONS

A.Z.	Abodah Zarah
B.	Babylonian Talmud
Bekh.	Bekhorot
Ber.	Berakhot
Bet.	Betzah
Erub.	Erubin
Gitt.	Gittin
Hag.	Hagigah
Hor.	Horayot
Hull.	Hullin
Kel.	Kelim
Ket.	Ketubot
Kidd.	Kiddushin
M.	Mishnah
Maim.	Maimonides
Ned.	Nedarim
Neg.	Nega'im
Pes.	Pesahim
R.H.	Rosh Hashanah
San.	Sanhedrin
Shabb.	Shabbat
T.	Tosefta
Tos.	Tosafot
Y.	Yerushalmi (Palestinian Talmud)
Yeb.	Yebamot

THE IMPACT OF THE ELECTRONIC MEDIA ON AMERICAN RELIGION

Waldo Beach

In the summer of 1987, the attention of the American public was drawn to the scandals surrounding televangelists like Jim Bakker and Oral Roberts, matters that seemed almost as newsworthy as the Iran-Contra affair. The "Holy Wars" that followed alerted the consciences of sensitive readers and viewers to the enormous powers of the televangelistic kingdoms of the "electronic church." These photogenic pieces about the religious racketeering of the money-changers in the temple, the Bakkers' air-conditioned dog-house, their condos and mansions in California and Tennessee, the two Mercedes-Benz automobiles, etc.,[1] are only symptoms of a much more serious and elusive problem: how has the new electronic technology of communication affected American religious belief and practice?

We come at this deeper issue with a perspective both descriptive and normative, i.e., an assessment of the facts, and also a normative evaluation from the standpoint of the Christian faith.

Research in Philosophy and Technology, Volume 10, pages 71-79.
Copyright © 1990 by JAI Press Inc.
All rights of reproduction in any form reserved.
ISBN: 1-55938-062-4

First, a few familiar facts. TV is now the major mode of communication in America today. Electronic communication has superseded the dominant forms of earlier centuries which were by word of mouth, and then by print. As one analyst of American culture has put it, "The most significant American cultural fact of the second half of the twentieth century has been the decline of the Age of Typography and the ascendancy of the Age of Television."[2] Currently, 98% of American homes have one or more TV sets, which are turned on about 7 hours a day.[3] Even with the recent growth of Cable TV and public radio and television, most viewers watch commercials channels.[4] Ever since Marshall McLuhan reminded us that *what* persons communicate is reshaped by *how* they communicate in the media[5], the content of the image on the screen is that of a direct visual impact, eliciting a transient emotional response. Of course, the transaction is one-directional, not dialogic. This in contrast to dialogic oral conversation, back and forth, and communication by print, which allows for at least a measure of cognitive, rational reflection and review of the content on the printed page. It is not strange, therefore, that, as President Reagan's addresses to the nation on TV illustrate, it is the image, the front, the style which impact upon the viewer, more than the substance or content of what is said.

Another range of facts has to do with the content of commercial TV programs. The daily "soaps" are dramas full of action, tensions, and violence. The half-hour nightly news intersperse the *bad* news from around the world— airplane crashes, riots in South Africa, oil tankers damaged by mines in the Persian Gulf—with the *good* news of the ads: the bliss of the happy, healthy life assured by high-fiber cold cereals, laxatives, aspirins, and all sorts of magic potions, or the beatitude and bliss that comes with the family's purchase of the new Subaru. The hidden assumption in all of these ads is that speed, power, comfort, convenience, and glamour constitute the truly good life. This is the gospel preached on commercial television, and the standard of moral worth is a quantitative one: more equals better.

With this spread of electronic communication, both by radio and television, recent decades have seen the rising empires of the televangelists. Each of these kingdoms centers on vivid charismatic personalities who are the "Prime-Time Preachers:" Billy Graham, Oral Roberts, Rex Humbard, Jerry Falwell, Jim Bakker, Jimmy Swaggart, Pat Robertson, and many other stars.[6] Each of these has built a highly efficient business organization with budgets in the multi-millions. Although Jeffrey Hadden, a sociologist who has made a close scrutiny of televangelism, points out that the claim once made by Jerry Falwell that his "Old-Time Gospel Hour" has a viewing audience of 50 million persons is grossly exaggerated, the numbers reached by these preachers is very high indeed. The budgets for maintaining the studios and for putting on their services of worship are steep. "The top four programs on television collectively took in over a quarter of a billion dollars in 1980."[7]

Computer technology of the most sophisticatd sort is used in raising money to sustain these kingdoms. Once your name gets on the computerized mass mailing lists of Pat Robertson's "700 Club," or Oral Roberts's "Faith Partners," you are dunned for money by a personalized appeal. Your name may be dipped into the text of the letter by a shrewd computer device that gives you the illusion that God himself is addressing you individually. Of course, humanitarian and philanthropic organizations of all sorts make use of the same technology in their mailing appeals. But there is an apocalyptic note in the fund appeals of the televangelist, whether made directly on the screen or by mail. Recently, Oral Roberts managed to fend off a death threat that God would take him "home" unless he raised eight million dollars, a fervent appeal that prompted one devotee in Florida, a dog-track owner, to send over a million to rescue him from death.

Still another significant sociological fact in the picture is the steady decline in membership rolls of the "main-line" Protestant churches. Certainly there are many other technological explanations for the downturn, but one plausible factor is the rise in popularity in the 1970s and 1980s of the electronic churches. The Sunday programs are right there in the living room or den, at the turn of the knob. The vivid appeal of color and sound, the mass choir singing with fervor the old gospel hymns, like "How Great Thou Art," the charismatic, dramatic preaching, the dramas of laying on of hands, the altar calls and responses, sometimes even the "speaking with tongues," all have an emotional pull lacking in the more staid and sober services of main-line Protestant churches.

The message that is preached by the electronic church is a curious mix. On the one hand, in keeping with the older Protestant evangelical tradition, the gospel is a simple message of salvation for those who turn from their evil ways and are "born again" by giving their hearts to Christ. This is a "me-centered," privatized faith. For those who are "born again," baptized by the Holy Spirit, there are material blessings and benefits that God will bestow. Puritan asceticism is replaced by a capitalistic ethic of plenty and pleasure. As the Bakkers said to their followers, "God wants you to be rich and enjoy the pleasures you thought were forbidden." They preached a cheerful materialism. "If you pray for a camper, be sure to tell God what color."[8] One cannot help but feel that the impact of commercial television's image of the good life as constituted by the abundance of material goods has been in good measure responsible for this reading of the fruits of piety promised by the televangelists.

On the other hand, the rise of the Moral Majority movement adds a new element to the content of the televangelist's message: a political concern which in some ways runs counter to the privatized, me-centered reading of the Gospel message. Jerry Falwell and many other evangelists now call America back to the God who has been forsaken, away from "secular humanism." They call for public policies that will recover the religious faith of our fathers.[9] Contrary to an entrenched Baptist tradition of a strict separation of church from state, the crusade of many in the New Christian Right is for the support of political candidates for office who would legislate to restore traditional American "family values." So the *public* message televised opposes pornography, abortion, divorce, ERA, homosexuality, sex education. It crusades for the legalization of "voluntary" prayer and Bible study in public schools, and the teaching of so-called "scientific creationism," which is the Genesis account of creation, to challenge the Darwinian evolutionary theory. The technologies of the mass media by mail, radio, or TV are used in fervent appeals to enact these Christian measures into public policy, and to save America. Christians are called to go to their school board meetings, to their city council, and to the polls in national elections, to enact these Christian ideals into law.

How may one justly evaluate the electronic church, both as to its means of communication and to the content of its message?

Though it is ridiculous to squeeze into a paragraph the basic tenets of Christian theology, we must recall, in very brief terms, certain basic ingredients in the classical Christian faith, theological and ethical. These are shared in common by the plurality of Christian churches, Roman Catholic, Orthodox and the wide spectrum of different forms of Protestantism. Roman Catholic worship centers on the sacraments, especially the eucharist, while Protestant worship centers on the preaching of the Word, but both the more sacramental and the more homiletical forms of worship share the same faith.

The basic faith-premise is a theocratic one: the rule of a transcendent God, Creator, Sustainer, and Redeemer of all, whose will for humanity is revealed in the patriarchs and the prophets and, in particular, Jesus the Christ. There are varied Christologies, but the one especially emphasized in the liberal Protestant tradition is the "prophetic" one, the Christ who challenged the religious establishment of his day, who called for justice and righteousness, concern for the needy and oppressed, as the authentic fulfillment of the covenant terms of God's relation to his chosen people.

The authentic response of the believer to the Providential rule of God is praise and thanksgiving, the core of true worship, where the self, in silence or words spoken or sung, individually or corporately, responds to the grace of God in gratitude. The immediate corollary to this response is the sense of obligation, the requirement of service, to love and serve one's neighbor and to care in stewardship for God's created order, to seek justice and to make peace. A Christian church is a community of persons who gather for worship and praise, and are then empowered to fulfill God's will by deeds of loving service to neighbors near and far, "to do justly, to love kindness, and to walk humbly." A Christian church should be servant to the community in which it is located, and the conscience of the public order.

When measured by these normative criteria of faith and ethics, has the sophisticated technology of media communication in the electronic church served to fulfill these classical norms or to pervert them? Are television and radio themselves the heroes or the villains of the piece?

There has been considerable research done recently assessing the impact of telecommunications on religious belief and practice in America, the most extensive a project sponsored by the National Council of Churches.[10] An incisive overview of the ethical and religious issues involved is to be found in William Fore's *Television and Religion: The Shaping of Faith, Values, and Culture* (Minnesota, 1987).

There is no categorical answer to the question as to whether the electronic media cultivate or pervert the expression of authentic religious faith, i.e., whether this technique of communication is an instrument of God or of the devil. The general evaluative conclusion of most of these studies is negative. Fore, for instance, concludes that TV "communicates a set of values, assumptions, and world-views which are completely at odds with religious values, assumption and world-views."[11] In part, the fault lies within the technique itself, and in part with the wills and motives of those using this revolutionary technology of television.

On the positive side, one can certainly concur at one point with the generalization of such writers as Ben Armstrong that television is "a miraculous instrument of God which now makes possible the fulfillment of the great commandment to preach the Gospel to all the world."[12] Television extends the vision of neighborhood. In New Testament times the assumed physical context in which the command to "love they neighbor" was assumed to be a narrow one: the person nearby down the village road. Now, the TV screen brings to sight the neighbors in our global village. Via satellite, the starving child in India or Zaire, the Hatian refugee, the rioting mobs in South Africa are brought vividly before us in a way more compelling than was possible through the printed word. So, if the far neighbors are brought near, we *may* be led by that vision to feel more strongly the obligation to serve the needs of far neighbors as the Great Commandment enjoins us to do.

In the phone directory, there is a consoling word, "The sound of a warm, familiar voice over the long distance telephone is almost as satisfying as a personal visit." Certainly, electronic communication overlaps distances and brings people together. Broadcast services, either from the local church or from one of the televangelist castles do indeed reach, with words of consolation and grace, the elderly, the infirm, the housebound, or those lying on a hospital bed. The televised Christmas Eve or Easter services from the great Cathedrals can give the viewer the sense of wonder, awe, reverence, and praise.

On the negative side of the score card, however, much of televised religion is a perversion, indeed a denial of what authentic Christian worship, faith, and practise should be. These are the most evident negative aspects:

1.   For one thing, if we have defined genuine worship as the turn of heart and mind and voice to God in reverence, prayer, praise, and thanksgiving, as well as supplication, then to sit in the living room and watch someone pound the pulpit and wave the Bible before you, or watch the purple-robed choir sway as they sing "In the Garden," is not genuine worship. The viewers are passive spectators watching a religious show.

As Neil Postman has stated, "On television, religion like everything else, is presented quite simply and without apology, as entertainment. There is no ritual, no dogma, no tradition, no theology . . . no sense of spiritual transcendence . . . . There is no way to consecrate the space in which a television show is experienced."[13] Consequently, to watch the televangelist is not worship, but entertainment. "Television is a form of graven imagery far more alluring than a golden calf."[14] Is it likely that viewers would join in singing the hymns, kneel before the TV set, or even say aloud the Lord's Prayer with the preacher? No. By the very nature of the technological medium itself, the relationship is one-directional, monologic, not dialogic. There is no active response. In this sense, the TV set is not an avenue to communion with God, but a barrier, separating the self from the object of worship.

2.   The electronic medium is conducive to the distortion of the authentic Christian worship and faith in another way. The focus of the camera is on the dynamic preacher, the musical lilt and rhythm of his style, his thunder of wrath, or his ingratiating humor. The substance of his message is of small account compared to his image and manner. Thus the "worship service" of the electronic church becomes not God-centered but preacher-centered. The eye of the mind and heart is distracted from the altar and the cross, the symbols of the transcendent and the holy, to the pulpit and the charisma of the preacher.

3.   When one does appraise the content of what is celebrated and preached, another distortion of authentic Christianity becomes evident. As earlier mentioned, the Christian gospel of the televangelist is commercialized. The new life in Christ promised is not one of simplicity and sacrificial love, but a life abundant in worldly possessions. The traditional Christian virtues of "faith, hope, and love" are replaced by technocratic values, and by the capitalistic values of wealth and the quantitative standards of worth. Illustrative of this commericalization is the generous offer of the televangelist to send religious trinkets and jewelry, Bibles, records, even samples of earth from the Holy Land[15] to all who make their pledges and contributions. This assures a cash flow to support the televangelists' kingdoms.

4.   Of late, the turn by the Moral Majority and the New Christian Right to the political message of "God save America" represents another distortion of the Christian faith. Here, the onus of blame shifts from the technique to

the tribal theology and the commercial morality of the "prime-time preachers." The televised "Washington for Jesus" rally on the Mall in 1980, and later a "National Affairs Briefing" in Dallas, drew enormous crowds. The theme was "God bless America," with a call to do battle against secular humanism at home and godless communism abroad. Even Ronald Reagan, in an address before the National Association of Evangelicals, joined this chorus in calling the U.S.S.R. an "evil empire." The disciples of the televangelists of the New Right defend a strong national military defense on biblical grounds, for, as Jerry Falwell said, "Nowhere in the Bible is there a rebuke for the bearing of armaments."[16] The public policy preached by such televangelists is the reversion back to the Holy War mentality, a simple distinction between a God-fearing America against the godless communism of the Russians. In fairness, we must insert a qualification of this generalization: in recent years, one of the leading televangelists, Billy Graham, out of fear of nuclear war, has turned to a more pacific reading of the Gospel and a concern for world peace and for mutual disarmament. In the main, however, the message of the televangelists is a narrow nationalism. The larger issues of Christian ethical concern for ecological justice, the care of the earth, for civil rights for minorities at home and abroad, for equal rights for women, for racial justice, and for disarmament and world peace are not heard. Martin Marty writes that "the normal activity of mass media is to convey the kind of value or opinion that is generated by a thoroughly secularized society with a religious veneer."[17]

The technology of mass communication itself is not to be blamed for this narrow and perverted interpretation of the Christian faith fed daily into millions of American homes. There are many programs, seen mostly on public television albeit under no religious auspices, like *Nova* or National Geographic Specials, that bring alive the wonder and mystery of God's created order of nature and the desperate need for an ethic of stewardship to care for the precious earth. Documentaries televising crucial and tragic epochs of our history like *Vietnam,* or the in-depth analyses of the Constitution in 1987, may arouse the conscience of the viewer to crucial ethical and religious issues. In short, the technology of mass media can be used either for humanizing or dehumanizing ends. It depends in good measure on the policies of the producers as to the content of what is filmed or broadcast. The National Televison Code sets an ethical norm which reflects a Christian moral standard:

> Program materials should enlarge the horizons of the viewer, provide him with wholesome entertainment . . . and remind him of the responsibilities which the citizen has toward his society."[18]

5. Finally, one must raise serious ethical questions about the fiscal policies of the giant electronic churches. As mentioned above, the shrewd business skills of money-raising are employed, with assurances of all sorts of spiritual and

material blessings promised to those who send in their tax-exempt contributions. And the computer mailing list appeal follows the tracks of a potential contributor relentlessly. As Hadden and Swann point out, "the computer provides a sort of technological equivalent of the Book of Judgment,"[19] assuring heaven to those who send in their money and threatening the pains of hell for those who do not. This practice is not unlike the medieval system of papal indulgences of the Roman curch, against which Martin Luther and the other Reformers protested.

Where do the millions of dollars go? The Bakker scandals brought to light the disillusioning fact that little of the revenue goes to serve the purposes of Christian ministry. A large portion of it goes to maintain the business organization of the televangelists' kingdoms, and to pay the high costs of telecasting programs. In 1979, Jerry Falwell raised some 35 million dollars, but he had to spend five dollars for every seven dollars he raised.[20] Much also goes to maintain a life-style of the televangelist and his family in a manner markedly different from that of St. Francis or Mother Teresa. Televangelism is a profitable business enterprise. If we are to judge these kingdoms by the normative Christian prophetic standards that the church exists in the world not for its own aggrandizement, but as the servant of society, to heal the sick, to feed the hungry, to clothe the naked, and to free the oppressed, the conclusion is plain: most of the giant electronic churches betray in practice the commands of the Gospel they preach.

In sum, the evidence would seem to lead to the evaluative conclusions that *both* by reason of the technology used in religious communication and the nationalistic, materialistic, exploitive purposes of the televangelists, the essential message of the Christian faith is perverted and secularized.

It would be ridiculous to propose, as a practical way out of this dark morass, that religious television should be banned, and that good Christians should go through their neighborhood throwing the TV sets out on the street. No, the way out as with all of the problems that technology has brought upon our culture, converting America from a theocracy into a technocracy, or what Frederick Ferré would call "Technolatry," is not to banish our techniques of communication, but to turn their content from dehumanizing to humanizing ends as inspired by the Christian faith.

Currently, there are some hopeful signs and signals. Some programs of mainline churches, such as "Insight," produced by the Paulist Fathers; "World Vision," by Stanley Mooneyham, which raises millions for world hunger relief; and "Catch the Spirit," produced by the United Methodists, convey vividly the social imperatives of the Christian gospel. Currently, an ecumenical TV program of some ten denominations, including Roman Catholic and United Methodists, are launching a cable network program to be broadcast nationwide. The content of these interfaith programs hopefully will have theological depth, persuasive messages of the social obligations of Christians to serve the needs of neighbors far and near, and the radical imperative to protect the precious order of God's creation. These messages can be made the more compelling by the impact of the TV medium itself and thus become an instrument, not of explotiation, but of service to humankind in obedience to the divine will.

NOTES AND REFERENCES

1. *Newsweek,* June 8, 1987.

2. Neil Postman, *Amusing Ourselves to Death: Public Discourse in an Age of Show Business* (New York, 1986), p. 8.

3. William Fore, *Television and Religion: The Shaping of Faith, Values and Culture* (Minnesota, 1987), p. 16.

4. See Waldo Beach, *The Wheel and the Cross: A Christian Response to the Technological Revolution* (Atlanta, 1979), chap. 6: "The Ethics of Communication."

5. Marshall MacLuhan, *Understanding Media* (New York, 1964).

6. Jeffrey Hadden and Charles Swann, *Prime Time Preachers: The Rising Power of Televangelism* (Reading, MA, 1981).

7. Ibid., pp. 47, 48.

8. *Newsweek,* June 8, 1987.

9. Jerry Falwell, *Listen, America* (New York, 1980).

10. Cf. National Council of Churches, George Gerbner, et. al., eds. *Religion and Television,* a research report by the Annenberg School of Communications, University of Pennsylvania and the Gallup Organization, Inc. (New York, 1984).

11. Fore, p. 71.

12. See Ben Armstrong, *The Electric Church* (Nashville, 1979), as quoted in Hadden and Swann, p. 179.

13. Postman, pp. 116, 119.

14. Ibid., p. 123.

15. Hadden and Swann, pp. 19, 115.

16. Falwell, p. 98.

17. Martin Marty, *The Improper Opinion: Mass Media and the Christian Faith* (Philadelphia, 1971), p. 47.

18. William Rivers and Wilbur Schramm, *Responsibility in Mass Communication,* 2nd ed., rev. (New York, 1969), p. 258.

19. Hadden and Swann, p. 105.

20. Fore, p. 93.

RELIGION AND TECHNOLOGY:
A LOOK AT TELEVISION EVANGELISTS
AND VIEWERS

Robert C. Good

Starting in the predawn hours of each Sunday morning, the largest religious gathering in America takes place, drawing almost 130 million people to their radio and television sets . . . . This amazing event takes place every week, all week, from early Sunday morning through the final midnight stroke on Saturday night. Making this possible is the awesome technology of broadcasting . . . . I believe that God has raised up this powerful technology of radio and television expressly to reach every man, woman, boy, and girl on earth with the even more powerful message of the gospel.'[1]

The management of the private consumer is a task of no slight sophistication . . . its most obvious instrument is advertising . . . and the uniquely powerful instrument of advertising is televison.[2]

Although the first quotation above may exaggerate the number of people who tune in to evangelical broadcasts, there is no doubt that television has made it possible for evangelists to be heard in the homes of millions of Americans

Research in Philosophy and Technology, Volume 10, pages 81-91.
Copyright © 1990 by JAI Press Inc.
All rights of reproduction in any form reserved.
ISBN: 1-55938-062-4

as well as by people in other countries.[3] Television evangelists are trying to convince those who hear them to commit themselves to religious faith, if they have not done so already. Also, there is usually the attempt on the part of such evangelists to persuade those who hear them to make financial contributions to their continuing ministry.[4] Trying to convince or persuade someone to do something normally presents no moral problems; however, an increasing number of people nowadays are leaning toward thinking that television evangelists may be controlling the behavior of those they reach through television.[5] Controlling the behavior of people, unlike the attempt to persuade, is the kind of activity people find to be morally objectionable.

Suppose that we say that people are controlled by television evangelists because many of their interests, wants, and desires are created by these evangelists. This would obviously be more than mere persuasion on the part of these evangelists. Saying that people are controlled by evangelists implies something that ought to be insulting to the intelligence of most of those who listen to television evangelists; namely, that they are not the best judges of their own interests. To decide if television evangelists control the behavior of some of their listeners, or if television evangelists are simply persuading their listeners to do certain things and to believe certain other things, with listeners being free to decide for themselves, would ultimately require a discussion of freedom of the will. A discussion of that substantial philosophical issue will not take place here. What does take place here is a discussion of arguments which try to show that television evangelists are involved in behavior control, and then objections to these arguments are considered which maintain that television evangelists are simply involved in persuasion.

John Kenneth Galbraith has discussed the effect that advertising, particularly that presented on television, has on the behavior of the American consumer.[6] His observations will help us to begin to probe the issue of whether television evangelists are involved in behavior control or in mere persuasion. Galbraith contrasts myth with reality. The myth is that producers are subordinate to the ultimate will of the consumer. In order to maximize their profits producers respond to the authority of consumers. According to the myth, the consumer is sovereign, i.e., self-ruled, supreme, and independent. Consumers make up their own minds about what they want, and producers respond to consumers' wants. According to Galbraith, the reality in contemporary America is quite different. The tastes and needs of the consumer fall under the authority of the producer, which means that the consumer is subordinate to the will of the producer. What is actually happening is that producers are managing consumers, bending them to their needs. Television advertising is the key instrument employed by producers to control the behavior of consumers. The goal of all advertising is to impress upon consumers that happiness will be associated with using a particular product. In general, advertising seeks to convince consumers that happiness will be the result of the possession and use of goods, and that such happiness will increase as more and more goods are consumed.

Of course, Galbraith thinks that we need to change the reality. He has been one of the most strident critics of business's attempt to control consumer behavior. Galbraith is completely convinced that consumer demand is created by producers, which means that producers control how consumers spend their money. What all this shows is that the law of supply and demand has been reversed. Rather than goods and services being produced in response to consumer demand, the sequence has been reversed, leading to consumer demand being a function of production. Galbraith submits that the result of this reversal has been that the production of public goods (education, health care, aid to the poor, etc.) has been sacrificed to satisfy the demand that has been created for private goods (designer jeans, video games, VCRs, etc.). One of the primary goals of advertising is to bypass the decision-making ability of the consumer. This attempt at such a bypass is objectionable from an ethical point of view. Consumers are not able to make up their own minds about what they want because they are inundated and overwhelmed by the blitz of television advertising which creates and controls their wants. Self-determination or autonomy is thereby threatened, and Galbraith suggests that this is an undesirable feature of contemporary America.

How does the preceding relate to television evangelists and their viewers? One might initially think that television evangelists are subordinate to the ultimate will of television viewers. A large number of people in America desire to listen to television evangelists at home, and television evangelists are simply responding to the authority of television viewers. Television viewers, one might think, are sovereign because they make up their own minds about what they watch. Peering through a Galbraithian lens at the relationship between television evangelists and their viewers, however, yields a quite different interpretation of the relationship. The wants and needs of the viewers of television evangelists actually fall under the authority of the evangelists, which implies that the viewers are subordinate to the will of the evangelists. What is happening in reality is that television evangelists are managing the behavior of their viewers, bending them to fulfill their own needs, many of which are financial in nature. Television is employed skillfully by many evangelists to control the behavior of their viewers. The goal of television evangelists is to impress upon their viewers that happiness (usually in the promise of eternal life) will be associated with believing what they say, and with sending money to further the ministry in question. In general, the message that television evangelists attempt to get across is that adopting the basic doctrines of the evangelist's religion and contributing to the evangelists' cause will lead to increased happiness through the ever-increasing confidence that one will have eternal life.[7]

One could argue that we need to change this situation in which television evangelists have so much control over the behavior of their viewers. There is something highly undesirable about the manner in which television evangelists are reversing the law of supply and demand. Rather than evangelical television shows existing due to viewer demand, the sequence has been reversed, so that now viewer demand is a function of the production of the large number of television shows featuring evangelists. The result of the reversal is that certain virtues and habits of mind that television viewers should be developing are being sacrificed to satisfy the demand that has been created by evangelists for spiritual satisfaction and the increasing confidence in eternal life for oneself that comes with more and more donations to the ministry. One of the primary goals of television evangelists is to bypass the decision-making ability of the viewer. This attempt at a bypass is objectionable from the moral point of view. Viewers of evangelists are unable to make up their own minds about what they wish to believe and what they do with their "spare" money because they are overwhelmed by the plethora of television evangelists who create and control the wants and needs of their television flock. Self-determination or autonomy is thereby threatened, which is an unfortunate fact about contemporary America. People ought to be able to think for themselves rather than having their behavior and beliefs controlled or dictated by television evangelists.

So far, we have looked at arguments that could be advanced to show that television evangelists control viewer behavior by creating wants and desires in their viewers. It is important to note that Galbraith's conclusions about advertising's effect on the consumer have been severely challenged, for example, by Ralph Winter.[8] Let us now take a look at Winter's observations about Galbraith with the goal of seeing how they might be adapted to serve as objections to the position explained above, that television evangelists control the behavior of their viewers.

In an attempt to show that Galbraith overgeneralizes about the effect that ads have on consumers, Winter points out that the impact a particular ad has on one person is often and usually different from its impact on another person. For example, an ad for a product may motivate one consumer to purchase it immediately while the same ad may have no effect on another consumer. This observation is supposed to show that Galbraith cannot generalize in the fashion he desires when he says that ads control consumer behavior. An analogous point could be made about the contention that television evangelists control the behavior of viewers. A particular evangelist's television show may motivate one viewer to subscribe to the evangelist's beliefs and to send financial contributions to the evangelist's ministry on a regular basis. That same television show may have no effect on another viewer who sits through the entire show and does not adopt the evangelist's beliefs, nor does he send the evangelist's ministry any money. Therefore, it makes no sense to say that television evangelists control the behavior of their viewers.

Conceding the point that television evangelists are faithfully followed and contributed to by some and not by others, one should go on to insist that the fact remains that a television evangelist does dictate the belief system and the donation behavior of his regular viewers. These faithful followers form the group that is having its needs, wants, and donation habits created by television evangelists. Rather than thinking for themselves regarding what they want and need, and rather than thinking independently about how to spend their "donatable" money, they want and need what the evangelist tells them they want and need, and they contribute to the ministry because the evangelist asks them to do so.

Winter goes on to assert that consumers are not as affected by ads as Galbraith alleges, because consumers are aware that advertisers are primarily self-interested and they are, therefore, skeptical of the claims made in ads. The thrust of Winter's point is that producers exercise no control over the naturally skeptical consumers we have in this country. An analogous point could be made regarding the nature of the effect that television evangelists have on viewers. Television viewers are aware that evangelists appearing on television are primarily self-interested insofar as their utmost concern is to accumulate money for their continuing ministries. Therefore, the television evangelist does not exercise any control over the behavior of the naturally skeptical viewers of television we have in this country.

The point that needs to be made here is that some viewers of television evangelists are skeptical about the claims and requests made by these evangelists, while some viewers are not. Some viewers are convinced that television evangelists are primarily self-interested, motivated only to acquire more and more money for their ministries and/or themselves. Such viewers will, of course, be skeptical of the evangelist's messages. On the other hand, some viewers surely believe that television evangelists are not at all motivated by self-interest. Such viewers may believe that television evangelists have received a calling from God to the ministry and that they are interested in "saving souls" by urging those who hear them on television to subscribe to religious faith. In other words, some viewers seem to believe that television evangelists are engaged in a truly altruistic activity, spreading the word of God so that more and more people will acquire religious faith and thereby gain eternal life. This sort of viewer does what the television evangelists ask— subscribe to a certain set of beliefs, and donate money to the continuing ministry. There is a strong case to be made that viewers such as these *are* being controlled by television evangelists in that their needs, wants, and desires are being dictated by such evangelists.

In a third effort to show that Galbraith misunderstands the nature of the relationship between advertisers and consumers, Winter points out that life is full of attempts at persuasion, and he goes on to argue that the techniques of advertising are no different from techniques used in other forms of persuasion. His point, then, is that advertising has no greater consequences on the behavior of people than do the other efforts at persuasion that others direct our way on a daily basis. A parallel point could be made regarding the nature of the television evangelists' messages to viewers. The television evangelists' attempt to persuade viewers to adopt certain beliefs and contribute money to the ministry is just one attempt among the many attempts at persuasion that a person deals with on a daily basis. The television evangelist's effort to persuade us to do certain things is not importantly different from, for example, our friends' efforts to persuade us to do certain things, e.g., buy a raffle ticket, support their candidate for political office, join them for lunch, etc. Our friends try to convince us that happiness will result from the activities they suggest in the same way that the television evangelist tries to convince us that happiness will result from the activities he suggests. Thus, the techniques employed by the television evangelists are no different in nature from the techniques employed by others who endeavor to persuade us. Television evangelists, then, are no more capable of controlling behavior than anyone else who tries to persuade.

The way to reply to the foregoing is to argue that the techniques used by television evangelists to persuade *are* importantly different from other attempts at persuasion that we encounter. Television evangelists present themselves to their audience as possessing special knowledge that goes beyond the knowledge of the average person who engages in persuasion. Television evangelists claim to have special contact with God, a claim which goes far beyond the claims to authority or credibility we are normally faced with in attempts at persuading us. It is this special contact they claim to have with God which enables television evangelists to assert confidently what it is that God wants us to do. What God wants us to do, specifically, is to have faith in Him, follow His word, and give money to His cause which is, of course, served by the evangelist's ministry. Eternal life is promised by the evangelists for those who believe in God and contribute to the ministry. Now, what happens to those who do not believe in God, according to the evangelists? The answer to this question varies according to the particular evangelist one consults, but suffice it to say that eternal life does not await those who do not believe in God, and, in fact, eternal damnation may be the result of this lack of faith. Most attempts at persuasion which we confront do not threaten us with loss of eternal life as does the attempt at persuasion in which the television evangelist is engaged. Furthermore, not to give money to the evangelist's ministry, in the judgment of many of their followers, is to run the risk of not acquiring eternal life.[9] Needless to say, the stakes that are established by television evangelists in their attempts at persuasion, eternal life vs. no eternal life, are far more hefty than the stakes established in most other attempts at persuasion. It is clear that many viewers of television evangelists do what the evangelists tell them to do *because* they are convinced that such evangelists know how people can acquire eternal life.

To that extent, it is arguable that television evangelists *do* control consumer behavior in a way that amounts to more than mere persuasion.

A fourth manner in which Winter objects to Galbraith's position on advertising, and the final one I discuss, is to submit that Galbraith overlooks the important function that advertising provides of informing consumers about what goods are available. Advertising acquaints consumers with the range of choices they possess, and it does so in a way that is very beneficial to consumers, since they could not possibly accumulate such information on their own. Advertising, then, enables consumers to make informed choices about what to buy, and it does so in an efficient and desirable fashion. One could take a similar stand on the nature of the relationship between television evangelists and their viewers. That is, television evangelists fulfill the important function of informing television viewers about certain benefits that will accrue to them if they hold certain beliefs and support the ministry. Television evangelists acquaint their viewers with a choice that they could make in their lives—to believe in God, which will enable them to live their lives in the proper way as well as to acquire eternal life.

It is extremely misleading to allege that evangelists are simply enabling viewers to make informed choices. They are telling their viewers that eternal life awaits them if they subscribe to certain beliefs. Of course, a viewer cannot verify in his time here on earth that eternal life awaits him or anyone else for that matter. The point is that the evangelist promises something that the viewer cannot determine if he will acquire or not. This makes the choice the evangelist offers to viewers crucially different from the choices advertisers offer viewers. When I see four men hoisting bottles of Michelob and saying, "It doesn't get any better than this," I am able to check in my lifetime if what they are saying is so. In general, it is misleading to characterize the evangelist as informing viewers about available "goods," where the evangelist's "goods" are the benefits of eternal life. The evangelists may be mistaken that the "goods" he promises are even available—that is, there may be no eternal life.

Throughout this paper we have been examining whether or not television evangelists threaten the self-determination or autonomy of their viewers. I close this paper by discussing Gerald Dworkin's analysis of autonomy, and how it relates to television evangelists and their viewers. To further our probe of the issue of whether or not television evangelism deprives viewers of autonomy, we need an account of autonomy, and Dworkin gives us an account which is plausible and insightful.[10]

Dworkin's analysis distinguishes between first-order desires and second-order desires, in a way which is now familiar. First-order desires can be reflected on by second-order desires, insofar as a person is able to step back and formulate an attitude, either of approval or disapproval, toward his first-order desires. Basically, Dworkin argues that Autonomy = Authenticity + Independence. An autonomous person does his own thing. The "his" aspect of this short, colloquial characterization of autonomy refers to authenticity, while the "own" refers to independence. Are a person's first-order desires *his*? In other words, is the person authentic? The key question is, "Does a person wish to have the first-order desires he does?" If the answer to this question is yes, the person is authentic. If the answer to this question is no, the person is not authentic. The second-order desires of an authentic person reaffirm his first-order desires; an authentic person desires that his desires are as they are. The second-order and first-order desires of an authentic person are in harmony. The second-order desires of an inauthentic person do not reaffirm his first-order desires; an inauthentic person does not desire that his desires are as they are. The second-order and first-order desires of an inauthentic person are not in harmony.

A person, even if authentic, still needs to be independent to count as autonomous on Dworkin's analysis. A person's desires may be *his,* his second-order desires reaffirming his first-order desires, without being his *own.* How might this happen? It happens when a person's desires have been brought about by manipulation, deception, or the withholding of relevant information. A person's second-order desires may reaffirm his first-order desires, but the person's second-order desires would not reaffirm his first-order desires if he were aware that he was being manipulated, deceived, or having information withheld from him. In fact, a person may not have the first-order desires he has if he were aware of such manipulation, deception, or information withholding.

How is Dworkin's analysis of autonomy relevant to the relation between TV evangelists and their viewers? The question that needs to be posed is: Do TV evangelists interfere with the autonomy of their viewers? Let us presume that nearly all the faithful followers of an evangelist are authentic, namely, that their second-order desires reaffirm their first-order desires, with respect to the evangelist's messages. That is, they have the first-order desires to adopt the beliefs the evangelist says they should, and the first-order desire to contribute money to the evangelist's ministry. In addition, they desire that their first-order desires are as they are; they approve of the first-order desires they possess. In order for a person to be autonomous, however, the person must be independent as well as authentic. What can we say regarding the independence of the viewers of evangelists? Is it the case that the desires of those who view evangelists have been brought about by manipulation, deception, or withholding of relevant information? A strong case can be made that this question should be answered in the affirmative.

Do television evangelists manipulate their viewers? One might argue that they do in the following sense. Evangelists tell their viewers that they will not receive eternal life unless they adopt certain religious beliefs and show the strength of their faith by donating money to the ministry. They are appealing to the fear, anxiety, and uncertainty their viewers have about what awaits them after earthly death. Many viewers are seeking a satisfying explanation of what will happen to them after earthly death. Being aware of this fact about viewers, television evangelists stand ready with a strategy viewers can follow to assure themselves of eternal life. What ultimately makes the activity of the television evangelists manipulative is that they are shrewdly managing their followers into thinking that they must do and believe exactly what the evangelists tell them to do and believe, that what the evangelists preach is the only acceptable way to live one's life if one wishes to have eternal life.[11]

Do television evangelists deceive their viewers? Certainly, an evangelist would be deceiving his viewers if he told them that their financial contributions went to further the ministry when, in fact, some of the contributions went directly into the personal bank account of the evangelist himself. If viewers were aware that evangelists to whose ministerial cause they had contributed had derived extraordinary personal financial gain from contributions, some viewers may not continue to have the first-order desires to adopt the beliefs that evangelists propose and to support the ministry by donations.[12]

Do television evangelists withhold relevant information from their viewers? One could argue that they do in the following way. Television evangelists often suggest that they know what it is that God wants us to do, or what it is that we can do to serve God. Television evangelists should be asked many of the questions that Plato tells us Socrates asked Euthyphro. Can you give us any proof that you know what it is that God wants? If we are to be able to determine whether or not a particular action serves God, must we not know what God's goals are? That is, how can we as servants serve our master unless we know what our master's project is? How does the television evangelist know what God's goals are, and what God's project is? Television evangelists present themselves as having knowledge of God's will. Why doesn't the evangelist say, instead, so as not to withhold information from his viewers, that what he recommends his viewers do is what *he thinks* God wants them to do?[13] Then perhaps some viewers might begin to speculate on the evangelist's basis or justification for thinking what he does about God's will. Such speculation should begin the process of acquiring certain habits of mind, like asking for evidence or justification, which are far more sensible to pursue in life than simply doing and believing whatever television evangelists tell one to do and believe.

Are television evangelists involved in behavior control or are they involved in mere persuasion? I think that the pendulum is swinging toward control. I hope that this paper will encourage others to reflect further on the question.

ACKNOWLEDGMENTS

Some of this paper was written when the author held a Summer Research Fellowship awarded by Rider College in 1987. The author is grateful to Rider for its financial support, and to Professor Frederick Ferré and an anonymous reviewer for *Research in Philosophy and Technology* for their valuable comments on an earlier version of this paper. Special thanks are owed to the author's colleagues Richard Burgh and Carol Nicholson for their insightful and encouraging observations about the general tone and structure of this paper.

NOTES AND REFERENCES

1. Ben Armstrong, *The Electric Church* (Nashville: Nelson, 1979), p. 7. Mr. Armstrong is the executive director of the National Religious Broadcasters, the trade association of the religious broadcast industry.

2. John Kenneth Galbraith, *Economics and the Public Purpose* (Boston: Houghton Mifflin, 1973), p. 137.

3. Jimmy Swaggart's television programs, which are telecast in the United States, and in dozens of foreign countries, reach 8 million viewers each Sunday. Jerry Falwell's gospel hour airs over 350 stations to 438,000 households, and over the Liberty Broadcasting Network to 1.5 million cable television subscribers. In April, *The PTL Show,* hosted by Jim Bakker, reached 13.5 million households via its own satellite network to 178 stations. The above information was reported in *Time* Magazine's cover story article of April 6, 1987, entitled "TV's Unholy Row."

4. *Time* also reported in its April 6, 1987 issue that the gospel broadcasters' total receipts likely come close to $2 billion a year and that Jerry Falwell's organization generates $100 million in revenues, while Jimmy Swaggart's 1986 revenues were estimated at $140 million.

There is no doubt that the evangelists need money to stay on the air, and that fundraising is one of their major tasks. Jeffrey K.Hadden and Charles E. Swann succintly make this point in their fascinating book, *Prime Time Preachers: The Rising Power of Televangelism* (Reading, MA: Addison-Wesley, 1981), p. 13: "Entrepreneurial religious broadcasting cannot survive without audience response that can be converted into contributions."

Television evangelists spend a healthy portion of their air time making financial appeals. In her *Televangelism: The Marketing of Popular Religion* (Carbondale: Southern Illinois University Press, 1987), p. 134, Razelle Frankl reports that Oral Roberts has spent 31.0% of his air time on financial appeals; Rex Humbard, 42.6%; Jerry Falwell and Jim Bakker, 23.0%; and James Robison, 36.0%.

5. See, for example, Gerard Straub, *Salvation for Sale: An Insider's View of Pat Robertson's Ministry* (Buffalo: Promotheus Books, 1986), and Peter G. Horsfield, *Religious Television: The American Experience* (New York: Longman's, 1984).

6. Galbraith, op. cit., Ch. XIV. See also John Kenneth Galbraith, *The Affluent Society* (New York: Mentor, 1969) and John Kenneth Galbraith, *The New Industrial State* (New York: Signet, 1967). I often rely on the excellent characterization of Galbraith's views as well as the perceptive description of the issue of consumer autonomy found in Joseph DesJardins and John McCall, *Contemporary Issues in Business Ethics* (Belmont, California: Wadsworth, 1985), pp. 136-141.

7. I am presuming that evangelists are expert in using television as a "technology-dependent social system in the business of selling products with techniques of mass persuasion" (Frankl, op. cit., p. 10). Virginia Stem Owens, in her *The Total Image, or Selling Jesus in the Modern Age* (Grand Rapids: W.B. Eerdmans, 1980), calls attention to the fascination evangelists have with mass commercial and advertising culture.

8. Ralph K. Winter, "Advertising and Legal Theory." This article originally appeared in *Issues in Advertising,* David Terck, ed., 1978 American Enterprise Institute. It is reprinted in DesJardins and McCall, op. cit., pp. 154-157. Other interesting articles which criticize Galbraith's views on the power of advertising are G. William Trivoli, "Has the Consumer Really Lost His Sovereignty?",

Akron Business and Economic Review, 1 ,(4):33-39, (1970), and Robert L. Arrington, "Advertising and Behavior Control," *Journal of Business Ethics,* (1982), pp. 3-12. For an effective defense of Galbraith's views, see Alan H. Goldman, "Business Ethics: Profits, Utilities, and Moral Rights," *Philosophy and Public Affairs,* 9(3):260-286 (1980).

9.   A letter that Rex Humbard reportedly sends wayward followers is followed by observations by the authors in Hadden and Swann, op. cit., p. 103:

> Dear Thomas,
> Last week I knelt at the prayer altar to pray for every member in the Prayer Key Family, and I wanted to pray for you . . . but your name was not there . . .
>
> Rex Humbard
>
> The Prayer Key Family Book is Rex Humbard's directory of sinners for whom Rex and his family will pray. You get listed there by contributing to his TV ministry. Rex never quite says you'll go to hell without his prayers . . . [but] . . . good things can come to you if you get your name back in the good book.

10.   Gerald Dworkin, "Autonomy and Behavior Control" (Institute of Society, Ethics, and the Life Sciences, 1979). It is reprinted in DesJardins and McCall, op. cit., pp. 159-166.

11.   Oral Roberts is particularly adept at manipulating his followers. In 1980, Roberts claimed a 900 foot tall Jesus visited him at his bedside and said he should build a medical center. Contributions to support this project began to pour in. And, of course, in March, 1987, Roberts said God would call him home unless followers contributed $4.5 billion for missionary work by the end of the month. One individual presented Roberts with a check for $1.3 million which led to the goal being achieved. Still, Roberts stayed in his Prayer Tower and asked for more money. Both of these incidents were reported in *Time* Magazine (April 6, 1987).

12.   The Charlotte Observer reported in 1987 that Jim and Tammy Bakker in recent years have acquired $700,000 worth of real estate and luxury cars. Many television evangelists are not ready to divulge what they do with the donations they receive. Jimmy Swaggart's recent tryst with a prostitute caused many to observe that he had deceived his viewers, given that he often condemned on his television shows the very behavior that he engaged in himself.

13.   Evangelists often disagree amongst themselves. Jimmy Swaggart and Jerry Falwell have recently argued that Jim Bakker and Oral Roberts have a misguided conception of what God wants them to do. The point is that different evangelists have different thoughts about how people should be serving God. See *Time* (April 6, 1987).

ARE SCIENCE AND TECHNOLOGY QUASI-RELIGIONS?

J. Mark Thomas

Can science and technology be understood as manifestations of quasi-religion? And, if they can be so understood, what is their relation to the other forms of quasi-religion? What are the necessary and sufficient conditions for the existence of a quasi-religion, and how would science and technology qualify?

First, if religion is understood simply as the aggregate of beliefs and practices of the traditions (including, perhaps, the "new" religions), then no concept of quasi-religion is possible. Religion must be understood as a *dimension,* rather than a sphere of human being. There must be a "religious" quality to existence, whether identified as the holy (Otto), the sacred (Eliade), ultimate concern (Tillich), societal integration (Durkheim), a system of order giving symbols (Geertz), or ideology (Marx). As a dimension of life, religion becomes susceptible to constructive understanding. Then, there may be seen to be a religious significance to overtly nonreligious actions, institutions, and symbols. Paul Tillich's definition of religion may serve as the paradigmatical case (and is central to this argument):

Research in Philosophy and Technology, Volume 10, pages 93-102.
Copyright © 1990 by JAI Press Inc.
All rights of reproduction in any form reserved.
ISBN: 1-55938-062-4

Religion is the state of being grasped by an ultimate concern, a concern which qualifies all other concerns as preliminary and which itself contains the answer to the question of the meaning of our life. Therefore, this concern is unconditionally serious and shows a willingness to sacrifice any finite concern which is in conflict with it. The predominant religious name for the content of such concern is God—a god or gods . . . . In secular quasi-religions the ultimate concern is directed towards objects like nation, science, a particular form or stage of society, or a highest ideal of humanity, which are then considered divine.[1]

A second condition necessary for the existence of quasi-religion is that it can arise only on the basis of secularism.[2] Not until an autonomous break with "theonomous" society has opened the possibility of a "secular" society can elements of that society adopt a religious status independent of temple and shrine. In citing the conditions for the existence of "civil religion," Phillip Hammond offers a similar criterion: there must be an institutionalized religious liberty—manifest in the American context as a "separation" of church and state which has *not* separated the use of religious symbols.[3] In other words, before there can be civil religion or quasi-religion, there must first be the possibility of a nonreligious sphere which is capable of "carrying" religious symbols independently.

Third, *quasi*-religion must be distinguished from *pseudo*-religion. Quasi-religion is not one which portrays itself to be religious despite the inauthenticity of the claim. Rather, it (e.g., science, the nation) functions religiously even if it passionately denies its "religious" character. A business enterprise attempting to incorporate itself as a "religion" in order to avoid taxation may legitimately be called "pesudo-religion." Fascism, even in its most virulent anti-Christian and supramoral phase, may be legitimately understood as a "quasi-religion." As Tillich summarizes, " 'pseudo' indicates an intended but deceptive similarity; 'quasi' indicates a genuine similarity, not intended, but based on points of identity."[4] Implicit in this condition is the lack of any criterion of volition. It is the appearance of a phenomenon as "religious" which qualifies it for the category, not the intentions of its funders, interpreters, or adherents—even should these be antithetical to "religious" intentions as they understand them.

Fourth, quasi-religion must encompass a transcendent ideology. It cannot be concerned only with the fragment, the partial, and the phenomenal in isolation. There must, indeed, be a concern with the comprehensive whole. In this sense of the ambiguous term "ideology," there can be no quasi-religion without an embracing system of ideas. Again, Hammond argues that a set of ideas allowing the nation to be understood in a transcendent manner—a "transcendent ideology"—is the first condition for the establishment of civil religion.[5] Tillich refers to the "quasi-religious" character of such *ideologies* as Fascism and Communism.[6] While it may be argued that not every "ideology" is "religious" in the sense of civil religion or quasi-religion, it is doubtful that any system of symbols less comprehensive than that implied in "ideology" could be called religious. Likewise, the ideological system must have a transcendent reference. It must refer things not simply to a relational context within which they may be perceived and perhaps manipulated, but within which they gain an ultimate significance and meaning. In Tillich's terms, it must contain "the answer to the question of the meaning of our life."

Can science and technology be understood as quasi-religious forces in the light of the conditions considered above? And if they can, how are they related to that liberalism which bears the conventional account of modernity?

In the history of ideas, it is significant that the bearers of classical liberalism and the philosophical apologists for a scientific and technological culture were essentially the same thinkers. The liberal war against the classical and traditional world was waged in terms both political (individual sovereignty, social contract, limited government), and cultural-epistemological (philosophy versus religion, fact versus prejudice, progress versus stagnation). Intimations of this movement had already taken place, of course, in the methodological attitude and social aspirations of such precursors as Francis Bacon. His utopia was a society dedicated to the "knowledge of causes, and secret motions of things; and the enlarging of the bounds of human empire, to the effecting of all things possible."[7] But the father of liberalism—John Locke—was undoubtedly also the chief advocate for the rise of technological society. He argued, as Sheldon Wolin concludes, that philosophy "should surrender its traditional concern with man's inner state and ultimate destiny, and turn instead to examining the kind of knowledge which would enable men to exploit the natural world."[8] Likewise, the unquestioned saint of liberalism, Adam Smith, protests that the "sublime contemplation" of God's wisdom ought not to be "the great business and occupation of our lives."[9] What should become the great occupation of our lives was the business of making human existence more commodious. Liberalism was becoming sublimely practical and active about transforming the world (including thought) into something of instrumental significance. The concept of truth was turning from the revolutionary idea of truth and justice to one of technical reasoning.[10] Reason had become, as Jeremy Bentham believed it to be, only the calculator of means for otherwise irrational ends.

Science and technology were hardly invented by liberal society. Disciplined observation (captured better in the German word, "Wissenschaft"), and instrumental action are apparently elements of being human. Without them, it is questionable whether one could speak of "human" beings as such. What was new about science and technology in liberal society was the shift in the *telos* of the human community itself, as Paul Tillich observed. In modernity, the *teloi* of classical humanism (the actualizations of all human potentialities, and the conquest of those distortions of human nature caused by the bondage to error and passion), and religious transcendentalism (the elevation from the universe of finitude and guilt to the reunion with ultimate reality), gave way to a scientific-technological one:

Rational man, the active center of the world, analyzing, controlling and changing it according to his purposes. Obviously, under the determination by this *télos*, science necessarily received a predominant place, and this place became more elevated the more the theoretical and practical success confirmed the claim of science to domination. The two older definitions of man's *télos* . . . were pushed aside. In most cases this did not happen intentionally; but the power of the world of technical means, including the means to increase them indefinitely, drove the mind into the horizontal direction to the neglect not only of the vertical elevation, symbolizing the religious aim, but also the circular enlargement symbolizing the classical aim.[11]

On the surface of it, science and technology appear as forces in direct contradiction to those of religion and ideology, and Tilich seems to confirm this in his analysis:

The drastic character of the present encounter of the world religions is produced by the attack of the quasi-religions on the religious proper, both theistic and nontheistic. The chief and always effective weapon for this attack is the invasion of all religious groups by technology with its various waves of technical revolution. Its effect was and is, first of all, a secularization which destroys the old traditions, both of culture and religion.[12]

There appears to be further support for this in Tillich's interpretation when he suggests that the real danger of the quasi-religions is "secularization," "profanization" representing "a process of becoming more and more empty or materialistic without any ultimate concern."[13] Taken literally, this would mean that the danger of the quasi-religions is that they destroy religion by destroying ultimate concern. This was certainly the dream of many of the liberal reformers and the socialists who inherited this dimension of the liberal ethos: science would displace religion, not replace it. Technology would make for a project of human abundance which would obviate earlier preoccupation with cosmological worlds. Were this the argument, it would necessarily stop here. Science and technology could hardly be said to be "quasi-religious" if their meanings were that they destroy ultimate concern.

But the emptiness of the quasi-religions must be seen as the complementary and paradoxical pole in a dynamic process. The other pole is characterized by the new *télos* they represent, a new understanding of the chief end of human being. In this sense, they certainly qualify as transcendent ideologies. There might be plural formulations of this *télos*, but insofar as societies participate in it, they enter into liberal modernity. That this new symbol of the fulfillment of humankind excludes any overt reference of the *ends* to be served by the vast instrumentality of the technological society is the mark of its "emptiness." The problem is not, however, that science and technology have no end, no final cause; it is simply that their final cause remains unsatisfying as an expression of meaning and value. The function of reason, explains Whitehead, is to "promote the art of life," through its "active attack on the environment" spurred by the "threefold urge: (i) to live, (ii) to live well, (iii) to live better. . . .

In fact the article of life is *first* to be alive, *second* to be alive in a satisfactory way, and *third* to acquire and increase in satisfaction."[14] "The quasi-religion of liberal humanistic tradition," Tillich believes to have been "politically expressed in the American Constitution and philosophically expressed in the United States by people like William James or Whitehead."[15] "Through the pressure of such groups as the American Civil Liberties Union," echoes Robert Bellah, "philosophical liberalism is rapidly becoming our orthodox civil religion."[16] Here, the obvious contradiction in terms embodied in liberalism manifests itself as paradox: the tradition which is opposed to tradition, the orthodoxy which eschews the orthodox; the common public faith of a public which confesses no common faith.

The question becomes: is it possible for contemporary persons to lose interest in—or better, not to be grasped by—the ultimate meaning of existence? The "religious" questions "are obviously not questions which occur to everyone, or indeed to the vast majority of people," answered a Harvey Cox celebrating the secular city. To the secular person of today "the world has always been void of any built-in meaning."[17] But this is the Cox who a decade later confessed that he had turned in his "search for gurus, for Christian versions of kalyanamitra," to the book of the saints and Benedictine monastery, to Buddhist mediation instructors, and Freudian psychoanalysts.[18] This seems to be the paradigm rather than the aberration of the liberal *ethos*. The disinterested ideal of science does not seem capable of becoming general, and the prolific production of means cannot become a satisfactory substitute for any question of ends. Can a society become radically "pluralistic" in the sense that there are no centrally integrating symbols or social structures in a true "market" of persons and groups? Were such a reality possible, were the "depth" dimension to be eliminated in all common cultural expressions, then the liberal project would have come to pass. But, as Tillich argues, the human spirit rebels against any such abstract emptiness. The forces of liberal humanism could not be sustained as merely critical realities.

> Whenever they had to defend themselves—as in matters of scientific autonomy, educational freedom, social equality or civil rights—they showed again their quasi-religious force. It was a struggle between faith and faith; and the quasi-religious faith could be radicalized to a degree where it undercut even its own roots, as, for example, in a scientism which deprives all nonscientific creative functions, such as the arts and religion, of their autonomy.[19]

"Scientism is a demonization of humanism," Tillich concludes. Scientism and technicism are not identical to science and technology; the former represent a distortion of the latter, and the character of this distortion is the elevation of one dimension of being to a hegemonic imperialism over all others. Demonization "occurs when particular symbols and ideas are absolutized and become idols themselves."[20] Thus, the difference between science and scientism, between technology and technicism, is not one primarily of quantity or complexity. It is rather the difference between an autonomous element of the whole which remains in relation to other elements, and one element gaining precedence over all others. Then, as Tillich says, other realms (e.g., religion, the arts) lose their autonomy and can be taken into the cognitive realm as only subjects of scientific analysis and technical manipulation. As quasi-religious forces, scientism and technicism draw all reality into the terms of their under-standing ("framing" in Heidegger's provocative language). In this way, methodo-logical "reductionism" is a spiritual child of contemporary quasi-religion.

Science and technology qualify as quasi-religions only as scientism and technicism, and it is within the womb of liberalism that they first take on this character. (Ironically, the Marxists adopt both the eschatological attitude of the Hebrew prophets, and the "bourgeois" attitude of those who expect science to overcome religion.) The ultimate concern expressed in science and technology is the progressive analysis and transformation of nature into a realm of human artifice. To borrow the argument from Hannah Arendt, "the issue at stake is, of course, not instrumentality, the use of means to achieve an end, as such, but rather the generalization of the fabrication experience in which usefulness and utility are established as the ultimate standards for life and the world of men."[21] And when, indeed, this has come to be, it is proper to speak of that transcendent ideology as "quasi-religion."

Several outcomes ramify from the identification of a phenomenon as quasi-religious. The first is that this "prevents intelligent dialogue with them."[22] It becomes taboo to touch critically those realities which have been "established as the ultimate standards for life." As common experience across American universities demonstrates, a cognitive struggle to establish independent intellectual status continues for those disciplines outside of the natural sciences or technological applications. This they attempt either by laying claim to the particular form of reason embodied in the structure of their inquiry, or (more likely) by legitimating themselves on the basis of their relation to the "hard" sciences. It might be argued that higher education is no less evangelical in the late twentieth century than it was in the late nineteenth, but that the object of piety has shifted from Protestant Christianity to liberal pragmatism, including its quasi-religious offspring, scientism and technicism.

A full exposition of the substance of the forces of science and technology as quasi-religions would require more than an essay to provide. Nevertheless, some indications may be made of what they mean as symbols of human destiny and potentiality.

First, there is the drive for union with more perfect forms lurking within the powers of technology, a vestigial remnant of the traditions proper:

> In the depth of technical creativity, as well as in the structure of the secular mind, there
> are religious elements which have come to the fore when the traditional religions have lost

their power. Such elements are the desire for liberation from authoritarian bondage, passion for justice, scientific honesty, striving for a more fully developed humanity, and hope in a progressive transformation of society in a positive direction. Out of these elements which point back to older traditions the new quasi-religious systems have arisen and given new answers to the question of the meaning of life.[23]

Although this substance may be continually emptied by the disinterested ideal of liberalism, where it still exists (or is intentionally preserved), ends are visible for technical activity and scientific analysis beyond mere instrumentality. Then, the residue of the traditions remains in the *télos* of technology. Knowledge is united with liberation, or the fulfillment of humanity, or the realization of justice—not simply with the perfection of disciplines within the academy (to whatever end assumed).

More common, however, is the tendency of the quasi-religions to create a new mythology. The cosmos was brought into being, says Carl Sagan, by a "meaningless" process. To understand this process is to resolve all things into their elements through analysis, grasp them through an understanding of their aggregation, and transform them through a new formula. There is no "whole"—much less a meaningful or moral whole—to which the parts relate. Here, the new myth of scientism is most evident and most objectionable:

> If representatives of modern physics reduce the whole of reality to the mechanical movement of the smallest particles of matter, denying the real quality of life and mind, they express a faith, objectively as well as subjectively. Subjectively science is their ultimate concern—and they are ready to sacrifice everything, including their own lives, for this ultimate. Objectively, they create a monstrous symbol of this concern, namely, a universe in which everything, including their own scientific passion, is swallowed by a meaningless mechanism. In opposing this symbol of faith Christian faith is right.[24]

Understanding the contemporary spiritual situation in terms of the hegemony of the quasi-religious forces of science and technology (scientism and technicism) changes the focus of the interpretation of modernity. Broken is the nonreflexive conventional view that it represents autonomy and objective knowledge over heteronomy and subjective orthodoxy. What becomes visible is a conflict between faith and faith: the faith of the Enlightenment in an automatic harmony (making each part work unwittingly for the whole), in tension with the synthesis of the transcendental drive for reunion with the ground of being and the classical drive for the realization of human in all dimensions. Of course, remnants of these earlier symbols of the human condition and destiny may be found in the "humanities" (at least in the catalogues of some colleges), and in the evangelical dimension of some churches. This is the faith conflict working its way out in the drive for technical education, the withering of the liberal arts, and the necessity for all institutions of higher learning to make claims (bold or subtle) about the utility of their educations. What is lost is not simply the classical traditions—as Allan Bloom has brazenly charged in *The Closing of the American Mind*—but *any* serious and sustained consideration of the whole in relation to the parts. *That* is considered "ideology" by the conventional liberal view. Neither does liberalism truly represent the complete destruction of a whole. Liberalism assumes a whole which is summarized by "market society," symbolized by the autonomous pursuit of science and technology in the disciplines, and grounded in the faith that a metaphysical harmony at the heart of reality will make all of these autonomous actions work for the best possible good.

If liberalism comes to be seen in this way, it becomes subject to its own criticism (historicity), and loses its role as the sole arbiter of truth (science) and rational action (technological and economic efficiency). Then, it can be seen in the depth of its symbols as a manifestation of public theology, even as the social science which emerges from it can be seen as public philosophy.[25] When this happens, the ideological criticism of the faith and ethics implicit in scientism and technicism can begin.

Some indications of this criticism can be made, but the full task must belong to the wider communities of learning and work which experience directly the limits of science and technology within the context of liberalism (and its variants).

First, the theodicy of technicism is inadequate, interpreting the problem of human existence in terms of its opposition to the parsimonious character of nature. Enlightenment thinkers are rife with phrases about the struggle of a suffering humanity to wrench life from the unforgiving hand of natural creation. This motif gained momentum during the nineteenth century as technology seemed to prove the point demonstrably. But what the utopias of the Renaissance and the arguments of the Enlightenment did not envision was the radically ambiguous effect of technological progress. Utopia was to be a place wherein well-analyzed practical problems had been efficiently addressed by well-engineered technical solutions. It was not conceived as a place wherein technical solutions would exacerbate human misery and threat, but this is the ambiguous reality observed by all advanced technological societies. Technical advances in the capacity to act and scientific understandings have contributed both to the amelioration and exacerbation of evil in the human situation. Scientific understandings and technical organization can and do serve irrational will to power and structures of destruction as easily as they serve powers of healing and construction. Any understanding of evil capable of taking this lived experience into account must transcend the theodicy of technicism.

Likewise, the soteriology of technicism fails to explain the fundamental failure of the "technical fix" to the human condition. Defenders of this soteriology, such as Talcott Parsons and Peter Medawar, offer a litany of achievements of technological culture in support of this doctrine. If technology creates problems, they argue, technology can also solve the problems it creates. Faith does not end before the door of empirical evidence. The radical ambiguity of technological creativity and destructivity is reduced by the soteriology of technicism to a remaining imperfection in the technical system.

Finally, the system of meaning and value inherent in scientism and technicism undermines noninstrumental values and objective systems of meaning which might otherwise give substantive direction to scientific and technological progress. In the liberal market culture in which scientism and technicism were born, it is difficult to speak of the value of that which is not of instrumental use. To say that something is "useless" is precisely to say that it is "worthless." Realities traditionally treated as ends and final causes in existence are undermined by their expulsion from rationality (God as projection), their reduction to some other more "basic" phenomena (morality as preference function), or by relativizing them according to a liberal understanding of pluralism (truth as cultural product). Lacking an anchored sense of justice, for instance, scientism and technicism can be turned in any direction by the powerful groups in a society without a coherent objection that such actions fail valid normative tests of social structures. Liberalism asks the question of authority in challenge to traditional ethics: who determines what justice is? The conventional answer in liberal society points once again to the concept of the marketplace, but who is to determine whether the marketplace should be allowed to destroy the ozone layer, for instance, making the surface of the planet incapable of supporting life? There is nothing more basic in the value structure of technicism to which an appeal can be made for an answer.

This, finally, reveals the insufficiency of these quasi-religious forces for a depth understanding of the human condition and for human fulfillment. For it is in the new myth of scientism of creation as a "meaningless mechanism" that the original humanistic intentions of the liberal ethos fall into ruin. Of course, there is nothing within the methodology of science which could provide the basis for a conclusion about the *meaning* of natural or human processes. This is a faith judgment of scientism. But it reveals the logical end of the movement to force all of being—including human being—into the model of analyzable objects. This new myth expresses the essential despair of scientism and technicism after they have purged the world of any existentially compelling human ends. The original hopes for science and technology that humankind might be made at home in the world—expressed in the utopias of the Renaissance—are contradicted by the myth of absurdity grounded in bettering a meaningless world.

Interpreted as quasi-religions, scientism and technicism reveal their demonic character, elevating an authentic element of existence to the whole. As forces which swallow up both creation and meaning in the threat of complete annihilation and absurdity, they must be resisted in the struggle between faith and faith.

NOTES AND REFERENCES

1.   Paul Tillich, *Christianity and the Encounter of the World Religions* (New York: Columbia University Press, 1963), pp. 4-5.

2.   D. Mackenzie Brown, *Ultimate Concern: Tillich in Dialogue* (New York: Harper & Row, 1965), pp. 31ff.

3.   Robert N. Bellah and Phillip E. Hammond, *Varieties of Civil Religion* (New York: Harper & Row, 1980), pp. 66-71.

4.   *Christianity and the Encounter of the World Religions,* p. 5. Interestingly, Hammond also speaks of "quasi-civil religions," such as ecclesiastical legitimacy and nationalism, phrased in sacred terms. Apparently, he also means to suggest authentic religious phenomena which lack intentional self-consciousness as religions proper. See note 3, above, *Varieties of Civil Religion,* p. 64.

5.   *Varieties of Civil Religion,* p. 52.

6.   *Christianity and the Encounter of the World Religions,* p. 7.

7.   Charles W. Eliot, ed., The Harvard Classics, vol. 3: *Bacon, Milton's Prose, Thomas Browne* (New York: The Collier Press, 1910), p. 181.

8.   Sheldon S. Wolin, *Politics and Vision: Continuity and Innovation in Western Political Thought* (Boston: Little, Brown, 1960), p. 298.

9.   Ibid.

10.   "The transformation of revolutionary reason into technical reason was the decisive feature of the transition from the first to the second period of modern society." Paul Tillich, "The World Situation," in *The Christian Answer,* Henry P. Van Dusen, ed. (New York: Charles Scribner's Sons, 1945), p. 4. [This essay can also be found in *The Spiritual Situation in Our Technical Society,* ed. and intro. J. Mark Thomas (Macon, GA: Mercer University Press, 1988)].

11.   Paul Tillich, "How Has Science in the Last Century Changed Man's View of Himself?" *The Current* 6(1-2):86-87 (1965). [This essay can also be found in *The Spiritual Situation in Our Technical Society,* ed. and intro., J. Mark Thomas (Macon, GA: Mercer University Press, 1988)].

12.   *Christianity and the Encounter of the World Religions,* p. 12.

13.   *Ultimate Concern,* p. 5.

14.   A.N. Whitehead, *The Function of Reason* (Boston: Beacon Press, 1959), pp. 4, 8.

15.   *Ultimate Concern,* p. 36.

16.   *Varieties of Civil Religion,* p. 36.

17.   Harvey Cox, *The Secular City* (Toronto: Macmillan, 1965), p. 69.

18.   Harvey Cox, *Turning East* (New York: Touchstone, 1977), p. 175.

19.   *Christianity and the Encounter of the World Religions,* pp. 10-11.

20.   *Ultimate Concern,* p. 5.

21.   Hannah Arendt, *The Human Condition* (Chicago: University of Chicago Press, 1958), p. 157.

22.   *Ultimate Concern,* p. 23.

23.   *Christianity and the Encounter of the World Religions,* p. 14.

24.   Paul Tillich, *The Dynamics of Faith* (New York: Harper & Row, 1957), p. 82.

25.   Cf. Robert N. Bellah et al., *Habits of the Heart* (Berkeley, CA: University of California Press, 1985), pp. 297ff.

THE JUDEO-CHRISTIAN TRADITION AND CRISES IN CONTEMPORARY TECHNOLOGY

Frank R. Harrison, III

Focusing on what is viewed as the negative impact of the Judeo-Christian tradition on technology, a typical claim is that this tradition bears much of the responsibility for the crises in contemporary technology. Different versions of this thesis have been popular since World War II, and have had, in the last fifteen or so years, a growing acceptance among philosophers and theologians. In numerous instances, these claims dominate discussions of technology and religion. In doing so, they set the boundaries for both the types of questions that can be raised in the range of permissible responses. This situation, I suggest, distracts many thinkers from considering far deeper problems of which a multitude of religious and technological crises in the Western world are only symptomatic. It is, therefore, critically important to examine these theses and to see where they must necessarily fail. To do this is not only important for the philosophies of religion and technology, but also for the advancement of

Research in Philosophy and Technology, Volume 10, pages 103-118.
Copyright © 1990 by JAI Press Inc.
All rights of reproduction in any form reserved.
ISBN: 1-55938-062-4

contemporary civilization, both Western and Eastern, as the Eastern world rapidly acquires not only Western technology, but assimilates western attitudes as well.

To aid in focusing my discussion, I use the now classic article of the medieval historian, Lynn White, Jr., "The Historical Roots of the Ecologic Crisis," as an instance of the position I am examining.[1] While it is the case that White stresses the ecological crisis of our times, I suggest that, with no injustice to this position, his remarks can be expanded to embrace wider notions of technological crises.

In assessing this broader "White position," first, I claim that there is a deep logical confusion in the use of "the Judeo-Christian tradition." The temptation is to understand this phrase as a definitive descriptor indicating a definite description of a particular concrete thing. The White position apparently falls prey to this temptation, and, in doing so, is forced to supply a specific referent for the phrase. That the White position does this is not surprising, for the article "the" is notoriously slippery in its use.

Consider the phrase "the whale." If it is said, "The whale is a mammal," more than likely "the" is operating as a universal quantifier. However, if it is said, "The whale over there is young," "the" is now being used as a definitive descriptor. To complicate matters, when used in the sense of a universal quantifier, "the" can function either in a definition about words or in an assertion about matters-of-fact. To say, "The whale is a mammal," might be to say something like "By 'whale' is meant 'a mammalian creature.'" Definitions are not assertive and, hence, neither true nor false. If, on the other hand, "The whale is a mammal" is used assertively, there must be some possible, even if not probable, counterevidence to the assertion. I suggest the White position confuses these uses of "the" when using "the Judeo-Christian tradition" in making its various claims. The claims appear to be universal in scope and factual assertions about a particular thing, while also being completely protected against even the possibility of any counterevidence.

I argue, however, that "the Judeo-Christian tradition" is not used as a definitive descriptor indicating a definite description of a particular concrete thing. It is not a referring phrase in the sense of having a specific referent that can be described by supplying either necessary, or sufficient, conditions, for it. Neither does it function in a definitional claim. Rather, "the Judeo-Christian tradition" functions as a family term. It has no specific referent or clearly established definition. It does suggest only a very broad and vaguely delineated family of activities, beliefs, customs, and the like.

This hypothesis opens the way to my second contention. In contrast to the White position, I argue that the crises in contemporary technology rest with the various uses to which technology can be put under the guiding influences of certain philosophical—not religious—assumptions concerning the philosophical categories of *nature, cognition, value,* and *person.* One widely held family of assumptions involving these categories is atomistic-mechanistic. Diverse formulations of general atomistic-mechanistic assumptions have been assimilated (sometimes quite unconsciously) over the last four hundred years into specific areas of both the the Judeo-Christian tradition and technology. Crises in the Judeo-Christian tradition and technology, then, are themselves related to a common source. This is a much different view than that suggested by the White position. It is at the level of philosophical assumptions delineating broad philosophical categories, and not the Judeo-Christian tradition, that the villain of the story begins to come into focus.

Using many of White's own phrases, a summary of the position he represents can be sketched in this way:

> The roots of Western technology go back to a striking tale of creation which Christianity inherited from Judaism. In this strongly anthropocentric story, man shares, in great measure, God's transcendence of nature, establishing a dualism not only between God and man, but also between man and nature. The acceptance of this story makes it both possible and compelling for man to exploit nature in a mood of indifference to its well-being. In fact, it is God's will, in this tradition, that man does exploit nature for his own human ends. There are some limits, however, placed on man's proper relation to nature. For, since God created all things, nature must be seen, and respected, as revealing God's existence, power, and goodness. "The Book of Nature," like Holy Scripture, is to be revered as a revelation of God to man. However, in the eighteenth century we find the hypothesis of the existence of the Judeo-Christian deity becoming unnecessary for many scientists. Nature is no longer seen as the handiwork of God, but rather merely as a lifeless machine mechanically composed of ever smaller machines, all mindlessly cranking through regular routines. Remaining of the ancient creation tale is only the essential distinction, and distinctiveness, of man from a nature to be manipulated by man for his own secular ends. And, according to the White position, we shall continue to have a worsening ecological—technological—crisis until we reject the orthodox Christian arrogant axiom that nature has no reason for existence except to serve man.[2]

Some have, from sociohistorical positions, argued forcefully against the White position. In *The Technological Society,* Jacques Ellul comments on the popular East-West hypothesis:

> *Christianity and Technique.* The East: passive, fatalist, contemptuous of life and action; the West: active, conquering, turning nature to profit. These contrasts, so dear to popular sociology, are said to result from a difference in religion: Buddhism and Islam on the one hand; on the other, Christianity, which is credited with having forged the practical soul of the West.
>
> These ideas are hardly beyond the level of the rote repetitions found even in the works of serious historians.[3]

Ellul proceeds to debunk this dichotomy, continuing by observing that "The technical movement of the West developed in a world which had already withdrawn from the dominant influence of Christianity."[4] Indeed, no appeal to *any* concept of *religious tradition* appears in the five reasons Ellul develops to explain the birth and development of contemporary technology.[5] "Rote repetitions" or not, "the Judeo-Christian tradition" suppositions are still very much in evidence in the White position.

An instance of an early and direct critical reply to White is found in an article by Lewis W. Moncrief, Jr., "The Cultural Basis for Our Environmental Crises." Moncrief takes umbrage with White, making the following observations:

> It seems tenable to affirm that the role played by religion in man-to-man and man-to-environment relationships is one of establishing a very broad system of allowable beliefs and behavior and of articulating and invoking a system of social and spiritual rewards for those who conform, and of negative sanctions for individuals or groups who approach or cross the pale of the religiously unacceptable. In other words, *it defines the ball park in which the game is played,* and, by the very nature of the park, some types of games cannot be played. . . . The fact that another culture does not associate spiritual beings with natural objects does not mean that such a culture will invariably ruthlessly exploit its resources. It simply means that there are fewer social and psychological constraints against such action.[6]

Moncrief devotes the remainder of this article to developing views concerning an "explanation of the environmental crisis that is now confronting us." In his particular elaboration, varying elements are woven together: The egocentric tendencies of human beings, a status hierarchy of positions and values, the universal desire for the "better life," the sociopolitical ramifications of both the French Revolution and the English Industrial Revolution, and the belief in an inexhaustible supply of resources.

> The forces of democracy, technology, urbanization, increasing individual wealth, and an aggressive attitude toward nature seem to be directly related to the environmental crisis now being confronted in the Western world. The Judeo-Christian tradition has probably influenced the character of each of these forces. However, to isolate religious tradition as a cultural component and to contend that it is the "historical root of our ecological crises" is a bold affirmation for which there is little historical or scientific support.[7]

On the whole, from the viewpoint of a sociohistorical contention, the weight of an acceptable position concerning relations between the Judeo-Christian tradition and technology appears to rest with Ellul and Moncrief, and not White.

It is not my intention, however, to enter into a sociohistorical debate concerning the White position, even though in passing I shall cite some historical examples that would count as counterevidence to the claims of the White position if that position is, indeed, a factual hypothesis. Without entering into sociohistorical debates, I can, however, suggest *philosophical reasons* for rejecting the White position. As previously suggested, my first major criticism of this position involves considerations of the use of "the Judeo-Christian tradition." By introducing these considerations, the *logical* legitimacy of raising, and responding to, general questions such as "What is (are) the (causal) relation(s) holding between the Judeo-Christian tradition and contemporary technology?" is brought into serious doubt. What meaning can we attach to an assertion that is vague enough to include everything that can be appropriately encompassed under the family phrase, "the Judeo-Christian tradition," but specific enough to permit concrete evidence *and* the attending possibility of counterevidence?

A simple parallel might be clarifying here. Suppose Jill's father claims that his daughter is not to go to dances, wear anything but very plain and simple dresses—certainly no makeup and jewelry—and never drink any alcoholic beverages. When asked to justify these restrictions on the activities of his daughter, the father points out that she has been raised in the Judeo-Christian tradition and Christians simply do not do these sorts of things. Certainly anyone can define "the Judeo-Christian tradition" in such a way that the comment of the father can be specifically used in relation to his claims about what his daughter is, and is not, to do. In that case, however, the response of the father to the request for supplying reasons is extremely close to begging the question. Whether it does or not depends on the formulation of his definition of "the Judeo-Christian tradition." On the other hand, if "the Judeo-Christian tradition" remains broadly vague enough to be faithful to that family of beliefs, attitudes, rituals, etc., within the tradition, appealing to the tradition cannot give support to the conclusion.

The White position assumes that the phrase "the Judeo-Christian tradition" acts as a definite descriptor, successfully referring to a particular concrete tradition that is delimited by a conjunction of necessary properties. The referent is taken to be a particular tradition which is homogeneous in its broad historical scope and specific in its content,[8] but this is not correct. To grasp why, consider another phrase, "the murderer of Ann Orr." This phrase is used, in fact, in a referring way. I do not know who, or what, murdered Ann Orr.[9] I do know this much, however. It is some particular thing, located in a specific manner, and having relatively determinate and constant characteristics which are logically relevant to whatever possess them, insofar as it is the referent of "the murderer of Ann Orr." If something is lacking any of these features, then it, logically speaking, cannot be the referent of that phrase. Given these considerations, what could be a possible—in a logical sense of "possible"—referent of "the Judeo-Christian tradition?" There is not found, ranging over approximately the last two thousand years, any specific set of beliefs, dogmas, or rituals univocally held or practiced by all those suggested by "the Judeo-Christian tradition." That, however, is to say that there are neither sufficient nor necessary properties needed to isolate a specific referent for "the Judeo-Christian tradition."[10]

Early in the development of the Judeo-Christian tradition, St. Paul was continually struggling with various conflicting assumptions guiding interpretations of the Christ story as it was then related within both Jewish and Gentile settings. The Patristic Period displays fundamental disagreements concerning Church doctrine. The harmony that was eventually realized was as much because of political considerations, and pressures, as religious ones.[11] Even excluding heretics, those who "by definition" fall outside of what is considered the faith, during the height of the Western medieval period there was not univocal agreement on matters of doctrine, faith, or practice.[12] Certainly, during and after the Protestant Reformation and the Council of Trent it becomes even more precarious to seek a specific referent for "the Judeo-Christian tradition."[13]

If "the Judeo-Christian tradition" is not a referring phrase having a specific referent, then *how* is it appropriately used? It functions as a *family term*. It is used as an open-ended vague collective term, broadly suggesting various and widely divergent activities, beliefs, customs, dogma, and the like,[14] only loosely connected in a multitude of differing ways. Literally, there is no particular thing to which "the Judeo-Christian tradition" uniquely and unambiguously refers. Nor are there any essential characteristics running throughout the tradition which can be isolated, and to which we can continually point. It is closer to the mark to say that "the Judeo-Christian tradition," as Moncrief suggests, "defines *the ball park in which the game is played* . . . [but] the kind of game that ultimately evolves is not itself defined by the ball park."

Even the suggestions of Moncrief are rather specific. Instead of imagining a ball park, envision a very ancient stadium. Some of the older parts have crumbled away, been discarded, and are forgotten in current times. Other ancient stones have been incorporated into newer facilities. There are other still newer sections built completely out of contemporary materials. Nor, at any particular moment in history, is only one game being played at the stadium. Within its vague areas, where walls give way to playing fields which in their turn slip into open meadows, all sorts of activities can, and do, take place— not ony ball games, and not only spectator sports. Many games have been played which are played no more. Others have yet to be played. All of them— past, present, and future—loosely form a large family *suggested by* the phrase, "the Judeo-Christian tradition."

To provide a concrete referent for "the Judeo-Christian tradition," albeit a pseudo one, the White position suggests, both explicitly and implicitly, a specific account of what it perceives as essential to that tradition. Concentrating on select passages from Genesis, a specific *interpretation* of "the" Judeo-Christian creation tale is presented.[15] The White position then attempts to generalize *this* interpretation to serve as part of that concrete referent needed for the supposed referring phrase, "the Judeo-Christian tradition." Once having this specific interpretation in place, the White position can talk of *all* Christianity serving as the necessary matrix of both technology and a particular attitude toward nature, and, consequently, having to bear much of the blame for contemporary crises engendered by technology. In this way, the White position suggests all manner of influences, tensions, and the like, for which a seemingly *specific* religious tradition must assume a large measure of responsibility. But there are only influences and tensions, if any, existing between *specific* interpretations of dogmatic claims made within the environs of the ancient stadium and assumptions and assertions of equally specific understandings of technology. The White position misses this important insight. Instead, the White position takes a limited portion of the Judeo-Christian tradition, gives it a specific interpretation, and then defines the entire tradition in terms of that portion while disallowing any counterevidence to the allegedly universal empirical claims the position sets forth.

Even more, imagine, with the White position, that "the Judeo-Christian tradition" is a legitimate referring phrase *and* that, in fact, it does have a proper referent similar to that suggested by White. Then how can we account for the various conflicting, if not contradictory, stances taken *within the tradition* toward religion and technology? For instance, Albert Borgmann contends that technology and Christianity are adversaries.[16] R. A. Buchanan, on the other hand, claims that religion must accept the methods and assumptions of science. No doubt Buchanan would extend his claim to include technology.[17] Or, we may take note of "Technology and Man: A Christian View," by W. Norris Clarke.[18] Clarke, a Roman Catholic priest, argues optimistically that technology is a positive "element in the total development of man as an image of God."[19] Yet Ellul, a Calvinist, says of technology that:

> It is the product of the situation in which sin has put man; it is inscribed exclusively in the fallen world; it is uniquely part of this fallen world; it is a product of necessity and not of human freedom.[20]

Such radically divergent views, all within "the" Judeo-Christian tradition, cannot be accommodated, or accounted for, given the White position.

The broader a tradition is perceived to be as it develops over space and time, the greater the likelihood is an increase in vagueness of any claims concerning that tradition. This becomes *logically problematic* when appeals are made to such very vaguely delineated traditions in order to justify or explain much more specific claims. It is not the case that historians, for instance, logically cannot appeal to broad and vague traditions to help clarify and substantiate particular claims of a specific nature. It is logically the case, however, that the broader and more vague the tradition, and the more specific the claim to be justified or explained, then the greater the likelihood that there are one or more fallacies in the attempted justification or explanation. The White position leads to a logically unfortunate position. If the phrase "the Judeo-Christian tradition" is understood as a definite descriptor indicating a definite description which does successfully refer to a particular tradition, then great segments of what would ordinarily be viewed as part of this tradition must be ignored. One can always *stipulate* a definite description for "the Judeo-Christian tradition" so that it does successfully refer to some narrow range of phenomena. If this is done narrowly enough, the White position may be justified for that limited range. But at the same time, I suggest that the White position would be uninteresting, if not also question-begging. The position, after all, takes part of its excitement from a purported insight into the totality of *THE* Judeo-Christian tradition and its bearing on technology. On the other hand, if "the Judeo-Christian tradition" is so universal in scope that the White position is exciting, then the questions and responses raised in that position are suspect, if not false or meaningless.

My second major criticism of the White position is that it neither correctly suggests *where* the difficulties creating so much havoc in technology are located, nor *what* we are to grasp, in some general way, these difficulties to be. They are not found in a broad Judeo-Christian tradition, although some specific areas of a family of traditions do reflect and even nurture them. Nor are they characterized by suggesting a particular interpretation of a creation story found in Genesis. How, then, are these difficulties to be characterized, and where are they to be located? Beginning to develop a solution to these two puzzles, I focus three important areas: *philosophical categories, philosophical assumptions,* and *first principles.*[21]

In the performance of any human activity there are always some *philosophical categories* which necessarily guide and coalesce in that activity.[22] While necessary for the performance of any human activity, *these* categories are not necessary in a strict logical sense. Nor are they, perhaps, necessary for the activities of houseflies or angels. Nor does this observation entail that sharp boundaries can always be neatly drawn between human activity and the activity of other sorts of creatures. Further, humans might have been different from what they in fact now are, and, in some future time, they may be different again. In such possible cases, *these* philosophical categories could be moot, in others not, but, as things now stand, these categories are necessary for human activity.

Philosophical categories of *nature, cognition, value,* and *person* are individually and collectively vague and tacitly grasped. This permits a rich, although not unlimited, range of articulating them for various purposes within particular ranges of human activity. None of these categories are specifically religious, scientific, technological, legal, and so forth. They are too nonspecific to be typed in such ways. In that each of them is reflected in more specific areas of human activity, however, they may each, and all, be viewed religiously, technologically, and so on. Philosophical categories are, then, extremely broad, nonchartered areas in which human activity is played out. While in themselves they have no *distinct* boundaries, nevertheless, they may be given diverse boundaries, with varying degrees of specificity, in different ways by different humans for different purposes on different occasions.

The more concrete ways in which philosophical categories are tacitly grasped, structured, accepted, and used from within the temporal viewpoint of humans—how they are *assimilated*– become the particular *philosophical assumptions* for a society or individual. It is this assimilation of philosophical categories, under manifold forms of philosophical assumptions, which both limits the range of human activity as well as guides that activity which does occur. The use of the term "assumption" can be misleading in this context. An assumption, in more ordinary uses, is always open to questioning from *within* some community or by an individual. There is evidence of differing sorts, arguments, explanations, and so on, which in numerous ways impact on assumptions to weaken or to strengthen them. In some cases an assumption is weakened to the point that it is no longer feasible to retain it within the system where it was presumed to be operative. Even so, the overall system remains essentially intact.

Philosophical assumptions, however, are not like that. Rather, they form the vague boundaries establishing what are to count as systems of beliefs, knowledge, facts, values, and the like, which in turn mold particular societies and individuate particular human beings. Sometimes, these systems are relatively rigorous. More often, they are only loosely coherent. In any event, philosophical assumptions fashion, and direct, attitudes and activities by which a society, or individual, establishes the world in which it dwells. Philosophical assumptions, then, become foundational, but not in a Cartesian sense, for those societies and individuals assimilating them. These assimilated assumptions set limits on, while also directing within those limits, what are counted as acceptable by a society or individual as appropriate general types of actions to be taken in particular circumstances. Indeed, what is perceived as bizarre activity by a society or individual is behavior *not* falling within the boundaries prescribed by the philosophical assumptions of that society or individual.

What the philosophical assumptions are for a society or individual are revealed, seen, and grasped through common practice, customs, activities, attitudes, and the like. This revealing, grasping, and seeing the assimilated assumptions are usually neither conscious nor reflective processes. Further, any activity or reflection on them is possible only after the framework has been established. Such reflective activity, like any human activity, always requires an established background to guide it, and within which it can be operative. One is born into, enveloped, and nurtured by a society already being established in its assimilated assumptions. For the newborn infant growing into adulthood through early childhood and adolescence, the world being established by his, or her, society reveals itself, not in isolated bits-and-pieces that are given, analyzed, and put together one-by-one as tinker toys. Rather, the world emerges slowly as an interrelated whole into which the human becomes integrated as part of a living whole.

In this process of integration and inculturation philosophical assumptions appear "natural." Indeed, they are the criteria by which a society or individual judges what counts as natural or not. Specifically, what assumptions a society or individual assimilates is not easy to discuss by those dwelling within them. It is in terms of these assumptions that something is determined to be an argument, explanation, description, and the like, and which of these is to count as acceptable, or not, and for what reasons. There must always be a background of some philosophical assumptions supplying criteria by which questions are raised and answers posed, even when such questions and answers are themselves about philosophical assumptions. When philosophical assumptions are focused by a society or individual, it is always, therefore, piecemeal. There are always some philosophical assumptions left tacitly serving as the guiding background for the particular examination of what is in focus. It is the assimilation of philosophical assumptions that is essential in molding societies and individuals, while establishing the worlds in which societies and individuals dwell.

Each society, each individual, tacitly maps out in the detail it requires the terrain of *nature, cognition, value,* and *person.* These mappings are themselves flexible and changeable throughout the history of a society or individual. Nonetheless, the process is guided by relative demands of varying degrees of usefulness in particular situations. These guiding factors, more often than not, include in some combination tacit appeals to consistency, coherence, simplicity, applicability, and relevance. These are operative within a pragmatic frame of the survival and well-being of the human organism. This is not to claim that the philosophical assumptions of a society or individual *are* consistent, coherent, simple, applicable, and relevant. Whether they are or not often remains unclear and unquestioned until basic physical or psychological conflicts occur in particular instances of human activity. Conflicts in activities both societal and individual are sure signs of conflicts in what are assimilated as the philosophical assumptions establishing in a vague manner the acceptable boundaries of *nature, cognition, value,* and *person.*[24]

Although different societies and individuals are fashioned by their philosophical assumptions, nonetheless there is always *some* commonality among these societies and individuals. For one thing, humans are more-or-less similar in biological structure and needs. For another, all philosophical assumptions, no matter how divergent they appear, are responses to vaguely felt philosophical categories whose various structurings are necesary for the survival of both society and individual. Further, these responses are fashioned and assimilated under the ubiquitous guidance of consistency, coherence, simplicity, applicability, and relevance, albeit in different degrees and mixtures. While there may even be enormous degrees of diversity among some societies and individuals, there are also necessarily and primarily many family similarities in which, and only in which, diversity is meaningful. Thus, even though philosophical assumptions both fashion societies and individualize humans, they are not radically dichotomizing.

In assimilating philosophical assumptions, a society or individual, over time, further concretizes them into *first principles* for both theories of, and practices in, consciously focused topical areas. Various sciences, scientific methods, principles and actions of morality, dogma and rituals of religious groups, legal dicta and practices, and the like, are all formulated and made concrete *within* confines of philosophical assumptions. First principles become consciously articulated within a larger community in the establishment of what is perceived as specialized communities of engineers, scientists, religious believers, lawyers, and so on, each with its particular family of activities. For those dwelling in these specialized communities, such first principles, like the philosophical principles guiding them, appear to be unquestionably natural and normal.[25] These specialized communities may, and often do, further divide into smaller groups along lines of even more concrete needs and understandings of overall categories and assumptions in which they dwell.[26]

It is very well to talk about philosophical assumptions being assimilated by individuals and societies, but this seems to have taken us far afield of any discussion of the White position regarding "the" Judeo-Christian tradition and religion. If the White position is in error, the question still remains *where* are to be found the specific difficulties engendering crises in contemporary technology, and *what* general remarks, if any, might be made about them? The White position claims, granting for a moment that sense *can* be made of it, that what is problematic is located in the Judeo-Christian tradition, and consists in a particular way of viewing nature and man's relation to it. A grave error of the White position is to assume that there are certain characteristics unique to, and defining of, the Judeo-Christian tradition. In this assumption the White position is incorrect. It is also dangerous. First, it encourages us to look in the wrong place for reasons for what we sense as radically wrong in large areas of our own society. Second, it invites us to look for the wrong sort of thing. Where, then, should we look, and for what?

I have argued that there is no specific thing to which "the Judeo-Christian tradition" could possibly refer in any universal and empirically meaningful way. Rather, the phrase suggests, or points to, a broad and nebulous family of many communities.[27] These communites are more sharply focused into further smaller groups.[28] Equally as important, phrases such as "contemporary technology" and "the ecological crisis in technology" are best understood as family terms, and not as referring ones. There is no specific thing to which "contemporary technology" refers. Nor, specifically, is there *the* ecological crisis in technology. Once more, there are families of activities that may be grouped together, in various ways for various purposes.[29] An important philosophical insight to grasp is that religious, technological, scientific, legal, and so on, traditions are very general attitudinal ways of assimilating differing philosophical assumptions which, in turn attempt to establish some sort of boundaries for philosophical categories necessary for human activity.

Heterogeneous societies of different traditions composed of many communities during different historical epochs have held similar philosophical assumptions. For example, in the fourteenth century a Ptolemaic perspective of the universe, with all of its attending influences and ramifications, could be found in many religious, technological, scientific, legal, and so on, traditions in the Western world. One did not have to be a scientist or a theologian to view the world in this fashion. The uneducated untraveled peasant also looked to the stars and beyond. This was the natural way to discover his or her future, to influence his or her luck, to aid in his or her health, and on and on. Nor was it that the writings of Claudius Ptolemaeus were the underlying reason for this powerful world perspective gripping much of Western medieval life. Rather, Ptolemy's writings were consciously accepted as correct because of philosophical assumptions already widely assimilated into societies of the time. These writings focused, in part, what was already deeply entrenched as the norm of things. In doing this, these works also supplied first principles for a particular system of astronomy, but philosophical assumptions partially focused by that system went far further than an astronomical system, as can be seen in the astrology of the day.

Under various pressures philosophical assumptions evolve, change, and are replaced. The Ptolemaic perspective slowly lost its hold, although it has not completely disappeared even today. Other philosophical assumptions began to be assimilated. Over the last four hundred years in the Western world,[30] diversified atomistic-mechanistic ways of mapping philosophical categories have become tacitly established for many societies and individuals. As the works of Ptolemy concretely focused numerous but related philosophical assumptions, so the works in physics of Isaac Newton have focused, for modern times, sundry atomistic-mechanistic assumptions. Newtonian physics does not create these assumptions. Rather, it concretizes some of them as first principles and establishes specific areas in which these principles are useful in achieving particular desired results. Moreover, these first principles and their perceived success in specialized cases reinforce general, tacit, atomistic-mechanistic assumptions which are not part of Newtonian physics itself. Thus, we can sense influences of the Newtonian perspective in all sorts of activities—religious, moral, legal, technological, to mention a few. While, for the most part, all of this may feel quite natural, nonetheless in some instances there may be feelings of disquietude, if not conflict.

In this family of assimilated philosophical assumptions is found the location of much of the genesis of many particular crises in technology. The location is not in Genesis. The nature of these assumptions is *suggested* by saying that they are differing atomistic-mechanistic perspectives of the world. That such assumptions have been adopted, and adapted, in various areas of both Judaism and Christianity should be of no great surprise. The White position is correct insofar as it senses this assimilation, yet the Judeo-Christian tradition cannot uniquely lay claim to any atomistic-mechanistic assumptions of *nature, cognition, value,* and *person.* These are *not* religious assumptions. They are philosophical ones that have not only been assimilated into areas of modern Judeo-Christian traditions, but also, for example, into areas of Western technological and scientific traditions, for, like the Ptolemaic perspective of the medieval world, atomistic-mechanistic assumptions guide much of human activity in that World in which we currently dwell.

P. Hans Sun has suggested that:

> Among those committed to philosophy there is even a lack of consensus about the specific problematic dimensions of technology. Together with the plurality of public beliefs, this becomes a practical warrant for the virtually unfettered pursuit of technology—unfettered at least by anything other than economic constraints.[31]

"The specific problematic dimensions of technology," from the perspective of a philosopher, lie in those areas of philosophical assumptions under which sundry activities in communities in the tradition of technology find their guidance. While there is a plurality of public beliefs in the larger society, there is also a commonality of background in both philosophical categories and their more specific mappings of philosophical assumptions which meld human beings into holistic societies with varying traditions. It is here, in the philosophical assumptions of a society, often reflected in its general traditions, and not only in its specific religious, scientific, or technological claims, that we can profitably look for the grounds of conflicts displaying themselves in different human activities.

In my essay I have taken some of the initial steps in looking for these grounds. First, I have raised serious *philosophical* objections against one influential collection of views, the White position, distracting our philosophical work. Second, and more constructively, I have pointed to, and outlined, those areas in which our philosophical work might be more rewardingly carried forth. The next steps in this journey to understanding ourselves and that world in which we dwell consist in careful descriptions of various interpretations of atomistic-mechanistic boundaries of philosophical categories, and the ways these interpretations are joined together as frameworks of large systems of human activity. Only then will philosophers of technology and religion be in secure enough positions to take their next move, which is to make guarded recommendations on how better—under the guidance of consistency, coherence, simplicity, applicability, and relevance—to begin a remapping of philosophical categories. But at that point, I imagine that philosophers of religion and technology will no longer be philosophers in so specialized a sense—a sense itself revealing an underlying Newtonian atomistic perspective—but, rather, lovers of wisdom in the ancient Socratic sense.

NOTES AND REFERENCES

1. Lynn White, Jr., "The Historical Roots of the Ecologic Crisis," in *Philosophy and Technology: Readings in the Philosophical Problems of Technology,* Carl Mitcham and Robert Mackey, eds. (New York: The Free Press, 1972), pp. 259-265.

I am using "the White position," as a family term suggesting a broad range of different, but related, views concerning the influence of what is called "the Judeo-Christian tradition" and its effects on technology.

2. See especially pp. 260-265 of White's article.

3. Jacques Ellul (trans. by John Wilkinson), *The Technological Society* (New York: Vintage Books, 1964), p. 32.

Lynn's "Crisis" article was written thirteen years after Ellul's *The Technological Society* appeared in French and three years after the English translation. Even so, White makes no reference to Ellul's work.

4. Ibid., p. 35.

5. "(1) A very long technical maturation of incubation without decisive checks before the final flowering; (2) population growth; (3) a suitable economic milieu; (4) the almost complete plasticity of a society malleable and open to the propagation of technique; (5) a clear technical intention, which combines the other factors and directs them toward the pursuit of the technical objective. . . . But the unique phenomenon was the simultaneous existence of all five . . . all of them necessary to bring about individual technical invention." Ibid., pp. 59-60.

6. Lewis W. Moncrief, "The Cultural Basis for Our Environmental Crisis," *Science* 170:508-512 (October 30, 1970), p. 31.

7. Ibid., pp. 36-37.

8. In all fairness to White, he mentions segments of the Judeo-Christian tradition, such as the Eastern Church (and note that there are *many* Eastern Churches forming a family), which do not fit, nor do justice to, his overall hypotheses concerning the Judeo-Christian tradition, the development of technology, and technological crises. Instead of abandoning, or revising his views, White abandons consideration of the Eastern tradition of Christianity. Here we see specific reference-making and apriorism at work as it controls hypotheses, discussions, and arguments.

9. Ann Orr, her sister, and her niece, were brutally murdered with a hatchet on August 15, 1987, in Athens, Georgia.

10. Certainly one can always, following the general pattern of White's treatment of the Eastern tradition, ignore some movement as being a "cult" falling outside the boundaries of the Judeo-Christian tradition. For instance, Christian Scientists, Mormons, Moonies, and Santerias may, by different groups and for widely different reasons, be called "non-Christians," or heretics. Nonetheless, members of these groups consider themselves to be Christians. To ignore such groups, or to define them as heretical, gives further credence to the claim that the White position suffers from the fallacy of apriorism. While it appears to be a general empirical position concerning the Judeo-Christian tradition, nevertheless "the Judeo-Christian tradition" is "understood" (i.e., defined) so as to eliminate the possibility of counterevidence.

11. An illustrative example is the "solution" of the Arian controversy. In 325, Emperor Constantine called, presided over, and politically directed a council of mainly eastern bishops at Bithynian, Nicaea. The issue to be decided, and one that could not be previously agreed upon by the bishops, concerned the multiple nature of God. This was not an issue settled one way or another in the Judeo-Christian tradition of the day. Athanasius cleverly led Arius into admitting that his interpretation of the nature of God was a form of polytheism. The Emperor then threw his influence to Athanasius, but not for religious reasons. The Emperor, personally, thought the entire debate was trivial from a religious viewpoint. What was of vital concern to Constantine were his attempts to use the Church in the uniting of the Empire. If Christianity were perceived as merely another polytheistic religion, then he could not use it effectively to achieve his political goals. The Council

of Nicaea, like the Councils of Ephesus (431) and Chalcedon (451), was called because there was no specific Judeo-Christian tradition guiding the Church in matters of interpretation of "the faith."

12.   One of the more bellicose moments in culture occurred with the introduction of radical new ideas brought from the Muslim world into the West. This was, of course, the arrival of Aristotle. The platonic God was about to be replaced, within a particular Christian epoch, by an "updated version." Certainly, Christians would still utter the words "I believe in one God"— no matter that this was a "trinitarian" deity—but the God of Thomas and Augustine is not altogether the same in the context of each of their particular traditions.

13.   When, on the eve of All Saint's Day in 1517, the monk Luther tacked his theses on the main door of the Castle Church of Wittenburg, he was following an old and accepted medieval custom of "publis disputation"; however, these disputations *pro declarations virtutis indulgentiarium* quickly led to multiple splits in any semblance of the (western) Judeo-Christian tradition established since the last of the great general councils before the eleventh century schism of Western and Eastern communions.

14.   Phrases such as "and the like" and "and so forth" are essential in understanding the use of family terms. There is no general rule to which we can appeal to continue the list of which only some members, forming such families, have been cited. Nonetheless, in specific cases, we can say or decide whether or not *that* case is part of the family—whether or not it would properly continue the list.

15.   The creation story told in Genesis is open to different interpretations. There is, for example, an ancient rabbinical interpretation which may remind one of Plato's *Timaeus.* In this specific rabbinical view, a formless "matter" coexists with the Deity. From this eternal chaos, this darkness, the Deity is continually bringing order into the Universe according to His divine plans. The Deity is understood as a craftsman, but more like a potter modeling material than as an eigthteenth century watchmaker putting together discrete bits and pieces of this and that. A potter coaxes, as it were, latent order out of the clay; a watchmaker forces order on the pieces with which he is working. Also, in speaking of various interpretations of the creation story, one should be mindful of the new "Process Theology."

16.   Albert Borgmann, "Prospects for the Theology of Technology," in *Theology and Technology: Essays in Christian Analysis and Exegesis,* Carl Mitchum and Jim Grote, eds. (Lanham, MD: University Press of America, 1984), p. 305.

17.   R. A. Buchanan, "The Churches in a Changing World," in *Philosophy and Technology: Readings in the Philosophical Problems of Technology,* Carl Mitcham and Robert Mackey, eds. (New York: The Free Press, 1972), p. 241.

18.   W. Norris Clarke, "Technology and Man: A Christian View," in *Philosophy and Technology: Readings in the Philosophical Problems of Technology,* Carl Mitcham and Robert Mackey, eds. (New York: The Free Press, 1972), pp. 247-258.

19.   Ibid., p. 247.

20.   Jacques Ellul, "The Relation of Man to Creation According to the Bible," in *Theology and Technology: Essays in Christian Analysis and Exegesis,* Carl Mitcham and Jim Grote, eds. (Lanham, MD: University Press of America, 1984), p. 135

21.   These areas form families in two ways. First, *within,* as it were, each area is a wide range of other overlapping areas. For instance, in grasping values there are political, social, aesthetic, religious, moral, and the like, values. But, second, *between* these larger areas there are a multitude of overlapping areas. There are no sharp distinctions except those which humans draw in various ways for various purposes. Indeed, what may count as a sharp distinction in one case would not in another.

22.   Holding beliefs and opinions about some thing or another, knowing that something is the case, hearing an excellent concert, playing a game of baseball are examples of what I call "human activities."

23.   I stress that these words are *used to act only as pointers.* Pointing is the very best that humans can do. In this pointing, I *attempt* to assume no stance on the meanings of these words, but I can only attempt to bracket them in a purified manner. Insofar as these words *are* words, they are part of a language, a culture, a way of life. As a human being, I am always necessarily dwelling in, and emerging out of, some philosophical assumptions revolving around these words, no matter how tacit these assumptions might be.

24.   Such conflicts, for instance, can readily be discerned in different instances involving AIDS. In these cases there are often revealed deep seated conflicts in what is regarded by a society or individual as constituting *nature, cognition, value,* and *person.* These conflicts reveal themselves in many ways such as indecisive action, quite open and bitter hostilities, disagreements over the rights of individuals versus the rights of societies, and so on.

25.   There are, however, in all societies and for all individuals, limits of tolerance which, if ignored, trigger a reaction against the offender, the one outside the boundaries, whether these boundaries be social, moral, religious, political, technological, scientific, and so on. These limits are usually overtly drawn by the society or individual only in particular cases. Over time, with persistence, such outsiders may bring about fundamental change in those philosophical assumptions that once excluded them.

26.   I am presenting a too well organized scenario. A human being, even within one society, belongs to many traditions, many communities, many specialized groups, all of which do not necessarily harmonize in their various assumptions and principles.

27.   Or "communions," as used in phrases such as "the Anglican Communion" or "the Orthodox Communion."

28.   For instance, within the Judeo-Christian tradition in only modern-contemporary times, one finds Protestantism. Within that large community are discovered Baptists, but that family subdivides into Northern and Southern Baptists, each of which further subdivides according to what *it* perceives as fulfilling *proper* doctrine of the Judeo-Christian tradition. Within the Baptist Communion, at least officially, such divisions stop with the individual worshipper, each of whom is able to read and interpret Holy Scripture in his or her own way according to his or her "own light."

29.   Neither contemporary technology, various crises in technology, nor strained areas of social adjustment to the multifarious activities of technology have been as broadly distributed over time and space as the Judeo-Christian tradition. Hence, in all likelihood, phrases referring to contempprary technology and its problems, while vague, are not nearly as vague as "the Judeo-Christian tradition."

30.   Another vague family term.

31.   Hans P. Sun, "Notes on How to Begin to Think about Techology in a Theological Way," in *Theology and Technology: Essays in Christian Analysis and Exegesis,* Carl Mitcham and Jim Grote, eds. (Lanham, MD: University Press of America, 1984), pp. 171-172.

MINDSET AND MORAL VISION

Larry Rasmussen

A NEW SETTING

Some new words have joined the vocabulary of moral responsibility. Most follow from heightened human power, and most of that power issues from scientific and technological developments. In 1973, Stanley Cohen and Herbert Boyer first spliced genetic material from one microbe into another to create a bit of life that never existed before. James Watson and Francis Crick had, in 1953, determined the chemical arrangement of DNA (deoxyribonucleic acid), the double helix strand which carries the hereditary blueprint of all living things. In 1987 the United States Patent and Trademark Office ruled that patents for new life forms can be extended from microbes to higher life forms, including mammals. "Biotechnology" entered the human vocabulary, as did "genetic engineering," "cracking the genetic code," and other phrases which signaled new powers and new spheres of moral concern and responsibility.

The list can be extended. "Nuclear fission" and "nuclear fusion" are of a vintage only slightly older. They specify new scientific-technological power so dramatic as to have actually dated the beginning of an epoch, August, 1945—

Research in Philosophy and Technology, Volume 10, pages 119-128.
ISBN: 1-55938-062-4

"the nuclear age." Humans are now capable of being uncreators as well as creators, in ways and degrees not given to previous ages. "Acid rain" is yet another entry. It signals heightened human impact on the natural environment, as does "planetary carrying capacity."

We can exaggerate the differences of present realities from past ones. U.S. Americans are prone to do so. That notwithstanding, a distinctive character trait of our time is amplified human power affecting a wider range of consequences and objects than earlier chapters of the human story have known. Scientific and technical knowledge and developments have been and are key for this enhanced power. Indeed, *the* distinctive configuration of our era might be this: a quantum leap in human knowledge and power; a close correlation between this knowledge and this power; and a novel range, with novel objects and consequences, of this knowledge and power.

THE CAST OF MIND

If ours is an epoch of scientific-technological power, what is its turn of mind? What kind of arching perspective fostered our particular orientation to the world? Is it possible to say what the commanding outlook has been, in practice at least, if not in the minds of the philosophers of the age?

What follows is simplified to a fault. Only the most elemental qualities in the bent of mind critical to understanding the reach of power in a technological age are sketched. But if they *are* most basic, that will suffice.

The engine of capitalist, and socialist, industrial civilization is applied science: scientific knowledge wed to technological power. The script is succinctly summarized in a recital of Francis Bacon's program: "Knowledge is aimed for power over nature and power over nature is aimed for improvement of the human lot."[1] We view ourselves over against [the rest of] nature, indeed over against the world, as subjects-working-on-objects. The natural environment is "stuff" for human knowing, human design, and human transformation. It is the object of active human control for perceived human good.

There is a more compact way to say this: For the post-medieval world, knowledge is power and power is control.

Bacon's object was the anvil of nature, upon which humans hammered out worlds of their own crafting, yet the uses of science and technique are hardly limited to nonhuman nature. We must add Karl Marx's name to what will become a quartet that stands in for a chorus of millions. Marx is a symbol, or shorthand, for the turn to *society* as the object of disciplined, scientific knowledge used for the human transformation of human reality. Society is itself science's object, following Marx and other contemporary pioneers in a new branch of knowledge, the social sciences.

If Marx places "society" on an agenda already listing "nature," Freud adds "psyche." The approach is continuous; the object of knowing changes. That is, science "knows" in a subject/object relationship, and technique is developed to effect a desired outcome. In this case, the self makes its very self the object.

What follows appeared on a bulletin board at the American University in Washington. It might have appeared most anywhere in our society.

> Interpersonal Skill-Building Groups: In these 10-session skill-focused groups, students will be taught to monitor and master anxiety, using . . . improved social skills by learning to be appropriately assertive.

The flyer goes on to speak of "designing experiences" and acquiring techniques for "establishing trust." The goal is to teach the self "to monitor and master" its own "anxiety" by positioning itself rightly in a web of relationships, of which it is part and which it can help "construct." The world of the psyche joins nature and society as external worlds known and controlled by human power.

It would be straightout wrong to claim that the knowledge/power/control complex is a uniquely modern one. That is not the precise contention here. The contention is that this complex is part and parcel of the great increase in knowledge and power which effects a novel range of objects and consequences. Nature and all else within our grasp is increasingly pulled up into human history. Even someone as cautious as theologian and ethicist James Gustafson writes: "the ordering of all life is shifting in a sense from God to humanity and doing so more rapidly in this century than in all the previous centuries of human culture combined."[2] "Now we can outdo evolution," boasts one Nobel laureate.[3]

This triumvirate—Bacon, Marx, Freud—doesn't yet include the member who makes it the modern quartet—Max Weber. Weber's studies in social institutions and the ethos of capitalist societies led to this conclusion: in our kind of culture effective organized movement is usually bureaucratic and managerial in mode. Means are adjusted to ends in the most economical and efficient way, and authority is justified as the possession of expertise in law-like knowledge which has manipulative power for achieving organizational ends. Employees have standing when they can deploy a body of knowledge efficiently for the purpose of controlling behavior towards stipulated goals. Such is the bureaucratic and managerial mode of controlling the environment in rational ways. (The very word "rational" now reflects this in one of its meanings. "Rationalization" as a term in economics and sociology means the division of knowledge and labor into specializations linked together as efficient means toward institutionally desired ends. Further, the triumph of this culture is now so complete that this approach pertains not only to the production and distribution of material goods, it is extended to services and uses of knowledge as well; witness the world of consulting firms and contracted research.)

Our summary, baldly stated, is this: whether as mastery of nature, society, or psyche, scientific knowledge and technique are keys to power for our era; power is used for control; and the dominant way of exercising power and control is via the rationalized systems of large organizations.[4] Furthermore, our era is marked by quantum leaps in this human knowledge and power sufficient that mass human behavior in this kind of world effects a novel range, novel objects, and novel consequences.

MORAL QUESTIONS

Another kind of analysis surfaces other dimensions. What has been the guiding self-image for those moderns who wield this kind of power in circles great and small?

The one-sentence, box-top answer is this: the master image of humanity in the West since the Enlightenment has been the image of mastery itself. The modern "project" has been the effort to attain nonprovincial rational human autonomy, and the goal has been control itself. Especially in circles of triumphalist bourgeois optimism, we have lived by the simple, driving conviction that we can have a world of our own making, and it can be good. The optimism and the innocence, coupled with human power to vastly affect surroundings, has been impressive, as measured by the sheer quantity of results. Equally impressive has been the cultural perseverence and indeed the resurgence of optimism, innocence, and human drive to remake the world in the Reagan years. H. Richard Niebuhr's theological caricature of Protestant liberalism decades ago rings true still: "A God without wrath brought men without sin into a kingdom without judgment through the ministrations of a Christ without a cross."[5] The language is theological, and appropriately so since it expresses a transformation of cultural ethos and outlook which distanced us far from the Calvinism of early beginnings. The doctrine of providence was transmuted into the doctrine of progress (with that went the notion of the presence of pervasive, persistent evil at the heart of things). The doctrine of creation was purged of elements offensive to rationalism (with that went humanity's immersion in nature). The biblical anthropology of sinful humanity was truncated in certain consistent ways (with that went the kind of cultural wisdom which would have asked whether the drive to control the world was not the *distortion* of our humanity, rather than its vocation).[6]

Whatever the remaining power of these deep-seated cultural habits of innocence, optimism, and almost unquestioning confidence in the power to fashion the worlds of nature, psyche, and society, we are considerably more sober now. Brute reality has rejected "control" and rational order as the proper names for our present world! Brute reality has also set us up for a deeper appreciation of nature, and forced a chastened admiration for technology. We are far more keenly aware of the interdependence of all life at all levels, and of the complexity and fragility of interlocking relationships in and across all spheres. We continue to pursue science with dedication, to be sure, and remain virtually addicted to technical solutions for human problems, but worries about the consequences of scientific and technological work surface much earlier and find a stronger voice than they did in the last century and the first half of this one. Heightened human power in a shrinking world, bundled together as it is in a shared fate, gives great pause today.

Noteworthy amid this new mood is the attention to moral questions and concerns. Freeman Dyson's comments about one arena—nuclear arms policy—echo those heard from other quarters. "If a political arrangement is to be durable," he writes, "it must pay attention both to technical facts and to ethical principles. Technology without morality is barbarous; morality without technology is impotent. But in the public discussion of nuclear policies in the United States, technology has usually been overemphasized and morality, neglected. It is time for us now to redress the balance, to think more about moral principles and less about technical details."[7]

If we shift the arena to biotechnology and the modification of present species or the creation of new life forms, moral questions quickly come to the fore. Who rightly possesses and wields such fateful powers? Who will be the "image-makers" and the decision-makers, and by what standards will they envision and decide? Who grants the right to experiment on and for future human beings and other life forms? Who regulates such experimentation? By what guides and gauges? How much freedom should free enterprise have here? How much government involvement? How are the claims of both future and present generations adjudicated when they are in conflict?

We stand dumb before many of these queries, yet we know they carry a seriousness not granted them in the past. Both the title and subtitle of Hans Jonas' book bespeak the new mood: *The Imperative of Responsibility: In Search of an Ethics for the Technological Age.*[8]

THE RENEWING OF MIND

The way we have perceived things reveals a will "to cognition and control, manipulation and mastery."[9] The results of this modern project are highly ambiguous, and some, extremely threatening. Thus, many today search for a recasting of our orientation, a basically different stance and disposition. The search is well underway. Multiple paths on multiple fronts are being taken. What follows here is the modest proposal that an ancient tradition be reconsidered; more precisely, that some selected themes from Jewish and Christian traditions be reassessed for the frame of mind they might help promote in our circumstances. We can only be suggestive. The following are offered as notions to think *with,* rather than simply concepts to think about. Four are offered: creation, neighbor, justice, peace.

Creation

Creation is the theological term for the totality of all things, together, in relation to God. Strictly speaking, "creation" is our term, since the verb form, not the noun form, is the one present in Hebrew scriptures. This not only underscores the sense of ongoing creating and sustaining, it also underlines the unfinished character of the world. In any event, the term carries a sense of energy, dynamism, and change, as well as suggesting persisting patterns that conserve and preserve.

There is also a vision here: all creation is one, and harmony and security are possible. The vision is nicely reflected in one of the many biblical ways of imaging the world—as an *oikos* (house and household). The English words economics, ecumenics, and ecology all share this root and reference. "Economics" means providing for the household's material and service needs, and managing the household well. "Ecumenics" means treating the inhabitants of the household as a single family, human and nonhuman together, and fostering the unity of the family. "Ecology" is knowledge of that systemic interdependence upon which the household's entire life depends. If English had adopted the Greek word for steward (*oikonomos*), we would immediately recognize the steward as the trustee or caretaker of the *oikos*.

For the United Nations 1972 conference on the environment in Stockholm, scientist René Dubos and economist Barbara Ward wrote the following, in striking confirmation of this ancient, unitary understanding of the created order.

> There is something clarifying and irresistible in plain scientific fact. The astonishing thing about our deepened understanding of reality over the last four or five decades is the degree to which it confirms and reinforces so many of the older moral insights of humanity. The philosophers told us we were one, part of a greater unity that transcends our local drives and needs. They told us that all living things are held together in a most intricate web of interdependence. They told us that aggression and violence, blindly breaking down the delicate relationships of existence, could lead to destruction and death. These were, if you like, intuitions drawn in the main from the study of human societies and behavior. What we now learn is that they are factual descriptions of the way in which our universe actually works.[10]

Neighbor

The meaning of neighbor follows from the understanding of creation. Neighbor is a universalized term: all are neighbors. Jesus of Nazareth voices the radical reach of this when he construes the enemy as neighbor, and instructs his followers to treat all neighbors with a regard equal to that which they accord themselves and their closest compatriots, i.e., when he instructs them to use the same frame of reference for considering their neighbors' needs as they use for their own.

We should note not only the universal reach of "neighbor," however, but its time frame. Contemporaries, whether near or far, friend or foe, are not our only neighbors. Unborn generations are neighbors as well, as are past generations. Moral responsibility here stretches through time and arches across space.

H. Richard Niebuhr, cited earlier, has articulated this understanding as succinctly as anyone. The following was written in the 1950s, before "ecology" became a household word, and during an intense period of the Cold War between the United States and the Soviet Union. That he did so is testimony to the roots of this understanding in his religious tradition, roots penetrating deeper than the shallow soil of modernity.

> Who, finally, is my neighbor, the companion whom I have been commanded to love as myself? [The neighbor] is the near one and the far one; the one removed from me by distances in time and space, in convictions and loyalties . . . The neighbor is in past and present and future, yet [the neighbor] is not simply [humankind] in its totality but rather in its articulation, the community of individuals in community. [The neighbor] is Augustine in the Roman Catholic Church and Socrates in Athens, and the Russian people, and the unborn generations who will bear the consequences of our failures, future persons for whom we are administering the entrusted wealth of nature and other greater common gifts. [The neighbor] is [humanity] and [the neighbor] is angel and [the neighbor] is animal and inorganic being, all that participates in being.[11]

As a fundamental moral orientation, the neighbor as "all that participates in being" is strikingly appropriate for the kind of world with the kind of human power discussed above.

Justice

While the vision of redeemed creation is that of harmonious, abundant, and secure life together, our actual experience is vastly different. It is creation laced with deep discord and stirred by profound need and want. Fissures of suffering, pain, and violation rend nature, psyche, and society every bit as much as joy, ecstasy, satisfaction, and fulfillment surface.

Ancient traditions shared the same experience and had a way of understanding it. With other peoples of the ancient Near East, the Hebrews shared a cosmology something like this. The creating of the universe by the gods or God was a mighty movement from chaos—matter as "formless and void"—to harmonious order. Yet chaos survives and continally intrudes. A struggle between creation and choas is joined, and never ceases in the experience of the world as we know it. The forms of chaos are many: famine and hunger, plagues and disease, mental illness, marital, familial and generational estrangement, deceitfulness and corruption, the ways of war and other violence, denial of goods to those in genuine need, and so forth. Later Christian theologians would use the term "original sin" for this pervasive disorder, Jewish theologians would speak of "the evil impulse." It is, in their ancestors' view, the presence of evil as an enemy of the ongoing created order.

Hebrew thinking about justice reflects this portrayal. Justice as a dynamic concept does not first appear with the great prophets of the eighth and sixth centuries BCE; it stems from this older understanding of cosmic reality as harmonious world order. When the Hebrew confession says again and again that Yahweh is "just," it means God fashions order from chaos, restrains the chaos, and balances things anew when chaos intrudes and triumphs. Justice is the push for harmony, often through severe measures. (In the prophetic oracles, whole nations and empires fall when their injustice provokes counterbalancing wrath.)

Since Hebrew minds were not given to separate history from nature (no word for nonhuman nature as a separate entity exists in Hebrew), justice does not participate in such a distinction. Differently said—and unlike modern notions—justice does not refer only to human relationships and welfare. It may refer one time to human events (Pharoah's horses and riders are tossed into the sea), and another to events we assign to nature (the tale of the Flood).

It is many-sided in other ways as well, reflected in the ensemble of words used in Hebrew. Sometimes justice is *sedekah* (righteousness), sometimes *hesed* (loving-kindness); elsewhere it is *emet* (faithfulness), *tom* (integrity), *miswah* (order), *torah* (instruction), *shalom* (wholeness, peace), or *mishpat* (equity). This is a considerably more comprehensive understanding than that which reigns in most Anglo-American moral traditions. Those traditions have focused on justice as liberty or equality, or some combination of these. Justice as liberty means guaranteeing the widest range of individual choice commensurate with such choice for others. Justice as equality means guaranteeing a comparative allotment of goods, services, and opportunities at a humane level for the largest number possible. Much debate, legislation, policy formulation, and regulation turns on which concept will prevail and the ways in which one might contemplate or correct the other. Vital though this notion be, it should not escape our attention that both dimensions share a common anthropocentrism; they assume the sphere of justice is populated by humans only and pertains to human welfare only, directly or indirectly. Creation imagined as an oikos does not eliminate concern for liberty and equality, much less for human welfare in general, but it makes the radical assumption that the basic "unit" of reality is the whole creation in God! For that reason, justice, biblically considered, is the rendering, amid limited resources and the conditions and constraints of a broken world, of whatever is required for the fullest possible flourishing of creation. That which makes for wholeness in nature, psyche, and society (to return to our divisions) is "just."

Peace

Justice introduces shalom, usually rendered as "peace." The rendering is not wrong, so long as it connotes shared well-being in every sphere, well-being extended to all creatures so that life is lived without debilitating fear. It is tranquility and serenity; it is also bread and dance.

The antonym of shalom is the chaos and anomie we have mentioned. It is the many forms of violence and violation. Or, positively, all that intersects the cure and care of creation belongs to peacemaking and peacekeeping. Shalom, then, is considerably more than the avoidance of war and the limiting of other forms of violence. But we must quickly add that in our age this ancient understanding of peace as the well-being of creation, and the ancient understanding of threats to it as the intrusion of chaos, have a stark, direct relevance. Weapons of mass destruction, whether nuclear, chemical, or biological, and the slow degradation of the envelope of life through environmental abuse, pose the unprecedented possibility of a massive victory of chaos over the piece of creation which is our only home. No previous war, however horrible its local manifestations, carried the awesome capacity to draw the curtain on the very *possibility* of having neighbors in the future. None had the capacity to render the planet itself virtually dead and its atmosphere hostile to the fertile evolution of teeming life. The literal meaning of "holocaust" is too real a human possibility now: the consumption by fire of all that is. Thus, while the full meaning of shalom is far-reaching, total well-being that includes everything from bodily care to nurturing the spirit to making treaties, music, and love, its minimum definition is the avoidance of nuclear fire and the biochemical devastation of the environment.

These "think with's" are only illustrative of resources for what is now underway in myriad ways in many circles, the renewing or recasting of mind. They are offered not only sketchily but modestly, in recognition that the very traditions of which they are part, Judaism and Christianity, are themselves contributors to "*the problematique humane*" of the modern technological world. Nonetheless, renewing of mind often happens by way of the free and imaginative interpretation and appropriation of the treasures of past peoples and their living traditions. "In Search of an Ethics for the Technological Age" (Jonas) will require moral wisdom old and new.

NOTES AND REFERENCES

1. Hans Jonas, *The Imperative of Responsibility* (Chicago: University of Chicago Press, 1984), p. 140.

2.   James Gustafson, *Ethics from a Theocentric Perspective,* Vol. I (Chicago: University of Chicago Press, 1984), p. 281.

3.   See the opinion piece by Al Cavalieri, "Genetic Engineering: A Blind Plunge," in the *Washington Post,* May 14, 1982, on the "op-ed" page.

4.   I feel constrained to underscore a disclaimer made earlier in the text. The use of Bacon, Marx, Freud, and Weber is not intended as a crisp summary of the project of each of them. They are convenient symbols for strong themes in modern cultural orientations. To regard the foregoing as anything other than this would be patently unfair to each of them, and especially their vast differences from one another.

5.   H. Richard Niebuhr, *The Kingdom of God in America* (New York: Harper and Row, 1937), p. 193.

6.   See the important discussion of Douglas John Hall in *Lighten Our Darkness: Toward an Indigenous Theology of the Cross* (Philadelphia: Westminster Press 1976), especially the initial section of the book. This is a critique of North American culture and North American Christianity.

7.   Freeman J. Dyson, "Demystifying the Bomb," *The New York Times Magazine,* 4/5/87, p. 54.

8.   See the earlier note for publication details.

9.   Cornel West, *Prophesy Deliverance! An Afro-American Revolutionary Christianity* (Philadelphia: The Westminster Press, 1982), p. 100.

10.   René Dubos and Barbara Ward, *Only One Word* (London: Penguin Books, 1972), p. 85.

11.   H. Richard Niebuhr et al., *The Purpose of the Church and its Ministry: Reflections on the Aims of Theological Education* (New York: Harper & Row, 1956), p. 38. The use of terms in brackets is done to avoid sexist language.

12.   The discusson of this last section, using creation, justice, neighbor, and peace, draws heavily from, and is an adaptation of, a longer discussion. See Larry Rasmussen, "Creation, Church, and Christian Responsibility," in Wesley Granberg-Michaelson, ed., *Tending the Garden* (Grand Rapids: Wm. B. Eerdmans Publishing Co., 1987), pp. 114-137. The earlier section of this article, on "The Cast of Mind," draws from my paper, "Socially Responsible Ministry: The View from Chrisitan Ethics," to be published by Pilgrim Press in a collection edited by Dieter Hessel.

THE FRAGILITY OF TIME:

ORWELL AND ELLUL IN THE

MATRIX OF THEOLOGICAL ORIGINS

Charles Mabee

INTRODUCTION: ORIGIN OF
THE THEOLOGICAL PROBLEM OF TIME

In a recent study relating theology and technology, Egbert Schuurman makes
the following statement concerning the theological perspective of Genesis 1-11:

> Since the fall, history has ceased to be the unfolding of creation through the fulfillment
> of man's cultural task. On the contrary, history has been running ever more aground. Of
> this the flood, the building of a Babel culture, and the biblical history of Israel are clear
> manifestations. Nor can man himself restore history. Rather, he is the cause of its many
> dislocations and destructions. Skills and techniques of all kinds may be admirable, but
> the tyrannical or greedy use of human power over nature is a failure deriving from human
> sin, not from God's intention in the creation.

Research in Philosophy and Technology, Volume 10, pages 129-148.
Copyright © 1990 by JAI Press Inc.
All rights of reproduction in any form reserved.
ISBN: 1-55938-062-4

He concludes, "Sin always involves a loss of 'earth' in some sense: alienation from God and alienation from creation go hand in hand."[1] This interpretation of the Old Testament materials has many of the traditional elements of Christian exegesis, and it correctly points to the underlying structural unity of creation and history, albeit a structural unity fractured by the traditional understanding of the Fall. In this view, the Fall severs history from creation in a primordial disruption that can only be reinstituted by God with the Call of Abraham in Gen. 12:1. In this way, while the concerns of the faith are grounded in the traditional Christian idea of the history of salvation, the goal of salvation history is the restoration of creation and general history.

In this paper I make an additional proposal in the interpretation of Gen. 1-11 that shares several of the features of Schuurman's reading, but one which also significantly differs from it. In particular, I find his perspective that sin always involves a loss of " 'earth' in some sense" to be penetrating and insightful, but one which can also be refined based on the problem of modern technology discussed in the work of Jacques Ellul and George Orwell. Both Ellul and Orwell refine the idea of evil in contemporary terms as the ability to manipulate time, or, more specifically, to utilize time as a means of protecting individual and political geographical space. What is not clear in either of their works is the insight that this perspective is already anticipated in the Primordial History of Genesis. I believe that the issue of the fragility of time helps explain how Gen. 3-11 is structurally linked to Gen. 1-2. Gen. 3-11 is the aborted attempt of humans to aggressively manipulate time (= history) for their own self-interests, beginning with the so-called Fall of Genesis 3; an attempt that culminates in the story of the Tower of Babel in Genesis 11. Importantly, the response of Yahweh to each of these outbreaks of human sin is not punishment in a legalistic sense, but consists of acts designed to protect further the fragile created order of the natural interrelation of space and time. This is in stark contrast to the act of retribution voiced by Noah in response to the sin of Ham in Gen. 9:25—"Accursed be Canaan. He shall be his brothers' meanest slave." Thus, as the events of the Primordial History unfold, we see God acting out of the posture of the protection of nature, whereas humans act out the evil machinations of their own heart. Schuurman is surely correct in his explanation of why alienation from earth and history [= time] go hand in hand. This explains why, according to the Genesis account, human efforts to coalesce human technique with the natural propensity for meaningful work are just as problematic as the fusion of human history and the discernment of God's activity in the world.

Before a more detailed discussion of the narration of primordial time is offered, it is crucial to point out the central place of Genesis 1:15 in the story for all that follows: "Yahweh God took the man and settled him in the Garden of Eden *in order to serve and watch it.*" This verse now stands in programmatic relationship to the remainder of Genesis 1-11. For the whole of this body of material, therefore, the shape of human work is defined by serving and watching (in the sense of guarding). Whatever sins are to follow in Genesis 3ff., all of them stem from rebellion against this fundamental human posture of serving and watching that the narrative conceives as intrinsic to the human condition. As Schuurman correctly indicates: "sin always involves a loss of 'earth' in some sense: alienation from God and alienation from creation go hand in hand." The earth is man's primordial home, and coming from the soil, all other forms of his existence must always come to terms with this fact.

GENESIS 1-11: THE THEOLOGICAL FOUNDATION OF THE PROBLEM

Everyone familiar with the Genesis 1-11 narrative recognizes that several key events take place that recount the emergence of human sin evoking divine response: the eating of the forbidden fruit, Cain's murder of Abel, the song of Lamech, the marriage of the daughters of men by the sons of God, and the construction of the tower of Babel. The German Old Testament specialist, Gerhard von Rad, argues that this material bespeaks a view of increasing deterioration in the relation of God and humans on the part of the major narrative source of the material, the so-called J writer. Furthermore, he saw the increase in human sin evoking the response of appropriate grace on the part of Yahweh that matches the expressions of human sin and paves the way for the inception of Israelite religion embodied in the Call of Abraham in Gen. 12. More recently, Old Testament scholars have questioned the idea of progressive intensification of sin operative in this narrative unit. In relation to our interest in the theological grounding of time, however, two basic exegetical issues emerge in the analysis of this material:

1. What is the underlying *meaning* of the human sin that is perpetrated by humans in the story?
2. Is the divine response to be framed in terms of these sinful acts, or in terms of the structure of creation?

The remainder of our discussion of the Primordial History is centered on these issues.

In order to clarify the meaning of human sin as it arises in Genesis 1-11, let us observe each occurrence of it in literary context. First, the eating of the forbidden fruit is born out of the human desire to become divine (3:5-6), knowing good and evil. The prohibition against the eating of this fruit of the tree of the knowledge of good and evil is stipulated in 2:17, and represents the only prohibition given during the time of the actual creation. What is particularly interesting about the story is the rationale for the punishment of banishment from the Garden that ensues upon the completion of the crime. Toward the end of the overall narrative we read:

Yahweh God said: "Behold, the man has become as one of us, knowing good and evil." And as a result, lest he stretch out his hand and take (fruit) also from the tree of life, and eat of it, and live forever: Yahweh God sent him from the Garden of Eden to serve the soil from which he was taken. [3:22-23]

What is particularly instructive about this passage is that Adam's banishment from the Garden takes place as a result of Yahweh's concern for *time,* in the form of the tree of life whose fruit will allow him to live *forever.* In other words, Adam is dislocated by Yahweh so that he will not be able to manipulate time in order to fortify his place in the Garden (to "live forever") by eating of the tree of life. Yahweh's punishment of banishment is not effected for the sake of punishment. In short, it is punishment that arises out of Yahweh's concern *for the fragility of time.* Whatever else it has accomplished, the human knowledge of good and evil has brought with it the possibility of human manipulation of time. This text points to this manipulation of time as the primary area where human sin can penetrate with the most damage against the basic structure of creation. The intended message is clear at this point: the utilization of time for the sake of space results in banishment.

Moving on to the next narrative sub-unit, the precise reason why Yahweh rejected the offering from the soil by Cain in Genesis 4 has been frequently debated by Old Testament interpreters. It is obvious that the text is not primarily interested in giving the *reason* for Yahweh's negative response. Rather, its focus is on the response itself and Cain's angry reaction to it that results in the murder of his brother out of envy. If we penetrate to the deeper levels of the brief narrative, we see the problem of the human control of time as underlying Cain's emotion of envy, but this control of time manifests itself in a different aspect than in Genesis 3 ("living forever"). Here we are dealing with time in an embryonic cause-and-effect relationship that bridges the present and future. In point of fact, Cain wishes to control the future (Yahweh's response to his offering), based on his act in the present (the presentation of the offering to Yahweh). In this sense, von Rad is correct in pointing to the issue of Yahweh's freedom as being fundamentally at stake in the narrative, even if we believe that certain intimations in the text point to a kind of rationale for the divine action (the ground has been cursed, or the like). The meaning of Yahweh's freedom is that the future is his, and not Cain's. Cain cannot force either Yahweh's future or his own by a rationalistic approach based on cause and effect. Whether Yahweh has "sufficient" grounds (from a human standpoint) to act in the way in which he does, is of no interest to the writer. This glaring omission in the narrative only emphasizes the point of Cain's desire to manipulate the future, yet his inability to do so. The protection of time from human control is hereby maintained in the course of primordial events. Even Cain himself is protected from further consequences of his deed by human hands when Yahweh places the mark upon him. This act continues the theme of the narrative of Yahweh's on-going intention of the protection of creation, rather than punishment of human sin.

From a literary-critical standpoint, one of the oldest texts in the Old Testament is the song of Lamech (4:23-24). It is generally classified as an oral boasting or revenge song, and is considered to have originated at a time when the law of blood revenge was circumscribed by little or no restraint. In this original setting, the song celebrated the power of the male hero who was able to protect his wives in a hostile envrionment devoid of written law code, or a state-controlled legal system. In this situation, it is not so much blood vengence that is at stake, rather it is the honor of the hero. In its adaptation to the written narrative of Genesis 1-11, however, the text underwent a radical transformation. In its new literary environment, it represents another instance of the outbreak of sin in the primordial context in the guide of Lamech's hubris and brutality. It is not blood vengence as such that characterizes the passage, but the extent of the blood vengence that reaches far into the future (seventy-seven fold vengence). As with the previous passage, we again find a narrative exposition of the human attempt to manipulate the future, only now set completely within the human context. The text does not actually narrate the future occurrences of this vengence, but the boasting of the manipulation of the future in the framework of a present time to the wives Adah and Zillah. That is to say, it is the reaching into the future by Lamech, and the celebration of his ability to conquer future events in the present, that gives the text its distinctive characteristic with regard to time. Thus, although the tree of life remains protected from man in the Garden, and Yahweh's own independence has been established through the Cain and Abel story, Lamech now nurtures the human aspiration for the control of time solely within the human realm. The path toward the destruction of the Primordial Flood is now firmly established.

The Flood itself is explicitly motivated in the narrative by the mating of the sons of God and the daughters of men (6:1-4). The implication is clear in this terse account that these events precipitate a major breakdown that fractures the proper relationship between the divine and human realms. The immediate result of the transposition of the divine beings into creation is a further circumscription of human time by God: "His days shall be not more than 120 years." By implication, the great danger of the mating of godly and human figures is the creation of beings who could mount yet another attack upon time by approaching the immortality of their divine fathers. Yahweh's response is necessarily severe and specifically addresses the problem of devasting human misappropriation of time. Only by limiting the length of human days can the fragility of time be protected and its integrity maintained. The attack upon time is expicitly indicated in the passage with the reference to the Nephilim and the designation "men/males/warriors of eternity" (6:4). Again, as in earlier instances of human sin, Yahweh's response is not conceptualized as punishment, but in terms of the protector of time in the created order.

The story of the construction of the Tower of Babel in Genesis 11 brings the human attack on time to a resounding climax in the Primordial History. While the top of the tower reaches the heavens, thereby symbolizing the human attempt to breach the created order, the fundamental rationale for its construction lies in its durability rather than its height. The purpose of the construction is clearly manifested in the statement that men wanted to "make a name for themselves."[2] This is also the reason why the materials of the construction are explicitly stated in far greater detail than would otherwise be expected. These are materials that are noted for their lasting qualities: " 'Come, let us make bricks and bake them in the fire.' For stone they used bricks, and for mortar they used bitumen." The tone of this story is as tragic as it is loathsome. Having failed in all other ways to deny the rightful place of time in the natural order, the building of the tower is the final human attempt in the Primordial History to manipulate time by capturing the future and bringing it under the power of human manipulation. The divine response of confusing human tongues and scattering them over all the face of the earth is again meant to thwart the human attack on time, not as a punishment. This is the final divine act before the inception of the religion of Israel that begins in Genesis 12. It is appropriate to state the matter as forthrightly as possible: the call of Abraham by Yahweh in Gen. 12:1-3, which moves the focus of the Genesis narrative out of the realm of universal primordial history to the story of the inception of Israelite religion, is meant to ameliorate the destructive forces manifest in the anthropocentric misuse of time. The problem is the peculiar fragility of time, a problem which the Primordial History simply asumes without rationale or etiology. It is certainly not the task of the theologian to provide imaginative answers where the tradition is silent. It is, however, incumbent upon us to move forward into the world as we know and experience it, and dialectically relate this tradition to it. I have chosen the work of Orwell and Ellul as particularly insightful expressions of the modern problem of technology and its misuse of time proleptically set forth in the traditional Genesis account.

ORWELL AND ELLUL: MANIPULATION OF TIME IN AN ANTHROPOCENTRIC WORLD

Introduction

Near the end of George Orwell's novel *1984,* the protagonist Winston Smith comes to the conclusion that "God is Power."[3] Such a perspective in the modern democratic context comes as no surprise to the dire prophecy of Alexis de Tocqueville given already in 1840:

> I believe that it is easier to establish an absolute and despotic government among a people whose special conditions are equal than among any other. I also believe that such a government once established in such a people would not only oppress men but would, in the end, strip each man there of several of the chief attributes of humanity. *I therefore think that despotism is particularly to be feared in ages of democracy* [my emphasis].[4]

For him, by the time that he wrote the second volume of *Democracy in America* in 1840, democracy and political tyranny had come to be almost synonymous words. For George Orwell, writing little more than a century later, democracy *as such* was likewise no absolute guarantee against political tyranny. In the midst of the popularity of *1984* among American readers, it may not be commonly known that one of the major totalitarian powers is the United States—Tocqueville's cradle of democracy. In the novel, Orwell explains the development of world totalitarianism in this way:

> The splitting-up of the world into three great super-states was an event which could be and indeed was foreseen before the middle of the twentieth century. With the absorption of Europe by Russia *and the British Empire by the United States,* two of the three existing powers, Eurasia and Oceania, were already effectively in being . . . . Oceania comprises the Americas, the Atlantic islands including the British Isles, Australia, and the southern portion of Africa [my emphasis].[5]

Britain carries the name of Airstrip One, and functions as an American outpost on the edge of the Continent, an area controlled by Russia. These two superpowers—Oceania and Eurasia—exist in a state of perpetual warfare, along with the third great power Eastasia (China and the countries to the South). Importantly, the great powers of *1984* are no longer "divided by any genuine ideological difference." Thus, for Orwell, it is false to juxtapose democracy and totalitarianism.

Orwell had the advantage of viewing over a century's more democratic experience than did Tocqueville, in both England and America, as well as the rest of the world. Yet, his vision is, in a real sense, the natural unfolding of Tocqueville's growing fear of democracy. Whereas the latter could only imagine the apathy and loss of liberty which centralization would bring, the former presupposed that and directed his intention, instead, to the offspring of an unfettered democracy—the *Party.* The Party represents, so to speak, the extraction of pure democratic rationality which has become pure irrationality: the democratic impulses of individualism and centralization of which Tocqueville warned, bereft of all mitigating social contact and conscience. *1984* is, therefore, first and foremost a political novel; more specifically, a novel of political power and corruption. Lionel Trilling's description is quite apt: "The exposition of the *mystique* of power is the heart and essence of Orwell's book."[6] As O'Brien, speaking as a Party spokesman, informs Winston Smith in the book: "Power is not a means; it is an end."[7] He describes for us what *might* become the ultimate development of the democratic state *if* we sufficiently lower our viligance vis-à-vis the efficiency which advancing technology affords the corrupt who can assume power even there. It is, we might say, the story of the marriage of democracy and technology; or, perhaps better, the graphic description of politicization of technology through the manipulation of time.

Orwell and the Language of Power

In spite of the fact that *1984* is not a novel about technology *per se*, it does provide us with some provocative thoughts on this subject as it enters the political sphere, one which carries significant theological ramifications for the issue of the fragility of time. As I have indicated, this book must be placed in the context of Orwell's overriding political interest. First of all, it is clear that he was acutely aware of the revolution which the machine which brought to societal structures. The machine represented a danger to the status quo of class society. A Quote from the heretical book by Emmanuel Goldstein in the text of *1984* (fictionally entitled *The Theory and Practice of Oligarchical Collectivism*) illustrates this point:

> From the moment when the machine first made its appearance it was clear to all thinking people that the need for human drudgery, and therefore to a great extent for human inequality, had disappeared. If the machine were used deliberately for that end, hunger, overwork, dirt, illiteracy, and disease could be eliminated within a few generations. . . . But it was also clear that an all-round increase in wealth threatened the destruction—indeed, in some sense was the destruction—of a hierarchical society.[8]

If a solution is to be found for the present human predicament, it lies in the release of the machine for the liberation from human drudgery and inequality. *1984* describes how the threatened power class, embodied in the Party, successfully maintains its control over the natural development of the machine. The Party utilizes techniques of oppression which are ultimately derived from the machine to ward off the powerless in the social realm which is spawned by the machine in the technical realm. Orwell continues (in the voice of Goldstein):

> In the long run, a hierarchical society was only possible on a basis of poverty and ignorance. To return to the agricultural past, as some thinkers about the beginning of the twentieth century dreamed of doing, was not a practicable solution. It conflicted with the tendency toward mechanization which had become quasi-instinctive throughout almost the whole world, and moreover, any country which remained industrially backward was helpless in a military sense and was bound to be dominated, directly or indirectly, by its more advanced rivals.[9]

Orwell does not seek a solution from the problems of the modern industrial world in a *retreating* to naturalism or romanticism. This is because the machine itself by the mid-twentieth century had become a "quasi-instinctive" part of human nature. It can no longer be arbitrarily removed. Orwell recognized this as the given quality of human existence in our time—a reality from which even art itself must proceed.

The promise for good, however, which had accompanied and nurtured the modern machine from its inception had failed to materialize in the twentieth century. Two world wars had painfully born this fact. In commenting on *1984*, Alfred Kazin puts the matter succinctly:

> Just at the moment when twentieth-century technology had shown itself capable of feeding the hungry, when unencumbered everything in sight justified Marx's testimony in The Communist Manifesto to the power of new productive forces and Whitehead's praise of "the century of hope" for "inventing invention," socialism in its original meaning—the end of tribal nationalism, of man's alienation from his own esssence, of wealth determining all values in society—yielded to the nightmare of coercion.[10]

What had gone wrong with the technological dream? Why had technology "yielded to the nightmare of coercion?" For Orwell, the answer seems to lie in the fact that technology had lost its way because it had served those *primal* intellectual associations that had initially fostered its development. Such associations were deemed *oldspeak* by the Party; concepts such as free[dom], honor, justice, morality, internationalism, democracy, science, and *religion*. In Orwell's terms, these words were all grouped "round the concepts of objectivity and rationalism."[11] By implication, therefore, technology embedded in the context of objectivity and rationality offered the single greatest hope of mankind. Perhaps the term "science" comes closest to capturing the essence of this view, if we conceive of the term in the broad sense of the free pursuit of knowledge according to rational and objective means. But totalitarianism had co-opted rational science and displaced its primary relationship with technology. As David Goodman writes: "The governments of *1984* are able to exercise such strict control over their citizens largely because they have adapted the fruits of science and technology to their own ends."[12] Similarly, George Woodcock notes that in the novel "science is *diverted* to producing refined instruments of torture, industry feeds a perpetual war that engenders the hatred on which power rests" [my emphasis].[13] Whether one speaks of "adapting" or "diverting," the end result is much the same. Technology has failed in *1984* because it has not been allowed to run its full, unencumbered force. Technology had become, in effect, anti-technology through the corrupting power of the Party. Faced with the liberating threat of technology, the Party's strategy was, in effect, to redirect the threat against itself.[14] The natural development of technology is arrested by the Party by turning politically controlled technology against it. In order to accomplish this, two aspects of human rationality are singled out by Orwell as fundamental to totalitarian control: *language* and *time*. By controlling language, the Party put itself in the position of controlling the human perception of time. By manipulating these two cognitive spheres, the politicization of technology was complete, and absolute power lay securely in the hands of the Party.

Language control makes possible a new way of thinking which alienates technological advancement from its native rational context, and sets it in a new irrational one. Orwell terms the new irrational context *doublethink,* a twilight word in which one holds "two contradictory beliefs in one's mind simultaneously," and accepts both of them as true.[15] *Doublethink* is the means by which the Party becomes transformed into the tyrannical technology of "communications and management."[16] Through the epistemological control of human thought processes which language naturally affords it, the Party extracts the rationality from technology in surgical fashion. Presupposed at this point is the insight that language/rationality operates fundamentally by means of *differentiation.* Rationality allows us to distinguish one thing from another by establishing separate, individual identities. It is precisely this power of differentiation that totalitarianism fears in its drive toward uniformity. Commenting on Winston Smith's reiterated phrase "it made no difference" found throughout the novel, Mark Crispin Miller writes:

> This is what the Party wants to do, what it has all but accomplished—to *make no difference,* to eternalize its own rigid hierarchy by wiping out all dissidence, eccentricity, variety, comparison. . . . The Party plans to make no difference whatsoever; and each time Winston Smith employs the phrase, each time he thus reveals that he cannot conceive some difference, he thereby wins a little victory for the Party, fulfilling, in his fatalism, the Party's program of complete erasure.[17]

This is the reason that language is one of the last issues to be contended between social democracy and totalitarianism; language determines whether or not we have a way to visualize differentiation. In this sense, all of the issues that we have been discussing—democracy, machines, and technology—in Orwell's view become increasingly reduced to a question of language in the present time. This explains his intensified interest in the subject in *1984,* embodied in the book's appendix, "The Principles of Newspeak."

Orwell's work encourages us to make clear distinctions within the individual categories of democracy, mechanics, technology, and even religion itself, in order to approach them from an enlightened standpoint in today's world. He reminds us that these rational, symbolic constructions are not absolutes in and of themselves. How we conceive of them and our relationship to them, is the ultimate question. In the appendix Orwell notes: "Newspeak was designated not to extend but to *diminish* the range of thought, and this purpose was indirectly assisted by cutting the choice of words down to a minimum."[18] In this regard, for example, Ellul's description of technique may already betray the narrow way that technology is perceived today. Ironically, it may represent already a sort of victory for Newspeak. The question is, does the particualr form of technology that dominates in the late twentieth century carry the implication that we have exhausted the depth of meaning of technology as such? If we find certain aspects of that technology oppressive, does that carry the implication that technology as such is oppressive? Orwell denies this way of forcing the issue in an either/or way of thinking. To fail to differentiate is to fall victim to those very same forces which one wishes to oppose. Only a thoroughly technologized mentality gives the choice, "technology or no technology." If Orwell is correct, the more our own technological impulse is used negatively to limit the total range of our technological response to life, the more nearly we ourselves already embody a totalitarian mentality.

Through the power of *doublethink*, the Party laid hold of its central tenet: "the mutability of the past."[19] The Orwellian insight is that time is not simply external to human existence, but is mediated to us by means of language. In this mediation, or heremeneutics of time, the Party had virtually eliminated it as an autonomous reality outside its own subjective interpretation: " 'Who controls the past,' ran the Party slogan, 'controls the future: who controls the present controls the past.' "[20] The sphere of time is viewed as an interrelated unity, with the entry point for Party interpretation being the control of the present. Those who controlled the present could rewrite the past, and this rewriting of the past programmed the future. The Party saw that "all history was a palimpsest, scraped clean and reinscribed exactly as often as necessary."[21] The key to political control, therefore, was essentially a linguistic, and ultimately metaphysical one; namely, the present stranglehold which the Party maintained by the function of historical record keeping. By maintaining its grip on the past through the manipulation of the public perception of it, the Party remained inviolable:

> Past events, it is argued, have no objective existence, but survive only in written records and in human memories. The past is whatever the records and the memories agree upon. And since the Party is in full control of all records, and in equally full control of the minds of its members, it follows that the past is whatever the Party chooses to make it. . . . When it has been recreated in whatever shape is needed at the moment, then this version *is* the past, and no different past can ever have existed.[22]

The real terror of the Orwellian vision now comes to light. It does not stop at simple totalitarian control of human behavior. If so, it would be a matter for political science and theory. As it is, it penetrates to the deepest layers of our perception of being, and thereby becomes an ontological problem of the magnitude that is portrayed in the Primordial History of Genesis.

Ellul and the Abstraction of Power

In 1964, a book appeared in the American setting that has become a primary text for the discussion of the problem of technology—*The Technological Society,* by Jacques Ellul.[23] Because this book contains the fundamentals of Ellul's approach to technology and establishes his central argument, I limit my discussion primarily to it. Ellul defines technology or technique as follows: "The totality of methods rationally arrived at and having absolute efficiency (for a given stage of development) in every field of human activity."[24] Although there are fundamental differences between them, we might say that this book more expressly unfolds the theological implications of Gen. 1-11 than does Orwell. His central insight is that whereas the machine stands as the point of origin of modern technology, and itself embodies pure technology, technology as such has become essentially independent of the machine in the modern world in the extracted rational form of technique. Indeed, it is the task of technique to assimilate everything within the machine: "the ideal for which technique strives is the mechanization of everything it encounters."[25] Ellul sees the growth and development of this machine-generated technique as inevitable throughout the modern world, and early in his book concludes that "all-embracing technique is in fact the *consciousness* of the mechanized world"[26] [my emphasis]. Clearly, for Ellul, technique has penetrated to the deepest layers of the psyche of contemporary man, and now represents a deeper reality than Orwell's party or other fundamental human realities such as sexuality (Freud) or economics (Marx).

Ellul clearly establishes the primacy of the machine in any discussion of technique. He writes: "Technique certainly began with the machine. . . . [and] without the machine the world of technique would not exist."[27] In another context, he notes that "capitalism did not create our world; the machine did."[28] In more specific historical terms, he locates the beginning of machine technique after 1750.[29] Today, however, this primal unity between machine and technique no longer exists. He continues:

> Technique has now become almost completely independent of the machine, which has lagged far behind its offspring. . . . It is the machine which is now entirely dependent upon technique, and the machine represents only a small part of technique. . . . [Indeed,] the machine is now not even the most important aspect of technique (though it is perhaps the most spectacular); technique has taken over all of man's activities, not just his productive activity.[30]

It is crucial, then, to understand Ellul's position that technique has become autonomous in our society, begins with this break from the machine which gave it birth. He describes in further detail how the dominance of technique has taken place:

Technique has enough of the mechanical in its nature to enable it to cope with the machine, but it surpasses and transcends the machine because it remains in close touch with the human order. The metal monster could not go on forever torturing mankind. It found in technique a rule as hard and inflexible as itself.[31]

The material divergence in the positions of Ellul and Mumford begins to arise with this characterization of the machine as "the metal monster." Faced with the inextricable reality of the machine that was essentially inhuman, technique arose in society to adapt it to human realities. Because this rational enterprise worked so well with reference to the machine, it increasingly began to be applied as an integrative force to all other aspects of society as well. In short, for Ellul, humans have become "the object of technique and the offspring of the mating of man and machine."[32] It is at this point that the genuinely philosophical and theological perspectives of technique emerge, including its relevance, as a result, for American biblical hermeneutics.

In a similar way that Marx argued that the proletariat class had been created by the industrialization brought about by the bourgeois, Ellul develops his thesis that the machine created technique in the vacuum created by its own inherent inhumaneness. He writes:

Technique integrates everything. It avoids shock and sensational events. Man is not adapted to a world of steel; technique adapted him to it. It changes the arrangement of this blind world so that man can be a part of it without colliding with its rough edges, without the anguish of being delivered up to the inhuman. Technique thus provides a model; it specifies attitudes that are valid once and for all. *The anxiety aroused in man by the turbulence of the machine is soothed by the consoling hum of a unified society* [my emphasis].[33]

Ellul, in essential agreement with Mumford, understands the impact of the machine on human existence to have been of such essential importance that it *fundamentally* altered our way of being in the world. The machine broke down whatever primal vestiges of unity existed between humanity and world.[34] Because humans cannot live for long in such a chaotic environment, technique arose as a way of reintegrating them into their environment. Better the ordered existence of the slave, than the disorientation of lost order itself. In a powerful statement that manifests the essence of Ellul's view of the machine, he writes:

Admittedly, the machine has enriched man as it has changed him. The machine's senses and organs have manipulated the powers of human senses and organs, enabling man to penetrate a new milieu and revealing to him unknown sights, liberties, and servitudes. *He has been liberated little by little from physical constraints, but he is all the more the slave of abstract ones.* He acts through intermediaries and consequently has lost contact with reality. . . . He no longer knows wood or iron or wool. He is acquainted only with the machine. His capacity to become a mechanic has replaced his knowledge of his material; this development has occasioned profound mental and psychic transformations which cannot be assessed[35] [my emphasis].

The liberation of the machine has, therefore, resulted in the slavery of abstraction. Humans have lost their primary associations with the marrow of life. As a result, nothing in human existence, including religion, is the same anymore.

Ellul interprets autonomous technique as the religion of our day in the sense that it has taken over, or overtaken, the traditional ideas and function of morality. In an extended description of this phenomenon, he writes:

> Technical autonomy is apparent in respect to morality and spiritual values. . . . Morality judges moral problems; as far as technical problems are concerned, it has nothing to say. Only technical criteria are relevant. . . . Thus, technique theoretically and systematically assures to itself that liberty which it has been able to win practically. Since it has put itself beyond good and evil, it need fear no limitation whatever. It was long claimed that technique was neutral. Today this is no longer a useful distinction. . . . The power and autonomy of technique are so well secured that it, in its turn, has become the judge of what is moral, the creator of a new morality. Thus, it plays the role of creator of a new civilization as well. This morality—internal to technique—is assured of not having to suffer from technique. In any case, in respect to traditional morality, technique affirms itself as an independent power. Man alone is subject, it would seem, to moral judgment. We no longer live in that primitive epoch in which things are good or bad in themselves. Technique in itself is neither, and can therefore do what it will. It is truly autonomous.[36]

Thus, for Ellul, technique has escaped the strictures of morality and traditional values, *by creating a new arena for its own activity*. In this sense, technique is *not* a direct attack upon the traditional values of our cultural heritage. If it were, it would doubtlessly be attacked as an enemy by the guardians of that heritage. This creative force is what allows technique to assume autonomous proportions, and to remain unhindered as it continues to extend its power in our lives. The result is that many interpreters frame the problem in the wrong way: the central point is not really the problem of the neutrality of technique (it can be used for good or evil), rather it is the fact that technique renders *our* traditional values neutral (our perception of good and evil is no longer meaningful). Technical solutions to problems have replaced moral solutions.

Technique as a creative force is the key to Ellul's description of it in terms of that aspect of existence we conventionally term the sacred, the spiritual, or the mysterious. Thus, although "man cannot live without a sense of the secret," autonomous technique works counter to it. He writes:

> The invasion of technique desacralizes the world in which man is called upon to live. For technique nothing is sacred, there is no mystery, no taboo. . . . Technique worships nothing, respects nothing. It has a single role: to strip off externals, to bring everything to light, and by rational use to transform everything into means. More than science, which limits itself to explaining the "how," technique desacralizes because it demonstrates (by evidence and not by reason, through use and not through books) that mystery does not exist. Science brings to the light of day everything man has believed sacred. Technique takes possession of it and enslaves it. The sacred cannot resist. . . . The mysterious is merely that which has not yet been technicized.[37]

Autonomous technique does not explain away the mysterious; it creates something new that reveals the mysterious to be unreal. If something exists outside the technical realm that claims human attention, then it is "assailed" by technique. By its very nature, technique cannot allow the independent existence of anything other than itself. Its creative force takes possession of everything which it encounters, religion being no exception to this rule. Because humans cannot live without a sense of the sacred, they follow the next logical course of action, they transfer their "sense of the sacred to the very thing which has destroyed its former object: to technique itself."[38] It is with the convergence of these two powerful forces—the human necessity for the sacred, and the autonomous creative power of technique—that Ellul lays the intellectual framework for theologically addressing technology. What, then, is the theological track record of the church for this technological challenge?

The answer to this question is to be framed in the larger one of the Christian role itself in technological development. Historically, the issue is clear-cut. Since technique rose to dominance first in the "Christian West," must not this religious tradition assume much of the blame of bringing to reality the harbinger of its own demise? Ellul finds that the answer is no, once the historical evidence has been properly analyzed. As Christianity rose to dominance in the Roman Empire, for example, he approvingly notes the decline of Roman organization. He maintains, therefore, that "it is not a coincidence that Rome declined as Christianity triumphed. The Emperor Julian was certainly justified in accusing the Christians of ruining the industry of the Empire."[39] This nontechnological character of pure Christianity is evident in Christian centuries subsequent to the break-up of the Roman empire. Thus, "the society which developed from the tenth to the fourteenth century was vital, coherent, and unanimous"; but it was characterized by a total absence of the technical will. It was a-capitalistic as well as a-technical. It is true that "very feebly a technical movement" began to take shape already in the twelfth century, but this "developed under the influence of the East." Therefore, he maintains that "the technical impetus of our civilization came from the East, at first through the intermediacy of the Judaei (a particular kind of trader) and the Venetians, and later through the Crusades." In this way, the following conclusion is established: *"The technical movement of the West developed in a world which had already withdrawn from the dominant influence of Christianity"*[40] [my emphasis]. Therefore, Christianity cannot be held accountable for the general course of Western civilization which has resulted in the dominance of technique.

Besides the chronological one of historical development, Ellul notes that two additional arguments have customarily been given for the theological point of view that Christianity "paved the way for technical development": (1) It suppressed slavery, an institution that held technique in check, and (2) it secularized nature, thereby giving rise to technique. Ellul disagrees with both of these conclusions. Concerning the fact, he finds that "there was in fact greater technical progress in civilizations where slavery was prevalent (for example, Egypt) than in others where that institution was practically unknown (for example, Israel)." Therefore, he finds no absolute relationship between technique and the absence of slavery. Second, he maintains that the association of secularized nature (which Christianity did, in fact, bring about) and the rise of technique is specious. Rather the promoting technique, a desacralized view of nature inhibits the natural tendency toward a form of prototechnique itself: magic. Christianity therefore, deprived man of the natural "powers," or gods of nature which man could put at the service of technique. In all instances, therefore, Christianity is exonerated historically as a force in the development of the technique of the East. Rather than aiding the development of technique, Christians consistently asked the moral question, *which came from outside technique itself,* "Is it righteous?" Once a particular technique was considered righteous "from *every* point of view, it was adopted, but even then with excessive caution" (author's emphasis). In this way, Ellul concludes:

> The search for justice before God, the measuring of technique by other criteria than those of technique itself—these were great obstacles that Christianity opposed to technical progress. They operated in the Middle Ages in all areas of life, and made history coincide with theology.[41]

Once the true historical record is known and Christianity is seen as an obstacle to technical progress, rather than an agent of it, the major question looms as to how faithfully modern Christianity has adhered to its own traditional critique of technique.

In general, Ellul is unforgiving in his criticism of Christianity in the modern West. The few prophetic voices, such as that raised by Kierkegaard, were to no avail:

> In the middle of the nineteenth century, when technique had hardly begun to develop, another voice was raised in prophetic warning against it. The voice was Kierkegaard's. But his warnings, solidly thought out though they were, and in the strongest sense of the word prophetic, were not heeded. . . . They were too close to the truth.[42]

The church had already adopted itself too closely to the rise of technique, especially in the more advanced industrialized nations. Witness the primary instance of this in England, where the Puritans "even after their political failure, were the predominant influence." He sees them as having "exploded all prevailing religious taboos and developed a practical and utilitarian mentality that emphasized the use of and even the exploitation of the good things of this world given by God to men." The Church of England itself had adapted "a kind of secularization of religion." For it, "religion is no longer the framework of society, it can no longer impose its taboos or forms upon it.

Rather, it integrates itself into society, adjusts to it, and adopts the notion of social utility as criterion and justification." The result of the loss of the religious framework of society was the rise of a certain plasticity which came to characterize other societies after the English experience, for example, France and America. In France, the monarchy took the leadership role in advancing technique through the propagation of scientific academies and institutes. The American setting itself benefited enormously from the entire European experience, especially this new social plasticity that the demise of Christianity brought forth:

> In the United States [the convergence of the state and private technical interests] took place at the beginning of the nineteenth century. Until then, the society of this country was inorganic. But at the time the American social milieu was favorable; moreover, the Americans profited from the technical consciousness evolved in Europe, and so they arrived immediately at a model for technique. Giedion has noted that the Americans began by mechanizing complex operations, which produced the assembly line, whereas the Europeans tended to mechanize simple operations, such as spinning. This American accomplishment was the result of the exceptional flexibility of the American milieu.[43]

The result is that Americans, who must have some sort of ordering principle in their society like everyone else, instigated something to substitute for the Christian church and the monarchy as traditional structuring forces. In particular, the fluidity of democratic America freed the way for the free, intense, and relatively unhindered development of technique. The new religion of technique would develop in this cultural ethos most intensely of all, with the Myth of Man as its centerpiece.[44]

Based on our discussion thus far, it is not surprising that Ellul argues that technique has penetrated the "deepest recesses of the human being."[45] This has been accomplished by the way in which it has modified the entire environment in which human existence now takes place. This environment includes "everything that goes to make up his milieu, his livelihood, habitat, and habits." But this modification extends beyond such practical considerations, and includes the more abstract realms of space and time. His discussion of space centers around the loss of *Lebensraum* brought about by the effects of the increased technologization of life. In terms of the problem of time, he finds Mumford's discussion of the centrality of the clock in the technical society to be directly on target. While the discussion of time does not seem to play as central a role in Ellul's text as it does in Mumford's, he clearly presupposes the work of the latter on this problem:

> Today the human being is dissociated from the essence of life; instead of *living* time, he is split up and parceled out by it. Lewis Mumford is right in calling the clock the most important machine of our culture. And he is right too in asserting that the clock has made modern progress and efficiency possible through its rapidity of action and the co-ordination it effects in man's daily activities.

The clock, therefore, is the machine par excellence that adapted humans to all other machines. Ellul dates this split of abstract time from lived time during the sixteenth century with the introduction of private clocks:

> Thenceforward, time was an abstract measure separated from the traditional rhythms of life and nature. It became mere quantity. But since life is inseparable from time, life too was forced to submit to the new guiding principle. From then on, life itself was measured by the machine; its organic functions obeyed the mechanical. Eating, working, and sleeping were at the beck and call of machinery. Time, which had been the measure of organic sequences, was broken and dissociated. Human life ceased to be an ensemble, a whole, and became a disconnected set of activities having no other bond than the fact that they were performed by the same individual. Mechanical abstraction and rigidity permeated the whole structure of being.

The real importance of this text lies in the way that posits the clock as the fundamental means whereby individual humans are disassociated from organic, physical processes. Human adaptation to the machine, in other words, could only take place once the primal unity with nature was severed. The human body was the final stronghold of resistance that fought the penetration of the machine into the center of human consciousness; the clock was the instrument of abstraction designed to overcome this resistance.

CONCLUSION: RELIGION, TECHNOLOGY, AND THE FRAGILITY OF TIME

The theology of technology ought to be grounded on the conception of the manipulation of time as indicated in the Primordial History of the book of Genesis. These texts represent the most basic understanding of evil which the biblical tradition opens up to us, an evil that seems to have accompanied the growth of big technology in the modern age. The insightful work of Orwell and Ellul assures us that this ancient perspective remains vital in the modern world. In the language of theology, Gen. 1-11 undergrids the long-standing Christian viewpoint that the full appearance of the kingdom of God is not something to be manipulated by man, nor forced by him into his own space. To "force" in the sense of the post-Genesis 11 environment in which we live, means to capture the kingdom under the terms of our manipulation of time and space. Modern technology, as Orwell and Ellul describe to us, operates in an environment where human power and ability to manipulate have achieved unforeseen levels of achievement. The theological implication of this is that, while humans have the ability to find security "for a time" in the defense of our self-defined space against the perceived chaos of nature and/or social relations through the manipulation of time (as frequently witnessed in modern technology), such acts rob us of the proper human role of "watching and guarding" the natural order. The concluding story of the Primordial History—the account of the Tower of Babel—is the enduring biblical symbol for the loss of the authentic human place in the world—a mythic description which ontologically establishes the framework for the phenomenon of modern technology as viewed by Orwell and Ellul.

The recognition that time is fragile, somehow mysteriously capable of being molded and shaped according to purely human instrumental ends, is perhaps the most distinctive ontological contribution which religious thought can make to the modern study of technology. The picture which emerges from the Bible is that only in a posture of non-aggressive interpretation of time may we achieve the means and purposes for which we were created. Only insofar as we allow time to remain outside the narrow anthropocentric interests which characterize modernity may we be truly open both to the creative power of God which time is meant to symbolize. It is in this sense that transcendence and the authentic humanness which proceeds from the full recognition of transcendence may become realities in our lives. Both Orwell and Ellul, albeit in quite distinctive ways, stand at the forefront of that chorus of modern prophetic voices which reminds us of the viability of this ancient insight that also forms the foundation of our biblical heritage.

NOTES AND REFERENCES

1. Cf. Egbert Schuurman, "A Christian Philosophical Perspective on Technology," in *Theology and Technology,* Carl Mitcham and Jim Grote, eds. (Lanham, New York, London: University Press of America, 1984), pp. 107-109.

2. Robert A. Oden, Jr., in "Divine Aspirations and Atrahasis and in Genesis 1-11," *Zeitschrift für die alttestamentliche Wissenschaft,* 93:2, 214, writes: "That they (the first humans) should immediately attempt to establish for themselves a lasting reputation, as did the masons in Gen 11, is predictable."

3. George Orwell, *1984* (New York: New American Library, 1984), p. 228.

4. Alexis de Tocqueville, *Democracy in America,* transl. George Lawrence; J.P. Mayer and Max Lerner, eds. (New York: Harper & Row, 1966), p. 670.

5. Orwell, p. 153.

6. Lionel Trilling, "Orwell on the Future," in *Nineteen Eighty-Four to 1984,* C.J. Kuppig, ed. (New York: Carroll & Graf, 1984), p. 162.

7. Orwell, p. 175.

8. Orwell, p. 126.

9. Orwell, p. 126f.

10. Alfred Kazin, "Not One of Us," *The New York Review of Books* 31(10):14 (June 14, 1984).

11. Orwell, p. 201.

12. David Goodman, "Countdown to 1984: Big Brother May Be Right on Schedule," in *Nineteen Eighty-Four to 1984,* C.J. Kuppig, ed. (New York: Carroll & Graf, 1984), p. 294.

13. George Woodcock, "Utopias in Negative," in *Nineteen Eighty-Four to 1984,* C.J. Kuppig, ed. (New York: Carroll & Graf, 1984), p. 87.

14. Kenneth J. Arrow points out that the Party does not even use all the technology available to it. This is seen, for example, in the fact that Orwell portrays an economy that has retrogressed

from its prewar levels. Cf. Kenneth Arrow, "The Economics of *Nineteen Eighty-Four,"* in *On Nineteen Eighty-Four,* Peter Stansky, ed. (New York: W.H. Freeman, 1983), p. 44.

15.   Orwell, p. 176.

16.   Lawrence, Malkin, "Halfway to 1984," in *Nineteen Eighty-Four to 1984,* C.J. Kuppig, ed. (New York: Carroll & Graf, 1984), p. 121.

17.   Mark Crispin Miller, "The Fate of *1984,"* in *1984 Revisited,* Irving Howe, ed. (New York: Harper & Row, 1983), p. 28.

18.   Orwell, p. 198.

19.   Orwell, p. 176.

20.   Orwell, p. 32.

21.   Orwell, p. 36.

22.   Orwell, p. 176.

23.   Jacques Ellul, *The Technological Society* (New York: Alfred A. Knopf, 1966).

24.   Ellul, p. xxv.

25.   Ellul, p. 12.

26.   Ellul, p. 6.

27.   Ellul, p. 3.

28.   Ellul, p. 5.

29.   Ellul, p. 111.

30.   Ellul, p. 4.

31.   Ellul, p. 4.

32.   Ellul, p. 146.

33.   Ellul, p. 6.

34.   In an article in which Ellul studies the first chapters of Genesis, he summarizes his theological position on technique and The Fall:

> I did not say that technique is a fruit of sin. I did not say that technique is contrary to the will of God. I did not say that technique in itself is evil. I said only that technique is not a prolongation of the Edenic creation, that it is not a compliance of man to a vocation which was given to him by God, that it is not the fruit of the first nature of Adam. It is the product of the situation in which sin has put man; it is inscribed exclusively in the fallen world; it is uniquely part of this fallen world; it is a product of necessity and not of human freedom.

See "Technique and the Opening Chapters of Genesis," in *Theology and Technology,* Carl Mitcham and Jim Grote, eds. (Lanham, New York, London: University Press of America, 1984), p. 135. Thus, he understands Adam as having a relation of *human necessity* to the world after "The Fall."

35.   Ellul, p. 325.

36.   Ellul, p. 134.

37.   Ellul, p. 142.

38.   Ellul, p. 143.

39.   Ellul, p. 34.

40.   Ellul, p. 35.

41.   Ellul, p. 38.

42.   Ellul, p. 55.

43.   Ellul, p. 58ff.

44.   Ellul, p. 390.

45.   Ellul, p. 325.

THE DIALECTIC OF APOCALYPSE AND UTOPIA IN THE THEOLOGICAL ETHICS OF JACQUES ELLUL

Darrell J. Fasching

ELLUL'S PARADOXICAL USE OF THE RHETORIC OF "APOCALYPSE" AND "UTOPIA"

Few claims about Jacques Ellul would seem more paradoxical (that is, "contrary to appearances") than the one I wish to make; namely, that he is a "utopian thinker." You do not have to read very far in Ellul before you discover that he considers utopian thought the primary myth of our technological civilization, whose sole function is to render human beings totally subservient to its necessities. We will put up with any dehumanization, he argues, we will accept any demand for efficiency and give up any freedom, as long as we believe we shall be rewarded with utopia. If there is such a thing as fate or necessity in a technological society, if technology has a certain autonomy, it is because we have been seduced into surrendering ourselves to

Research in Philosophy and Technology, Volume 10, pages 149-165.
ISBN: 1-55938-062-4

its demands in return for the promise that it will fulfill our wildest utopian dreams for comfort, for pleasure, and for success. The technological society will "not be a universal concentration camp," Ellul tells us,

> for it will be guilty of no atrocity. . . . Our deepest instincts and our most secret passions will be analyzed, published and exploited. We shall be rewarded with everything our hearts ever desired. And the supreme luxury of the society of technical necessity will be to grant the bonus of useless revolt and of an acquiescent smile.[1]

Ellul considers utopian thought to be an escapist reaction to that which cannot be prevented, and a "consolation in the face of slavery."[2] Constructing such utopian fantasies, he says, is the favorite pastime of intellectuals. But the fantasies of a Campanella, a More, or a Fourier, Ellul argues, "do not seem to have played the slightest historical role in the past nor foretold any future reality. . . . I fail to see a positive value in utopian views. They do humanity no good. Whenever men have taken utopian descriptions seriously, the result has been disastrous."[3]

Despite this, we continue to feed on a diet of technologically and politically utopian hopes, seeking freedom and fulfillment, only to end up in slavery and alienation. The technology that promises us freedom and security seems to create a progressively less free and more insecure world, day by day. In a technological society, every positive action seems to generate in an equally negative reaction—a world of plenty becomes a world of pollution, and a world made secure by "star wars" becomes the most insecure world of all. We are attracted by the utopian possibilities of technology, only to find ourselves faced with an apocalyptic future.

These are the dominant symbols of the sacred and the profane in a technological society—the sacral face of a technological utopia of security and abundance and the profane and terrifying face of an apocalyptic atomic holocaust. *The central myth of a technological society is the ambivalent Janus-faced myth of apocalypse and utopia.* Its very ambivalence tells us we are in the presence of a new sacred reality—for the sacred is readily identified, as Rudolf Otto pointed out, by the ambivalent emotions of *fascination and dread.* In our case it is a fascination with utopia, and a dread of an abrupt apocalyptic end to the human race.

The sacred always manifests itself through whatever form of power is experienced as ultimate (i.e., as the power determining human destiny). In the pre-modern world, that power was nature. Nature promised all the good things of life, and at the same time revealed herself as capable of arbitrary and capricious life-taking violence. As such, nature induced emotions of fascination and dread, and human beings sought to placate this awesome power by myth and ritual through which they conformed themselves to her order. Today, says

Ellul, it is technology which plays the role nature once did. Because technology is that power which desacralized nature, it has come to replace nature as the ultimate power that governs human destiny. Today it is technological civilization which inspires us with fascination and dread and the motivation to conform. Even as nature once seduced peoples into making human sacrifices in exchange for its promised benefits, so today it is technology which exacts these requirements. So we are led into ever deeper levels of subservience to the technological phenomenon by the shining hope of a utopian future, even as we paradoxically find ourselves daily moving closer to the precipice of apocalyptic self-destruction. The more we seek the first, says Ellul, the closer we come to the second. Our hope paradoxically seems to create a hopeless situation in which each person feels as if they are unable to act, unable to make difference, "unable to make history, and . . . knows that now there is no other person making it either, only blind mechanisms, obscure powers, inexplicable interactions."[4]

But Ellul, in his usual iconoclastic manner, inverts the meanings of *apocalypse* and *utopia* in his own theological writings. *Where the world embraces utopian hopes and fears apocalyptic scenarios, Ellul embraces apocalyptic hopes and fears utopian scenarios.* The slight of hand by which this reversal occurs is what he calls thinking in congruence with the dialectic of Biblical thought.

DIALECTICAL METHOD AND ELLUL'S ETHIC OF NEGATION

Ellul's basic analysis of our technological society divides it into three interlocking components; efficient technique, political illusion, and mass media myths. The root phenomenon is the use of the most efficient techniques in every area of human endeavor. Once efficiency becomes the dominant criterion for all action in society, all freedom to organize social life according to any other scale of values is doomed to failure, because the less efficient cannot compete with the more efficient. Hence techniques become totalitarian and autonomous, requiring humans to conform if they wish to survive. People have the illusion, however, that they are in charge of their technology through the mediation of politics. But it is just that, says Ellul, *an illusion.* Upon closer examination, behind the scenes, we find that politicians have become amateurs in a world of experts upon whom they depend to provide them with the most efficient solutions to our technological problems. As a result, politics has become no more than an empty ritual which helps to conform us to the technical demands for efficiency. But the key component which sustains this combination of necessity and illusion is the mass media.

If, as Ellul argues, technology has become the new bearer of the sacred and politics a kind of religious ritual for bringing us into conformity with its demands, it is the mass media which provide the mythologies which turn us into willing automatons. It is the media which promote the mythologies of the utopian progress of history via the techniques of science and the science of techniques. These utopian mythologies, by promising us the world of our dreams, seduce us into a total, although unconscious, surrender of our will to the demands of technical efficiency as the price of entry into this utopia. This surrender results in giving to technique an unwarranted autonomy without really having consciously decided to do so. Hence, our utopian hopes become the means whereby technology becomes our fate. It is as our fate, then, that the dark side of our technical society comes back to haunt us with the inverse side of the utopian mythos, persistent media images of impending apocalyptic doom, primarily envisioned as nuclear holocaust. Thus, apocalypse and utopia are inextricably linked mythic themes in a technological society.

Ellul tells us that he is an admirer and proponent of the dialectical theology of Karl Barth, although he makes it clear that he does not hesitate to depart from Barth when he finds himself in disagreement with him. What he admires and emulates in Barth is his faithfulness to "the remarkable dialectic that appears throughout the Bible, even in the least of its writings."[5] "We need," says Ellul, "to maintain the rigorous Biblical dialectic" of judgment and grace emphasized by Barth.

> The "Yes" of God is pronounced in relation to a previous "No." Without the "No," there is no "Yes". . . . The "No" pronounced by God over man and his works and his history is a "No" which is total, radical and ever present. . . . "Yes" makes no sense unless there is also the "No," and I regret to point out that the "No" comes *first,* that death comes before resurrection.[6]

As Ellul explains it, the dialectical tension that the Gospel sets up in its hearers, the tension between the Gospel and the world, became embodied in his work in a dialectical conversation between the Bible and *Das Kapital.* Caught in the conflict and tension of these two opposing ways of looking at the world, he refused to give up either. Marx, he says "changed the way I read the Bible. . . . I absolutely could not divorce the Biblical demand from the concrete economic or political reality. For me the two necessarily went together."[7] If Karl Barth eventually came to help him appreciate this tension between the Gospel and the world as itself Biblical and dialectical, Marx helped him correct the most glaring inadequacy in Barth's thought, his abstractness. Barth, he argues, failed to insert his dialectic into the real world of the twentieth century. His examples tend to imagine the world too abstractly, and portray it as a world more typical of the nineteenth than the twentieth century.[8] What is needed to make Barth's dialectic effective in our world is someone like Marx, who has taken the trouble to do a detailed analysis of our actual social world; but Ellul has no more taken over Marx wholesale than he has Barth. Marx, too, needs revision. He needs to be brought up to date, for it is no longer economics, he argues, but technology which dominates society and has become the engine of history. Thus, as with Barth, Ellul rethinks and reworks Marx, and develops his own theological position in a dialectical tension between these two Karls.

As Ellul fleshed out this dialectic in his life's work, now numbering over forty books, a kind of Kierkegaardian strategy of authorship took shape. Although not populated with as many *personae* as Kierkegaard's authorship, it soon became apparent that there were two different Elluls. There was the unflinching sociological realist who painted a picture of the technological society that was so bleak that he was commonly portrayed as a fatalist. And many assumed from this work that Ellul was either a sectarian or a romantic who wished to escape from this world into some simpler past world, or some remote pocket untouched by our technological civilization. Nothing, however, could be further from the truth. To see what Ellul was up to, however, one had to read the "other" Ellul—the theologian. In his theological work Ellul doesn't suddenly turn into some kind of naive optimist, but here he does speak, at least modestly, of hope and freedom as a possible within a technological society.

Is Ellul's goal really to transform the technical society, or simply a strategy to make the best of a bad situation? For the most part his rhetoric (even his theological rhetoric) deliberately chooses a pessimistic, almost sectarian, tone that seems to suggest that if we have to live in this world, the best we can hope for is to limit, to some modest degree, the demonic impact of technical necessity. Is that all we can hope for? Or is it possible that we might actually transform our civilization and enable technology to be an instrument of human freedom rather than the imposition of an impersonal fate? Ellul insists that freedom and transcendence (i.e., the ability to "go beyond" the world as given) can only occur through a radical Barthian "No" to our technical society. *The question is:* "Is this "No" truly dialectical, as Barth advocates, or is it a nondialectical negation of the world? Is Ellul's "No" that of the revolutionary bent on transforming society, or that of the sectarian advocating withdrawal from our technological culture?

Ellul's position on this, it seems to me, is ambivalent. In *The Ethics of Freedom* he tells us that his dialectical ethics embraces Barth's distinction of the three stages or moments in the relation between the Word of God and our culturally human words. First the Word *appropriates* our words (i.e., speaks to us by using our language), then the Word *contradicts* our words (i.e., the "No" of judgment which seeks to bring about repentance, rebirth, and a transformation of meaning), and finally the Word *expropriates* our words to convey the freedom of the Gospel (i.e., the "Yes" of God to our words now transformed so as to communicate transcendence).[9] There are times when it seems as if Ellul has abandoned this dialectic and the "No" he pronounces has become an absolute "No," an end in itself. There are other times when it seems as if Ellul can really envision a "Yes" following upon the "No."

In the first case, much of *The Meaning of the City* comes to mind, where Ellul speaks pessimistically of "the illusion of improving the world."[10] Here he seems to suggest a sectarian ethical model, a living in exile, as Israel once did in Babylon. In this sectarian model the situation of Christians is viewed as one in which "the city cannot be reformed ... [and] the church is in captivity," and must learn to live within this captivity.[11] At other times, he talks as if the goal is to bring about a fundamental social and cultural transformation. In one of these moments Ellul argues: "There is no possibility of turning back.... It is our duty to find our place in our present situation and in no other. Nostalgia has no survival value in the modern world."[12] He insists that the ethical challenge can be summed up in two questions:

1. Is man able to remain master in a world of means?
2. Can a New Civilization appear inclusive of technique?[13]

While both of these attitudes are present in Ellul's work, usually the "No" receives greater emphasis than the "Yes." The question is whether this greater emphasis leads to a breakdown of his dailectic into a sectarian dualism. To answer this question, we need to turn to an analysis of a level of complexity in Ellul's dialectical ethics which we have ignored up until now.

A TYPOLOGICAL ANALYSIS OF ELLUL'S DIALECTICAL ETHICS

In his ethics, Ellul draws on the work of Karl Barth and the nineteenth century philosopher Soren Kierkegaard. His fundamental stance on Christian ethics goes back even further, to the theologies of the Reformation, and especially of Martin Luther. H. Richard Niebuhr characterized Luther's theology of paradox as embodying one of five fundamental types of Christian ethic.[14] The extremes are embodied in *Christ against culture,* or sectarian Christianity, at one end of the spectrum, and *Christ of culture,* or cultural Christianity, at the other end. The first rejects society as totally corrupt and stands against culture, withdrawing to live behind sectarian walls (e.g., certain of the apocalyptic Anabaptist movements of the Radical Reformation). The second so identifies Christianity with the cultural status quo that the ideals of the Gospel become confused with, and reduced to, the ideals of the culture (e.g., certain forms of Christian liberalism).

According to H. Richard Niebuhr, there are three types of Christian ethic which have tried to mediate between the extremes of the *against culture* and *of culture* positions. For our purposes, two are of immediate interest. The Augustinian-Calvinist model of Christians *transforming culture* and Luther's *paradoxical model* of the relationship between the Christian and culture. In his own paradoxical way, I believe Ellul combines these two with the *against culture* model. To borrow from the phraseology of Noam Chomsky, I would argue that the *surface structure* of Ellul's ethic sets the *against culture* and *paradox* models in dialectical tension in order to generate a *deep structure* which is *transformational*.

The surface structure, which forms the explicit horizon of Ellul's ethical thought, is in large part derived from the ethics of paradox embodied in the work of Martin Luther. But this surface structure is doubly paradoxical, for it combines sectarian apocalyptic rhetoric with a Lutheran rhetoric of paradox. Ellul draws on the apocalyptic sectarian traditions of Christianity with their ethical pure-ism, harsh judgments of the world, anarchism and anti-institutionalism. Although he draws inspiration from these traditions, he is not a sectarian. Far from it.

One of the core insights of Luther's theology is the paradox that every Christian is always, at the same time, both a saint and a sinner. Luther's notion of "justification by faith" grew out of his experience that, although moral perfection is impossible, he was still acceptable to God through his faith. God accepted him, he said, as if he were blameless and a saint, in spite of being a sinner.

The paradox of being a saint in spite of being a sinner leads Luther to a paradoxical ethic. Thus, for instance, unlike the sectarian, he sees no problem in someone being both a hangman and a Christian at the time.[15] These two roles reflect the dual modes of God's rule over the world through state and church—the left hand of God's justice and wrath, and the right hand of God's grace and mercy, respectively. The secular public role of the hangman reflects the need for an ethic of realism about the corruption of the world. In spite of that, the possibility remains, for this same hangman, in his personal relationships, to transcend this cynical realism and exercise compassion and forgiveness. In any given society, one must be prepared to play both roles, in Luther's view, since even a society of saints would remain a society of sinners.

Luther's ethic is basically pessimistic. Its rehetoric is very similar to that of sectarian Christianity whose pessimism is so great that it gives up all hope in this world and seeks to withdraw from it. Such sectarianism, however, is really a peculiar kind of naive optimism which believes that it is really possible for an individual to leave the corrupt world behind, stop being a sinner, and become a saint, instead. Luther finds that incredible. Realistically, the best one can do, he thinks, is accept the paradox that we will always be both a saint and a sinner. In Luther's view, there will always be a need for two distinct ethics, mediating the corresponding paradox of God's justice and mercy. In this context Luther comes to understand "vocation" as a calling from God to be in the world paradoxically.

Ellul advocates a similar position in his "ethics of freedom," but with an important difference. Where Luther reconciles these two ethics by making one public and one private, Ellul insists that both be exercised in the public realm. In place of Luther's insistence that the public order is divinely decreed and cannot be changed, Ellul argues that God decrees both order and (eschatological or apocalyptic) openness to change and transformation.[16] Where Luther's paradoxical ethic establishes a complementarity between two separate spheres (private/inner and public/outer), Ellul's paradoxical ethic establishes dialectical tension between two mutually limiting public modes of action (political/technical ordering and apocalyptic/eschatological freedom), each of which requires the other. For Ellul, there really is no such thing as "a Christian ethic," only the ethical inventiveness of Christians. Christian ethics is invented out of the irreconcilable dialectical tension between the Gospel and the world. In our world, that translates into a dialectical tension between the Gospel and the technological ethics of efficiency. The point is not to resolve this tension but, rather to maintain it. It is this very tension which prevents the ethics of efficiency from making an absolute claim on one's life, and thus from realizing its totalitarian potentiality.

For Ellul, it is *apocalyptic* hope which creates this tension and introduces the possibility of an ethical freedom to revolt against at least some of the determinations that converge upon one. An ethic of freedom, he argues, requires the possibility of transcending or going beyond the world as given. In our situation, that means breaking with the utopian order of efficiency. Such a thing is not possible as long as all our hopes are embodied in the technical society. Only one who has a hope in something *wholly other* than this society can exercise the freedom to contravene its order and live by a scale of values other than that of the utopianism which keeps us conformed to the world. Thus, only communities of Jews and Christians who live by such a hope in the Wholly Other can introduce authentic freedom into our technological civilization. Ellul calls this enabling hope apocalyptic, not because he literally expects the world to come to an end, but because the kind of hope represented in the Apocalypse (i.e., *Book of Revelation*) is a hope in the "Wholly Other" which brings about a radical break with the world as it is, in order to inaugurate a new creation. The communities of apocalyptic hope become the mediators of God's transcending freedom whereby the old world is brought to an end and a new creation begins. Thus, Ellul's dialectical thought leads us into a reversal of the popular culture's position of "utopian hope" and "apocalyptic dread," to embrace instead, an *apocalyptic hope* and a *utopian dread.*

This radical hope gives birth to an ethic of holiness, that is, of separation from the world. Unlike the sectarian, he is not speaking of physical separation but of psychological and spiritual separation (i.e., a change of hopes) from the claims for hope and meaning offered by a technological society in favor of hope in the Wholly Other. It is, he says, "separation only for the sake of mission. The break has to come first but it implies rediscovery of the world, society and one's neighbor in a new type of relationship."[17]

Like Luther before him, Ellul displays a certain pessimism about altering human nature. He totally objects to all ideologies of revolution which argue that if we can only transform our social infrastructure, then all our problems will be solved. An ethics of freedom is possible, he argues, only if we recognize that freedom occurs in dialectical tension with, and transgression of, the limits of any and every social order.[18] The notion that we can pass through a social transformation and arrive in some realm of pure freedom is simply fantasy. Rather, freedom is a constant task requiring a "permanent revolution" in which we must continually transgress the limits of social order in the name of higher values in order to keep society open to further development. An ethic of freedom can only be one which is constantly opening up a breach in the present order so that freedom might be possible within it.

And yet there is a kind of remote and guarded optimism in Ellul. He seems to suggest that in the long run (although probably not in our lifetime), such an ethic of paradoxical tension can actually have a transformative effect on our technological civilization, making it possible for technology to be the servant of humanity rather than the master. The technological society was formed by numberless individual decisions over centuries and its transformation will have to occur in a like manner. The ultimate goal is to create a new complex of civilizational values which transcend yet include technique, such that technique will serve human development. For "life is given us in order that we accomplish these works and make scientific progress."[19] Thus, the deep structure of Ellul's thought reflects the Augustinian-Calvinist goal of transforming culture, and stands in some tension with the surface structure of the ethics of paradox. It is as if Ellul were saying that *the ultimate paradox is that the ethic of paradox is really an ethic of transformation.*

This ethic of paradox emerges out of the dialectical tension created when Ellul fuses the Lutheran ethic of dual roles with the apocalyptic ethic of anti-institutional anarchism. Ellul's placing of the Lutheran ethic of paradox in dialectical tension with the apocalyptic sectarian ethical tradition seems to have eliminated the worst and drawn the best out of each stance. From Luther he has retained the importance of paradox without accepting Luther's institutional fatalism. Ellul counters that fatalism with the anti-institutional anarchism of the apocalyptic tradition, but forces that tradition out of its sectarian withdrawal in order to unleash its anti-institutional force right in the middle of our technological institutional order. In so doing, the apocalyptic element acts as a catalyst upon the paradoxical element in the surface structure of his ethic, and that potent mixture in turn promotes an ethic of transformation at the level of deep structure.

ELLUL'S DIALECTIC RECONSIDERED:
FROM APOCALYPSE TO UTOPIA

Using Niebuhr's typological analysis of fundamental stances in Christian ethics, I have tried to unravel the complexity of Ellul's dialectic in order to show why Ellul often appears to be holding contradictory positions. Fundamentally, I think Ellul's position is this: In the short run the only way to make a dent in our technological civilization and have any impact on it is to assume a sectarian attitude of negating the world. But one must do so without leaving the world—hence the paradoxical element in his ethic. In the long run, however, I think Ellul believes that such an ethic can have a transforming impact upon even a technological society, fundamentally altering the relationship between human beings and technique, so as to transform techniques into instruments of human freedom. Hence, the dialectic in the surface structure of his ethic generates a transformational ethic in the deep structure. The surface structure determines the short range effects of ethical action, and in the process sets in motion the long range effects of the deep structure. Ellul's contradictions at the level of surface structure are strategic, serving the logic of transformation at the level of deep structure.

That complex dialectical logic is not carried through in his apocalyptic and utopian rhetoric. Rather than being related dialectically, these two themes seem to represent a non-dialectical dualism in his thought. Insofar as that is true, the "No" in his ethics is in danger of becoming an absolute, dualistic, and sectarian "No" rather than a dialectical and transformative "No." At this point, Ellul's phobia about the word "utopia" seems to overcome his good sense as a dilectical thinker and leaves him with a blind spot. As a result, he fails to follow through on his own dialectical logic, and he fails to see that the Biblical apocalyptic tradition is a prophetic or iconoclastic form of utopianism.

Ellul's treatment of the theme of revolution offers us a direct analogy for assessing his dialectical logic. In general, Ellul opposes violent revolution. He sees it as an expression of the sacralization of technique. Revolution, he argues, is the sacred time of chaos whose sole purpose is to reestablish sacred order. Just as the ancient kings of Babylon were ritually dethroned during the new year festival only to be ritually reenthroned to reestablish sacred order, so every revolution since 1789, Ellul argues, has only served as a ritual for reestablishing the sacral order of the technological nation-state.[20] The names may change but the structures remain the same, for the period of the anarchic revolutionary inevitably gives way to the reestablishment of order under the guidance of bureaucratic administrators.[21] That is why a technological civilization can permit the "useless revolt" with an "acquiescent smile," as Ellul puts it.[22] Revolution itself has been co-opted and integrated into the system through the power of the sacred.

One might expect, therefore, that Ellul would forbid Christians to be involved in revolutionary movements. But that is not the case at all. On the contrary, he argues that Christians ought to be involved in revolutionary movements in order to insert the element of freedom into them. The task of the Christians is to desacralize and demytholigize revolutionary movements, on the chance that they will be able to insert a real element of transcendent freedom into these movements and enable the participants to break free of their political and technological illusions. If that were to happen "political absolutes" and "technological solutions" would be replaced with the art of compromise. Instead of seeking meaning, fulfillment, and salvation from politics and technology, these would come to be seen as useful and helpful, but no cure for human finitude, and no substitute for human choice. Technology and politics no longer being absolutes, the possibility of spontaneous social development, and the subjugation of politics and technology to other values could then occur. That would be a true revolution, and one which can only be initiated by those who have a hope in that which is other than the political-technological order. Thus, Ellul urges Christians to be involved in revolution in order to *rehabilitate* the meaning of revolution and make a true revolution possible.[23]

Implicit in this scenario is the Biblical/Barthian dialectic of appropriation, contradiction, and expropriation. The Christian revolutionary begins by *appropriating* the common meaning of "revolution," then seeks to *contradict* its common meaning by demythologizing and descralizing it, and then finally seeks to *expropriate* the term "revolution" to communicate a new meaning, one that introduces genuine transcendence and transformation, and not simply a reestablishment of the old sacral order. This dialectical process Ellul calls "rehabilitating the sacred."[24]

Contrary to popular usage, Ellul uses the terms "sacred" and "holy," not as synonyms but as antonyms. The sacred is the reverse image of the Holy (i.e., the Wholly Other). The sacred is part of this world, a part "willed by God for its preservation."[25] The sacred is created by God to establish order and stability in the human world, but it is intended to remain open to its source and goal. However, to the degree that sacral order becomes an autonomous order separated from God, it becomes a fixed and demonic order, a reverse image of the Holy, which renders the institutional order of society into an absolute and totalitarian oppressive order. If the Holy can be reintroduced into and dialectically related to the sacred order of society, that order can be "rehabilitated" so that it once more becomes a true image of the Holy, eschatologically open to further development in the direction of the freedom and justice characteristic of the Kingdom of God as envisioned in the Biblical vision of the New Jerusalem.

For instance, Ellul argues that when the state assumes the sacred aura of an absolute power, the law becomes an ideological expression, protecting the special interests of those who hold power. But when the state is desacralized and is seen as a limited and relative institution, then it becomes the guardian of the law and is itself answerable to the demand for justice. The law develops spontaneously and autonomously, and keeps the nation centered in justice. The law mediates a transcendence which, while providing society with an order, at the same time serves to keep society open to further development and transformation which is not ideologically skewed in favor of ruling elites. In such a situation, the future is no longer subject to the whims of human ideological politics but rather reflects the *politics of God,* the reign of transcendence through which society assumes an eschatological orientation.[26]

The ethical task of those who live by apocalyptic hope, as Ellul envisions it, is to insert the dialectical tension of the Wholly Other into this closed world and through the dialectic of appropriation, contradiction, and expropriation, rehabilitate the sacred by desacralizing and sanctifying it (i.e., claiming it for the freedom and transcendence of God), which opens the sacral order to eschatological transcendence and transformation.

Now the question is: if *revolution* as sacral phenomenon can be rehabilitated, why can't *utopia*? Ellul argues that utopianism is the dominant myth of a technological civilization which both expresses and reinforces its sense of sacral technical order. It, like revolution, seems an excellent candidate for dialectical rehabilitation. Instead, Ellul treats utopianism like the plague. Perhaps he is reluctant to spell out the long range transformative or utopian effects of his ethic of negation because he believes that, once the short range strategy of negation desacralizes the social order, its ultimate transformation is no longer in human hands. It depends now upon the politics of God. But if so, then why is he willing to spell out the transformative effects with respect to revolution?

Utopianism as an expression of human hope, it seems, is beyond the pale of God's saving and transforming power. At this point, Ellul breaks with his own dialectical logic and transforms his dialectical negation into an absolute negation. In so doing, he has violated one of the cardinal rules he laid out for an ethic for Christians in *To Will and To Do*; namely, "whoever receives the revelation of God should give heed to men's hope, not in order to tell them that they are deluded ... but to help them give birth to their hope."[27] Human hope in a technological civilization takes the form of a utopian hope for a new world, a better world, a transformed world. By the logic of Ellul's own dialectic, he ought to be seeking to "rehabilitate" this hope. Indeed, insofar as the long range goal of his ethic is transformation, he is in fact seeking to do this, but his attempts are self contradictory to the degree that he refuses to entertain the same possibility for utopianism that he entertains for revolution.

The problem is that Ellul fails to appreciate the utopianism of the very apocalyptic tradition which stands at the center of his thought. In this regard, he could learn from his theological colleague Gabriel Vahanian, and from Karl Mannheim's sociology of knowledge. Karl Mannheim, one of the founding fathers of the sociology of knowledge, constructs a very interesting argument in his book, *Ideology and Utopia,* for the roots of utopianism in the apocalyptic tradition, and of the importance of that tradition to the making of history.[28] Utopias, he argues, introduce a tension into the present order of things which is creatively disruptive. Without this tension we would live "in a world in which there is never anything new, in which all is finished and each moment is a repetition of the past. ... With the relinquishment of utopias, man would lose his will to shape history and therewith his ability to understand it."[29] If one substituted the word *apocalypse* for the word *utopia,* Ellul could have written this very same statement and, in substance, has.

Even more to the point, however, is that in tracing the history of utopianism, Mannheim identifies the apocalyptic tradition as the most important source for his kind of radical utopianism. He cites the apocalypticism of Thomas Munzer as an example, and argues that this kind of apocalypticism embodies a radically utopian mode of transformative consciousness "in which the impossible gives birth to the possible and the absolute interferes with the world and conditions actual events."[30] This utopian consciousness introduces an attitude of "tense expectation" in which "the promise of the future which is to come is not ... a reason for postponement, but merely a point of orientation, something external to the ordinary course of events from where he (i.e., an individual) is on the lookout, ready to take the leap." Such apocalyptic utopianism "sees revolution as a value in itself, not as an unavoidable means to a rationally set end."[31] Again, these could just as easily be Ellul's words describing the intervention of the Wholly Other in the world of technical necessity through the mediation of apocalyptic hope.

For Mannheim, the utopian mentality is revealed in those "hopes and yearnings" which give rise to an inherently iconoclastic mode of consciousness "incongruous with the state of reality within which it occurs." It is the mode of consciousness which inspires those actions which tend to "shatter, either partially or wholly, the order of things prevailing at the time ... [and] break the bonds of the existing order."[32] The problem as Mannheim sees it is that utopias get confused with ideologies, and for good reason, since an ideology deliberately masquerades as a form of utopian consciousness but actually serves to maintain the status quo. Ideologies promise change but deliver more of the same old thing, whereas the utopian mentality unmasks such ideologies and forces transformative change. The relationship between ideology and utopia is rendered extremely problematic by the fact that in the real world the two are almost always found intermixed. Every ideology contains utopian elements and every utopia contains ideological elements. One sure sign of an ideology, however, is its propensity for making absolute claims upon the social structure. To the degree that these claims are relativized by the power of the apocalyptic element, to that degree the utopian can be liberated from its ideological straight jacket and serve to shatter and transform the existing order of things.

Mannheim's distinctions, however, could offer Ellul a way of recovering the rehabilitative dialectic which he seems to have abandoned with respect to the utopian. All Ellul needs to do is admit that there is more than one kind of utopianism. The kind of utopianism which Ellul wishes to renounce is ideological utopianism—the ideology of a technological civilization which promises change and substitutes the illusion of change. This would not, however, preclude the rehabilitation of the utopian mentality through an iconoclastic introduction of an apocalyptic utopianism. An apocalyptic utopianism would be a utopianism stripped of its ideological components under the impact of a genuine apocalyptic mode of consciousness. Such a utopianism would be the result of the relativization and desacralization of technological utopianism so as to open it up to that genuine change and transformation which Ellul characterizes as an eschatological openness to the future.

The thrust of Gabriel Vahanian's theological critique of Ellul, partially rooted in Mannheim's work, has been precisely to chide Ellul for not recognizing that there is such a thing as a Biblical form of utopianism, an iconoclastic form of utopianism which Vahanian would take to be normative for recognizing an authentic utopianism.[33] Ideology, argues Vahanian, "from the classless society to valueless ethics ... afflicts man with visions of another world. By contrast, utopia, like the kingdom, is moved by the vision of a new world, radically other than the 'other world' itself. ... Echoing, as it were the biblical view of the world as creation, utopia holds that only the *novum* is realizable, everything else being nothing but repetition."[34]

Like Ellul, Vahanian would claim that if our world has been desacralized, the sacred has disappeared in one form only to reappear in another. It is as "supernaturalism" that the sacred has met its demise, but only to give way to the sacred as "the utopian arena of transcendence."[35] The human, which becomes a possibility through the word, is limited neither to nature nor history, but transforms both through speech—the word made flesh and a new creation (*novum*). It is as a creature of language that the human comes to expression as technological and utopian. "Far from being a robot, technological man is the man who makes himself."[36] Indeed, "there is no humanity without technology. The human itself depends on techniques, and utopia is ultimately nothing other than a technique of human technologies."[37]

It remains only for the utopian to be linked with eschatology, Vahanian argues, in order to give birth to the *novum,* a genuinely new creation of the human in which we discover our utopianism in the image and likeness of the God who has no image.[38] The Christ event, the word made flesh, is but the affirmation of the coming of the human, the affirmation that human destiny is tied not to nature, nor history, nor the utopian techniques through which it comes into being, but to the eschaton.[39] In Christ the human person is not trapped in a "human nature," but experiences a truly utopian invitation to become a new creature, here and now.[40]

In Vahanian's view, the deliverance of technological utopianism from its propensity to become an ideology depends on an ecclesial revolution as the foundation for a cultural revolution.[41] For the Church to engage in this revolution, which could open up the language of technological utopianism to its eschatological possibilities, it must first of all *appropriate* the language of technological utopianism so that it might *expropriate* technological utopianism as a language of faith.[42] Make no mistake about it. Vahanian preaches no "Christ of Culture." He is not baptizing technology. "Utopia is not the kingdom. Utopia is to the kingdom as nature is to creation, or as history is to redemption, or, simply as the flesh is to the spirit. If there is a relationship between them, it is one of radical otherness."[43] It is this relation of radical otherness which gives to faith its iconoclasm, that pivotal "No" of the Barthian dialectic which makes a revolutionary expropriation of technological utopianism possible.

Vahanian has followed through on the Barthian dialectic precisely at that point where Ellul has remained reticent—at the point of transition from *negation* to *expropriation*. In a way that Ellul has not, he has been willing to imagine what it would be for the word to become flesh in a technological civilization, an imaginative act which is at once both eschatological and utopian. For "technological utopianism is focused neither on the past nor on the future, but on the present, on the time of the human, the only time with which God could be contemporary, the only time attuned to the fullness of the time, pleroma of the God who comes."[44]

To be sure, Vahanian, like Ellul, also has his phobias. If Ellul is phobic about utopianism, Vahanian is phobic about apocalypticism, which he equates with an ideological dualism more concerned with *changing worlds* than *changing the world*. Ellul's work should serve as a reminder to Vahanian (who already acknowledges a large indebtedness to him) that Biblical apocalypticism is not about *changing worlds* but precisely about *changing the world*. The mutual recognition of this fact would allow for a distinction between "ideological utopianism" and "apocalyptic utopianism"—one which would serve both Vahanian's and Ellul's purposes well. For Vahanian's eschatological *novum,* like Ellul's *apocalypse* of the eschaton, is nothing other than the presence of the Wholly Other in the here and now which makes all things possible and all things new.[45]

What I hope this discussion of Mannheim and Vahanian does is make clear that Ellul has an option which he has not fully availed himself of, one which would make his position more consistent with his own stated canon of dialectical logic. If the language of a technological society can be characterized as a language of technological utopianism, then it is crucial that the Barthian dialectic, which Ellul subscribes to, be carried through to its logical conclusion. It is not enough to say "No" to technological civilization. One must follow the "No" with a "Yes," a "Yes" to the utopian possibilities of technological civilization as the vector of new beginnings and new creation. There are signs that, in fact, Ellul has begun to move in this direction. In a letter to me he indicated, to my surprise, that in fact he found Vahanian's treatment of utopianism "very convincing."[46] Also, Ellul refers to the theme of utopianism in his book, *The Humiliation of the World,* in a way that is unexpected and uncharacteristic of him. Here, for the first time, insofar as I can tell, Ellul refers to "utopias" as belonging "to the order of truth ... known and created by the word."[47] Perhaps, after all, Ellul is prepared to extend his project of "rehabilitating the sacred" to a rehabilitation of utopianism. This I think could lead to a rethinking of the possible relationships between *technique* and the *word,* linking biblical utopianism to technological utopianism, inaugurating new creation, and new beginnings for our technological civilization.[48]

NOTES AND REFERENCES

All references are to books by Ellul unless otherwise noted.

1.   Jacques Ellul, *The Technological Society* (New York: Vintage Books, Random House, 1964), pp. 426-427.

2.   *The New Demons* (New York: Seabury Press, 1975), p. 117.

3.   "Search for an Image," in *Images of the Future,* Robert Bundy, ed. (Buffalo: Prometheus Books, 1976), pp. 24, 25.

4.   *Hope in Time of Abandonment* (New York: Seabury Press, 1973), p. 42.

5.   *The False Presence of the Kingdom* (New York: Seabury Press, 1973), p. 9.

6.   Ibid., pp. 23-24.

7.   *Perspectives on Our Age* (New York: Seabury Press, 1981), pp. 5-7.

8.   *The Ethics of Freedom* (Grand Rapids: William B. Eerdmans, 1976), p. 457.

9.   Ibid., p. 164.

10.   *The Meaning of the City* (Grand Rapids: William B. Eerdmans, 1970), p. 37.

11.   Ibid., p. 57, 72-73.

12.   See "The Technological Order," in *The Technological Order,* Proceedings of the Encyclopedia Britannica Conference, Carl F. Stover, ed. (Detroit: Wayne State University, 1963), p. 19.

13.   Ibid., p. 14.

14.   H. Richard Niebuhr, *Christ and Culture* (New York: Harper & Row, 1951). The five types are: (1) the Christian *against* culture, (2) the Christian *of* culture, (3) the Christian *transforming* culture, (4) the Christian and culture in *paradox,* and (5) the Christian affirming a Christ *above* culture.

15.   Paul Althaus, *The Ethics of Martin Luther* (Philadelphia: Fortress Press, 1972). See especially Chapter 4. The example of the hangman is discussed on p. 74.

16.   See my book, *The Thought of Jacques Ellul* (New York and Toronto: Edwin Mellen Press, 1981), especially the discussions of the sacred and the Holy on pp. 115-121, 162-176.

17.   *The Ethics of Freedom,* p. 7.

18.   Ellul says that he favors anarchism as a political strategy of revolt against the authority of all political institutions. He does not think anarchists can be successful in destroying the state. But in a world where all nation-states tend to absolutize their power, only a strategy of anarchism (non-violent in his case) can make a dent in the bureaucratic social order so as to make some modicum of freedom possible. See *Ethics of Freedom,* pp. 395-398.

19.   *The Meaning of the City,* p. 180.

20. *Autopsy of Revolution* (New York: Alfred A. Knopf, 1971), pp. 160ff, and *The New Demons,* Chapter 3. The Babylonian illustration is mine, but the point is Ellul's.

21. *The New Demons,* pp. 84-87.

22. *The Technological Society,* pp. 426-427.

23. See *The Ethics of Freedom,* p. 398ff, and also my discussion of Ellul's treatment of the role of Christians in revolutionary movements in *The Thought of Jacques Ellul* (New York and Toronto: Edwin Mellen Press, 1981), pp. 156-161.

24. See *Ethique de la liberté* (Paris: Labor et Fides, 1975), tome II, p. 48.

25. *The Presence of the Kingdom,* pp. 134-135.

26. *Theological Foundations of Law* (New York: Seabury Press, 1960), pp. 137-138.

27. *The Presence of the Kingdom,* p. 81.

28. Karl Mannheim, *Ideology and Utopia* (New York: Harcourt, Brace & World, 1936). See especially Chapter 4, "The Utopian Mentality."

29. Ibid., pp. 262-263.

30. Ibid., p. 213.

31. Ibid., p. 217.

32. Ibid., pp. 192, 199.

33. See Gabriel Vahanian, *God and Utopia: The Church in a Technological Civilization* (New York: Seabury Press, 1976).

34. Ibid., p. 38. The *novum* referred to here should be understood as that which is genuinely new and not just the kind of change which is superficial. The *novum* clearly must not be equated with some ideology of progress. On the contrary, *novum* suggests "new creation," new beginnings, the grace or forgiveness which enables one to start afresh. It approximates what Ellul would characterize as the eruption of the apocalyptic or eschatological end (i.e., God) here in this present moment which gives birth to a transcending and transforming freedom.

35. Ibid., p. 49.

36. Ibid., p. 137.

37. Ibid., p. 44.

38. Ibid., p. 137.

39. Ibid., pp. 45, 46, 54.

40. Ibid., p. 71.

41. Ibid., p. 92.

42. Even as supernaturalism once appropriated and expropriated the language of nature.

43. Vahanian, *God and Utopia,* p. 137.

44. Ibid., p. 154.

45. Vahanian tends to treat "apocalypse" and eschatology" as terms with opposing meanings which one must choose between, whereas Ellul tends to virtually equate these terms.

46. Dated May 2, 1982.

47. *The Humiliation of the Word* (Grand Rapids: William B. Eerdmans, 1985), p. 230.

48. Since writing this article, I have had further confirmation of a shift in Ellul's thinking on this matter. At the conclusion of the major address which Ellul gave to the Society for the Philosophy of Technology conference on *Democracy and Technology* at the University of Bordeaux in the summer of 1989, after a somewhat pessimistic assessment of prospects for the future, he concluded by saying that the only hope for the future lay in the direction of "utopianism" in the sense that "my good friend Vahanian uses that term." When I asked him about this change after the speech, he said that for a long time he resisted Vahanian's utopian approach, but gradually he became convinced by it.

ARTIFICIAL INTELLIGENCE AND WESTERN CULTURE:
A CHRISTIAN APPROACH

Gabriel Vahanian

Such is the paradox of our age and its strange predicament that the most technologically-oriented of all civilizations, the civilization of the West, should seem impervious to the spiritual energy it has all the same unleashed. Although all cultures are rooted in the past, none have ever been so beckoned by the future as has Western culture, and that by reason of its own religious tradition. Also, no other culture has so squandered its religious tradition as to be so uncertain of its own future. Undecided, Western culture thus either betrays its past, or returns to the past and buries itself in it as an ostrich does its head in the sand.

Research in Philosophy and Technology, Volume 10, pages 167-183.
Copyright © 1990 by JAI Press Inc.
All rights of reproduction in any form reserved.
ISBN: 1-55938-062-4

TOOLS TO CYBERNETICS

No derision is intended here. Ambivalence about the human reality runs deep in the core of our being, and has done so for so long that we can't remember where we come from. Or else, that is all we can remember, if only because, suddenly, we are unable to remember where we are going, with the result that our ambivalence is quite out of proportion both with our knowledge of what human reality actually is like, and our sense of its mystery. We forget that, whether God-made or man-made, the human potential—ever a hope of man and/or woman—lies nowhere except in that exclusively human ability, speech. Human potential lies nowhere except in the embodiment of language, just as God is to be found nowhere except in and through the Word become flesh, an embodiment ultimately bound to remain irreducible whether to physiology, or to biology and psychology, or to cybernetics, or to whatever else is at hand. Born of language, the human reality lies beyond man or woman, and human it remains, unsurpassably, insofar as its condition is a verbal condition, and hence is indebted to a technique, to language, however at once natural and cultural or, for that matter, artificial, it may be.

"Nature diversifies and imitates. Artifice imitates and diversifies," wrote the same Pascal (1976, 84; fragment 120) who defined man as "a thinking reed," and invented a calculating machine as if to show that the difference between nature and artifice is as heavy or, eventually, as thin as technique—even so thin, indeed, that no technique makes it possible to tell the difference, except by making it impossible to reduce the human to that by which it is seduced. Even as nature always is to the artificial second nature if not *technē*, a metaphor of language, so too technology is technē if not second nature and, again, a metaphor of language. "Natural" and "artificial," thus being metaphors of language, find in speech their point of greatest convergence as well as of greatest divergence, as illustrated by phrases like "thinking" *reed* and "thinking" *machine*. Obviously, Pascal is concerned neither with the reed, nor with the machine, but with the thinking that takes place in spite of them, the verb that transfigures them; not with the analogical relation between reed and machine, nature and artifice, but with the language of which they are each a metaphor. Language is, indeed, as different from either as metaphor is different from analogy, or the human from both reed and machine. Or, again, logos from logic. Language is incarnate, while to humans, nature, like artifice, is always second nature or technē, a metaphor of language. Language has, therefore, a logic of which the logic of either reed or machine is ever shy, although they each supply language with a metaphor and, ultimately, not only the technique we deserve, whether by way of tools or by way of cybernetics, but also a philosophy. "The thought of every age is reflected in its technique," Norbert Wiener pointed out in a rather pregnant fashion (1948, 49), while we realize that the thought of our age still needs to be fleshed out.

Bedazzled or nonplussed as we may be today when confronted with the apocalyptic prowess of humans and the magic quality of our technology, we must at least admit one thing, namely: that if the computer, a more complex and flexible mechanism than any so far invented, threatens the supernatural vision of the real, it also liberates us from sheer materialism. Or, to put it more appropriately, it liberates language from those twin distortions spawned by the principle of analogy at either end of its spectrum, whether in terms of materialism or supernaturalism, and in any of their surrogates. Indeed, the greatest lesson of technology is precisely that analogy can be simulated. Not so the metaphor.

Words are to language as are data to the computer, or nouns to verbs, or analogy to metaphor—or thinking to speaking. Like language, a computer "thinks": it simulates. Unlike language, it cannot "dissimulate" itself; it cannot cross itself out and give way to the metaphor, the verbal point beyond which language can only be surpassed by language, and the human by the human even as Adam is surpassed by the Christ, or Babel by Pentecost; or, on yet another level, as nature is by Creation, and history by Redemption, when, through the paschal metaphor, the human reality lies beyond both nature and artifice—in the Word, in language.

Nature, history, or, for that matter, technology may help provide language with appropriate metaphors, from thinking reed to thinking machine. Their symbols, however, tend in the end to become mere symbols, as is the case with mathematics. They die. But then they must die if language, and language alone—because it is essentially metaphoric (A is and is not B)—is to be surpassed by language and become as embodied as the human is irreducible and is irreducibly meant to escape the snares of analogy (A is to B as C is to D).

Admittedly, analogy has been a hallmark of Western thought. In spite of its roots in both the Greek and biblical notions of logos or of *nomos* and torah, analogy has, throughout its history, consisted in a continuous record of a failure whose nadir is reached when spirit and the flesh, subject and object are split from one another. Not that it all begins with Descartes, but, impressed like Leibniz by clockwork mechanisms, Descartes considered the animal as a machine and, in his *Traité des passions de l'âme* of 1646, likened the human body itself to a machine. To be sure, he did not take the final step: a small one, inevitably to be taken, as it was by La Mettrie when he wrote *L'homme machine*, a book now probably more famous for its title than for its content (Ashby, 1966, 98-99). Technology is already as fascinating as magic once used to be—unless, of course, magic itself was already a form of technology, whether in the shape of the Greeks' theatrical *mechanē* or their more philosophical understanding of technē. And it is technē that lurks behind many a definition of the human, from Plato's featherless biped and Aristotle's rational animal, to the brain as a computer; from the myth of man, to the human as a technique.

Great, to be sure, is the difference between a tool and a computer, between a machine and artificial intelligence or—to use a more proper phrase—expert systems. It is as great as the difference between the determinism of a calculating or any other kind of machine, and an expert system based on heuristics. It is a difference which, perhaps, must be understood less in terms of a shift from determinism to some principle of uncertainty than, for example, in keeping with the fact that light can be understood both in terms of particles and in terms of waves, two theories which cannot be reduced to one another, and yet are carried by one and the same language, as are the natural and the artificial.

What is specific to language is that, through it, humans both break off with nature and escape from artifice. If the natural is not reflected by it without ceasing to be merely natural, neither is the artificial processed by it without ceasing to be merely artificial. Human beings do not simply grow wings instead of building airplanes; we do not simply operate on the principle of analogy but on that of metaphor. Is it, then, any wonder that the thought of every age should be reflected in its technique (Wiener, 1948, 49; cf. 50-51)? Without language, there would have been no technique.

Interestingly, the more language is symbolic, the more technology is rudimentary. From the hammer to cybernetics, even while technology moves from muscles to brain, and becomes more symbolic, language itself—the very condition of all that is human—ceases to be merely symbolic. The Good Life itself is no longer to be understood in terms of changing worlds but—in keeping with the biblical tradition—in terms of changing the world; not *after* death, but *in spite of* death.

At this point, there is no reason left to be surprised at the claim made by Hubert Dreyfus when he contended that it is our philosophical tradition itself that leads straight into artificial intelligence. He wrote: "With the exception of Merleau-Ponty, from Socrates to Husserl through Plato, Descartes and Kant, philosophers have tried to determine rules that govern human conduct as well as the conditions, both sufficient and necessary, of understanding." Even for Husserl, Dreyfus argued, "mind grasps reality as an ensemble of graded rules just as do information engineers when they set up their models" (1985, 30). Whether, or how, Dreyfus sustains his case is surely, for our purposes, beside the point. It deserves consideration if only because it recalls another argument which dealt, not with the Greek heritage, but with the biblical tradition, and, at the height of the ecological crisis, blamingly attributed the devastation of nature and its technological plundering to the Judeo-Christian tradition (White, 1973). Leaving aside the question whether technology or, for that matter, ecology itself was properly assessed through that kind of sweeping criticism, what concerns us here is the contention that technology does have more than superficial affinities with the biblical tradition and its conception, both of Creation as such and the human role in and over-against nature on the one hand and, on the other, of the human reality as determined by its exclusive relation to God rather than to nature—regardless, if not just because, of physiology or biology or any other type of consideration. Not that nature as such is denied. What is denied is the idea of a *saving* nature: only God can save. Nature was never meant to be devastated, but kept up just as, subsequently, medieval theology affirmed the world by affirming that grace does not abrogate, but perfects nature. Which means that, in the biblical perspective, the Good Life is never severed from the goods that sustain life.

At any rate, whether technology harks back to the biblical tradition or stems from the Greek heritage, two things must be pointed out: appearances to the contrary notwithstanding, affinities between the Greek mind and the biblical vision are by far more substantial than all the superficial dissymmetry that may leap to the eye; on the other hand, by developing technology, Western culture has been consistent with itself and bears out the premises of its twofold origin in Athens and Jerusalem (about which Tertullian, unlike Saint Paul, missed the point altogether [as I have tried to show in "Ni Juif, ni Grec..."]).

But then, what is technology? In the light of this present sketch, suffice it to say that, as tool, technology simply consists in extending the human hand and that, by contrast, considered in terms of cybernetics and so-called artificial intelligence, it tends to alter what is meant by human nature as well as our understanding of ourselves. Formerly dealing with physical ability, it now deals with intellectual ability and already can even simulate the brain. But, lo and behold, it cannot quite simulate the brain without, at the same time, pointing out what, after Kierkegaard, can be called an infinite qualitative difference between the brain and the mind or the spirit. A difference which language alone can account for, and is for that very reason constantly *deferred*—through language—to language. Through language, is the human not that which can be traced back to its origins, but that which is *without precedent*? The idea of creation ex nihilo is thus *theologically*, if not logically, correct. From a biblical point of view, the ultimate question does not deal with what things are in themselves; it deals with the contention that, whatever is, is once and for all. Put differently, nothing is—except de novo. Temporality is not procrastination, but prolepsis, anticipation and hope. There is no being except in terms of a *new being*. Hence, only through language is man that which he is not and is not that which he is. Likewise, *simul justus et peccator*, the sinner is the only one who can say "I believe." The past having no claim on him, he now is *without precedent*. Like Adam, like the new creature in Christ.

Hence, not only the thought but also the spirit of every age is reflected in its technique. If artificial intelligence is consistent with Western culture and its understanding of reality, human and otherwise, the fact is that the real is nowhere so real as when it depends, not on an analogical understanding of things, but on the metaphorical power of language. In light of this, nothing, for example, is spiritually true unless it can also be literally true, just as the flesh is the condition of the spirit, or the human is the condition of God, and language is the condition of the word which is with God and is God (Jn 1).

THE MIND IS NOT A BRAIN

We need a new symbolic order. To that end, however, we must first avoid conclusions reached, although perhaps much too understandably, on the basis of hasty considerations concerning the rather awesome character of mechanical and electronic or even biological devices that, indeed, outperform all hitherto known human performance. At first physical, now intellectual, one wonders what level the process is going to reach next. It is a process that, in the last fifty years, has outdone what previously had been accomplished in one or two hundred thousand years! This process has been so sudden and has occurred so quickly that the feeling of a malaise is no figment of the imagination. Such a malaise, however, is one that affects us not only technologically, but also intellectually; not only materially, but also spiritually. It affects us scientifically and philosophically, as well as theologically, culturally and religiously.

In order to cope with this malaise, patchwork solutions will not do. It runs so deep that the remedy calls for a radical about-face of such a magnitude as can occur only if we do not turn our back on Western culture, especially since technological civilization already encompasses at once the West and the whole planet. Tradition is the price of such a cultural mutation; just as a cultural mutation is the price of tradition. The remedy needed is a symbolic order, freed from the shackles of a world view once dominated by a sacral understanding of reality and the various types of dualism and dichotomies thereby brought down to our age. True, technology desacralizes everything. However, we must remember that religion is not wedded to the sacred, at least not from the perspective of the biblical principle of iconoclasm, in the light of which God, and God alone, is holy. Thus is ushered in a dialectic of the holy and the not yet holy, and its dynamics, in contrast to the static dichotomy of the sacred and the profane (Cf. Vahanian, 1986a and 1986b). Indeed, the process of desacralization—as ambiguously experienced as it is ambivalently assessed— did not have to wait for technology in order to start moving. It was already set in motion by biblical religion and its singular exclusion of either temple or any other type of sacred precinct from the Garden of Eden or from the New Jerusalem; in a word, from its utopian vision of the world—a world in which swords are changed into ploughshares and the lion lies down with the lamb (Is 11; Gn 1; Rev 21:22). Ever since the first tool entered into human service, up to the most complex computerized mechanism, the sacred has progressively yielded to utopia, and the environment (*Umwelt*) to the world (*Welt*). Likewise, being and the thing-in-itself have yielded to language and the word, to communication and relatedness, or *communion*. At the same time, technology reaches another level of the human reality.

Take, for example, a bulldozer. For certain tasks, it is doubtless more efficient than a man. It affects him, however, only externally; but the bulldozer is and remains lame without human intervention. The situation is quite different when we consider the significance of a machine that thinks and can command machines, which command still other machines (Warnier, 1984, 101); as well as when we are led to admit, as did Wiener, that "the logic of the machine resembles human logic" (1948, 149), and that, as even H. Simon acknowledged, with machines that think, learn and create, the gamut of problems they will be able to treat will soon reach such a level that they will equal if not surpass the human mind (Olivet, 1986, 17).

But, then, has the human mind not always surpassed itself? If, to paraphrase the earlier quotation from Dreyfus, artificial intelligence is the secret of Western logic, what is new is not so much computing as the computer. Once that is admitted, it must be noted that, marred as Antiquity was by the cleavage between intellectual and manual activity, it had nevertheless managed to liken the functioning of the mind to that of what today would be called a computer (Dreyfus, 1985, Olivet, 1986). The fact is, however, that now the computer is realized, the logic of it remains essentially the same. Nor will it, one can surmise, differ much if and when, as scientists expect, today's electronic computer gives way to one built on, or including, molecular biology as well. At worst the precariousness of human existence will be felt in another key, at another level, and the human task will be no less demanding than it has ever been, whether ethically or otherwise.

Far more significant is the question that remains: whether the human reality is reducible to logic. However complex the program, a computer deals with data, whether digital or symbolic, whether deterministically or heuristically oriented. It will *simulate* intelligence: at first, to be sure, only a part of it; and later, regardless of how large that part becomes. As Hubert Dreyfus pointed out, human intelligence is a global phenomenon mobilizing the whole of our knowledge from the moment of perception onward (1985, 32). It makes no difference whether "that very man who can conceive logical processes and can build the machines meant to handle them is himself not able to do rigorously what he knows how to have done by those same machines" (Warnier, 1984, 20; cf. Couffignal, 1964, 118). To be sure, we have moved from machines that did what man could not do, to machines that do what man can do. But they proceed differently: machines proceed sequentially and only simulate the human brain, which proceeds globally and thinks with the whole body (Warnier, 1984, 110; Couffignal, 1963, 93; Faugeras, 1984, 156). The human brain minds, and reminds us that the mind is not a brain.

BEYOND INTELLIGENCE: THE HUMAN

The computer treats data; thought deals with knowledge. Whatever degree of correspondence is set up between data and knowledge, they must not be confused, if only because they are not of the same nature (Warnier, 1984, 16). Simulation, should it ever achieve what is beyond expectation, will nevertheless remain, Bolter stated, nothing more, if nothing less, than "a matter of educated trial and error, of balancing one option against another, of minimizing evils and maximizing benefits" (Bolter, 1984, 11). At best, simulation shows that artificial intelligence is "an exercise in symbolic logic" (ibid.), the "system" of which is, perhaps, not unlike that of a living organism (Dreyfus. 1972). Given this kind of understanding of what a system is, it is most likely that, eventually, "we shall make human thinking less mysterious and machine operations more so"(Good. 1971), as is already the case with expert systems dealing with medical diagnosis.

Does it follow that the human act of intelligence is thereby devalued? An experienced pilot does not "literally" think about what he does but remains intelligently in control. By contrast, a simulator forces the apprentice pilot to follow the rules step by step until the point is reached when, unless he "survives" the simulator, he will not qualify as pilot. Even the most expert medical system remains under the control of a human expert.

In view of such considerations, it seems evident that, far from debilitating human knowledge, the more an expert system becomes efficient, the less it dispenses with human control, even if, we must add, the latter's still unprogrammed part of knowledge is gradually reduced to 10, to 5, or to 1 percent. The human expert will then work, if not in another field, at least on another, not yet "domesticated," method. More important still, the human expert works on what he does not know, while a computer works only on what it "knows." But does it ever know what it does not know? And if not, is it anything more than a prosthesis?

To be sure, a prosthesis is a prosthesis, whether it consists of a transplanted human organ or of an electronic piece of equipment. The difference, existentially if not physically, is rather thin, or is bound at least to become thinner and thinner. However, no one thinks of a type of surgical operation, affecting us physiologically or even biologically, as devaluating in itself—so long as, of course, the existential question, "Who am I?" remains a live option. Indeed, who am I when some other body's heart beats in mine?

Or has technology, by the same token, come to mean something quite different from what it has meant so far; thus, perhaps, explaining why it is felt, or perceived, to be devaluating the human person rather than "relocating" it? Could it be that this idea of devaluation is itself a result of the first industrial revolution, when technology was geared to a rather particular field of human activity—economics? If so, debatable as artificial intelligence may be, is it not the case that, through it, technology has moved from an earlier materialism towards a set of concerns that address the human quest in realms other than that of economics? Does it not follow that the closer technology comes to simulating one human activity after another, the more it presses us into raising precisely those questions in the light of which the human reality remains irreducible, and irreducibly religious?

For that reason, Norbert Wiener seems less than convincing when he observes that, the first industrial revolution having resulted "in the devaluation of the human arm by the competition of the machinery," chances are that "the modern industrial revolution is similarly bound to devalue the human brain act at least in simpler and more routine decisions" (1948, 37). The irreducibility of the human must have escaped his attention: not to mention the fact that, in each case, it is only "routine" activities that are struck with so-called devaluation. Wiener acknowledged that "just as the skilled carpenter, the skilled mechanic, the skilled dressmaker have in some degree survived the first industrial revolution, so the skilled scientist and the skilled administrator may survive the second" (ibid.). Does Wiener then mean that he would prefer a society governed by less-than-skilled administrators? Of course, he doesn't. Something keeps him from stating clearly what he means when, "taking the second [or the third and nth] revolution as accomplished," he adds, laconically, that by then "the average human being of mediocre attainments or less [will have] nothing to sell that is worth anyone's money to buy" (ibid.)! Why? At least, in that respect, the situation will be no worse than it has or should have been. At best, it could well be that, by then, we will have moved closer to a society based, globally speaking, "on human values other than buying or selling" (ibid.)—on the idea of the Good Life entailing the goods that make it a good life. Utopia? Maybe, but a utopia neither more nor less realizable than the Old Testament vision of a land where the rich have nothing too much and the poor lack nothing (Ex 16:18; II Cor 8:15); or than the apostle Paul's vision of the Body of Christ, a church where there is neither Jew nor Greek, neither male nor female, neither master nor slave (Gal 3:28).

Calling man a thinking reed, Pascal himself never imagined he was devaluating him. However, in 1836, Heine visited England and noted that machines seemed like men, while men seemed like machines (Pollock, 1957, 131). Echoing an age-old commonplace, he overlooked the fact that, in Pollock's words, "technology has always transformed man" (ibid., 132); indeed, it consists in humanizing even the human. Through technology, the human puts itself into question, and that question is basically a religious question, if only because religion is ultimately less bound up with nature than it is with culture and, hence, with technology. Religion is bound up with "archeology" much less than it is with eschatology. Religious man is an artificer, a *pontifex*— bridging the ideal and the real or, for that matter, God and Caesar, by precisely rendering unto Caesar what is Caesar's and what is God's unto God. Lying between God and Caesar, the human also lies between the natural and the artificial and is reducible to neither: human is, indeed, that than which, or for which, God is radically other. And it makes no difference whether one regards the human as basically religious, or considers the human as irreducible except to that which is human.

This approach seems to me far more significant than all the self-congratulatory statements of those who, delusively, would assign the human to some reservation still off-limits to technology (even as, presumably, American Indians, in their reservations, or God, in the role of filling gaps in nature, were somehow held off the limits of science and technology). For instance, it is entirely beside the point to argue, as Couffignal did, that once mechanisms could reproduce, their "offspring" would no longer be artificial (1963, 100); or, more sedately but in an equally "reservationist" mood, to take comfort, as did Bouveresse, in the fact that, if simulators have invaded practically every field of Homo sapiens, they are met with strong resistance by Homo sentiens (1985, 7; cf. Dreyfus, 1985). The fact is that today a machine can already read a book aloud, and in English, or see its way in a room.

Except for Narcissus, why should one mistake for oneself one's image reflected by a mirror? Does one need anything other than one's own image to look at and say, "This is not human," as does Magritte of his celebrated picture of a pipe with the legend: "This is not a pipe?"

True enough, at present, computerized systems still rely exclusively on electronic devices. When biomolecular components are also included in the make-up of such systems, and the human brain is directly connected with them, when some kind of symbiosis is thus achieved, will Homo sapiens have then surrendered to some Machina sapiens? Addressing himself to this question, René Du Bost simply recalled what, of all people, La Mettrie once said: "Man is so composed a machine that it is impossible to have any clear idea of it in the first place, and consequently to define it" (Du Bost, 1972, 5). Or else how could that other achievement, "the great achievement of electrical engineering," also be "the most philosophical of all machines" (Bolter, 1984, 12)? Nor is there any way for the mirror *not* to be a mirror. Narcissus turns into Narcissus only because he loses control of the mirror, I mean, of himself. No machine escapes human control. Only the human, being all too human, can lose control of the machine (Warnier, 1984, 108). For that very reason, whatever the problem, it is not a technological problem: it lies beyond the purview of technology as such (Couffignal, 1963, 103-104).

Put differently, so long as artificial intelligence (though a misnomer) remains artificial, and is yet much more efficient than human intelligence, their respective operations will differ *toto coelo*. No matter how much know-how, if not knowledge, on its arcane, or mystical, or, simply, existential dimension is transferred to computers of the future, human moral obligation will be left whole and wholly inalienable.

EXPERTISE AND DECISION:
THE HUMAN EXPERIENCE

It used to be that we spoke not only of God as a mystery, but also of the mysteries of nature, and marvelled at them: nature lies beyond all human achievement, regardless of the extent to which its operations may be controlled and *simulated* by the human mind. This is another way of saying that the corollary of human independence from nature, and the latter's domestication, entails nothing short of human dependence on nature. This will be true as long as the desert can be changed into a garden and, to paraphrase W. H. Auden, ports have names for the seas on which humans venture into life; it will hold as long as shortage can be changed into plenty, scarcity into abundance, and life severe into life abundant.

Similarly, the much maligned Descartes said: "I think, therefore I am." Thought lies beyond fear and wonder, the muteness of the body, and the speechlessness of the soul. In this way Descartes stands between Aristotle's wonder at why there is anything at all, and not nothing, and Pascal's fear amidst the eternal silence of infinite spaces: thought, that is, lies beyond wonder or fear. Thought breaks off with nature, if only by shifting the grounds of mystery from the system of nature to the nature of thinking *systems*, or, simply, from the language of nature to the nature of language—oblivion of which can alone result in the split between subject and object. What was significant for Descartes was less the mystery of nature, than the instrument through which that mystery is grasped.

Remember that, with the advent of artificial intelligence, we move into the area of machines that can handle symbols and imitate mental acts (Pitrat, 1985; Couffignal, 1964, 118). We deal with *thinking* systems (Bolter, 1984, 6) to which, however, no data could be transferred, stored, or processed without mathematical logic. Inescapable as logic may be, it is the same logic that permits the simulation of numerical operations, as well as of symbolic ones. Like the calculating machine, the talking machine does not *speak*, "it 'functions' in a logical universe, in a world made by man in a language he has chosen" (Warnier, 1984, 92). This language, furthermore, implies and necessitates that one and the same word must always have the same meaning. With the word thus "canned," so to speak, in a "frozen" universe of discourse (ibid.), "the difference between the living and the inanimate, between thought and its object, is no longer one of nature but of degrees of organization" (Slama 1986), of programming. Such is the case with Orwell's *Newspeak*, which can only function in a world so disincarnate as to be the very denial of utopia and, by the same token, of language. Only if utopia is grounded in language, as it must be, can it not be confused with any *final solution* or, which amounts to the same thing, with any religion of the book, whether the book of nature or otherwise. Western religion is a religion of the Word, pointing to both human grandeur and wretchedness: language is indeed as rich as it is poor (Warnier, 1984, 92); unable to make anything *happen*, yet *it* does happen, drawing the whole world in its wake and renewing it instead of merely programming it.

Oddly enough, the more efficiently artificial intelligence functions, the less it appeals to intelligence (Olivet, 1986, 163; Serres, 1984) or, rather, would do so were not human intelligence based on the distinction, even the separation, between knowing and programming (Olivet, 1986, 22). However thin the line of demarcation, it does exist. Perhaps that is the reason why specialists disagree on what artificial intelligence can or cannot achieve, and whether the feeling of danger or the more creative type of work can be simulated (Dreyfus, 1985; Couffignal, 1963, 96). Perhaps, too, the line of demarcation is nothing other than—between the two extremes of the angel and the beast—the space left to the human, and nothing but the human, caught as it is between instinct and wisdom, between experience and decision. But, because artificial intelligence deals with expertise, does it also deal with experience? True, expertise rests on experience; but expertise calls for logic, whereas experience calls for decision. Unlike expertise, experience calls for a cutting short, a decision; that is, it calls—as does language, in von Humboldt's view—for an infinite use of finite means.

The question is: Where will programming stop? Will it spill over into human behavior and, then, will it be too late when we realize it? Or will it be so conceived and controlled as to promote the kind of society and human behavior that will be spared from both "intellectual totalitarianism" and the "police state," as Friedmann contended (1957, 8)? We should be mistaken if, however optimistic we allow ourselves to be, we forget that military considerations have played a larger role in the pursuit of artificial intelligence, or expert systems, than have the medical, agricultural, or legal fields. On the other hand, pessimistic as we might be for good reasons, we should not forget or overlook the fact that, after all, artificial intelligence does not repel truly human intelligence; it only repels forms of intelligence of which—in terms of dogmas, of do's and don'ts, of unexamined faith, and of unexamined life—humans have been more guilty than has usually been acknowledged throughout the ages. Lucky's oft quoted monologue in Beckett's milestone, *Waiting for Godot,* naturally comes to mind at this point (1954, 28).

As Michael Polanyi wrote, "human intelligence lives only by grasping the meaning and mastering the use of language" (1964, 36), and it is through language that the whole range of data collected by our senses, even by the body, is processed. Thus, "our seeing is an act of comprehension for which we rely in a most subtle manner on clues from all over the field of vision, as well as on clues inside our body, supplied by the muscles controlling the motion of the eyes and the posture of the body" (Polanyi, 1964, 34). One speaks with one's whole body, and just for that reason, never is language merely body language; or else, extending as it does the body, it could never "include things outside it" (Dreyfus, 1985, 30; Polanyi, 1964, 35). Embodied, language does not confine the human within the body. There is no short-cut to the human except at the price of the human. One speaks with one's body; but then, the body being that with which one speaks, speech is the way one comes to be, the human way of being.

Accordingly, human intelligence consists, as Dreyfus puts it, not in what we know so much as in what we are, having a body endowed with physical aptitudes and a capacity for emotions (Dreyfus, 1985; Bouveresse, 1985). Like all animals, humans belong to a species; computers belong to a series (Warnier, 1984, 105). Regardless of how close the computer ever comes to the brain, "information is information, not matter or energy," if only because "the mechanical brain does not secrete thought 'as the liver does bile,' as the earlier materialist claimed, nor does it put it out in the form of energy as the muscle puts out its activity" (Wiener, 1948, 155). Belonging to a series, computers replace one another. Unlike them, no human can replace another. Unlike animals, on the other hand, humans can break with nature and the "tradition of instinct" and extend their organism by adding a tool to it or linking it to some other technical device (Duhamel, 1933, 31). Human intelligence, too simple and too complex, as rich as it is poor in efficiency, is the kind of intelligence that tells the difference between the Mona Lisa and a snapshot (cf. Ganascia, 1985), between speaking and programming, or memory and expectation, and, again, between analogy and metaphor.

SYMBOLS OF LANGUAGE: HOMO LOQUENS

In this light, it would seem obvious that, if the thought of every age is reflected in its technique, then something more than mere technology is to be understood by technique, namely language. By which I mean that, if in one respect technology is what makes us aware of nature today, in another respect it makes us aware of language as that which is specific to human nature. Saying that the computer is now, as the clock used to be, what provides us with a metaphor of the human (Bolter, 1984, 7; 18) is spared from becoming a cliché, only as soon as we realize that the metaphor, instead of reducing the human to a clock or a computer, points precisely to what is specific to the human—language without which even thinking would be "thoughtless" and the human without a human nature.

To be sure, computers can *master*, but they can *only* master a language by lowering it to the level of a feedback mechanism, or of logical choices from among available data, or, again, to an analogical comparison between this and that. By contrast, human beings cannot master a language unless they also *submit* to it. Through language, we adapt to the environment, and invent a world: Du Bost called this a process of creative adaptation (1972, 7-11; cf.

Dreyfus, 1985, 32), the successive stages of which are even attested by the development of technology. Since we do not grow wings and fly, we *simulate* flight, instead of imitating birds, by dissimulating the wings we lack—and behold, the Concorde takes off the ground! And we remain all the more human.

Humans cannot master, or dominate, except by subjecting themselves to their object, and then the question is no longer one of domination but of *efficiency*, or, put differently, of *correlation*—that is, the subverting of subject and object. This even metaphysics dreamed of through the principle of identity and difference, through the principle of analogy. Analogy succeeds only by turning the infinite qualitative difference between God and man into a dichotomy, an opposition of nouns, of substances, whose correlation can only take place by changing worlds (as when the soul is reunited with its God) and not by changing the world, as when humans, meant to be perfect as God is, become therefore more human and fly, though precisely not by growing wings. They fly or, for that matter, live only poetically, metaphorically, at the level not of the noun but of the verb.

The human condition, unlike the computer in verbal capacity, not only accounts for this or that, it is also responsible (Warnier, 1984, 114): which means that, for humans, destiny is what we can assume rather than merely be programmed into. We are neither featherless bipeds nor clockwork mechanisms, nor even thinking "machines," if by *machine* is meant that which abides by the rules and definitions of a body of knowledge (Dreyfus, 1985, 32).

That simulators of human intelligence can reach higher and higher levels need not mislead us. Computerized mechanisms will be so efficient as to learn from their mistakes or keep track of and "memorize" the results of their operations. Would that be, however, tantamount to what is called experience? Would it equate, in other words, to that without which there would be no human intelligence? Is memory nothing other than merely a storage room, which can collect past experiments? Surely, human experience must be something more than the (re)collection of the past (Brunet, 1967, 1014), of choices already programmed and made. In order for experience to give way to decision, must it not first break off with the past, as the summer fruits break off with the tree of winter?

As verb is to noun, so is decision to experience; or, for that matter, "creative adaptation" to mere feedback, or homeostasis; and just so is human intelligence to artificial intelligence.

Pointing out that in biology and in psychology (as in many another field probably) "the notion of mental content [has] dominated that of mental process," Norbert Wiener remarked: "this may well have been a survival of the scholastic emphasis on substances, in a world in which the noun was hypostatized and the verb carried little or no weight" (1948, 141). That was a world where analogy dominated over metaphor, and likewise being dominated over language, over *Homo loquens*—a world that forgot that even God is word, and that as the word becomes flesh all dichotomies, all cleavages, are wiped out. As Saint Paul puts it, cleavages are wiped out between Jew and Greek, male and female, master and slave or, for that matter, between nature and artifice—if only because in Christ, verbal condition of God, the human, to which all belongs, belongs to God (I Cor 3:23). The future is, in other words, not something to which we are sentenced. It must also be *willed*, as Du Bost convincingly suggests, when he points out that humanity consists precisely in diverting, if not subverting, the *logical future* dealt by natural or scientific determinism into a *willed future* (1972, 6).

Rightly or wrongly, it has become customary to presume that science has had much to do with the obsolescence and the superfluousness of the God-hypothesis. What is odd, however, is that science is also today what puts sheer materialism into question (Wiener, 1948, 155), and forces us to redefine technology (Du Bost, 1972, 11). From its inception on, it has been rather closely wedded to economics and all that is implied by way of exploitation, oppression, or simply inequity and social, or cultural, deprivation. It is perhaps the merit of expert systems, even so-called artificial intelligence, to have through computerized mechanisms kindled in us the consciousness of technology as a further human opportunity: to the extent, indeed, that Paul Goodman once considered it a branch of moral philosophy (1982), while others now see it as a branch of political philosophy (Ferkiss, 1974; Dickson, 1977; Stanley, 1982).

This would, of course, require another vision of society, of another kind of society. First, it must be one, if not wholly freed from the market economy, at least in which—put in biblically utopian terms—the rich have nothing too much and the poor lack nothing. Second, it must be a society in which language—neither Esperanto nor Newspeak—reflects, not the search for some sacral principle of universal explanation nor for some scientific key to the universe—i.e., for some unitary vision of the world (Morazé, 1986), that Babel-like dream still plaguing us—but of the variety of human experience. An experience as diverse as it is complex, as common to all as it is unique—this experience is one *without precedent*, so long as it bespeaks one to whom God is closer than is one's own self, or own *person*, embracing both inward self and theatrical, outward *persona*—in the sense of simulator.

Has there ever been a society that has not itself been a simulator of the person, e.g., in terms of Jew and Greek, male and female, master and slave, and so on; against which simulation, the church above all should have been the iconoclasm? Technological or otherwise, no society can ever so simulate the person as to prevent, any more than did nature or history, human uniqueness from its vocation to praise God for being human, all too human, and yet so wondrous a creature (Ps 139:14).

REFERENCES

Ashby, Wm. Ross. See below, Sablière.

Beckett, Samuel. *Waiting for Godot* (New York: Grove Press, 1954).

Bolter, J.D. "Artificial Intelligence." *Daedalus*, 113: 3 (1984).

Bouveresse, Jacques. "Billet: Les machines sont-elles intelligentes?" *La Recherche* 170: 1126-1127 (Oct. 1985).

Brunet, André. "L'homme et les machines à penser." *Nouvelles de la Cause*, 31: 292 (1967).

Couffignal, Louis. *La cybernétique* (Paris: P.U.F., 1963).

Couffignal, Louis. *Les machines à penser* (Paris: Editions de Minuit, 1964).

Dickson, David. *The Politics of Alternative Technology* (New York: Universe, 1977).

Dreyfus, Hubert. *What Computers Can't Do* (New York: Harper & Row, 1972).

Dreyfus, Hubert. "L'intelligence artificielle est impossible." *Le Monde de l'éducation*, May 1985.

Dreyfus, Hubert, and Stuart Dreyfus. "Why Computers May Never Think Like People." *Technology Review*, January 1986.

Du Bost, René. "Les machines et les hommes." *Télé-Médecine*, 5 (August 1972).

Duhamel, Georges. *L'humaniste et l'automate* (Paris: Paul Hartmann, 1933).

Faugeras, Olivier, and Martin Vasculick. "Les chemins de l'évolution." *Autrement*, 57 (1984).

Ferkiss, Victor. *The Future of Technological Society* (New York: George Braziller, 1974).

Friedmann, Georges. "Préface." In Frederick Pollock's *L'automation, ses conséquences économiques et sociales* (Paris: Minuit, 1957).

Ganascia, Jean-Gabriel. "La conception des systèmes experts." *La Recherche*, 170: 1142-1151 (Oct. 1985).

Good, I.J. "L'Intelligence de l'homme et l'intelligence artificielle." *Impacts of Science on Society*, 21 (4): 343-362 (1971).

Goodman, Paul. "Editorial." *The Antaeus Report*, Fall 1982.

Morazé, Charles. *Les Origines sacrées des sciences modernes* (Paris: Fayard, 1986).

Olivet, R. "L'Inintelligence artificielle." *Science et Vie*, 823 (1986).

Pascal, Blaise. *Pensées* (New York: Modern Library, 1941. Reprint, Paris: Garnier/Flammarion, 1976).

Pitrat, Jacques. "La Naissance de l'intelligence artificielle." *La Recherche*, 170: 1130-1141 (Oct. 1985).

Polanyi, Michael. "The Scientific Revolution." In H. White, ed., *Christians in a Technological Era* (New York: Seabury, 1964).

Pollock, Frederick. *L'Automation, ses conséquences économiques et sociales* (Paris: Editions de Minuit, 1957).

Sablière, Jean, ed. *De l'automate à l'automatisation* (Paris: Gonthier/Villars, 1966).

Serres, Michel. "La haute couture de la connaissance." *Autrement*, 57: 178-184 (1984).

Slama, Alain-Gérard. "La grande crise de la science." *Le Point*, 705 (24 March 1986).

Stanley, Manfred. "Technology, Society and Education." *The Antaeus Report*, Fall 1982.

Vahanian, Gabriel. "Ni Juif ni Grec ...: l'utopisme chrétien comme prélude à la modernité." *Archivio di Filosofia*, LIII (2-3), (1985).

Vahanian, Gabriel. "Tra Dio e l'uomo: sacro e santità." *Il sacro*. Massimiliano Pavan (ed). *Fondamenti*, 4 (1986a).

Vahanian, Gabriel. "Dieu et l'utopisme du langage." *L'être et Dieu* (Paris: Editions du Cerf [Cogitatio fidei], 1986b). English translation, "God and the Utopianism of Language." In Robert Scharlemann and Gilbert E. Ogutu, eds., *God in Language* (New York: Paragon House, 1987), and also in Edith Wyschogrod, David Crownfield, and Carl A. Raschke, eds., *Lacan and Theological Discourse* (Albany: State University of New York Press, 1989).

Warnier, Jean-Dominique. *L'homme face à l'intelligence artificielle* (Paris: Les Editions d'Organisation, 1984).

White, Lynn, Jr. *Dynamo and Virgin Reconsidered: Essays on the Dynamism of Western Culture* (Cambridge: MIT Press, 1973). Originally published under the title *Machina ex deo....* 1968.

Wiener, Norbert. *Cybernetics* (New York: John Wiley & Sons/Paris: Hermann et Cie, 1948).

TECHNOLOGY AND THE RICHNESS OF THE WORLD

Robert Cummings Neville

The Biblical convertibility of swords into plowshares and spears into pruning hooks suggests that the morality of technology lies directly in the uses to which implements might be put. When Plato discussed instruments and craftsmen, it was to highlight the fact that technological expertise requires a specialized understanding of the real nature of the matter at hand, even if that expertise could not be generalized to philosophic scope. Thus, in the ancient roots of our civilization technology was viewed at worst as morally neutral, and its habitual employment was a source of learning the natural joints of nature and the good.

Of course, modern technology is more problematic. Leonardo da Vinci, whose technological imagination surely equalled Thomas Edison's, Alexander Graham Bell's, and Buckminster Fuller's combined, had a bleak vision of the consequences of technology. In his *Atlanticus,* for instance, he propounded a riddle, the answer to which is "metals."

Research in Philosophy and Technology, Volume 10, pages 185-204.
Copyright © 1990 by JAI Press Inc.
All rights of reproduction in any form reserved.
ISBN: 1-55938-062-4

There shall come forth out of dark and gloomy caves that which shall put the whole human race into great afflictions, dangers, and deaths. To many of its followers, after great troubles, it will offer delight; but whoever is not its supporter shall perish in want and misery. This shall commit an infinity of treacheries, prompting wretched men to assassinations, larcenies, and enslavement; this shall hold its own followers in suspicion, this shall deprive free cities of their liberty, this shall take away the lives of many people, this shall make men afflict upon each other many kinds of frauds, deceits, and treacheries. O monstrous animal, how much better were it for men that thou shoudst go back to hell! Because of this the great forests will be deprived of their trees and an infinite of animals will lose their lives.[1]

Metal is the source of the machine technology Leonardo did so much to design. As depicted in the riddle, metal shall afflict the whole race, being active where humankind is passive, though treacherously seeming the opposite; it will educe the full range of human sins and destroy the natural environment.

The later Romantic reaction to "nature dead," in Whitehead's phrase, included an attack on technology as tools for the murderous dissection. Whitehead's analysis in *Science and the Modern World* argued that modern technology, symbolized by the Charing Cross Railway Bridge, made possible the accomplishment of human purposes without regard for the massive depth of the context; hence, technology and the instrumental pursuit of human purposes lose coherence with the whole of life and become violent and ugly.[2] Heidegger's *The Question Concerning Technology* argues that the culture of modern technology leads us to view the world exclusively as if it were a set of resources for our own use. The world then loses the status and richness necessary to command any profound uses, and our culture thus exhausts itself in useless passions.[3]

These general points are hardly new, and many recent studies have drawn useful distinctions among various technologies and analyzed their differential effects. Less attention has been paid to the nature of the world that is impoverished by technology. That is the topic here. How should we conceive the "richness of the world" that technology threatens or destroys? Perhaps if some conception of the rich world were not taken for granted, more qualifications could be added to the typical picture of technology as villain.

I

Why has the topic of the natural richness of the world been neglected? That is a complex story. First of all, Kant's philosophy destroyed the philosophy of nature, substituting for it two disciplines: physical science itself, and the philosophy of science, an epistemological enterprise. By virtue of its dependence on the methodology of the controlled experiment, modern physical science is sufficiently allied with technologies of control as to be subject to the criticisms applied to technologies in many respects. Since the philosophy of science accepts the scientific articulation of the world to be the principal, or only, kind of knowledge, the nature of the world prior to, or apart from, scientific analysis just doesn't register. One of the consequences of the Kantian philosophy is that discussions of the "richness of the world" are relegated to metaphysics, mysticism, or symbolic theology. These three allegedly noncognitive domains are sources in themselves for skepticism about knowing the richness of the world. The next several points inquire whether they are in fact noncognitive.

Second, regarding the metaphysical articulation of the nature of reality as densely rich, Kant was but one of several forces that have tended to delegitimate that discipline. Despite the demise of logical empiricism, in our own time phenomenological positivism, Rorty's Neopragmatism, and deconstructionism all conspire to suggest that metaphysics is not only intellectually illegitimate but immoral as well—an imperial, coercive imposition of a "transcendental signifier" on a truly less organized world, to use the jargon of deconstructionism. This is a new version of Kant's claim that metaphysics is transcendental illusion.

Nevertheless, all these criticisms are beside the point in that they assume falsely that metaphysics must be a set of ideas that alleges to "determine objects," as Kant said, to be a mirror or reading off of the forms of things. The criticisms also assume that since metaphysics is about the most basic and general traits of existence, it must be certain and foundational for all other kinds of knowledge if it is anything at all.

These assumptions simply are false with regard to metaphysics as it has been practiced for the last century by pragmatists and process philosophers. Beginning with Peirce, metaphysics has been conceived within the context of interpretation: a metaphysical idea is an hypothesis that interprets a subject matter, subject to the variety of tests appropriate for hypotheses of such great generality. Even well established hypotheses are by no means certain. And metaphysics is foundational only in the sense that it is sometimes *about* foundations. By no means is metaphysics itself a foundation upon which other knowledge is to be built. Indeed, the very complexity of testing metaphysically general hypotheses means that they are highly vulnerable to the vicissitudes in all the other kinds of knowledge called in to probate them. So, metaphysics as hypothetical inquiry about "generic traits of existence," in Dewey's terms, is by no means subject to an attack on certainty and foundationalism. Indeed, as a philosophic genre metaphysics is alive and well today.[4]

Third, there is deep suspicion about talk of the infinite depths or richness of the world because such discussions seem so intuitive or mystical. The authors who have evoked the mystery and majesty of the world are poets, and many take it to be a criticism of the later Heidegger that his evocation of the world relative to technology is "poetic." The poets and poetic philosophers, such as Emerson and Thoreau as well as Heidegger, don't write clearly, where that means being able to correlate their references to discriminable objects. The richness of the world is never satisfactorily represented in a finite set of terms, and the fact that depths shine through depths suggests that "representation" may be misguided from the start. Poetic speech evokes *experience* of the richness of the world. So do religious meditations and life-styles close to nature; these don't help allay criticisms of the noncognitive status of claims about the world's richness.

What should allay criticism, however, is that metaphysics can step in to provide clear interpretants of those intuitive or mystical experiences. An intuitive feel for nature (or for nature and culture together, for that matter) is holistic, and it registers levels of depth. Yet it is internally differentiated by the interpretations it harmonizes within its own texture. Therefore, intuition is not certain, however aesthetically "right" it feels subjectively.[5] The degree of plausibility in its cognitive claims depends entirely on the merit of the interpretation internal (and also external) to the intuitive process. There are, of course, many symbols that interpret intuitive experiences of the sort in question here. Those provided by metaphysics can be made clear, well-defined, verifiable in many contexts other than the intuitive ones, and thoroughly public. The quality of an experience (intuitive or not) depends not only on the reality encountered, but on the store of interpretive resources brought to it. If metaphysics provided the only interpretants for intuition or experiences of the nature-mysticism sort, these would be impoverished by their abstraction. Fortunately, interpretants of metaphysical generality can be integrated with interpretants from as many symbolic domains as address the scope of the experience. These are the sources of the poetic imagery expressing nature-mysticism.[6]

Fourth, in a move parallel to the delegitimation of metaphysics, theology has been criticized as a cognitive disicpline, and relegated to the study of symbols. Without accepting that criticism, it is worth pointing out that theology is, indeed, among other things, the disciplined appropriation and development of religious symbols. It allows us to bring to the discussion of matters such as the "richness of the world" the appropriate funded experiences of the great religious traditions. We thus have access to the traditions of the world as God's creation, as created in and by the Logos, as well as to the traditions in India calling up nature as the dance of Siva, as the infinite faces of Krishna, and to the great Chinese traditions of the Tao. By themselves, these symbols are uncoordinated and controlled only by the particularistic communities using them. Or, more often in today's world, by the communities that abandon them for the bits and bytes of technology. When integrated under the guidance of metaphysical ideas, however, these symbolic theological expressions can be ordered as testimony for an understanding of the richness of the world. Metaphysics, intuition of the nature-mysticism type, and symbolic theology thus are mutually reinforcing tools for approaching the topic of the richness of the world.

A fifth and last reason for the neglect of that topic is that in the contemporary situation many people believe the "richness of the world" is sufficiently expressed by the mere acknowledgment that no one set of categories or representations constitutes an exhaustive description. As Popperian philosophy of science has argued, descriptive theories can be falsified, but not positively verified. Verification is of the indirect sort that indicates that such a theory identifies differential aspects, in a controlled experiment, of the nature of the subject matter; or, more generally, that make a difference as to what can be done and observed in active experience. In principle, there is no limit to the number of theories that can be verified this way, although each might be incommensurate with the others. We employ those theories our culture appreciates, that we fancy ourselves, or that are particularly useful for identifying what is important for our purposes. Derrida's emphasis on *"differance"* simply pushes this notion so far that there is little point to distinguishing the descriptive process from the reality described. The moral regarding the richness of the world is that the world is capable of sustaining an indefinite, if not infinite, number of descriptions, each from its own angle. The difficulty with locating the warrant for the richness of the world on the metalevel of richness of description is that, although valid as far as it goes, the point is not helpful regarding technology. Since technologies themselves greatly affect the descriptive schemes with which we regard the world, they can easily suggest that, of the indefinite number of descriptions, only those abetting technology should count. Indeed, even the plausibility of the hermeneutical strategy itself presupposes that the world can be conceived of as interpretable in an indefinite number of ways.

Therefore, relative to technology, it is worthwhile to attempt to articulate the infinite richness of the world "on its own terms." These terms, developed in the following pages, are metaphysical and theological, and they serve to interpret the experience of the "whole world" people feel is threatened by at least some forms of modern technology. The discussion of the reasons for the neglect of the topic of the richness of the world has, backhandedly, presented the methodology for discussing it, that is, metaphysics related to religious symbolism.

II

The infinite density of the world is a theme represented in a great many metaphysical systems. In Whitehead, for instance, any actual occasion is a synthesis of an infinity of apprehended antecedents, with each of the antecedents given some particular valuation. For Spinoza, *natura naturans* is the infinitely deep productivity of God's self-nature, and the known attributes of *natura naturata,* thought and extension, are but two of an infinite number.

In Leibniz's world, each monad is a determinate reflection of an infinity of other monads. Even Aristotle's system, conceived long before the theological motif of an infinite God imaged in an infinite-and-finite world, allows that substances have a finite essence but an infinity of contextualizing accidents. Where these systems differ is less in the acknowledgment of infinite complexity in finite things than in the accounts each gives of the kinds of relations among the elements that form the whole. Whitehead's are temporally causal; Spinoza's, eternally causal; Leibniz's, reflective like mirrors; and Aristotle's, environmental.

To provide a viable contemporary account, it is necessary to operate at a level of very great abstraction, greater than in those theories just mentioned. The reason for this is that an abstract account must be able to be illustrated in any more specific account of the natural world that has some plausibility, from the viewpoint of the particle physicist, to that of the Dakota Indian, the landscape painter, or the musical composer. Charles Peirce called this "vagueness," the capacity of abstractions to be made specific, or to be illustrated in each of several conceptual or symbolic systems on a less abstract level that might be wholly incompatible with one another. In addition to being specifiable in the terms of the less abstract systems just mentioned, a metaphysics appropriate for discussing "the world" threatened by technology needs to be specifiable by the relevant religious or theological symbols.[7]

I put forward two principal hypotheses to describe the richness of the world at a level of metaphysical abstractness. (1) The first is *that to be determinate is to be a harmony of essential and conditional features created ex nihilo by an indeterminate ground.* It follows from this that, because the essential and conditional features are themselves determinate, they, too, are harmonies, and so on down and around, indefinitely. Whereas the first hypothesis is pure ontology, and says little about the layout of the world, the second thesis is more cosmologically descriptive. (2) It is *that the world is a process of subprocesses that each separately, and all collectively, illustrate four categories called by Plato (in the* Philebus) *the Unlimited, Limit, Mixture, and the Cause of Mixture.* Each of these four is a special slant on the world's richness, and each expresses something necessary about existing as such. Furthermore, each of the four has been thematized in religious or theological symbols. Thus, the first hypothesis says that the world is created as infinitely rich, and the second says what that infinite creation consists of.

The first hypothesis, that to be a finite thing is to be a harmony of essential and conditional features, has a metaphysical and an ontological dimension. The metaphysical dimension is a description of determinate identity. The "argument" in the metaphysical description is that, on the one hand, to be determinate is to be determinate with respect to something else. Hence, there must be conditional features relating a determinate thing to those other things with respect to which it is determinate. On the other hand, a thing must have an essential character of its own to give it standing relative to other things; without essential features a thing would collapse into its relations with others, and thus could not even sustain those relations. By acknowledging only conditional features, we would be reduced to a monistic metaphysics of internal relations, with Bradley's result of internal lack of differentiation. By acknowledging only essential features, we would be reduced to an atomistic pluralism of diverse things not at all related to one another. By acknowledging both essential and conditional features we rest with a metaphysical pluralism in which things require one another without being reduced to those requirements.

That things are *harmonies* of features means that, at the highest level of integration, the top level features just fit together dyadically. If they were harmonized by some higher "third term," their essential features over/against each other would be lost. Therefore, the top level harmony is what Whitehead called a "contrast," an immediate togetherness of several things. This contrast is thus always finite; it is a "this and not that," and is determinate by virtue of what it excludes as other possible relations among its top level constituents. The contrast-character of the top level in any thing also applies to any lower level; finite definiteness is achieved by harmony as contrast. Yet, because any contrast requires that each of its components be a harmony, any contrast is infinitely deep. That is, each harmony contains essential and conditional harmonies that themselves contain essential and conditional harmonies ad infinitum. A determinate thing, thus, is both finite and infinite: finite in its contrastive nature, and infinite in its components. If one were to make this metaphysical hypothesis specific by applying it to the Whiteheadian cosmology, for instance, the data apprehended would be conditional features, and thus infinite in the stretch back through time, whereas the subjective forms giving new individual definiteness would be essential features, and the bearers of finitude for each new occasion.

The ontological dimension of the hypothesis about harmony appears when we ask how two or more harmonies can be together. As a function of cosmological causation, or cosmological relations, they condition one another by their conditional features. Because the conditional features of a thing would be indeterminate without the thing's essential features, mutual conditioning would not be possible were there not a more profound level of ontological togetherness. In the ontological context of mutual relevance, even the essential features of different things must be together. In order to prevent the representation of the ontological context from eliminating real plurality by turning the essential fetures into mere conditonal ones, the ontological context cannot itself be determinate. If it were, it would be a containing "third term." The ontological dimension of the hypothesis, therefore, is that the ontological context of mutual relevance is the ontological creating of the determinate things ex nihilo. There is no determinate creator apart from the creating, only the creating itself, resulting in the world of mutually determinate but irreducibly plural things. the language of "creation" obviously arises from the Western theological tradition; the point is expressed in Lao-tzu's distinction between the Tao that can be named (the mutually determinate world of the ten thousand things), and the Tao that cannot be named (the indeterminate ground of the named Tao).

The ontological dimension of the hypothesis about harmonies thus gives a nontemporal vector character to the world. Any determinate thing, or set of mutually determinate things, has a character of its own, which is contingent on the creating of the mutually determining order of which it is a part. Within the orders of the world there are obviously temporal vectors—early things causing or conditioning later changes. Temporal vectors are cosmological, however, as constituted by conditional relationships. The ontological vector is nontemporal and unites without blending both conditional and essential features of things. One must be careful not to represent the nontemporal ontological vector character of the created world by means of temporal symbols, such as *totum simul* or everlastingness. All representations of ontological contingency or the ontological vector character of things must be properly "eternal."

The ontological dimension brings a new element of infinity to the world. The infinity of the metaphysical dimension of things consists in their infinite internal complexity, topped by contrastive finitude. The infinity of the ontological dimension is the infinite inclusiveness of the vectoral togetherness of all things in the determinateness of any one. To be finite is thus to be "with" an infinite creation. Each thing is infinitely deep metaphysically, and infinitely "associated" ontologically. Because of the ontological vector characer of the association, an individual thing's identity is in one sense indifferent with respect to whether it refers to its own finite character or the inclusive character of the whole. "That am I" (*Tat tvam asi*), is an experience of mystical union expressed in many different ways and cultures. It recognizes the mutual requirement of finitude and infinity in the determinate world.

The second hypothesis, calling upon Plato's four categories, is a specification of the first. If the first is metaphysical tending toward ontology, the second is metaphysical tending toward cosmology, and can be called a Primary Cosmology. Each of the categories is definite by virtue of exhibiting essential and conditional features. To be an *actual* determinate thing is not only to have essential and conditional features, but to have (1) some features that provide Limit or patterns, (2) some that provide the Unlimited or subprocesses that are to be ordered by patterns, (3) some that determine Mixture or the definite haecceity of existence, the set of contrasts constituting finite nature, and (4) some that are the Cause of Mixture, the balance or fit of the thing with other things and with its own components.

(1) Let us suppose, as is surely the case, that nearly all of things in the world are processes, whose components are other processes, and that themselves are run through larger processes. "Things" thus denotes an enormous spectrum of kinds of processes. Viewed as a matter of pattern, some things have tight organic integrity, such as biological organisms, whereas others are organized more loosely, such as events, specific causal vectors, situations, cultural artifacts, social institutions, etc. Our culture tends to name things according to their pattern, and according to the roles they play in other patterns.

(2) Things can be analyzed from the standpoint of their components as well. A situation, for instance, has to be able to pattern together enduring individuals, social habits, pervasive moods, historical crises, institutions of many sorts, climatic conditions, and many other factors. An enduring individual, such as a human being, has components as diverse as its internal organ systems, as biological systems such as the metabolic in which it participates but that extend far beyond it, as semiotic systems of language and gestures in which it participates with other people, as roles in social systems, as stages in maturation, as historically defined factors, as particular relations with place and persons, as personal purposes and goals. Because so many things are mutually determined, a person is a component in a situation in one set of ways, whereas the situation is a component in the person's life in other ways.

To analyze any one thing is to see it as containing a variety of components organized according to patterns that deal with that variety. Furthermore, each component is itself a harmony of components of bewildering variety, on down and around. Each component of a harmony has something of a career of its own, according to the nature of its own process. Sometimes a component is wholly dependent for its very possibility on being harmonized with the other components of the thing at hand, as a person's economic livelihood depends on being integrated with other factors in an economic system. In other cases, a thing's components have a great deal of independence, and the harmony of the whole must respect the laws of the components, as physical or chemical elements always behave in their set ways when combined into physical and social objects. In all cases, if one takes away in analysis the overall pattern of a harmony, its components are to that extent then "unlimited," and will either cease to be possible, change radically, or go their own way irrespective of the thing under analysis. Any level of pattern or order is thus fragile with respect to the coherence of its components. There may be other factors in the environment that guarantee a certain order, but that order is thus dependent on the environment. From the standpoint of any given harmony, its fragile identifying order is constantly in jeopardy to the separate, usually blind, processes that are its components and context. The Unlimited is not pure lack of order but the relative chaos resulting from lack of a specific order. Depending on the kind of patterns in each level of components, a thing has levels of relative stability and relative instability, and these levels can be of diverse kinds. As

Plato recognized, no form or pattern can last for long because the components of the complex formed are constantly changing.

Regarding the components of a harmonic process, it is one-sided just to fear their potential for destruction of the organizing patterns. The other side is that the quasi-independence of the careers of many components are the source of vitality and novelty. This is not metaphysical creativity or spontaneity, but rather the force of freshness and change that comes from the fact that any process is itself but the temporary coherence of many other processes, each going its own way. Whereas the inevitability of change always means that any order is only temporary, it need not mean that change is always for the worse. No system can be so totalitarian that some birth at wrong season can't break it and improve it (to play with Plato's image in *Republic* VIII).

(3) As a Mixture, a concrete process is to be understood not only according to its patterns and components, but also according to its existential definiteness. Within process there is a temporal passage that effects transformations of things through the three temporal modes. The future is an organization of possibilities, utterly vague in the infinite yet-to-come, and progressively more specific relative to the present, as the possibilities have to be possible outcomes of present changes. The present is the temporal mode of changes in which fixed past events are altered to become new things according to the proximate possibilities for the moment. The conclusion of a present moment is a completely determinate state of affairs, which is thereby past. The past consists of all finished changes, coordinated in the structures and matrices of the spatial and causal vectors of forces. There are, thus, three senses of alteration in the mix of processes. The future alters the structure of possibilities as it faces different present states. The present is existential change, altering possibilities into actualities. The past alters by the accretion of more actualities, extending the lines of actualized causal influence.

Possibilities are disjunctive but lack the force of the excluded middle, as Paul Weiss has argued.[8] That is, my possible posture five minutes from now is "sitting-or-not-sitting"; "not sitting" has to be determinate on its own to be a real alternative (i.e., have its own essential features), so the possible posture is "sitting-or-standing-or-lying-down-or-walking-etc." That inclusive possibility has to be actualized some way or another (assuming that the other possibilities for things allow me to be around in some posture), but five minutes from the event each of its internal disjuncts can still be actualized. Because the real possibility is the inclusive disjunct, the principle of excluded middle does not apply to the possibility itself. At the point of actualization, the disjuncts must be made determinate, and all the internal alternatives but one must be excluded. In one sense, actualization is the eliminiation of all vagueness, of all alternative specifications, from possibility.

The determinateness of possibility comes from the definiteness of actuality, not from some eternal grab bag of forms. The future in itself, apart from its connection with the present, is pure formal unity, utterly indeterminate without some plurality to form up. The differentia come from the possibilities having to be relevant to actual things. If there were no animals, there would be no possibilities for posture; if there were only snakes, the posture possibilities would include lying down and crawling, but not sitting, standing or walking. Because the determinateness of possibilities derives from actuality, it is a mistake to think of actual entities as merely complete definite selections of universals, with every universal either "in" or "out" (this is Kant's conception). Rather, actualization is the making definite of possibilities, the achievement of complete haecceity, of existential individuality.

A universal is a common nature; it retains some vagueness even when it is embodied in an actuality that participates in it. All descriptions of the usual sort involve reference to the common natures that get actualized, but usually without mentioning that the real actualized thing is not just the common nature but an haecceity even more specific than that. The exception to common description is in morals. If Chang had the real possibility of robbing the bank or not robbing the bank, and actualized the robbery, ever after he is the one who robbed the bank but could have done otherwise. Similarly, Chang actualized the possibility of having a button nose; but not just any button nose— it is exactly "this" shape. An accumulation of qualifications of "button nose" can describe Chang's nose more accurately, but cannot exhaust it, since each descriptive predicate is a common nature, and is embodied in some even more specific way in Chang's actual face. Chang's actual face includes both the common nature "button nose" and the specific embodiment of it, Chang's haecceity, just as his actual moral character includes both 'robbing-and-not-robbing-the-bank" and "actually robbing." Chang's full existential being cannot be completely described because he is more than the sum of his common natures.

The existential depth of actualization of individual haecceity is not reducible to the possibilities of the future, or to the patterns of the past. Rather, both of those depend on the conjunction of future, present, and past in actualization. Existential philosophy and theology have recognized the importance of this, for instance as expressed in Tillich's notion of the depths of Being. Often, however, existential thought has focused on the passage from possibility to actuality in the present without attending to the essential features of future and past. At any rate, the concrete reality of Mixture has to do with processes of actualization, with definite individuality.

Because there are many processes in the Mixture of affairs, there are many scales to time, and these have various coordinations. The scale according to which a mountain range is actualized through a collision of continental plates is different from the scale of a human being's maturation, from the diurnal rhythms of everyday life, from the development of an idea in conversation, from the degeneration of an atomic structure in radioactive decay. The remarks made above about the interweaving of components in a harmony are complicated by the different time scales of actualization. To think that the world as a whole proceeds moment by moment, where "moment" means the tick of some kind of astronomical or physical-particle clock, is a gross abstraction, sometimes helpful to physicists and trainmen, but often mischievous. The mischief lies in its obscuring the richness of the interplaying temporal structures of the various processes of the world; the mischief consists in the ruination of processes that require a complex sense of balance, such as education or care of an environment that is used for immediate needs.

(4) The Cause of Mixture is the category apparent in the last point. Plato characterized it as balance, proportion, measure, and the like. It is the normativeness involved in conforming all things, all processes, to bring out the values in possibilities to be actualized. Each possibility has the flat value of being a way of actualizing its components together. The richness of the world consists in the greater harmony of the values of all the ongoing processes, adjusted to each other so as to maximize the values in each. Because of the Cause of Mixture, the various processes of the world are the Tao, the Way of integral movement. Each process is what it is not only in terms of its essential and conditional features, displayed in the career of its actualization, but its identity consists also in its place in the larger movement of things.

It is unlikely that any good sense can be made of the notion of "the whole of things." Kant's arguments against "totality" are good ones. Still, when we think of everything we can imagine together, and enlarge that imagination as much as possible, we approach a kind of aesthetic perspective on value. The aesthetic perspective is almost not a perspective at all; it is the consideration of any given thing—however arbitrarily demarked—as possessing and displaying its value in its world. From an aesthetic point of view, each thing is the center of its own world. The Cause of Mixture is the coordination of all things in an aesthetic way, giving each its due at its own standpoint. Those "standpoints," of course, are processes with their own temporal scales. Morality, in contrast to aesthetics, requires a fixation on some one finite set of perspectives, taking the array of environing processes as subordinate in value to the values of the defining set of perspectives, e.g., the values of human civilizations. The aesthetic Tao of process is, to use Whitehead's phrase, "a little oblivious as to morals."

The reality of the Cause of Mixture, of the whole of process, is not apparent except in refined experiences, as in nature mysticism, religion, "the peace that passes understanding."[9] It is the most obvious place where misplaced technology interferes with the integrity of the world. Yet the Cause of Mixture is that dimension of reality most difficult to describe, because its description consists in showing what value is achieved by having the mixture of processes adjusted this way rather than that. The difficulty is in attaining the "infinite perspective" from which the values of the alternatives can be compared.

III

The senses of "richness" articulated by the two metaphysical hypotheses are implicit in the above remarks, and perhaps even obvious. It remains to make them explicit and connect them with the religious symbols that embody them in our concrete culture. At the same time we can reflect on the class of technological "dangers" associated with each. In general "richness" means a finite something that contains or reflects an infinity of somethings, an infinite "contrast," or an "actual infinite." The following six points spell out some of what this can mean.

1. Infinity of Eternal Identity

According to the first hypothesis, the identity of a thing consists in its essential and conditional features. By virtue of the latter, it is connected with an infinity of other things cosmologically; the significance of this is brought out in the senses of infinity associated with the Primary Cosmology (points 3-6, here). By virtue of being a *harmony* of essential and conditional features, a thing's identity is dependent on being together with all other things, with respect to which it is determinate with their essential features. This ontological togetherness underlies all temporal kinds of togetherness, and is the basis for identity as such. It is properly eternal, and is the community of identity of all things.

The Indian religious traditions, perhaps more than other traditions, have developed the theme of the underlying ontological unity of all things, the mutuality of identity. Even in the theistic traditions, there have been mystical strains that experience an internal dialectic in which the individual's true identity is not the differentia exhibited in the plurality of the world, but rather the positive force of the divine. That force is equally expressed in all other things, and there is thus a commonality of identity that still respects the differences of one thing from another. If God is our true identity, then we enjoy that identity in other things as well. For there to be finite identity as such, there must be the mutual identity of all.

At the deepest level, technology can be taken to be a disrespect for identity as such, denying the mutuality of identity by subordinating "others" to use. This is the profoundest truth in Heidegger's concern about taking the world simply as resources. Here, technology's threat is not to be understood instrumentally. The problem is not that, if we don't respect others, our own identity is threatened. The problem, rather, is that if we don't respect others, or ourselves, identity as such is betrayed. The infinite reality of the finite as such is betrayed by instrumental thinking that does not acknowledge the infinity of togetherness in the identity of the thing used. Of course, this does not mean that we cannot use things or think instrumentally; that is part of the real identity of all living things depending on an environment. What it means is that we need to attend reverentially to the things we use so as to acknowledge their identities and the fact they are in complete solidarity with our own and that of the world as such. The Native Americans, who reverenced the Buffalo while slaughtering them and using every part, had the right attitude toward the eternal infinity of things. Kinds of technology that prevent this reverence, that require forgetfulness or gallows humor, destroy our attunement to this sense of "richness of the world."

2.   The Infinite Contingency of the Finite

The vector character noted in the ontological context of mutual relevance, in eternal identity, presents another sense of infinite richness. That we or the world exist does not proceed from antecedent determinate principles. There is no formed potential for divine creation in some God, nor a disposition to ontological fecundity in Mother Nature. There is simply the eternal act of ontological creation, eternal because of the eternity in ontological identity. Temporal things are among the creatures, and so ontological creativity manifests itself in each particular moment of change, but the modes of temporality are not in time, and hence are together in eternal ways.

The shock of contingency, and sense of dependence on an ontological ground, have been registered in the religious traditions with symbols of creation. In most such traditions, the conception of the creator has been associated with conceptions of local gods, generalized perhaps to a cosmic God. Yet the experience of contingency has motivated a dialectical search for an interpretant that does not attribute determinateness to the creator. The Neoplatonic tradition, first in Islam, then in Christianity and Judaism, funded a conceptual search for symbols of simplicity and unity in the Godhead. Without the theistic association of the ground of contingent reality with an individual god, other traditions have readily symbolized the infinity of ontological contingency. The Buddhist doctrine of the emptiness of form is perhaps the most obvious, the dependence of finite being on ontological nonbeing.[10] The relation between the Tao that can be named and the one that cannot, in Taoism, and the generativity of *jen* in Chu Hsi's theory of *jen* also illustrate the point.

The spiritual content of the shock of contingency is, at least, wonder and thankfulness. To the extent technology gives us the sense that we control things, that we are the authors of things, it blights that spiritual content. Of course, we do control what we control; but that is to be analyzed into our powers for affecting the forces of the world. We are indeed authors of our deeds, and have moral responsibility because of that; but we are not authors of the ontologically contingent context of our actions. There may be many causes of the loss of wonder and thankfulness for existence. Technology is among them when and as it suggests that we depend on ourselves, obscuring the fundamental contingency of things.

3.   The Infinity of Order

Immanuel Kant found the sublime in the starry heavens above and the moral law within, and he was surely right to do so. The heavens above symbolize the fact that any finite order with which we identify our place is itself part of a larger order, which is part of a yet larger order, and on without end. The moral law within symbolizes that the value we make is nested within an infinity of other worthy orders, all affected by the rightness or wrongness of what we do. Indeed, the very discovery of the hermeneutical structure of understanding—that things can sustain an indefinite number of interpretations, each with its point—indicates the infinity of order or Limit in any finite thing. Moreover, as Plato emphasized, no order by itself is adequate for either the existence or the representation of a finite process, because the process is always on the way to some other order.

The idea of a creator imposing order on the world, both structural and moral (if those are distinguished) is about as universal an element of mythology as any. Indian, Chinese, Semitic, Greek, and Norse mythology express that element. It is the symbolic theme behind the Sky God, the gods of thunder and lightning, as well as the more complex divinities of monotheism. Frequently, the imposer of order is one god among many, or one aspect of a more complicated monotheistic god, or a symbolic figure in a nontheistic tradition such as Confucianism or Buddhism. As an expression of Limit, the divinity of order-making is part of what it must mean to be ontologically contingent.

Many thinkers have observed that modern technology is this patriarchal dimension of culture run wild. Technology is the imposition of (human) order over nature that has its own, less finitely ordered, state. There is a great truth to this, but order itself has its infinity that can be distorted by the technological imposition of human order. Human orders, the goals of technology, are precisely the ones that do not ordinarily register the infinite nestings of the world's orders. Ecological mistakes are mistakes about the real order of things. Moral mistakes are mistakes about the real structures of value. The traditional critique of technology, as in Roman Catholic thinkers of antimodernity, is usually a valid critique of a technology's distortion of the infinity of orders.

4.   The Infinity of the Unlimited

It seems redundant to say that the Unlimited is infinite, but the obvious redundancy is a mistake. The Unlimited is not pure lack of order, but the separate integrity of the components of any given ordered thing. A thing is a harmony of its components, each of which is a harmony of its components, on down and around. This is an obvious case of "actual infinity," where the finiteness comes in the fact that the harmony itself is a contrast, indeed perhaps a contrast with haecceity.

The religious symbolism for the infinity of the unlimited often has to do with nature, with Mother Nature, the Earth Mother, the creative procession of subprocesses, with accidental birth out of season, with powers of causal vectors that stampede blindly through the delicate orders of human society. From the standpoint of a patriarchal culture, the religious recognition of the Unlimited smacks of the demonic, of forces that are disrespectful and destructive of imposed order. In religious cultures that balance the yang and yin, Siva and Shakti, there is an appropriate recognition of the infinity of components in definite process, and of their partially independent powers that are oblivious to higher orders.

Insofar as technology inculcates pride in human order, nature takes her revenge. Our wells fill with soap suds, our skies with smog, and our psyches with trash. Soon we cannot taste pure water, see clearly, or have real feelings. Where technology must assume that the lower-order components do not count, our experience is impoverished by being limited to the recognized components, and the very being of those high-level components depends upon their infinite depth of internal components. The limited experience of things then becomes the experience of a mask. The reality behind the mask will get its revenge.

5.   The Infinity of Existence

Actual things include not only their common natures, their vague possibilities made specific, but also their exact haecceities. Just as having order and having components are elements of contingent ontological creation, so is the fullness of actual existence. There is a strange coincidence of opposites in the infinity of finite existence. In the very achievement of final individual definiteness there is an infinity of detail: any universal feature is specified further in actuality. The Scottish poet, Gerard Manley Hopkins, revelled in the haecceities of things, dappled beauties shining forth like shaking foil.

From "I Am That I Am," through Thomas's conception of the world as participating in God as Act of *Esse,* to Tillich's and Buber's existential conceptions of Being, the infinity in finite existence has been a theme of Western religions. In Islam, the Sufi tradition has elaborated the same theme. The Taoist emphasis on particularity; the Confucian, on filiality; the Buddhist, on suchness; express the point in other ways.

Technology can threaten the richness of the world in this sense when it takes things according to their types and manipulates them according to the separate natures of their components. The former is a function of the abstractions involved in Cartesian objectivity. The latter is a function of a mechanistic metaphysics. Twentieth century existentialism is a proper protest against the technologism of modernity precisely in its rejection of the reduction of things to their orders (types) and components (mechanisms). With one exception, this sin of technology is the most important, for it pervades our whole culture. And it has a multiplier effect in conjunction with the other threats of technology. Reducing things to their orders, technology also can misconstrue the true orders of things. Reducing things to their components, technology can obscure the infinite depths of components. The result is a cultural world that is like a child smashing around a china shop while in a dream. This compounds technology's threat to wonder, thanks, and the sense of the infinite togetherness of identity. The one more important sin of technology arises in consideration of its threat to the Cause of Mixture.

6. The Infinity of Harmony in the World

All religions thematize the problem of finding a tao, a path that leads one (or one's people) into harmony with the whole, however the whole is conceived. The conception of the whole is extremely problematic. On the one hand is the problem mentioned above with the notion of totality as such. On the other is the problem of imaging connections among things on a scale large enough to be relevant here.

"Harmony" is perhaps the best word to describe the comprehensive connections, because it connotes both the interdependence of the various components of the world and also their independence: their intrinsic values are to be enhanced by their juxtapositions in harmony with other things. Harmony, however, has unfortunate connotations as well. Clearly, the deep processes of nature are often violent—exploding masses, colliding stars, destructive transformations of environments, and the like. On the human scale it has seemed in nearly every part of the world that sometimes the path of righteousness requires one to fight. As is made clear by the Earth Mother's violence on the one hand and the Sky God's call to arms on the other, the harmony of the whole cannot be all sweetness and light. Religions have recognized this paradox. The peace that passes understanding is incomprehensible because it includes the endurance of crucifixion. Arjuna's encounter with the comprehensive faces of Vishnu resulted in his resignation to the duty to slaughter his mentors and relatives. The sense of the whole is a deep mystery transcending moral considerations, as God remarked to Job out of the whirlwind.

From the abstract position of metaphysics we can note that the Cause of Mixture requires a reconciliation of ontological identity with cosmological connections. That is, the harmony of the whole requires that the integrity of all things' harmony with essential features be recognized in the cosmological relations to be established among them. Thus, the Cause of Mixture commands a kind of piety that may have the appearance of morality. It is deeper than morality, however, because it demands an aesthetic appreciation of the worth of each thing from its own standpoint, and a positioning of oneself so as to harmonize with those interacting but independent worths. Because of the vast array of overlapping time scales of actualization, people in various religious traditions tend to view the task of this appreciation as one of finding and attuning to a center. There is no real cosmic center, of course. Nor does the relevant piety entail that one treat one's own standpoint as privileged. Rather, the appropriate center is one of personal harmony with things such that one's own position is irrelevant, and the center can be moved or expanded anywhere.

One more aspect of the mystery of the whole needs to be mentioned. Whereas it appears that finding one's center and pursuing one's way along the path are matters of grave individual responsibility, paradoxically the view from the path enlightens one to the sense that the deep rhythms of things are what count, and that one's personal agency is a trivial puff. More strongly, the path involves surrender to ontological grace, to the generative movement of the Tao, to the spontaneity of Buddha Mind. It would be a mistake to put too much emphasis on the common themes in obviously different religious symbolic traditions; yet there is a common reinforcement of the mystery of the infinite harmony of the world.

The greatest sin technology can commit is to suggest, because of the enhanced powers it delivers up to the human will, that the world is not ultimately mysterious. That sin has the ancient dignity of being the sin of pride. It leads to a profound misapprehension of what is real and good, and very quickly to a diminishment of the potential of human life. Perhaps in the great harmony of things, human life is due to be diminished, like a bacterium that in flourishing chokes itself out. Perhaps sin itself is but the mortality of our species as inflexibility was the death of the dinosaurs; surely the Calvinists were right, that sin is bigger than we know, a profounder phenomenon than immorality. Nevertheless, we are indeed finite creatures with an infinite content in an infinite world, in at least the ways specified here. As finite, our visions, actions, and goods are limited, and our moral obligations stem from the reality of our finite nature. We are not gods whose taste is purely aesthetic, and therefore transcendent of morality.[11] Consequently, we should sin not. In particular, we should circumscribe our technology so as to prevent it from diminishing the richness of the world.

CONCLUDING REMARKS

The arguments of this last section have been less in the nature of a conclusion and more of a project proposal for further research. Six senses of "infinite richness" have been sketched and correlated with religious symbols to reinforce their cultural significance. It remains to pursue those symbols systematically, to see how the differences among the various traditions from which they are drawn really imply different nuances in the general point symbolized. It remains also to identify just what kinds of technology, in what contexts, lead to the diminishment of each sense of richness. By focusing on the potential threats technology poses to the richness of the world, the argument here has fallen into the common habit of assuming that technology is monolithic and bad. On the contrary, certain technologies can put us in closer touch with certain aspects of infinite richness, with the starry skies above, if not the moral law within. The scheme presented here offers a potential for appreciating as well as depreciating various kinds and aspects of technology. For the argument to be moved to the position to do that, however, the present consideration of the richness of the world would have to be supplemented by a parallel discussion of the nature of human behavior, experience, and purpose—another topic. Perhaps enough has been said here to indicate something of the richness of the world.

NOTES AND REFERENCES

1. From the *Codex Atlanticus,* folio 370r, ca. 1495, cited by Ladislao Reti in "Elements of Machines," in *The Unknown Leonardo,* Ladislao Reti, ed. (New York: McGraw-Hill, 1974), p. 287.

2. See Whitehead's *Science and the Modern World* (New York: Macmillan, 1926), Chapter Five, "The Romantic Reaction."

3. See Heidegger's "The Question Concerning Technology" in the book by that title translated by William Lovitt (New York: Harper Colophon, 1977). The Harper Colophon edition, ironically, has a misdrawn Leonardo gear on the cover.

4. In addition to the great contemporary systems of Peirce, Dewey, Whitehead, Hartshorne, and Weiss, see *New Essays in Metaphysics,* Robert Cummings Neville, ed. (Albany: State University of New York Press, 1987).

5. On the fallibility of intuition, see my "Intuition," *International Philosophical Quarterly,* 7:556-590 (December, 1967). The argument there is that Peirce's theory of interpretation, contrary to his claims, requires a kind of intuition, but a fallible kind.

6. By "nature-mysticism," I mean not only pantheism and romantic evocations of nature but any mystical approach that sees nature holistically, and as being or bearing the divine. The ontological-aesthetics of the Tao in Confucianism and Taoism, for instance, would count as nature-mysticism, as well as much else.

7. This sense of metaphysics as vague abstraction derives from Peirce. I have discussed it, with the texts from Peirce, in *Reconstruction of Thinking* (Albany: State University of New York Press, 1981), Chapter 2.

8. See his splendid *Modes of Being* (Carbondale, IL: Southern Illinois University Press, 1958), prop. 2.13.

9. See Whitehead's discussion of Peace in *Adventures of Ideas* (New York: Macmillan, 1933), Chapter 20.

10. See, for instance, *Absolute Nothingness,* by Hans Waldenfels, translated by James W. Heisig (New York: Paulist Press, 1980), or *Religion and Nothingness,* by Keiji Nishitani, translated by Jan Van Bragt (Berkeley: University of California Press, 1986).

11.   Concerning the reinstatement of the finite moral perspective in an infinite aesthetic world, see my *Puritan Smile* (Albany: State University of New York Press, 1987). Aestheticism itself is the greatest sin of pride—the ascription to ourselves of a godlike capacity.

TECHNOLOGY:

OUR CONTEMPORARY SNAKE

David E. Schrader

There is a well-known miracle story, repeated in all three of the synoptic gospels, in which Jesus asks the assembled teachers of the law whether it is easier to say to a paralytic, "Get up, pick up your stretcher and walk," or "Your sins are forgiven." It is clear from the text that Jesus thinks that the latter task, forgiveness of sins, is the more difficult, the more characteristic of divinity. (Matthew 9:1-8, Mark 2:1-2, and Luke 5:17-26) Modern technology has given humankind the power to heal the lame, to "leap tall buildings at a single bound, change the course of mighty rivers," even modify life itself. The language in which we speak of modern technology is filled with such epithets as "divine," "God-like," etc., yet modern technology has not given humankind the universal power to forgive sin.

Given technology's immense capacity to increase human power, the most central challenge that modern technology poses to religion lies in humankind's tendency to think that technology has enabled us to achieve power equal to that of God. In this sense, technology tempts us like the snake of old, promising

Research in Philosophy and Technology, Volume 10, pages 205-215.
Copyright © 1990 by JAI Press Inc.
All rights of reproduction in any form reserved.
ISBN: 1-55938-062-4

that if we partake sufficiently of its fruits we shall attain equality with God. We fall prey, all too easily, to the idea that humanity is the central ordering force in the universe, that we can save ourselves from whatever perils might beset us, that we are therefore worthy of our own worship.

To the extent that we view God primarily as a, or the, principle of order in the physical universe, as some strains of theology surely have done, modern technology may well lead to an understanding of universal order which makes the existence of God a dispensable hypothesis. Moreover, to the extent that modern technology can lead us to view humankind as having a power close to omnipotence, that technology may equally well distract us from the central kind of problem in human experience, the problem of moral insufficiency, over which we lack significant power. In short, technology in its contemporary form carries the potential to allow us to transform humanity into an idol.

I argue that this potential of modern technology to tempt humankind to turn itself into an idol carries with it an important message to the theologian. If theologies are to ring true to human experience in the world, they must be developed first and foremost as addressing the problem of human moral inadequacy; in traditional terms, the problem of "sin," rather than problems surrounding natural power.

Given the immense creative (in a sense even redemptive) power that technology has given us over the physical world, I would contend that the best that we can ever get from a theology that conceptualizes God primarily in terms of divine supremacy over the physical universe is a conception of God as a creative force, perhaps prior to, but in large measure of the same character as, human creative power. Only if our concept of God is developed primarily along moral lines are we likely to recognize a God who is sufficiently of a different order from humankind to be worthy of genuine worship.

Moreover, the story from the gospels, with reference to which I started this paper, would seem also to suggest that such a moral theology likewise lies closer to Christian origins, although not perhaps to the Christian tradition as it developed at the hands of either its medieval Catholic, nor its enlightenment Protestant systematizers.

I

In the story from the gospels we see contrasted two fundamentally different kinds of causal power. First, there is the power to heal the paralytic. This is the power to affect causality in the realm of physical nature; to restore the proper function of disfunctional body parts; presumably also the power to control weather, the movement of schools of fish, hoards of locusts, frogs, etc.; the power to transform one kind of substance (water) into another (wine), part the Red Sea; and a whole host of other "nature miracles." Second, there is the power to forgive sin. This is the power to affect causality in the realm of moral nature, to mitigate the causal results of moral deficiency (sin), whether those results be conceived of as a kind of morally paralyzing guilt, punishment in some future "other world," the (Hindu) cycle of rebirth conditioned by karma, or yet some other means of reaping what we sow.[1]

It is undeniable that God has been held to have power in both of these senses in most major theistic religious traditions. It is equally undeniable that different theological formulations have placed different relative emphasis on these two aspects of divine power.

In "Karl Popper as a Point of Departure for a Philosophy of Theology," I argued that if theological formulations are to be rationally assessable, they must be framed as solutions to particular problem situations.[2] Equally, if theological formulations are to be taken by ordinary people as having any relevance to human life, they must also be framed as solutions to particular problem situations. Lacking such a framing, theological formulations will take on the appearance, both to the ordinary believer and to the philosophical critic, of intellectual cobwebs, spun out of nothing more than the fertile imaginations of theologians. While such systems may well satisfy the academic theologian, they surely cannot prove sufficiently substantial to support flesh-and-blood communities of believers.

Theological emphases on those two different notions of divine power reflect concerns with different types of problem situations. In the article just noted, I identified four different types of problem situations to which at least some historical theologies have purported to give solution: (1) the problem of control over natural phenomena; (2) the problem of the ultimate explanation of natural phenomena; (3) the problem of providing justice—happiness commensurate with virtue—in an unjust world, a world in which an individual's virtue seems regularly unrelated to his or her happiness; and (4) the problem of sin, how humans can face the inevitable conflict between our moral behavior and our highest moral aspirations.[3]

The first two of these kinds of problem situations conceptualize God primarily in terms of divine supremacy over physical phenomena. The last, by contrast, conceptualizes God primarily in terms of divine power over moral phenomena.

The third, the problem situation which provides the point of departure for Kant's so-called "moral theology," is ambiguous with respect to the contrast with which I am concerned here. I would argue that the notion of divine power at the center of this third approach to theology is more akin to that involved in the first two approaches than to that involved in the fourth. It seems primarily to involve God's power to create an after-world, a realm in some sense beyond that in which we presently live, in which moral beings, assumed to survive their death in the present realm, are then given reward or punishment, or some combination of the two, in proportion to the virtue of their lives here on earth.

I would not, of course, wish to suggest that these four problem situations are the only ones which have spawned theological solutions, but the four are surely historically important. Moreover, each of them requires a clear conceptualization of divine power. Among them we see three quite distinct approaches to divine power over the physical order, and one approach, perhaps in some sense two approaches, to divine power over the moral order. Among them, they provide a clear contrast between theological approaches which focus on the two very different kinds of power contrasted in the gospel story.

II

Technology, above all, is power over physical nature. In its contemporary form, technology gives human beings the power to alter nature in quite radical ways, the power to overcome the boundaries that nature had previously imposed upon us, even the power to create such fundamental kinds of things in physical nature as new chemical elements and forms of life. It is the capacity of humans to use technology to modify our physical environment even at its most basic level that has led Buckminster Fuller to speak of humanity as the "anti-entropic" element in the universe, that component of physical reality which counteracts the natural tendency of the rest of physical nature toward a state of increasing disorder.[4] As nature of its own accord winds down, according to the second law of thermodynamics, the creative force of human technology works in the opposite direction continually to build up and renew nature.

There is no need to rehearse here the positive and negative impacts of technology on human society. Both are immense. On the grand scale we see both the power we now have to make the lame walk and heal the sick, and the power we now have to destroy the world many times over with nuclear weapons. At the far more modest level, we see both the remarkable little microcomputer with which I am writing this paper, and the occasional "down" store computer which makes it impossible for us to purchase anything, or the "down" university computer which makes it impossible to secure a student transcript. Technology is pervasive at both the grand and the small scale, and at every point in between.

Of itself, as a kind of power, technology is as good or as bad as its various products. Given the magnitude of power that technology has provided, its products have encompassed the very good and the very bad, but there is one danger that seems to be an almost invariable accompaniment of power. Power is a seducer to whoever possesses it.

To the extent that technology increases human power to the point where we tend to see ourselves along the lines suggested by Fuller, as the (or even a) fundamental source of order in the universe, it tempts us to see ourselves as replacing God, at least his capacity as lord of the physical universe. As Harvey Cox recognized in *The Secular City,*

> we meet God at those places in life where we come up against that which is not pliable and disposable, at those hard edges where we are both stopped and challenged to move ahead. God meets us as the transcendent, at those aspects of our experience which can never be transmuted into extensions of ourselves. He meets us in the wholly other.[5]

Thus, the technology extends the limits of the pliable and disposable, as technology tends to move further out those edges at which we are stopped, as technology reduces that part of our experience which we cannot transmute into extensions of ourselves, technology also makes smaller the range of places at which we may meet God.

Accordingly, it is surely natural to see a connection, as Cox did now almost a quarter of a century ago, between urbanization and technologization, on the one hand, and secularization, on the other. Cox rightly recognized that one of the most central features of the contemporary city is that it is "the place of human control, of rational planning, of bureaucratic organization."[6] Surely one of the key differences between urban and rural culture is that in urban culture the major problems confronting people are problems of organization and technology. Traffic, trash removal, even crime, seem to be problems that the people of the contemporary city can resolve if only they can implement the right kinds of human organization and the right kinds of technology— a new transit authority with shiny fast subway trains, a no-strike clause in the contracts of sanitation workers and the latest technology for converting trash into usable materials, a highly professional police force and state-of-the-art burglar alarms.

Beyond the city, even though the weather continues to set up some remaining "hard edges" which challenge human control over rural life, even there the advent of new irrigation techniques, advances in veterinary medicine, a host of advances in horticulture, and a vast variety of other products of agricultural technology also contribute to the diminuation of the realm wherein transcendence is to be encountered. While technology may well contribute to making the city seem almost exclusively a "place of human control," it has likewise extended the boundaries of human control in rural life as well, and as dramatically.

Throughout contemporary society technology has vastly increased human power over physical nature, to the point where it is very tempting to see ourselves as masters of that nature. Yet as human power over physical nature has increased, the power to create and the power to improve (redeem) that nature, the need to recognize another power over that same physical nature must inevitably diminish.

III

As the gospel story of the healing of the paralytic makes clear, we do not encounter God's power exclusively, or even most characteristically, in the control of physical nature. Rather, divine power, in its most characteristic form, relates to the moral order. Gustav Aulén, for example, writes:

> God's "omnipotence" is not the causality of the divine will in relation to everything that happens, but the sovereignty of love . . .
> If God's sovereignty has this character, what is then implied in the *omnipotence* of God? It is clear at once that we need not be concerned with a number of meaningless questions about God's omnipotence which have appeared even within technology. Can God do everything? Can he transform a stone into an animal? All such questions are beside the point and completely meaningless. They have nothing to do with faith. They are based on a conception of the will of God as entirely capricious, which fails to understand that it is here a question about the power of love and nothing else.[7]

Aulén does, I fear, overstate his point somewhat. God's sovereignty over the whole of creation, over nature both physical and moral, is *precisely* what is at stake in the traditional notion of divine omnipotence. Christians could hardly maintain a belief in God as the "maker of heaven and earth" if sovereignty over physical nature had "nothing to do with faith." Yet while they do have *something* to do with faith, Aulén is surely right to remind us that there is much more to God's power than his control over rocks and floods.

When Aulén speaks of the "power of love," he is speaking essentially of a power that operates over the moral realm. It is a power to abrogate the normal chain of moral causality, as Ronald Green would express it, to "not necessarily determine the fate or worth of moral agents in keeping with their own moral judgments."[8]

The notion of moral causality at play here is no doubt troublesome, and is susceptible to a wide variety of conceptualizations. Minimally speaking, it is the idea, which seems bound up with the very idea of morality, that certain forms of behavior seem appropriately followed by certain forms of consequences. As a general rule, we are saddened by the death or suffering of a child (who is morally innocent) in a way that we are not saddened by the death or suffering of a terrorist bomber who is harmed by his or her own bomb. In the former kind of case, the suffering or death strikes us as undeserved, while in the latter kind of case it seems deserved.

Obviously, questions of moral deserts, of the moral consequences of particular forms of behavior, are much more controversial than questions of the physical consequences of particular forms of action. At least so long as we avoid both the cosmic and the subatomic level of physical reaction, we find people in substantial agreement about what should be expected to follow, for example, from the collision of two bodies of given masses. Yet, again speaking minimally, it does seem essential to the entire project of morality that certain forms of behavior should be followed by moral disapproval or moral condemnation. The recognition, or sometimes mistaken belief, that one's own behavior is of a form that is appropriately followed by moral disapproval is, of course, that which we all know as guilt.

If every such notion of moral consequence fails to make sense, it would seem to follow that the entire enterprise of morality is but a grand illusion. Practically speaking, there would be no difference between doing right and doing wrong. If, on the other hand, some such notion of moral consequence makes sense at all, then we find ourselves with a form of causality entirely different from physical causality, we find ourselves with something that we might speak of as "moral nature." While technology has clearly given humanity great power over physical nature, it has not advanced us a bit in gaining power over moral nature.

Granted, various types of chemical and conditioning technologies have given those who control societies the power to shape the behavioral patterns of the controlled to a considerable extent, but this is something far different from the power to abrogate moral causality. Such technologies have not given humankind the power to forgive sin, to break the causal bond between morally condemnable behavior and moral condemnation. Moreover, they are likewise incapable of giving us the power to eliminate sin. In giving humanity greater power over physical nature, technology has given us the power to behave in ways that have greater consequence. In the moral realm this means only that our sins, as well as our good deeds, are, some of them at least, a lot larger than they might be without the assistance of technology. Moral nature, in short, is an area wherein technology has not made humanity even a small bit closer to God.

IV

God's domination over physical nature is, as I note above, an essential commitment of Christian theology. That commitment is the central determinant in shaping a Christian understanding of the individual's relationship to the totality of his or her environment; but a theology that conceptualizes God primarily in terms of his dominion over physical nature will have great difficulty motivating its own acceptance among humans in a technological age.

Perhaps my point might be most clearly expressed by borrowing some terminology from Imre Lakatos's philosophy of science.[9] God's dominion over moral nature must lie at a tenable theology's theoretical "hard core," that part of the theology which is fundamentally definitive of its basic theoretical project. By contrast, its conceptualization of the relationship between God and physical nature should lie in the theology's "protective belt," the part of the theory which may be significantly modified in response to new discoveries about the nature of physical reality without thereby doing violence to the fundamental theological program.

To see why this is the case we must return to my earlier claim that theologies, like other kinds of theories, are evaluated as they succeed in competition with rival theories which purport to resolve the same problem situations. Clearly, theology cannot simply ignore natural science (although natural science can surely pursue far and away the largest portion of its program while completely ignoring theology). Theologies both can and must conceptualize God in terms consistent with the best of current science. A theology which fails to do this much must inevitable seem arcane to literate people in an age in which science informs the dominant view of the physical universe. Still, history clearly shows the danger posed to the entire theological project that follows when theology goes beyond this, and starts to frame itself primarily as an answer to what are fundamentally scientific questions.

Theologies which conceptualize God primarily in terms of his power over physical nature will so conceptualize him because the central problem situations to which such theologies address themselves concern power over physical nature. Other kinds of problem situations will require other kinds of conceptualizations of the deity. If we examine for a minute the kinds of problem situations which concern power over physical nature, we will find that such problem situations, at least in an age of technology, receive their most plausible solutions in terms of human power generated by technology. In the present day, if we should find our city overrun by rodents like the storied Hamlyn, we would not look for the solution to the problem in either prayer or a wandering "pied piper." Rather, people of the contemporary technological world would look for someone to invent a better mousetrap (or poison).

Whatever speculative questions we might have about the original power that created physical nature, when contemporary people look for a power to *redeem* physical nature, a power to solve the problems which confront us in our relationship with physical nature, we look to the power of human technology. We may hear stories about the "mighty acts of God" in the biblical past. We do, of course, pray for safe journeys, relief from flood and famine, and various other events in physical nature. For most people in a technological age, however, such prayers seem to be more symbolic acts of devotion than genuine attempts to get the physical situation changed.

From time to time we even see genuine appeals to divine power as attempts to deal with some problem in physical nature. The faith healer would be one example here; yet modern people expect the solution to physical problems to come, if at all, from human technology. Faith healers enjoy both less esteem and less success in our world than do surgeons.

Success is the key issue here. When we evaluate rival solutions to practical, physical problems, it would be clearly irrational not to choose in the direction of that approach which has proven more successful. The success of human technology, its record of generating solutions to a multitude of physical problems which have beset humankind, make it eminently reasonable to place our faith in human technology when it comes to facing the problems of physical nature. As Ian Barbour notes, "the essence of faith is not doctrinal belief but trust and confidence. What do you trust?"[10] In our present age people trust human technology. Moreover, that trust in human technology is generally well founded. Human technology is surely not a magical key that opens every door, yet when it comes to solving the problems we either find or create in physical nature, human technology is still the best option we have. Barbour is right to caution against an "unqualified devotion to technology,"[11] but, within its own sphere, technology has no particularly plausible rival for our trust.

As I said above, human technology does not address the speculative question of creative power. Rather, it addresses the more practical question of redemptive power. The problem of creative power alone, without redemptive power, as Hume well argued so long ago in Part V of the *Dialogues,* does not lead us to anything close to the living God of any living faith.[12] At very most, some sort of deism might be warranted. It is only in the search for a redemptive power that we might find such a living God, and yet technology has clearly enabled humankind to supplant, at least as a redeemer of physical nature, such a living God.

V

It is, I would submit, only in a theology that conceptualizes God primarily in terms of his power over moral nature, his power to forgive sins, that we may expect to find a theological approach which can speak to contemporary humans. As I argued above, technology can do nothing to bring human moral fallibility within the realm of human control. Our moral failings continue to present us with what Cox called "those hard edges where we are both stopped and challenged to move ahead." While technology, as well as the lastest advances in natural science, must inevitably affect the "protective belt" of any viable Christian theology, the moral "hard core" of such a theology can remain largely constant, little changed over nearly two millennia. Technology may well effect the *scope* of human sin, but in *kind* there is little difference between the hubris which can be generated by contemporary technology and the hubris illustrated so long ago by the Old Testament story of the Tower of Babel.

Encountering those moral "hard edges," a Christian theology can offer the promise of a forgiving God. If Green's account of Judaism and Hinduism are at all plausible, at least some non-Christian theologies can also offer a kind of answer to the problem of moral limitation which contemporary technology cannot even approach.[13]

I shall not argue here that the solution proposed to the problem of moral limitation by any Christian theology is preferable to that posed by any particular kind of rival theory. I shall not even argue that the solution proposed to that problem by some variety of Christian theology is even an intellectually warrantable solution, although I think that a strong case can be made for that conclusion. At present, my sole concern is to note that it is only by so focusing theology that theology can avoid being driven off the field of competition for popular allegiance by the impact of contemporary technology.

Today, in a time which has seen the triumph of human technology, we may again ask, far more aptly than in the time of Jesus of Nazareth, whether it is easier to heal the paralytic or to forgive sins. Most of the time, today, human technology can give us the power to heal the paralytic, enabling him to pick up his stretcher and walk. It is far more difficult, as it was two thousand years ago, far more characteristic of God, to be able to forgive the paralytic's sins. As long as we recognize that fact, as long as our theologies focus on that fact, we may very well find ourselves encountering God as we face the fact of human moral finitude.

If we fail to attend to the priority of God's power over moral nature, if our theologies tell us to look for a God whose dominion is best revealed in power over physical nature, then we shall most likely see only our own image, magnified by the power of technology. Focused on the power over physical nature, contemporary technology, like the snake of Genesis, holds out to us the ultimate temptation, the temptation that it can make us equal to God.

NOTES AND REFERENCES

1.   For a valuable analysis of this notion of divine power over the course of moral causality, see Ronald M. Green, *Religious Reason: The Rational and Moral Basis of Religious Belief* (New York: Oxford University Press, 1978).

2.   David E. Schrader, "Karl Popper as a Point of Departure for a Philosophy of Theology," *International Journal for Philosophy of Religion*, 14:193-201 (1983).

3.   See ibid., p. 200.

4.   See R. Buckminster Fuller, *No More Secondhand Gods and Other Writings* (Garden City, NY: Doubleday & Co., 1963), p. vii.

5.   Harvey Cox, *The Secular City* (New York: Macmillan, 1965), p. 262.

6.   Ibid., p. 4.

7.   Gustav Aulén, *The Faith of the Christian Church*, Eric H. Wahlstrom, transl. (Philadelphia: Fortress Press, 1960), pp. 122, 125.

8.   Green, p. 109.

9.   See Imre Lakatos, "Falsification and the Methodology of Scientific Research Programmes," in *Criticism and the Growth of Knowledge*, Imre Lakatos and Alan Musgrave, eds. (Cambridge: Cambridge University Press, 1970), esp. pp. 132-135.

10.   Ian G. Barbour, *Science and Secularity* (New York: Harper & Row, 1970), pp. 70ff.

11.   See ibid., pp. 70ff.

12.   David Hume, *Dialogues Concerning Natural Religion,* Norman Kemp Smith, ed. (Indianapolis: Bobbs-Merrill, 1947), pp. 165-169.

13.   See Green, pp. 125-158, 201-246.

TEMPTATIONS OF DESIGN:
A MEDITATION ON PRACTICE

Martin H. Krieger

City planners rarely design slums. Planning and design—whether for the physical environment, in social policy, or in engineering—are meant to provide a deliberate and good order. The technologies planners and designers employ are meant not only to provide that order, they ought provide the deliberate justification for it. This is no mean achievement, and the design professions have always had an intimate (if unacknowledged) relationship to other disciplines which are under the temptation of design, such as science and religion.

If we think a platted city is orderly, we are even more impressed by the natural sciences' account of the order of the universe:

> After the big bang, the universe rapidly cooled down, and as it did so the elementary particles appeared, or "froze out" in their current varieties. Eventually, much later, the stars formed, and the different elements as we now find them were manufactured by nucleosynthesis in those stars. If the universe is open,

Research in Philosophy and Technology, Volume 10, pages 217-230.
Copyright © 1990 by JAI Press Inc.
All rights of reproduction in any form reserved.
ISBN: 1-55938-062-4

and if we wait long enough (10^{10}-10^{100} years), not only will the stars cool off, and the planets and stars detach themselves from each other and from the galaxies, but the black holes will decay, and matter will seem to liquify and flow, even at zero temperature. Eventually, the atomic matter will fuse or decay into iron. Along the way the sky will be filled with galaxies, now strongly red-shifted. And at least for some time we shall have lots to do, for life will go on, albeit in perhaps curious forms. [NOTE: I use *universe* to denote the universe as understood by the physicists and the chemists, while I use *world* to refer to the world we live in and experience. This distinction cannot be hard and fast, and what we might call the biological realm must lie somewhere "in-between." Understanding the universe and understanding the world have been at times thought to be the same problem.]

Thus, science connects the history of our physical universe with its composition and its finer structure. While that order may not be a matter of divine providence, it is no casual fact. For in this account, the world we live in and experience is composed: actively composed in its being made, analytically composed of its elements, and composed in an articulate and orderly fashion in its design. Its history, aliquotion, and structure are intimately connected. Its technology and its philosophy are congruent.

Composition is a mode of understanding the world that is comprehensive, supposed to leave out nothing. But the modes of composition are historically specific, with different forms and manifestations at different times. The historical sequence of forms and manifestations may be called scientific progress or religious enlightenment; the sequence itself is an extension and part of that comprehensive understanding of the world. The history of the forms and modes of description, and their structure, then shows that each mode is one more act of composition—not to speak of the history itself being an act of composition.

Each level of composition feeds the others—as in a complex historical novel with scenes of action that go from the intimate, to the political, to the world-historical. Each of the levels possesses its own autonomy, but then finds that it is deeply indebted to the others for articulating and epitomizing its meaning. Such a panoply of levels is a provision of the world, and such a book may be a model of our knowledge of the world—nature being "the volume of God's works," as Bacon put it. Now, our knowledge of the world, including, of course, the story of the big bang, must meet the demands of rhetoric, the forms and practices of persuasive argument. If the world is God's will encoded, in the last several hundred years we have come to see that encoding not only as a matter of Creation and art, and of symbolic and allegorical presentation, but also of mechanism and invention and manufacture, of engineering and instrumentation.

There is no city plan, no utopia, no ecology that is so systematically ordered, no fantasy of design which is so pervasively recurrent. This is one reason why the design professions are drawn to being scientific. It is in that realm that the fantasy of unity has been pressed so consistently.

Such a composition, however, is also a temptation. A temptation lures us to evil and puts us to a test. *The* temptation is the sin of pride, our desire to be God, to control and to perfect the world. Now, in our everyday lives we surely have a provision of the world that is ours, or at least mostly so. We get along reasonably well, managing nicely. Why not then just possess the whole world itself, all of it—perhaps by a natural extension of our provisional mode of being? Then the stuff we every day, ordinarily, cannot quite get into line would be under our command, and we could get it right, all of it. There would be a single mode of composition, one that is repeated everywhere, covering the world. It is a Chinese bronze vase thatched totally with its serpent motif, serpent tiles of various shapes and sizes covering all of it. It is the dream of decoration. And so we put city plans on our walls, and admire photographs of technological artifacts such as silicon chips.

There is no reason, to be sure, that our provision of the world is anything more than just a provision that works for us now. To be a complete and total tiling is perhaps asking for too much. The return of repressed residues and excreta is not so much the problem. We might be able to handle that, employing tricks of ornamentation. Rather, different parts of the world are perhaps best managed in their own ways. Polytheism may be more practical than is monotheism. Pluralist planning and schematic design are employed every day in actual practice, but their justifications have never proved so attractive as that of the monotheistic modes.

The most insidious of the temptations are for knowledge of the world. (Following Kant, I call them "dialectical," referring to the logic of illusion.) It is perhaps the sin of pride to *hope* for a single design for the world, but that we could *know* that design is surely more prideful. The world might well be designed, perhaps even designed by God, as we discuss a bit later; but need it be designed in accord with our conceptual powers (or vice versa), so that we might be able to understand it? That would be most wondrous, a design suited to our intellectual design. Kant argued that we assume that the world is designed, and designed for our conceptual powers, so as to organize our inquiries into the nature of the world. Such an "ideal of pure reason" regulates our thoughts about nature. He describes how we are tempted to see that ideal as something we *know* to be true, how we are confused by that temptation, yet how we are encouraged to do great work under its sway. Whether or not the world actually is designed, or by whom, or what that might prove, we are in the grips of a dialectical temptation.

That temptation has provoked us to make rich and powerful theories of order, planning, and design which encompass randomness, evolution, mechanism, and human social interactions. What makes the technology so attractive is the room for invention and discovery made possible under its discipline.

Complete composition and perfection and design are not needed for everyday life. Without falling apart, the world might be a little less composed, sprinkled with glitches, more absent of our intentions. Things would go along smoothly enough, not much worse than they would otherwise. But *we* would not be the persons we are without the desire for composition and perfection, the temptation of design, and the urge for absolute knowledge. Wholeness has an actual felt reality for us, we struggle and hope for it, and we sometimes come close in our poetry and our science. The experiences of wholeness are robust, resistant to the destructive powers of our critical intelligences.

An accounting of our temptations will not eliminate or avoid them, but such an accounting can be a vindication of God's justice in permitting evil in the world. Such an account is called a "theodicy." Of course, theodicies and justifications are but one more of our temptations.

The diabolical does not destroy us most of the time; we can recover from our bouts with it; we get along nicely and uneventfully. The world's potholes, quicksand, whirlpools, and craters attract us, but we have learned to walk or swim gingerly around them, and when we are caught we seem not to fall in all the way. We are almost always "on rope," as they say in the circus. We have a sense of closure and order, and a sense of graceful failure. We can make sense of the world. To planners, who are nowadays acutely aware of evil and imperfection, what should be most remarkable is how influential planning is at all, for it sets the stage for those inventions we might call entrepreneurship, arbitrage, and just plain cheating.

Also, we can act as if there are manifestly safe and manifestly dangerous places, the pure and the polluted, the clean and the dirty. All we need do is to stay on the safe side, cross on the green, and keep ourselves pure. When carefully examined, the potholes and quicksand are everywhere; the pollutions are ever-present; the pure is bastard; the traffic lights are muddied. This degeneracy or overlap does not harm us much, and so we can for the most part maintain the contention that we can divide the world into clean and dirty places. The repressed may well return but it asks no revenge, and our denials of the repressed are not so insidious in their side-effects.

The world is much roomier than we tend to believe, less rigorous, less likely to add up and be vengeful, more capable of absorbing bankruptcies and misalliances. There really is no accounting that will find the missing few pennies or even the missing millions. (Things are, however, not infinitely roomy.) The world seems generous because in fact it is more generous than we want to believe in our monitory moments, yet our sense that we pay for our sins is true at least some of the time. That we pay for so few of them is what makes us think twice.

The world is degenerate, polluted, bastard, and mixed—and generous, comfortable, and roomy-enough. The City of God may be just; cities, as such, are the places where justice is possible at all. And what is curious about the methods and techniques of planning is that that justice (and injustice) is explicitly articulated—whether it be in terms of sewer pipes or social security.

ARGUMENTS FROM DESIGN

Let us return to our temptation in its least diabolical, most heady form, when we merely hope to be natural scientists.

> In crossing a heath, suppose I pitched my foot against a *stone,* and were asked how the stone came to be there, I might possibly answer, that for anything I knew to the contrary, it had lain there forever: nor would it perhaps be very easy to show the absurdity of this answer [although modern glaciology and plate tectonics suggest otherwise and give rather good reasons for where it came from—MHK]. But suppose I had found a watch upon the ground, and it should be inquired how the watch happened to be in that place, I should hardly think of the answer which I had before given, that, for any thing I knew the watch might have always been there. Yet why should not this answer serve for the watch, as well as for the stone? Why is it not as admissible in the second case, as in the first? For this reason, and for no other, viz., that, when we come to inspect the watch, we perceive (what we could not discover in the stone) that its several parts are framed and put together for a purpose, e.g., that they are so formed and adjusted as to produce motion, and that motion so regulated as to point out the hour of the day; that, if the several parts had been differently shaped from what they are, of a different size from what they are, or placed after any other manner, or in any other order, then that in which they are placed, either no motion at all would have been carried on in the machine, or none which would have answered the use that is now served by it.
>
> William Paley, *Natural Theology* (1802)

> Look round the world, contemplate the whole and every part of it: you will find it to be nothing but one great machine, subdivided into an infinite number of lesser machines, which again admit of subdivisions to a degree beyond what human senses and faculties can trace and explain. All these various machines, and even their most minute parts, are adjusted to each other with an accuracy which ravishes into admiration all men who have ever contemplated them.
>
> David Hume, *Dialogues Concerning Natural Religion* (1779)

William Paley and David Hume agree about the wonder of the world's manifest complexity, and its seeming composition and order and purposefulness, but the significance of such wonder for an argument for the design of the universe is not at all straightforward. For Bishop Paley, the Argument from Design was a powerful one supporting God's existence. For Hume, there need not have been a single designer. A crew of reasonably competent workmen can produce a seaworthy vessel, their predecessors having by trial-and-error figured out how to do it right. A similar crew could have produced the world, "the art of world-making" having matured after having been "botched and bungled" in many previous attempts. And we moderns might add that chance and evolution may have done some of the work. More generally, as indicated in my bracketed remark about Paley's stone, what we take as a wonderful fact of design depends on what we take as subject to theoretical inquiry and understanding.

Earlier authorities on the mechanics of the universe differed as to how much needed was God's will. Leibniz believed that the world was just mechanical, and nature self-sufficient so as to achieve its own order and perfection—once God had set the system into motion. Newton thought of God as a tuckpointer, justifying and patching up the imperfections and breakdowns in the world's mechanical order, so endowing the world with vitality.

Kant thought the Argument from Design at best suggests the existence of a supreme Architect. (That we believe it proves the existence of God is a dialectical illusion, one which Kant tries to dispel in the *Critique of Pure Reason*.) More likely, the Argument demonstrates our need for the notion of a designed universe, to guide and regulate our inquires about our world. It is our nature that such regulative principles must be invoked. Nature does not tell us anything, but if we believe that she speaks in scannable lines, we hear the poetry of her muse, and so we have coherent and composed knowledge of the world.

The great and admired cities are a product of mercantile greed, royal ambition, speculative rapaciousness, and unregenerate slavery. Modern day planners and designers almost always work in teams, or at least have to face the consequences of ersatz collaboration and negotiation. Often, chance and the effects of combination dominate fortune and intention. The architect has to bargain away his dream in order to get built. Yet, and this is crucial, we are still entranced by an order that is decipherable by us. Only then does technique embodied in a profession lead to a calling.

Imagine if one could show that the design and order of the universe is repeated (as a structural homology) in its history and in the history of our knowledge of the universe: the structure, its development in time, and the history of science displayed the same design and principles. Hegel claimed such an overwhelming and pervasive ordering in his logical, historical, and epistemological description of the universe and the world. His claim follows as the next step in the description. And God is the ultimate fruition of such a hierarchy.

Thus, the temptation becomes more encompassing, and our distance from it is decreased. We might argue about details of the modes of homology and repetition, about how particular concrete facts fit into the larger schematic story, but that story, in all its levels, fills the space of our inquiries. What seems to Kant like formal logical traps (dialectical illusions) turn out to be just the structures we need to understand the world in all its complexity and concreteness. The dialectical temptations are formal, defeated by the facts of life in their detailed variety and in their systematic organization. Only when we are abstract and disembodied, ignoring the details and particulars, will the dialectical temptations mislead us. The issue is not the limits to our knowledge, as Kant believed, but whether we are up to the conceptualization of life itself. That natural and social science, and the techniques they employ, have come to be influential in the design professions is a sign of temptation. That we have then ignored their entreaties is a sign of our capacity to finesse temptation when we want to get done and be on with it.

We might be able to have such pervasive knowledge of the world because our own natures parallel the world's nature. The forms of cognition and the forms of the world are the same. This is, perhaps, too strong a claim. We may take the insights of Paley and of Hegel, and combine them into a more encompassing design for the universe, what has come to be called the Anthropic Principle. We *might* note (besides our intelligence and its usefulness for understanding the universe): the adaptation of all the other organisms to the environment; the fact that the inorganic world has the right prerequisites of temperature, elements, and pressure so that life is encouraged, and we are around to appreciate the universe; the aesthetic value of nature for man, and its effectiveness in educating his soul; the way that culture educates us so that moral virtues are developed in our interactions with the world; and, finally, the progressiveness of evolution. The laws of nature, the configuration of the universe, and our own biological and conceptual constitutions are such that the world may be said to be the way it is so that we may have knowledge of it. If I am just one more piece of meat from Nature's stew, I am a piece of meat who has the capacity for a particular kind of intelligence, and so the world is intelligible for me. ("And God saw that it was good.")

The argument may be made a bit more strongly and in a seemingly more modest fashion. Each of the various versions of a modern physical cosmology might be distinguished by its assumptions: about the size of certain parameters, such as the strength of gravity (if there is such a force in the cosmology), or the kinds of particles it allows. It turns out that only a small number of these cosmologies will also allow for a notion of intelligent life that could ask just these questions about design. If such a theory must incorporate gravity, and have at least three spatial dimensions (so that complex organismic life, such as we are, might exist in it), and have less than four dimensions (so that planets will not fall into the Sun and electrons continue orbiting nuclei), then in fact there are few candidates for a good theory—at least now, given our knowledge. Composition and order, as we know them, lead to a unified design for our universe. The recurrent hope for a theory of planning, for an ideal of design, for a method that is transcendental, is the mundane version of this sacred desire.

Thomas Wright (1750) argued that the infinity of God is suggested by the unending stream of galaxies we encounter. But in the modern picture, in what seems like an unending infinite time, we shall need only finite energy to survive, and we will have the capacity to remember our past, and so to have a history, within those energetic limits. Thus, the cooling down of the universe will not be without interest. From this physicist's eschatology, we might conclude that truly the universe is made for us, or at least we are made well enough to suit ourselves to it. I suspect that the Anthropic Principle has become of widespread interest because it provides a seemingly scientific way for us to make ourselves at home with the universe. Historically, the Anthropic Principle is "the same" as the existence of a City for Man, in which justice and society mirror our deepest needs—namely politics.

> The composition is the thing seen by every one in the living they are doing, they are the composing of the composition that at the time they are living is the composition of the time in which they are living. It is that that makes living a thing they are doing.
>
> Gertrude Stein, *Composition as Explanation*

Hume's and Kant's objections still apply. That the world *seems* to be made for us is just that, a wonderful semblance that guides us to greater knowledge of it. That dialectical illusion, that temptation to composition, works well enough, and we get along with its inadequacies. We do not even have to think about the composition of the world, yet we are, as well, creatures who can find themselves enthralled by the prospect of perfection and order and composition, knowing full well there is imperfection and sin and evil in the world.

There are leftovers from design, as well as evil and pain and defect. Evil actions are real; pain feels awful; and there are still many unturned stones in Bishop Paley's world. We do not know, through reason or otherwise, what will turn up on the next heath. There seem to be lots of undesigned parts of the world, left over, suboptimal, just sitting there drifting. It could be (following Leibniz) that all of these less than good and perfect elements are actually aspects of a larger scheme, functional and necessary, and that in time we shall come to have knowledge of the world's true perfection and order.

Alternatively (Newton), believing in God's vitality as well as his existence, the world might actually be paradoxical and playful, less than totally and systematically ordered, perhaps whole but riven with contradiction. No single overarching principle could encompass it. God's freedom for action is ultimately arbitrary, so that even when we come to understand some of the play in the world's constitution, that understanding will never restrict his will. It will never guarantee us intellectual dominion over other parts of the world. There will always be surprises we could not conceive of, that we could not conceive not conceiving of. Hence, rationality and intelligence, while they may seem to be all we need to comprehend our world, are not enough. In fact, they are temptations, ones whose spell we are fated to fall under. We know that in this mundane world we tend to presume on God's will, that we have "perverted" the Good and spoiled it. That is our sinful nature, or at least our lack of perfect lovingkindness. So goes an Augustinian account for the existence of evil and pain in our world.

Within this theodicy, there are arguments about how we might do better, how we ought to live more righteously. Pascal argued for faith in God and His Word, since the benefits would be very great if God existed, and the losses small if he did not. Similar arguments have been made for more "conserving" lifestyles, in this case respecting the limits of Entropy rather than of God's Will. All of these arguments for a righteous life say little about the possibility of conflict among the various interpretations of God's Will or of Entropy's limitations, and about how those conflicts might be resolved in our mundane and political, imperfect world. They tend to undervalue the costs of belief if they turn out to be false idols.

Without God, one might reconstruct the argument of the last few paragraphs in terms of the value and danger of a commitment to a universal design. God's freedom for action and His Will is now expressed in terms of the limits of our understanding of the presumably designed world, and Pascal's bet now concerns the payoff from a commitment to teleology in our investigtions of the world (the payoff of believing what Kant called an ideal of pure reason). The temptations of design become Baconian idols, again misleading us. Such is the moral psychology of design as it is encountered phenomenologically.

In actual design practice, the technologies we employ reflect the theologies to which we are committed. Leibnizians are fascinated by method (while of course in actuality they adjust methods to work in each situation). Newtonians pay more attention to tradition, institutional factors, and historical peculiarities. And just about all planners and designers, at least on the Sabbath, believe in the rationality of Pascal's bet.

To reiterate, the world seems imperfect and incomplete, subject to instabilities and confusions, dialectical and actual. Yet we get along quite nicely, not at all destroyed by imperfection or skepticism. We make a world that is sensible for ourselves—as long as we do not push it too far, and we seem not to do that too often. We manage well enough in our everyday lives, not haunted by our dreams, or confused by our speculative reflections.

Like carpenters we are craftsmen equipped with a tool kit which we employ to do our work. The tools are flexible, and we are adept in figuring out how to use them; for the most part, they are used in conventional ways, and we take on tasks much like ones we have taken on before. We become more adept, learn new things, and fail once in a while; but we rarely fail spectacularly. We know how to mend our errors, to save a job from disaster. We have mastered the tricks of the trade. We have a harmonious provision of the world even though it is incomplete and imperfect.

The techniques of design are not simply a sham, meant to hide entrenched conventions and modes of domination; nor are those techniques sufficiently prescriptive that a designer need only follow their guidance. Techniques surely employ conventional archetypes, yet they also give us a chance for invention, and, most importantly, they provide a handle on otherwise intractable situations.

Harmony is perhaps not so surprising once we recall the stuff that has been abandoned and botched. Underneath the harmony, there are forbidden chords and steps, and music we are not permitted to make. Our lack of knowledge of the forbidden is willful, a result of our commitment to the tool kit we have, the simple world we have made, and the stuff we have forgotten and hidden so things would be clear.

To make things clear, we set them down, focus on what counts, and "bring up the contrast." There are times when we more carefully and deliberately do make things clear, enforcing on ourselves a more strictly formalized representation of the world *as* the world, claiming we have got it right.

At this point, a city plan or an architectural model has no people, no garbage, and no congestion; but the so-called pure forms of life are rather unclean. Symbolic algebra is encrusted with literal pictures and local cultural features; architectonic structures are ornamented and decorated with the vernacular and idiosyncratic; genres are mixed; and even if we could believe in a race or in pure blood then octoroons are never simply 1/8, and "purebloods" are mixed and spreckled. Purity requires a great deal of maintenance work. We have to keep up the taboos so that we can believe in lines of provenance and naming. Since those lines have always been crossed, taboos are modes of restoring a bastard monarchy and its peerage. No wonder we have to be obsessed with taboos if we want to be sure of following them exactly. Nature is not on our side.

"Suppose that truth is a woman," as Nietzsche suggested, and is deceptive, misleading, impure, and contradictory (as women were supposed to be). Or, if I hold up an apple, and then ask you how much of it you see, the right answer is "all of it," but the reflective and problematic and "true" answer is the front half surface. We ask questions about the world that assume our alienation and objective distance from it. And just so, we are tempted by reality. What is interesting is that we live with such temptations and even desire them.

MAKING DO

The temptations of design are not half so potent as is our absorption in our everyday lives, an absorption in getting things done. The obsession with clarity, purity, and reality is remarkably controlled, staying in reserve. Our everyday maintenance activities reassure us that the world is just "the way it is." Tools are adapted to new circumstances, fit comfortably into our tool kits, and so we need not abandon being mundane, down-to-earth carpenters or plumbers. Actual technique is practical, almost despite the pretentions of method.

Now we have disciplines of art and rhetoric, cuisine and genre, and religion and philosophy, to take care of questions about clarity, purity, and reality, respectively. Disciplines convert disturbing observations into work and tasks, taming wonder and anxiety, and eventually producing material and intellectual artifacts such as artworks and theories that put the world in its place. Even a Socratic dialogue, no matter how aporetic, immaterial, and in a sense unsatisfying, keeps us off the streets in those times of distress.

These various disciplines permit us to see the world as sensible and problematic, and to ignore or resist, at least for a while, the temptations of residual fetishes, taboos, and skeptical mysteries. For all its variety and complexity, the world is regionalized, divided up so that we may live in one region of the world and more or less ignore the other regions. We are able to carve out a region in which we may enact our lives with comparative liberty. So we have a neighborhood in which we are at home, although across a wide street is a heathen district.

One of the curious facts about the physical universe as we have come to understand it is that it is possible to define regions so that the forces of nature appear in a hierarchy of strengths. Then, we may treat physical problems "perturbatively," that is, as if each situation were set up for the most part by all the stronger forces, while its special features can be understood by watching how the next weaker ones disturb that set-up. Most interestingly, the hierarchy is just the one that is revealed in the cooling down of the universe after the big bang. The stronger forces may readily display themselves, freezing or crystallizing out at earlier, more energetic, hotter times, while the weaker ones must wait until things cool off sufficiently so that the general background heat does not overwhelm them.

When things are cool enough, freezing sets in, and a force's particular order in the universe shows itself, just as a crystalline structure shows itself. The universe may be said to relax from a state of great complexity and turbulence, to a more orderly, smooth, linear world. Along the way, of course, there are regions which display turbulent eddies and waves. What is worth noting is the possibility of extended regions of smoothness itself, nonturbulent flows, the universe being capable of bearing stress without breaking down.

The story about our physical universe is not always so simple. If we have a large number of similar individuals interacting with each other, as in a crowd of people or in a crystal filled with electrons, it is often quite difficult to develop any perturbative approach. The world does not seem to rationalize or hierarchize properly. It is resistant to discipline. Still, there are saving graces. Sometimes it is possible to group a bunch of the individuals into a more coherent scheme, so that an ocean of water molecules becomes a fluid perturbed by wavelike motions. Sometimes we may develop a way of accounting for the disparate individuals which puts them in their place, such as when we count out and divide a group of people into the evens and the odds. So just when we do not seem able to tame the world, we may still find there are ways of saying what we are up to that make it simple and clear.

Whatever the order we have been endowed with historically, it demands as well a synchronic structural account. So the accumulations of history are to be rational; the artifacts of technology are to be functional.

We live with temptation and otherness. We are constituted by our capacity for dialectical temptations (such as the ones Kant describes), temptations to know the ideals of reason, not only to appeal to design in understanding the world, but also to make an Argument from Design.

We are constituted as well by our capacities for alterity or otherness: to be anxious, ecstatic, desiring, hungry. We can be distant from, yet drawn to, our everyday world. Consciousness, that capacity for alterity, demonstrates a gap or hiatus between our involved lives and something other. We may stop and think, or slip into a reverie; but then we resume what we were doing, paying it a quiet nonjudgmental attention.

The world we live in has enough room within it for other worlds, worlds which are just as real as this world. Our sensational and ideational capacities are suited to discovering other worlds—whether peninsular or subsurface to the world we live in. Acts of divine forgiveness, altered states of consciousness, fetishes and taboos, and skeptical inquiries are in *this* world. Design, initiation, and will are still possible in our already-designed world. There is a reflective play between ordinariness and otherness that allows us a sense of initiative. The aura and authenticity possessed by cities, homes, and objects is real, but it is real in this world.

Genesis had this world to model itself after. God, in the form of the Hebrew fathers, had a comparatively easy time creating Genesis. They knew how it had to come out. Their great invention was finding a morally satisfying cosmological path. Later, if the New Testament were to be authentic, it had to be a typological repetition of the Scripture (now the *Old* Testament).

There never was a first time, before design. We are redesigning a world that has always been composed. Our arts are always under the formulaic spell of genre and typology.

Just how the world actualizes its potential is what gives us a sense of a "first time." Say we wonder why the initial universe was electrically neutral, without any net rotation, and equally balanced between matter and antimatter, as our current evidence about the early universe suggests. One possibility is that this highly symmetrical configuration is the most likely one—but it turns out that a vacuum is even more symmetric. So why not have the initial universe be a vacuum? But then why is there something rather than nothing? Because the less symmetric (but still highly symmetrical) matter/antimatter filled world is, it turns out, more stable and less energetic than is the vacuum. Imagine that some matter/antimatter pairs appeared as fluctuations in the vacuum, and, like a bit of freezing in a supercooled liquid, this more stable, ordered, less symmetric configuration grows and makes up all of space: So we have a first time. One of the great mysteries is just why cities do have centers. And such accounts are about what a city is.

We make do. We are in accord with the harmonies of the universe and of reason, yet of course we are sinful. We design and initiate around both the harmonies and the sins. We are comfortable, blessed, and loved—at home and at peace with the facts of life. We also desire and will, and are tempted and tested; and so we work our way back home, provisioning our world comfortably enough, using the natural kinds of stuff in ways we had not thought of before. The actual imperfect world is roomy enough so that we can make sense in it, yet there are all sorts of stuff which show up the limits of our sense-making. In our designs, we leave out some of that stuff since it does not fit, yet we do not suffer for its being missing.

It is almost surely the case that not everything fits and is in the right place, that not everything happens for a (good) reason, that things are not getting better all the time. Paleontology, which once supported a more neatly designed universe, now suggests that adaptationism, determinism, and progress are not quite fulfilled. There are leftovers and free riders. Still, the world turns out to be adequate and orderly enough for us. We ask if these characteristics are the world's nature or our own, whether the world is telling us something or we are telling it to ourselves. The questions form a sequence of entanglements. If we have a desire for a description of things as they really are, just so, we are also willing to settle for a provisional description, not worrying so much about its ontological status. We stop asking questions in so general a form, and then get on with actual designing and everyday work. Arguments from design are just a part of the composition of the world.

NOTE

On cosmology see Barrow and Tipler, and Dyson, Weinberg, Hawking, Wilczek, and Prigogine. Barrow and Tipler is devoted to the Argument from Design, but see as well Carre, Allston, Plantinga, and Tennant. Obviously, I have in mind Hegel of the *Phenomenology,* and Kant of the first and third *Critiques.* On planning and design, Lynch provides a fine synopsis.

REFERENCES

Alexander, C. *The Timeless Way of Building* (New York: Oxford, 1979).
Allston, W.P. "Teleological Arguments for the Existence of God" in P. Edwards, ed., *Encyclopedia of Philosophy,* vol. 8, pp. 84-88 (New York: Macmillan, 1968).
Barrow, J.D., and Tipler, F.J. *The Anthropic Cosmological Principle* (New York: Oxford, 1985).

Carre, M.H. "Physicotheology" in P. Edwards, ed., *Encyclopedia of Philosophy,* vol. 6, pp. 300-305 (New York: Macmillan, 1968).

Clarke, T. "Seeing Surfaces and Physical Objects" in M. Black, ed., *Philosophy in America,* pp. 98-114 (Ithaca: Cornell University Press, 1967).

Dyson, F.J. "Time Without End: Physics and Biology in an Open Universe," *Reviews of Modern Physics,* 51:447-460 (July 1979).

Gould, S.J. *The Panda's Thumb* (New York: Norton, 1980).

Hawking, S. "The Goal of Theoretical Physics," *CERN Courier,* 21:3-8, 71-74 (February and March 1981).

Ignatieff, M. *The Needs of Strangers* (New York: Viking, 1985).

Krieger, M.H. *Advice and Planning* (Philadelphia: Temple University Press, 1981).

Krieger, M.H. "Planning and Design as Theological and Religious Activities," *Environment and Planning B: Planning and Design,* 14:5-13 (1987).

Krieger, M.H. "Where Do Centers Come From," *Environment and Planning A,* 19:1251-1260 (1987).

Krieger, M.H. *Marginalism and Discontinuity: Tools for the Crafts of Knowledge and Decision* (New York: Russell Sage Foundation, 1989).

Leach, E. *Genesis as Myth* (London: Cape, 1969).

Lynch, K. *Good City Form* (Cambridge, MA: MIT Press, 1984).

Plantinga, A. *God, Freedom, and Evil* (Grand Rapids: Eerdmans, 1978).

Prigogine, I. *From Being to Becoming* (San Francisco: Freeman, 1980).

Stein, G. *Selected Writings of Gertrude Stein* (New York: Random House, 1946).

Tennant, F.R. *Philosophical Theology* (Cambridge: Cambridge University Press, 1928).

Weinberg, S. *The First Three Minutes.* (New York: Basic Books, 1976).

Wilczek, F. "The Cosmic Asymmetry Between Matter and Antimatter," *Scientific American,* 243:82-90 (December 1980).

COLLOQUIUM SECTION

HUMANAE VITAE AND THE CURRENT INSTRUCTION ON THE ORIGINS OF HUMAN LIFE

Jane Mary Trau

The Church's recent instruction on the origins of human life[1] addresses the moral licitness of reproductive technologies such as artificial insemination, in vitro fertilization and embryo transfer, and surrogate motherhood. Much of the document appears reasonable to those who already accept the Church's teachings with regard to sexual relations, marriage, and parenting. Even among faithful Roman Catholics, however, there is a question, if not an outright objection, concerning the Church's conclusions on homologous in vitro fertilization.[2] The position taken by the Church on this particular issue is problematic because it conflicts with certain aspects of *Humanae Vitae,* and because it begs the question against the use of technology.

The conflict the current instruction raises with *Humanae Vitae* can be shown only after a central problem with the earlier document is made clear. The question-begging fallacy with regard to in vitro fertilization and embryo

Research in Philosophy and Technology, Volume 10, pages 233-242.
Copyright © 1990 by JAI Press Inc.
ISBN: 1-55938-062-4

transfer is fairly obvious, and follows from a more fundamental question regarding the use of technology.

One possible consequence of the difficulties with the current instruction is a reaffirmation of inherent problems in *Humanae Vitae*. A second consequence is the denial of available technology to members of the Church. This denial must be sufficiently justified if the faithful are to accept it, and this justification is precisely what the document has failed to provide.

The rationale offered by the document on the origins of human life appeals to the nature of sexual relations within marriage and the nature of the technology whose use is proposed. This rationale fails because the characterization of conjugal relations does not follow from what *actually* is professed in *Humanae Vitae*, and because of what appears to be an underlying presumption against technology in favor of natural means. Thus, one must first reconsider the flaws of *Humanae Vitae* and the presumption about technology, if one is to understand the instruction on in vitro fertilization.

CONSISTENCY WITH *HUMANAE VITAE*

Much has been said about the internal consistency of *Humanae Vitae*. One objection, which by now can be called the "traditional" criticism, is that the conclusions of the later sections do not follow from the initial claims of the document.[3] At the outset, the instruction insists that the nature of the sexual act is *always* both unitive and procreative in nature; and that these two aspects, though intellectually distinguishable, are never actually separable. The encyclical concludes that the separating of these two aspects betrays the true nature of sexual activity, and thus is morally wrong.

What should follow from this insistence is that it is never morally permissible to intend to act or to act contrary to the true nature of the sexual act. Later sections of the document state that there *are* certain conditions under which a married couple can enjoy the unitive aspect of sexual activity while deliberately intending to frustrate the procreative nature.

> If, then, there are serious motives to space out births, which derive from the physical or psychological conditions of husband and wife, or from external conditions, the Church teaches that it is then licit to take into account the natural rhythms immanent in the generative functions, for the use of marriage in the fecund periods only, and in this way to regulate birth without offending the moral principles which have been recalled earlier.[4]

This seems to suggest a sort of prima facie obligation to always intend both the unitive and procreative aspects of the full sexual act, except when these expressed conditions are met. This allowance for exceptions within the document cannot be denied. It is clearly the basis for the recommendation of the rhythm method. If the encyclical did not admit these justifiable exceptions, then the use of rhythm would also be illicit as a means of preventing conception. Thus, we do have a precedent for the justifiable separation of the unitive and procreative aspects of the conjugal act, within *Humanae Vitae*.

The Church teaches that, given these acceptable conditions for unity without procreativity, there is only one acceptable method, and that is the one that cooperates with, rather than interferes with, nature. More is said about this in the next section of this paper. For our purposes now, it is sufficient to say that, regardless of the method approved, the separation between the two aspects of the act has been made, and cannot be denied by interpreters and defenders of *Humanae Vitae*.

We are left with two understandings of the nature of the conjugal act. First, there is the *theoretical* pronouncement that the two aspects can never be separated; and second, there is the *practical* pronouncement that under certain, justified conditions one aspect can indeed be enjoyed without the other. This apparent equivocation will be crucial to the criticisms of the current instruction on homologous in vitro fertilization.

In rejecting artificial methods of birth control, *Humanae Vitae* states that, although the use of natural and artificial methods reflect the identical intention, the former are proper and the latter are not:

> In reality, there are essential differences between the two cases; in the former, the married couple make legitimate use of a natural disposition; in the latter, they impede the development of natural processes. It is true that, in the one and the other case, the married couples are concordant in the positive will of avoiding children for plausible reasons, seeking the certainty that offspring will not arrive.[5]

The *intention* to avoid procreation while enjoying the unitive feature of conjugal love is defended by the *method* used to accomplish the intention. This amounts to the peculiar moral principle that the method of achieving an end, rather than the end intended, is the source of moral rightness or wrongness. This position could be construed as holding that the means justifies the end.

The Church condones the *intention* to avoid procreation by recommending a natural *method* of contraception, but fails to explain the bad-making characteristics of artificial methods to accomplish this intention. Once the intention is considered licit, the nature of the means must be considered as an independent question. Thus, if it is morally permissible to avoid procreation, what feature must the means possess to be an appropriate means to a proper end?

The answer which appears to be given is, if technology destroys a natural process, either permanently or temporarily (depending upon the method used), it should not be used. But this is precisely the question: when nature fails or must be limited, is the use of artificial technology licit? If one answers that it is not licit precisely because it is artificial, one simply begs the question.

Assuming that the Church would not make so simple an error, one must look further for a justification for rejecting the artificial means.

TECHNOLOGY AND NATURE[6]

Implicit in *Humanae Vitae* is a prejudice in favor of nature over technology, i.e., the natural accomplishment of a licit end or goal is generally preferred to an artificial means. Furthermore, technology should not destroy or replace a natural process or phenomenon, but should assist or supplement.

If this is the Church's position, it is problematic because it limits technology beyond its capabilities. By analogy, this line of argumentation would allow the use of eyeglasses to assist the eye in its function of sight, but would not condone the replacement of an eye by means of a transplant. The Church, however, clearly does endorse transplants *when the natural organ or function of an organ has failed.* In the same way, artificial contraception can replace where nature has often failed, i.e., the rhythm method, and in vitro fertilization can replace where nature has failed, i.e., in utero conception.

Since the Church has supported organ transplants it is fair to say that the presumption in favor of natural means does not exclude the use of technology where the natural function has ceased. Thus, it appears that an accurate assessment of the Church's position is that where natural means are functioning one cannot opt for the use of artificial methods in place of natural ones. On this account, the proper use of technology is to assist in the full functioning of a deficient natural process, or the replacement of it when it has completely failed.

Given this position, it is difficult to explain why the Church rejects the use of artificial birth control when natural methods fail, or why in vitro fertilization cannot be employed when natural methods fail.

The rejection of artificial contraception seems to stem from a confusion of intention with the means to accomplish that intention. This is analogous to labeling a handgun an offensive rather than a defensive weapon. The weapon itself is neutral. It is the intention of the user that determines whether it is used to aggress or defend. We condemn or condone the use of the weapon according to the intention with which it is used. There is no good-making or bad-making characteristic which the handgun possesses that is sufficient to determine the moral lictiness of its use. Similarly, the intention to avoid procreation is licit or illicit independently of the means used to accomplish that end, and the means of contraception is licit, illicit, or neutral independently of the end it accomplishes.

Some Church men and women argue that rhythm fails because people fail to use it properly. Alas, there is too much evidence that even under the most careful scrutiny the method is not as accurate as that offered by technology.

Additionally, the method is tedious, inconvenient, and requires much more of the user than any of the artificial methods require to succeed. We are led back to the inescapable question: If the artificial method is superior to the natural for the accomplishment of a legitimate end, why not use the artificial means? The value of technology is that it allows the efficient and accurate accomplishment of good ends. If the avoidance of procreation is a good end, then one must have good reason for rejecting artificial means. Once the end is approved, rationality demands that we allow people the best possible means to accomplish that end.

The approval of specific technologies can be determined by first evaluating the need of the technology; i.e., its use should not be gratuitous. For example, one could suggest that the artificial methods be used only when the natural means have failed completely or are inferior to the artificial means. This recommendation would maintain a preference for nature. Furthermore, it could be determined whether the benefits of the artificial methods outweigh any risk to the user. It could also be established that people use artificial means voluntarily, and that they are informed of the risks and costs of technology. If these conditions are met, and the use of any given technology does not involve some moral evil, e.g., unjust distribution of resources, excessive risk to future generations, deprivation of rights to innocents, then there appears to be no justification for rejecting the technology as morally illicit. Indeed, under the conditions stated, any given technology exemplifies the merits of technology as the product of rational persons for the furthering of rational and appropriate goals.

In a Natural Law vein, one could argue that the failure to use artificial means in the accomplishment of proper ends, when those means are available and superior to natural means, is in itself contrary to the fulfillment of the rational nature of persons. It is perfectly consistent with Natural Law ethics to adopt as a guideline the following principle: Technology is a product of rational human beings, and is properly used to assist them in the efficient accomplishment of proper aims.

Given that the enjoyment of the unitive function of the conjugal act is under certain conditions licit without the procreative function, it is legitimate under this understanding of technology to use artificial means to accomplish that end. Once the exception was made in *Humanae Vitae* to the inseparability of the procreative and unitive aspects of the conjugal act, it would, and indeed does follow logically that artificial means are licit to accomplish that end. These are two internal inconsistencies in *Humanae Vitae*: the practical separation of the two aspects while maintaining that they are theoretically inseparable, and the rejection of artificial means without adequate justification. The current instruction on the origins of human life inherits these two errors.

HOMOLOGOUS IN VIRTO FERTILIZATION

In the current instruction on the origins of human life, the Church does state its appreciation for the value of technology and give brief mention to a guideline for proper use.

> Basic scientific research and applied research constitute a significant expression of this dominion of man over creation. Science and technology are valuable resources for man when placed at his service and when they promote his integral development for the benefit of all.[7]

> Thus science and technology require for their own intrinsic meaning an unconditional respect for the fundamental criteria of the moral law: That is to say, they must be at the service of the human person, of his inalienable rights and his true and integral good according to the design and will of God.[8]

These passages affirm the Church's support of technology. Critical to this discussion, however, is the emphasis on the congruence between the use of the technology and the "integral good according to the design and will of God."

Apparently, the criteria for proper use of science and technology are that they serve human persons, their rights, and the true and integral good of persons *according to the design and will of God.* This last criterion is fundamental to the position on in vitro fertilization.

The Church's rejection of the licitness of in vitro fertilization rests on two key claims: first, the technology should not gratuitously replace natural methods; and second, that the use of technology should never violate the natural design of God for the good of persons. The understanding of the nature of the conjugal act thus becomes vital to the Church's reason for rejecting the use of in vitro fertilization.

Both documents imply, though never articulate and justify, an understanding of the nature of the conjugal act which stands to be threatened or violated by the introduction of technology. The instructions claim that the natural and divine design of sexual activity cannot be served for the good of persons either by artificial contraception or by in vitro fertilization.

The document on the origins of human life emphasizes the totality of the conjugal act, as does the theoretical position in *Humanae Vitae.* The principle reason for rejecting conception outside the womb is that it dissociates a particular and specific procreative act from its accompanying and simultaneous unitive aspect, "Homologous in vitro fertilization and embryo transfer dissociates from the conjugal act the actions which are directed to human fertilization."[9]

The emphasis here is on the simultaneity of the procreative and unitive act. The test tube conception is assessed as lacking the human action which has as its end the procreation of life. It is thus inextricably bound to the claim that procreation and unity must always coincide. The only proper human action directed towards procreation must be one that is also unitive. This description of the nature of the conjugal act is inescapable in both instructions.

A further problem with the Church's response is that it begs the question against nonnatural conception outside the womb. The nonnaturalness of the technique is not at question. It is clearly nonnatural, nonphysical, nongenital. The point which the document fails to address is precisely the identification of the good-making or bad-making characteristics of the procedure. The affirmation of the nonnaturalness of the technique does not move off the question. We are again left with an open question as to the appropriate use of technology.

The Church rejects in vitro fertilization as a licit use of science and technology because it violates what the Church considers to be the natural order of human sexual activity, and because it seeks to replace a natural function. The reference to the nature of the conjugal act and the preference for natural means is paramount in *Humanae Vitae*. The *Instruction on Respect for Human Life in Its Origin and on the Dignity of Procreation* is fundamentally derivative of these positions.

The claim that artificial means cannot be used because they are not natural clearly begs the question. A deeper claim is that they cannot be used because they violate the natural order or the divine will for the good of persons. This deeper claim begs the question as well, for it assumes that the natural order for human procreation (as the Church understands it) is always preferable to the use of technology.

Technology should not be rejected merely because it is technology. We know that the technology in question is not in the realm of the normal marital conjugal act. The point is, whether it is morally permissible to use it. The mere nonnaturalness of the technique does not adequately assess relevant moral characteristics. If the technique is available, and it is used with proper moral intentions, then the technique would seem to be acceptable. The propriety of the intentions is a separate matter from the moral licitness of the technique itself.

It could be accepted that the Church rightly insists that in vitro fertilization be homologous, and that it not be used to routinely replace or demean the proper conjugal act. But when the conjugal act is performed with all proper intentions and natual conception is impossible, we need a valid reason not to use the technology, if it is the only hope for the accomplishment of the intention of the act. The fact that the technology is external to the persons is obvious, but this fact does not in and of itself offer any self-evident justification that it be rejected. To say that the technology is wrong because the conception does not occur as a direct result of the conjugal act does not tell us why it is wrong to conceive indirectly.

A further problem with the document is that its conclusions are drawn from an assumption concerning the perfection of conception to be its natural occurrence within the context of marriage.

> In homologous in vitro fertilization, even if it is considered in the context of de facto existing sexual relations, the generation of the human person is objectively deprived of its proper perfection: namely being the result of and fruit of a conjugal act in which the spouses become "cooperators with God for giving life to a new person."[10]

This claim begs the question, as has already been shown. The fact that the fertilization is in vitro does not argue against the cooperative nature of the spouses with God.

The document claims that every child has the right "to be the fruit of the specific act of the conjugal love of his parents." It is not clear that this right is violated simply because the child is not the result of a specific conjugal *act*. If the child is the fruit of conjugal *love* and is born into a loving home, this right may be met in the most important context of the right, i.e., the child is willed as an expression of conjugal *love*, albeit not one specific *act*. The document states, "Such fertilization is neither in fact achieved nor positively willed as the expression and fruit of a specific act of the conjugal union."[11] The conception may indeed be positively willed as an expression of the *love* of the conjugal union, even if it is not the result of one specific act.

If the Church were to require that *every act intend,* not merely be open to the possibility of conception, then consistency could not condone even the rhythm method of birth control. But if the Church maintains merely that each act be open to the possibility of conception, rather than that each specific act *intend* conception, then homologous in vitro fertilization could be seen as licit without contradicting the Church's present position on birth control.

As I have shown, the practical pronouncement of *Humanae Vitae* is that every particular conjugal act does not require the intention of procreation. Thus, by denying that the totality of conjugal love is sufficient to legitimize in vitro fertilization, the statement on in vitro fertilization actually contradicts the Church's position with respect to the nature of specific conjugal acts, as previously expressed in *Humanae Vitae*. However, the current document is perfectly consistent with *Humanae Vitae* in that both documents beg the question with respect to the naturalness of method.

In the current doctrine on the origins of life, the Church condemns conception that is not the fruit of an act which specifically intends that fruit, yet fails to describe the bad-making characteristics of artificial methods for conception. At the same time, in *Humanae Vitae*, the Church does allow (even though She doesn't admit it) that the "'finality of the procreation pertains to the ensemble of conjugal life,"[12] but denies that very claim with regard to in vitro fertilization.

If the totality of conjugal life justifies both aspects of the conjugal act, procreative and unitive, then the conjugal act can be licit when it avoids procreation, and the conjugal act is thus also licit when procreation is impossible. As regards the licitness of procreation when it is the direct result of the proper conjugal intention but not the fruit of a specific act, the Church can appeal to the ensemble of conjugal life. We could thus conclude that the procreative act is licit even when it is not unitive. The physical actuality of this last case is in vitro fertilization.

The only remaining ground for rejecting in vitro fertilization would be some bad-making characteristic of the method itself. This evidence has not been presented.

The document suggests that, "Spouses who find themselves in this sad situation (sterility) are called upon to find in it an opportunity for sharing in a particular way the Lord's cross, the source of spiritual fruitfulness."[13]

The recommendation to replace physical fruitfulness with spiritual fruitfulness might not seem so burdensome if there were good reason to reject in vitro fertilization, but the Church has not demonstrated the moral illicitness of in vitro fertilization. Thus, it seems almost cruel to insist that married couples, willing to conceive as an expression of their conjugal love but unable to do so, should reject available technology to assist them in the accomplishment of the proper end of their act.

We could be true to most Catholic moral teachings on marital love and sexual relations and still hold that under certain conditions (e.g., a married couple wills but is physically unable to conceive), that in vitro fertilization may licitly replace the conjugal act.

For example, we could say that the obligation to conceive naturally and within marriage is a prima facie moral obligation that can be violated only when natural conception is impossible. We could also add the provision covered by the document, that no extra or spare embryos be conceived and destroyed. But with love as our guide, and the proper sense of obligation to our prima facie moral obligations, we can at once be true to Catholic teachings, meet the needs of good and loving people, and provide an ethically acceptable model for the proper use of technology.

NOTES AND REFERENCES

1. "Instruction on Respect for Human Life in its Origin and on the Dignity of Procreation," *Origins* 16, No. 40 (March 19, 1987).

2. Ibid. The document defines heterologous in vitro fertilization and embryo transfer as "the technique used to obtain a human conception through the meeting *in vitro* of gametes taken from at least one donor other than the spouses joined in marriage"; and homologous in vitro fertilization as "the technique used to obtain a human conception through the meeting *in vitro* of the gametes of the spouses joined in marriage."

3. Many theologians have discussed the merits and flaws of *Humanae Vitae*. For a concise and thorough philosophical analysis, see Carl Cohen, "Sex, Birth Control, and Human Life." in *Ethics*, No. 4 (July 1969).

4. *Humanae Vitae*, II, Section 16.

5. Ibid.

6. I am grateful to Rev. Dr. James J. McCartney, O.S.A., Director of the Bioethics Institute at Saint Francis Hospital, Miami Beach, Florida, for his comments and suggestions on this section.

7. *Origins,* op. cit.

8. Ibid.

9. Ibid.

10. Ibid.

11. Ibid.

12. *Humanae Vitae*, I, Section 3.

13. *Origins,* op. cit.

ON REENCHANTING THE WORLD

John F. Post

Those who would reenchant the world have so far failed. Indeed they have radically underestimated the challenge, which finds expression in the precise question, "In a world of scientific law, how can one speak of divine immanence?"[1] To put it another way, can those who live in a scientific world "affirm intrinsic meaning and value in the natural order? . . . Is a theology of nature . . . compatible with natural science?"[2] Or must we conclude with Berman and all those we may take him as speaking for, that "disenchantment is intrinsic to the scientific world view"?[3] If so, we may have to give up enchantment or give up science.

The first two sections explain just what the challenge to us reenchanters is, why it has been so nearly insurmountable, and wherein previous efforts to meet the challenge have failed. Then, drawing on more detailed work elsewhere, the following sections explain how those who live in a scientific world can affirm, after all, not only intrinsic meaning and value, but divine immanence.[4] The argument is not merely that such reenchantment is logically consistent with an austere scientific naturalism, but that we may form a synthesis of the two, in which each enriches the other while correcting the other's occasional extremes.

Research in Philosophy and Technology, Volume 10, pages 243-279.
Copyright © 1990 by JAI Press Inc.
All rights of reproduction in any form reserved.
ISBN: 1-55938-062-4

THE CHALLENGE

It is easy to see why these problems are so urgent. On the one hand, modern technology, or at least our inclination to pursue it in certain ways, results in planet-wide environmental and human degradation so appalling that we are compelled to question the world view or views apparently involved in any pursuit of that technology, and to grope for something better. On the other hand, few of us wish to reject the science on which so much of the technology is based. The physics, the chemistry, the biology—even their applications—all tell us important truths about the world, ourselves included. Berman is right that "in the seventeenth century, we threw out the baby with the bathwater," when we rejected "a whole landscape of inner reality."[5] How ironic if today we were to avoid that mistake only to fall into its opposite, by denying or disparaging the outer reality the sciences describe. And yet scientific description of that reality seems profoundly inimical to the reenchantment we seek.

Obviously, we must do better than the seventeenth century. But how? Begin by asking what exactly is supposed to be so inimical about the scientific description of things. In particular, consider the description of a sunset as a certain scattering of photons by particles in the atmosphere. This is clearly a true description, indeed objectively true, which suggests to many that the sunset is really or objectively nothing but such a scattering. To say so is to take the physical description as exclusively or monopolistically true; any description that is not a physical description, or not reducible to one, cannot be true (or false), and is not a genuine description after all, but perhaps a report on our feelings about the sunset, as when we call it beautiful. The beauty, such as it is, is not in the sunset, not in nature, but somehow merely in us, as we project our feelings outward; beauty is only "pleasure objectified."[6] So, too, for any other value, meaning, or enchantment it might please us to attribute to the sunset. Strictly speaking, the sunset is inert, or "dead."

Here in miniature we see what it is about scientism or naturalism in general, and physicalism in particular, that is supposed to be inimical to human being. Such views seem necessarily to reduce everything to nothing but collections of entities such as those the natural sciences are about (physics especially), and to restrict what can properly be said of the collections to what can be said in the sciences. Since value judgments—esthetic, moral, religious, whatever—cannot be reduced to or otherwise derived from scientific description, or indeed any description, they are not strictly or objectively true (or false), and the values they express are not in the world, but only in us.

Likewise, the subjective point of view, such as what it is like to be the persons we are, experiencing valuing and conscience as we do, and time and mystery, cannot be expressed in the sciences, or in any objective idiom. For objectification omits perspective, or the subjective point of view, precisely because viewing things objectively is to view them, so far as possible, from no point of view.[7] It seems that there can therefore be no place, in a scientific view of the world, for the perspective of a particular person in that selfsame world.[8] Consciousness, intentionality, religious and mystical inner states, our experience of time, and much more are cast adrift. Our lives can come to seem objectively insignificant, without point or meaning, and it can be correspondingly difficult to commit ourselves to worthwhile projects, even urgent ones.[9]

Clearly, this is the stuff of alienation, but that is not the end of it. Not only are values, meaning, and the subjective point of view threatened, so too are many familiar and often cheering ordinary properties of things—their color, fragrance, flavor, sound, and touch. These secondary qualities, as they are pejoratively called, are not primary or objective qualities, and evidently not reducible to them. It follows, we are told, that thinking of secondary qualities as real properties of things is a "falsification of the way things are," and contributes to the "delusion that the characteristics of the universe tie in closely with the doings of human beings."[10] Thus do objectivists in general, and physicalists in particular, characteristically warn against the evils of anthropocentric distortion of reality, and against projecting our idiosyncratic quality-spaces onto a world in which really there is no color, no sound, and no cheer.

Where is God, or any divinity, in this scheme? Nowhere. Expressions of divine immanence are irreducible to scientific description, to say nothing of purely physical description, and accordingly must be false or meaningless or otherwise defective. The same goes for all talk of "a theology of nature," all talk of nature's "participation in the drama of redemption," of nature as "sacramental," of "creation," of the world as "essentially good," and of us as "trustee or steward" of the ecosystem, responsible to some absentee creator.

Irreducibility of religious talk aside, is there a God in the first place? Naturalism evidently has no need of the hypothesis, no need to posit an extra, supernatural entity in order to give a satisfactory account of the world and its processes. If and to the extent that the existence of God is a matter of extra entities, Occam's razor comes into play, and we must conclude that there is no God.[11] If, on the other hand, the existence of God is not a matter of extra entities, then it seems that either God is a natural entity, or there is no such being at all. If God is a natural entity, it seems impossible to do justice to the divine transcendence, however admirably the divine immanence may have been accommodated; and if there is no such being at all, it is hard to see how the God-talk can be true, and with it the talk of a theology of nature.

HOW NOT TO REENCHANT THE WORLD

It does no good to object to this picture, as I've heard distinguished theologians and philosophers of religion object, simply that it is unbelievable, absurd, or at odds with faith. The objection neglects the powerful evidence and argument in favor of naturalism, and fails utterly to do justice to the genuine strengths of the position.[12] As Compton says, "It is misleading and . . . self-defeating, to refuse to grant this reductive approach any value whatever."[13] Simply to dismiss it *in toto* not only is question-begging, but neglects the venerable distinction between the baby and the bath.

We do better to face up to the fact that naturalism, true or not, is widespread and deeply entrenched among philosophers and reflective people generally. For better or worse, it is the dominant view in some of the most influential parts of our culture, no doubt in large measure because of its relation to scientific technology, and "has become such a profoundly established pattern that we now measure Christianity and theism against it."[14] Those who would reenchant the world, if they hope even to gain a hearing for their views in an increasingly secular world, must somehow come to terms with the teachings of an austere naturalism, either to accept them or to modify or reject them on the basis of informed, responsible argument. To compose theologies of nature as though there were no real difficulty from this quarter, as many have—to write glibly of divine immanence, of the gods of forest and stream, of a new animism— is unlikely to be taken seriously, or even read, by those whose views and behavior most need to be changed.

So let us retrace our steps, and reflect more carefully on the matter of the sunset. Scientific descriptions of it, we may concede, are true, even objectively true (meaning simply that their truth is independent of evidence, perspective, consciousness, understanding, and the like).[15] In particular, the sunset is indeed a scattering of photons by atmospheric particles. The problems begin when someone goes on to claim that really it is nothing but such a scattering, thus taking the physical description as exclusively true. And what lies behind this monopolistic or totalizing claim of exclusive truth is primarily the doctrine that what is not reducible to a physical description is somehow defective. Reject the doctrine, then, and the way lies open to other kinds of true description of the sunset, truths that could be just as important as scientific truths about it, if not more so.

It follows that what is inimical to human being and reenchantment is not science, after all, but reductive and monopolistic interpretation of its lessons. It is not "modern science [that] got into trouble by claiming to be the one true description of reality,"[16] and not "science [that] decides, in a normative fashion, that the world consists in nothing other than the picture drawn by science,"[17] but totalizing varieties of metaphysics based on reductive and monopolistic interpretations and exaggerations of what science does tell us.

Powerful support for antireductivism comes from a number of sources, but none so telling, perhaps, as that from physicalists themselves. In recent years, physicalists in growing numbers have acknowledged the barriers to reductive accounts in biology, psychology, semantics, and more.[18] They have rejected reductive approaches in favor of various *non*reductive physicalisms, according to which nonphysical properties and states need not be identical with physical properties and states, and nonphysical descriptions need not be definable by or translatable into physical descriptions.[19]

The trouble is that merely rejecting reductivism hardly suffices to reenchant the world. From the fact that the sunset is not nothing but some collection of physical entities and processes, it does not follow that it has any intrinsic meaning or value, let alone one's favorite, only that we cannot deny meaning and value solely on the ground of physical irreducibility. Likewise, from the insight, shared by many, that the sciences cannot claim to give us exclusive truth about the world, it does not follow that we may henceforth speak with serene conscience about the gods of forest and stream, or much else. Liberating though the rejection of reductivism is, it is after all only an opening, and much depends on what sort of positive account goes with it.

Physicalists face a parallel problem. One of the few merits of reductivism, after all, is that it tells a moderately clear story about what the relation is supposed to be between the nonphysical and the physical. Nonphysical properties and states (biological, mental, semantic, and the rest) are just identical with or at least in some strong sense equivalent to physical ones, and nonphysical descriptions are necessarily coextensive with (and in that sense reducible to) physical ones. But if this is rejected (except for a few cases where such reduction does obtain), what positive account of the relation, or relations, between the physical and the nonphysical can physicalists—or anyone else— put in its place? What, for example, is the relation between the atmospheric scattering of photons and the perceived colors of the sunset that so impress us? What is the relation between our brain states and mental states? Between physical time and subjectively experienced temporal becoming?

It happens that in the last dozen years or so a few physicalists have developed a positive account of an appropriate relation between the physical and the nonphysical. The relation is one of nonreductive determination, also called supervenience (or a variety of it). A set of nonphysical properties or states is determined by (or supervenes upon) a set of physical properties or states, just in case any two physically possible worlds that are alike as regards whether or not something in them has the latter, are also alike as regards whether or not it has the former. To fix its physical properties (*including* its physical relations to a wider environment) is also to fix its nonphysical properties (and relations), even though no nonphysical property (or relation) need be identical with or otherwise reducible to any physical property (or relation). The thing need not be, and typically is not, nothing but a physical thing, nor are physical descriptions of it exclusively true.[20]

The resulting nonreductive varieties of physicalism bear crucially on the typical reenchanter's would-be rejection of physicalism. For when we reject a view (or support it), we must first identify its distinctive minimal theses—

the least it can claim and still be the sort of view it is. Otherwise we are likely to be rejecting (or supporting) a straw man. To my knowledge, *no one who would reenchant the world has attempted to identify the minimal theses of physicalist materialism, or physicalism.* Yet, ever since the seventeenth century, this is the world view (or cluster of views) that in one version or another has been most powerfully at odds with reenchantment. The result is that many a reenchanter's discussion leaves the opposition's minimal core untouched. Objections to reductivism, for example, however well-founded and eloquent, have no effect on a nonreductive physicalism.

What, then, are the minimal physicalist theses? Elsewhere, I argue in detail for the following three: (i) every entity whatever is a mathematical-physical entity; (ii) there can be no difference between things without some mathematical-physical difference between them; and (iii) all truth whatever, whether in the sciences or beyond, is determined by truths at the level of mathematical physics.[21] Experience suggests that simply asserting (i)-(iii) can generate the same hostile rejection out of hand as does requiring universal physical reducibility. No doubt this is largely because (i)-(iii), on first hearing, can seem equally reductive, or at least to give a kind of primacy to the physical that is inimical to human being and the reenchantment of the world.

Before rejecting them out of hand, however, one should inquire not only into the evidence for them, but also into the ways the minimal version of physicalism they express differs from—and is superior to—the more familiar reductive and monopolistic varieties.[22] What are the differences? To begin with, unlike these inimical varieties, the minimal version does not exclude emergent and wholly novel entities and properties (such as, presumably, persons, art works, languages, and so on, plus certain of their properties). Nor is the minimal version eliminative. It does not entail, for example, that there are no thoughts, emotions, sensations, intentions, or whatever. Nor does it entail that talk about such things is somehow defective, or that it ought someday be replaced by talk about purely physical things.

Further, minimal physicalism is not an identity theory, typically so-called (according to which all properties and states of things are just identical with physical properties and states). True, like all versions of physicalism, the theory requires that any entity—a person, say—is identical with something or other in the physicalist's inventory of what there is. In this trivial, limiting sense the minimal theory is an identity theory, meaning, in the jargon of the trade, a token-token identity theory. But in this sense *any* metaphysics is an identity theory (that is, a token-token identity theory), insofar as it must claim that everything is somehow token-identical with or composed or constituted from certain basic entities or processes, whether physical, mental, organic, spiritual, or whatever. Yet even though a person, say, is thus token-identical with some collection of basic physical entities, the person need not be (and will not be) nothing but such a collection, or even individuatable as a person by some purely physical or other scientific term. Indeed, what determines what a person is, or anything else, need not be the properties of its physical parts alone, but can be (and often is) those properties only in relation to a wider environment. Minimal physicalism entails no narrow atomism, but is entirely congenial to holistic thinking.

Nor does the minimal version violate the methodological and hermeneutical autonomy of the various disciplines or domains of discourse. Each domain continues to enjoy its own methods of inquiry and interpretation, its own vocabulary for describing and explaining things within its scope. Each can proceed without waiting to see how its terms, its descriptions, or its interpretations connect with some domain closer to physics. No domain need fear that physical terms or methods are necessarily superior to its own with respect to matters within its scope. Indeed, physical terms and methods will often be inferior with respect to such matters.

Nor need everything real be brought under some objective description. Thus, there can be (and are) objectively inexpressible subjective states, such as, say, what it is like to be a bat,[23] or what it is like to be the person I am, experiencing time and death as I do, and conscience and mystery. The subjective point of view, however ineffable, not only need not be left out of account, but can be accorded the kind of priority it often deserves. So, too, for secondary qualities and emotions. The former, suitably construed, can be seen to be among the important ways things are, and the latter can correspond with the facts, so that "to feel about something may in certain privileged cases be the last, most penetrating way of knowing what the thing is."[24]

Nor is the minimal version committed to some mirror theory of truth, or even to some causal relation between words and the world, in virtue of which there is an objective fact of the matter as regards the reference of our terms. It does not even require the terms to have any precise reference, determinate or otherwise. The physicalist can heartily agree that vagueness and tortured, novel usage often are indispensible, in everything from poetry to physics, for creating momentous and irreducible new ways of seeing ourselves and our world or worlds. Metaphors especially are essential in this regard, and it is reassuring that a physicalist accommodation of metaphor presents no very great difficulty. Even though there is a sense in which metaphorical truth is physically determined, reduction to the literal, let alone to aseptic precision, is nowhere envisaged, and metaphorical truths can be accorded their appropriate sort of priority.

In these and other ways, then, minimal physicalism is compatible with so much that physicalism traditionally is supposed to deny or disparage. And this means that the usual objections to physicalism are all blocked. The usual objections have all been to the effect that physicalism cannot account for, or is actually incompatible with, or in some other way cannot do justice to one or another of the matters listed here. Indeed, so long as physicalism is reductive and eliminative, and therefore denies much of what clearly is the case, it will be an obviously inadequate account; those who would reenchant the world will be entitled to remain correspondingly undisturbed by what such a view would imply. But a nonreductive, nonmonopolistic physicalism of the sort outlined above (and defended in detail elsewhere) cannot be so easily dismissed. Indeed, the usual reactions against physicalism now must seem obsolete, flogging as they do the dead horse of reductivism and monopolistic or exclusive truth.

Thus is the evidence on behalf of a minimal physicalist version of naturalism powerfully multiplied. For, instead of explaining away so much of what clearly is the case, it explains it, nonreductively and holistically, by way of showing how it is determined by matters at the level of mathematical physics, even while explanations and interpretations in other terms are accorded the primacy they so often deserve.[25] And the more a theory successfully accounts for, the more support it thereby acquires. We begin to see why no casual or piecemeal arguments against the minimal core of physicalism will work. Instead, as is so often the case with powerful theories of large scope, it takes a theory to kill a theory. There is as yet no equally powerful competing theory on the scene, or so the physicalist is prepared to argue. Indeed, much of the seeming strength of the competitors—process metaphysics, for example, and most existentialism and phenomenology—has derived from their ability to give an account of matters that reductive and totalizing versions of physicalism have omitted or even denied or vilified. But a nonreductive, tolerant version of physicalism, pluralist in spirit, can likewise accommodate such matters, sometimes even giving a better account, and in any case suffers in no such comparison with these competitors. Their seemingly greater strength in this respect thus evaporates.

We see, then, why the challenge to us reenchanters has been so nearly insurmountable, and wherein previous efforts to meet the challenge have failed. They have failed because they have not identified the minimal core of physicalism, and thus have not come to terms with it one way or another. The core is untouched by arguments against reductivism, eliminativism, type-type identity theories, atomism, monopolistic and totalizing claims to exclusive truth, and so on. And yet, alas, the core does not seem very congenial to reenchantment, because it is hard to see how the core could be compatible with there being intrinsic meaning and value in the world. The core theses, again, are that every entity whatever is a mathematical-physical entity, that there can be no difference without a mathematical-physical difference, and that all truth is determined by mathematical-physical truth. How, in the face of such theses, can we say that the world has, or contains, intrinsic meaning and value? Where is the divine immanence, let alone the gods of forest and stream, when everything in the world is a physical entity and all truth is determined by physical truth? How, in other words, can one speak of divine immanence or of a theology of nature in a world of scientific law? Mustn't we conclude after all that disenchantment is intrinsic to a scientific world view?

Such difficulties will tempt many to say, "So much the worse even for a minimal physicalism." Of course, that is one logically possible path to take, at odds though it is with our best evidence and argument. Another, at the opposite extreme of reaction, is to say, "So much the worse for reenchantment." This, too, is unsatisfactory. A third is to declare that there really is no logical inconsistency between physicalism and reenchantment. But this response is in its way just as unappealing as the other two, for we would want to know *why* they are not inconsistent, despite so many appearances to the contrary, and we would want to know what the nature is of the deeper consistency. We crave coherence and unity, and in the long run no mere logical consistency between a couple of disparate perspectives is enough. Better by far would be a fourth response, namely to seek some sort of synthesis of physicalism and enchantment, however uneasy and tentative, in which each enriches the other while correcting the other's occasional extremes. To this we now turn.

PHYSICALISM AND VALUE

The first step toward reenchanting the world is to get values back into it. So long as values are merely projections of our desires onto a normatively inert world, or merely our internal response to causal stimulation by the world, we cannot affirm intrinsic value in the natural order, and the world cannot be said in the intended, objective sense to contain an element of value. We need therefore to reflect a moment on how the values disappeared from the world in the first place.

They disappeared, of course, in the seventeenth century, or at least were well on the way to disappearing, when the world began to be identified with what could be expressed in the language of natural science. Since no value judgment is derivable from or reducible to such language, or so it came to seem, it looked as though the world could contain no entelechy, no *telos,* no element of value whatever, but instead could only be nothing but the objective world of matter in motion. Values were banished from nature, along with much else that matters to us. All efforts to get the values back in have seemed unconvincing, evidently because it has seemed that "any objective description of the world would have to be value-free."[26] Indeed, no such effort can possibly succeed, so long as the world is identified with the totality of objective, nonnormative fact, and the only sense in which the world could contain or exhibit an element of value is via derivability from or reducibility to such fact.

What underlies this history is a set of assumptions and inferences that amount to what Mackie calls an "argument from queerness"[27] against objective values—against values that are "part of the fabric of the world."[28] The argument is that so-called objective values would have to be very queer sorts of things, because their relation with the facts is so mysterious, being a matter neither of derivation (or entailment or implication), nor of reduction (or definability or translatability), nor even of supervenience or "resultance" (the latter two notions being either unclear or, even if clear, not robust enough to capture the relation required by objectivists about value.)[29] Better by far to replace the alleged objective values with some sort of subjective response that can be causally (and therefore intelligibly) related to stimulation by the natural features on which the alleged values are said to be resultant or consequential.

Mackie himself explains why the argument from queerness is indispensable for subjectivists about value. Without some such argument, the mere fact of widespread disagreement about values does not by itself imply that there are no objective values about which to disagree, no more than disagreement in science implies that there really is no truth of the matter there. Or, as Nozick remarks about moral values, "It is because we do not see how an objective ethics is *possible* that we worry about irresolvable moral disagreements."[30] Indeed, if anything, the presumption should be that there *are* objective values. For this is what ordinary usage of normative terms overwhelmingly presupposes, as does most of our actual normative reasoning. Hence, as Mackie sees, subjectivists like himself are compelled to advance an error thesis: our ordinary usage and reasoning, entrenched for millenia, are massively in error, for there really are no objective values. And Mackie is far more candid than most subjectivists in acknowledging that the burden of proof is on those who advance any such thesis. The argument from queerness is meant to discharge this burden.

It follows that if we can undermine the argument from queerness, by showing the falsity of one of its assumptions, then not only is the presumption that there are objective values undefeated and in full force, we are free to treat ordinary usage and ordinary normative reasoning as powerful independent evidence against subjectivism, and in particular against its thesis that a couple of genuinely conflicting value judgments can be equally correct, there being no real truth of the matter in the first place. If we can undermine the argument from queerness, by showing how objective values are possible, we need not worry so deeply about irresolvable normative disagreements. Without the argument from queerness, or something very like it, subjectivism has little to be said for it.

In the argument from queerness we encounter yet again the twin themes of reduction and exclusive, or monopolistic, truth. The idea is that, unless talk about values can be reduced to or derived from or in some like way related to the privileged, monopolistically true factual or descriptive discourse, such talk cannot be strictly true (or false), and the values it expresses are really just our subjective responses to causal stimulation by the world. *It follows that a nonreductive, nonmonopolistic physicalism might well have the resources to overcome the argument from queerness and the tradition it underlies.* Such physicalism—or indeed *any* nonreductive, nonmonopolistic metaphysics—is free to deny that the world must be identified with what some privileged, factual discourse is about, natural science included, and also to affirm that in any case the possible relations between such facts and the values are not exhausted by relations of derivation, reduction, "resultance," or even supervenience (in one sense).

Instead, the relevant relation could be nonreductive determination.[31] That is, the purely descriptive or natural facts about the world (including us) might nonreductively determine which of our value judgments are true. If in turn the totality of descriptive fact is determined by facts at the level of mathematical physics, as the physicalist contends, then the objective world of matter in motion would contain an element of value after all, in that the mathematical-physical truths about the world would determine the correct distribution of truth-values over our value judgments, even if we often do not know just what that distribution is. We would no longer be forced to conclude, bleakly, that "any objective description of the world would have to be value-free,"[32] or that "the facts of science possess no meaning in and of themselves"[33] (unless of course we continued to assume, uncritically, that the facts can possess meaning only if meaning is reducible to the facts). A purely scientific description of us and the world would not be value-neutral or inert, despite long tradition to the contrary, and we would be free to regard nature and values as ontologically reunified.

Bold talk, and yet there is a way to make good on it. To begin with, the argument from queerness against objective values can be shown to be based on a false assumption. The argument assumes that there are only four sorts of relation that could obtain between the values and the facts: derivation, reduction, "resultance" (or some watery supervenience), and causation. Unfortunately, to show that this assumption is false it is not enough simply to assert that a relation of nonreductive determination might obtain. One must also show that this is an intelligible and plausible alternative to the listed four. Otherwise, opponents of reenchantment could reply that, although it is abstractly possible for there to be an alternative to the listed four, no one has given any reason to suppose that it actually obtains.

How, then, can we make clear what the alternative relation is? In particular, what would it mean to say that the facts determine the values? Part of the reply is that determination is a familiar relation, and basically a simple one. In ordinary parlance, to say that one thing determines another is just to say that the first delimits or fixes how the second can be; or, that given the first, there is one and only one way the second can be. Thus, to say (perhaps falsely) that the outcome of the battle of Lake Trasimene was determined by the terrain and the commanders' initial disposition of forces (or lack of it), is to say that, given the terrain and disposition, there could have been one and only one outcome. This is equivalent to saying that given any other battlefield in which the terrain and disposition of forces were the same as in this one, the outcome would likewise have been the same. Or, in the possible-worlds idiom that has become so useful, any two physically possible worlds that are the same as regards the battlefield's terrain and the disposition of forces are also the same as regards the battle's outcome.[34]

Similarly, to say that the facts determine the values is equivalent to saying that any two physically possible worlds that are the same as regards the facts that obtain in them are also the same as regards the values that obtain in them. Or, since this may seem to commit us to the existence of facts and of values as extra entities, over and above the admitted furniture of the world, let us reformulate in terms of that furniture, and speak only of natural or nonnormative entities and traits (relations included) on the one hand, and our value judgments about them on the other. To say that the one determines the correctness of the other, then, is to say that given any two physically possible worlds W1 and W2 in which the entities have the same natural traits, the same value judgments are correct in both W1 and W2. That is, given the natural traits and relations of the world's entities (ourselves included), there can be one and only one correct distribution of truth-values over our value judgments. (Not that the value judgments need be strictly true or false, only that if we pretend they are and distribute those values over them, then there is one and only one correct distribution.) This helps make it clear that the existence of objective values is not a matter of extra entities but of there being a truth of the matter as regards the correctness or incorrectness of our value judgments, a truth of the matter determined by objective, natural features of the world. Values need not be thought of as denizens of some shadowy, Platonic realm "out there," perhaps beyond space and time.[35]

There is also a weak sense of determination, a sense in which even opponents of objective values would agree that natural fact determines value. In this sense, the natural properties of people and things, *in conjunction with the normative principles one happens to hold,* determine one and only one distribution of truth-values over the value judgments. In the strong sense, by contrast, the natural properties alone determine the correct distribution over our value judgments, one's own normative first principles included. This is the sense defined above. Of course, it is this strong sense that is meant when one suggests that the world objectively contains an element of value after all, via nonreductive determination of value by fact.

Is this determination relation clearly nonreductive? Some have doubted it, yet the leading argument that the relation ultimately is reductive is based on a faulty presupposition.[36] And there are other technical questions about the relation (or its possible-worlds explication) that can be answered satisfactorily, although this is not the occasion to rehearse the details. The relation has emerged as a powerful and essential tool in the clarification of minimal physicalism as well as much else.

Thus, it can be made clear enough what the relation is. But is there any reason to suppose that the relation actually obtains between fact and value? That it does follows from two premises, one of them unproblematic, the other less so. Before presenting the premises and the derivation of the determinacy of valuation from them, we need to be very clear what we are trying to do at this stage of the discussion. We are *not* trying to give either a non-question-begging proof that the facts determine the values or a non-question-begging refutation of subjectivism as regards values. Instead, we are (only) trying to show that there is an intelligible, unqueer, plausible alternative to the relations between fact and value listed in the argument from queerness. This means that we do not have to claim at this stage that our two premises are *true* (or even probable), only that they are intelligible, unqueer, plausible principles that jointly entail the determinacy of valuation. Notice also that since the issue at this stage is whether the argument from queerness is sound, and in particular whether one of its assumptions is true, the argument from queerness cannot be appealed to in order to cast doubt on the premises that jointly entail the determinacy of valuation. To do so would beg the question of whether the argument from queerness is sound.

The first premise in the argument for the determinacy of valuation is unproblematic; indeed, it is shared by all parties. The idea is that there can be no difference in value without some relevant natural or descriptive difference. Even Hare, no objectivist about value, subscribes to this principle, as when he asserts that if St. Francis is a morally good person, so is anyone who is relevantly like St. Francis in natural respects.[37] And Harman, likewise no friend of objective values, also accepts the principle: "If it is wrong for someone else to do something, it would be wrong for me to do that in a similar situation."[38] In like manner, if I claim that a certain painting is great art while another is not, I must be prepared to point eventually to some relevant descriptive difference between the two (something to do with color, texture, design, subject, technique, etc.). This includes the case in which the second painting is a perfect forgery—even an exact replica down to the last microparticle. In that case the descriptive difference in virtue of which one is great art and the other only great technology would presumably have something to do with who made it—O'Keefe, say—and how she did it.

Since we are to treat like cases alike, such "equity" requires further that the principles to be followed in treating one case are to be followed in treating any relevantly similar other. The first premise, then, comes to the following Equity Principle:

EP.   For any two physically possible worlds W1 and W2 that are relevantly similar as regards the natural properties and relations of their entities, one thing has a certain normative status in W1 if and only if it has that same status in W2; and a normative principle is true (or at least correct or to be followed) in W1 if and only if it is true (or correct or to be followed) in W2.[39]

EP, like related notions of "universalizability," provides no criteria for what are to count as the normatively relevant natural properties and similarities. Such criteria are to be supplied by the substantive principles of one's value theory. Fortunately, the argument for the determinacy of valuation nowhere requires such criteria to be specified.

The second premise is a generalization of the principle that a couple of genuinely conflicting value judgments cannot both be correct; if the two exhaust the alternatives, just one of them should be given assent (whether we know it or not), and in that sense is correct. (Why this is not question-begging we see in a moment.) This is a kind of bivalence for value judgments, although it stops short of attributing truth or falsity to them. More generally, given any exhaustive set of two or more mutually conflicting value judgments, just one member of the set is correct. That is, just one should be given assent; or, if we are in a mood to pretend they have truth-values, just one should be assigned truth. This in turn implies our second premise, or what may be called Meta-Normative Anti-relativism:

MNA.   If we pretend that our value judgments are true or false, and distribute those values over the totality of the value judgments, then among all the possible mutually conflicting such distributions, only one is correct.

MNA is to be taken in a strong sense, not weak. In the weak sense we could "universalize" our principles in line with EP, distributing truth-values over the value judgments accordingly, thus arriving at the one and only one "correct" distribution induced by our principles in conjunction with the facts; and all the while others could do the same with *their* principles, arriving at their very different one and only one "correct" distribution. In the strong sense of MNA, there is only one distribution allowed, and one of these differing distributions, our own included, may or may not be it; among all the possible mutually conflicting principles persons might use in making their own distributions, only one is correct (or to be given assent).

Doesn't invoking MNA amount to assuming what is to be shown, namely that the facts determine which of our value judgments are to be given assent? No. Even if just one member of an exhaustive set of genuinely conflicting value judgments should be given assent, and likewise just one distribution of truth-values over our value judgments, it does not follow that *which* distribution is to be given assent is determined by the facts or by anything else. Thus the determinacy amounts to much more than MNA, just as it amounts to much more than EP. But the determinacy does follow from the conjunction of EP and MNA, as we see next.

Consider a physically possible world W1 together with its entities' natural properties (and relations). Suppose that in W1 the value judgments are to be assented to or not, hence that in W1 they are correct or not, to be followed or not, or whatever. Thus we may pretend they are true or false in W1. In line with MNA, this is to suppose that in any set of mutually conflicting value judgments, one at most is true in W1, first principles included; truth-in-world-W is nonrelative, in the sense that, given an exhaustive set of conflicting alternatives, exactly one member is true in W, and one's favorite candidate may or may not be it. Likewise, exactly one distribution of truth-values in W over the value judgments is correct.

Now, suppose, contrary to what is to be shown, that there is another physically possible world, W2, in which the entities have the same natural properties as in W1, yet there is a value judgment true in one of W1 or W2 but not the other. This is to suppose that a change in distribution of truth-values over the value judgments, such as the change between W1 and W2, does not require a change in the natural properties (or relations). But because W1 and W2 are the same as regards natural properties, the persons, acts, and circumstances in either world are indiscernible from those in the other in all natural respects. It follows that the persons, acts, and circumstances in the two are similar (because indiscernible) in all natural respects, hence in all *relevant* natural respects. Thus, they are relevantly similar, as are the worlds W1 and W2 which contain them. And this is true even if we haven't the faintest idea which natural respects are normatively relevant.

If W1 and W2 are relevantly similar, then according to EP, an item has a certain normative status in W1 if and only if it has that same status in W2. Also, according to EP, a normative principle is true in W1 iff it is true in W2 (where "iff" abbreviates "if and only if"). Furthermore, every value judgment asserts either the normative status of some particular item or some general principle or rule, first principles included. It follows that there is no value judgment true in one of W1 or W2 but not in the other after all, first principles included; a change in truth-value of a value judgment does require a change in the natural properties. That is, given any physically possible worlds in which the entities have the same natural properties, the same value judgments are true in them as well. But, as seen, this amounts to saying that the facts determine the values.

We cannot yet draw the stronger, cognitivist conclusion that the value judgments are true or false. From the fact that there is no value judgment true in one of W1 or W2 but not the other, it does not follow that there is some value judgment true in one of them, or in any other world. Nevertheless, what we may conclude is nearly as strong. Given the purely natural properties of people and things, then whether or not the value judgments are true or false, if we pretend they are and distribute those values over them, there is one and only one such distribution allowed, even if we do not know which one it is.

Why doesn't using MNA beg the question against the subjectivist? If at this stage of the discussion we were advancing the argument for the determinacy of valuation as a non-question-begging proof of objectivism, or as a non-question-begging refutation of subjectivism, then using MNA certainly would beg the question. For, in accepting MNA, we would be accepting what the subjectivist denies. At this stage, however, we are only trying to show that there are intelligible, unqueer premises that jointly entail the determinacy, and therefore that the alternatives listed in the subjectivist's argument from queerness are by no means exhaustive. That is, we are only trying to undermine the argument from queerness by showing that its major premise is false.

The argument for the determinacy does indeed undermine the argument from queerness. It does so first by explicating a simple, familiar relation—determination—which is a clear alternative to those listed, and then by showing that such determinacy follows from a couple of intelligible, unqueer premises, namely EP and MNA. Since the determinacy does follow, subjectivists must reject at least one of EP and MNA. Since they themselves accept the unobjectionable EP, they must and do reject MNA. It is *not* the case, they believe, that among all the possible mutually conflicting distributions of truth-values over our value judgments, just one is correct, meaning that it should be assented to by all parties (whether they know it or not). But subjectivists thereby merely deny what MNA affirms; and the denial or negation of an assertion is presumably itself unintelligible if the assertion is. Thus, it might seem that subjectivists cannot be rejecting this premise on the ground that it is unintelligible. Instead they must be rejecting it as false or incorrect. If so, they must concede that the premises as well as the conclusion of the argument for determinacy are intelligible, even if not both true, and that the relations listed in the argument from queerness do not by any means exhaust the intelligible alternatives as regards what the consequential link might be between facts and values. It would therefore seem that the argument from queerness fails, being based on a false assumption.

Unfortunately, subjectivists often do not reject MNA for being unintelligible in the sense in which the denial of an unintelligible assertion is itself automatically unintelligible. Rather, they reject it for being unintelligible in the sense of being explanatorily impotent. They believe that objective values can play no appropriate explanatory role in our accounts of natural events, and therefore that MNA can play no such role either. That is, positing as does MNA that just one member of an exhaustive set of conflicting value judgments is correct cannot explain, or can add nothing to our purely naturalistic explanations of various natural events, including making the value judgments we do. All the explanatory work is done by other, nonnormative disciplines, such as psychology and anthropology. In this regard, positing uniquely correct judgments independent of the normative principles we happen to hold is like positing witches, and is explanatorily unintelligible.[40]

Nevertheless, it is increasingly clear that positing such correctness does play an important and ineliminable explanatorily role, and is therefore explanatorily intelligible.[41] There are real regularities in the world that are identifiable only by appeal to normative properties construed as realized or not, independently of our principles. Such regularities include natural beauty's inspiring awe, honesty's engendering trust, justice's commanding allegiance, depravity's arousing condemnation, and so on. In this way, various normative properties figure in many of our best explanations. Since the normative properties involved evidently are irreducible, the explanations in which they appear evidently are ineliminable.

This reinforces our verdict that the argument from queerness fails to exhaust the intelligible alternatives as regards what the link or links might be between facts and values. Since the argument fails, it cannot be used to support subjectivism, nor can it be used to support the rejection of MNA, as so often in effect it has been, and as ultimately it must be.[42] And independent of the arguments from queerness and for determinacy, the weight of the evidence, including various facts about actual normative reasoning and other usage of normative language, including the explanatory, is heavily in favor of MNA.[43]

Recall the consequences of undermining the argument from queerness. Once the argument is undermined, not only is the presumption of objectivity undefeated and in full force, we are free to treat various facts about actual normative reasoning and other usage of normative language, including the explanatory, as powerful independent evidence against subjectivism, and in particular against the subjectivist's rejection of MNA. Without some such argument as the one from queerness, the mere fact of normative disagreement, even widespread, does not imply that there are no objective values about which to disagree, and subjectivists have no way of discharging their burden of proving that our ordinary normative reasoning and usage, entrenched for millenia, are in reality massively in error.

In view of all this—including the clear evidence of actual normative reasoning and other usage of normative discourse, again including the explanatory—let us henceforth assume that MNA is true, and therefore (granted EP) that the determinacy of valuation obtains. Thus, not only is physicalism consistent with objectivity as regards values, the objectivity follows from a couple of assumptions the physicalist could easily accept, and it is not after all "hard to see how objective values fit into a physicalist perspective."[44] We are not forced to concede that for physicalism "there is really nothing left in objects but their value for something, or someone, else."[45]

We can even define "correspondence with the facts" for a value judgment J: J corresponds with the facts iff J is true in the one distribution allowed by the purely descriptive facts about the actual world. The fact with which J corresponds is simply the conjunction of those facts that just suffice to determine J's truth-value in the distribution as true. More precisely,

CD. Where J is true in the one distribution allowed by the world, what J corresponds with is the smallest piece of the world to determine J's truth-value.

A piece of a world W is simply a subset of W's entities, possibly spatiotemporally scattered, plus their natural properties and relations. W_J is a smallest piece (or a least, or just suffices) to determine J's truth-value iff W_J, but no proper piece of W_J determines J's truth-value. W_J determines J's truth-value iff, given any W relevantly similar to W_J, J is true (false, neuter) in W iff J is true (false, neuter) in W_J. When J is not true in the one distribution allowed by the world, we say J corresponds with nothing.[46]

Philosophers have often questioned what it could mean to say that a value judgment makes a truth-claim, and just what the claim could possibly be (other than one that expresses, say, the speaker's attitudes.)[47] There is now a ready reply. The truth-claim J makes is the one that expresses the fact with which J would correspond were J true in the one distribution allowed over the value judgments. J's truth-claim is the class T_J^* of those descriptive truths that would, were J true, just suffice to determine J's truth-value as true. These truths express the descriptive matters in virtue of which J would be correct, even if (or even though) J is not derivable from or reducible to any description, *including* the description expressed by the conjunction of the members of T_J^*. It follows that unmoved spectators of the actual do have something to observe that would confirm J (whether they knew it or not),[48] namely those phenomena that just suffice to make J correct, or (what comes to the same thing) the purely descriptive facts with which J corresponds. If two people agree on these facts, then (whether they know it or not) they ought to agree on J, even when J is itself a first principle rather than a particular judgment made in light of such a principle.

Philosophers have also wondered how values could be "part of the fabric of the world," so that a change in the former would require a change in the latter. Here, too, we have a ready reply. They are part of the fabric in the sense that the correctness of a value judgment is determined by purely natural facts. A world W whose fabric makes various natural facts obtain in W would be one whose fabric thereby makes certain value judgments correct in W; a change in their correctness would require a change in the natural facts.

Thus, it seems ever more strained and artificial to withhold strict truth and falsity from value judgments. There is a fact of the matter as regards their correctness; they make truth-claims; they can correspond with particular pieces of the world; and they are confirmable by various descriptive phenomena even when we happen not to know what phenomena those are. A distinction between judgments for which all this holds (and more), and judgments which in addition are strictly true or false, looks like a distinction without a difference.[49]

Metaphysicians of every sort, not just physicalists, may take advantage of the present approach. If the truths about the metaphysician's unifiers suffice to determine all descriptive truth, then automatically they suffice to determine normative truth, thanks to the descriptive determinacy of valuation. There is no need to posit two realms of being and knowledge—noumenal and phenomenal, say—in which values and science go their separate ways.

We can therefore achieve an ideal of many philosophers from Plato on: to ground normative truth in what there is. Yet we can also agree with Sartre and all those we may take him as speaking for, in effect, when he says, "Ontology . . . cannot formulate ethical precepts. It is concerned solely with what is, and we cannot possibly derive imperatives from ontology's indicatives."[50] The reason we can follow both Plato and Sartre is that the normative imperatives are grounded in nonnormative fact, in the sense of determination, even if such grounding by itself enables no one to formulate or derive the imperatives from any indicatives.

To this day, physicalist varieties of metaphysics tend to echo the Democritean argument, "In reality there are only atoms and the void; therefore our values are mere conventions." The inference to mere conventions presupposes that the values are not determined by the physical phenomena. The presupposition is reinforced by the presumed failure of all efforts to show determination via either reduction or derivation, together with the further assumption that there is no other way to do so. The idea is that, since ought can neither be reduced to nor derived from is, "the distinction of vice and virtue is not founded merely on the relations of objects," so that "morality is nothing in the abstract nature of things," if we may use Hume's words to this effect.

Contrary to this whole multistranded tradition, we are entitled to the courage of our conventions. If all descriptive truth is determined by truth at the level of physics, as physicalists contend, then the objective world of matter in motion exhibits an element of value after all—intrinsic value—in that the physical truths about the world determine the correct distribution of truth-values over the value judgments. A purely scientific description of us and the world is not value-neutral or inert or "dead," despite long tradition to the contrary, and we are free not only to regard nature and value as ontologically reunified, but also to argue that "value pervades all life."[51] Although values seemed banished forever from nature, they were always there. It is we who may now return from long exile, imposed by too-ready acceptance of reducibility and derivability as the only ways to show that the physical world contains an element of value.

PHYSICALISM AND REENCHANTMENT

We see, then, how one can speak of intrinsic or objective value in a scientific world. But what of divine immanence and the other elements of enchantment? One such element is the subjective point of view, or the perspectives of particular persons in the very world that science describes. In some way we must do justice to what it is like to be the persons we are, experiencing mystery and time as we do, and valuing and choosing. Omit or deny what it is like, and our lives will seem insignificant or meaningless.

The problem here is partly that what it is like to be a particular subject evidently cannot be expressed in any objective idiom. Such objectification omits perspective, or the subject's point of view, for the simple reason that viewing things objectively is to view them, so far as possible, from no point of view. As Nagel puts it, "Every subjective phenomenon is essentially connected with a single point of view, and it seems inevitable that an objective, physical theory will abandon that point of view."[52] It would follow, of course, that there is no way that what it is like to be the subject can be reduced to purely physical or other objective discourse: "The reduction can succeed only if . . . the specific viewpoint is omitted from what is to be reduced."[53] If the specific viewpoint is omitted, then it is hardly accounted for by physicalism or by any other objective approach.

The problem actually is deeper, as Nagel suggests. There are certain experiences or mental states that not only are not expressible in any objective idiom, but are not expressible at all. Such states doubtless include varieties of religious and mystical experience, as well as much else, but Nagel makes the point especially vivid by emphasizing the experience of alien species. Thus, there is something it is like to be a bat, even though facts about what it is like are very peculiar. Some may be so peculiar as not to consist in the truth of any humanly expressible propositions. "We can be compelled to recognize the existence of such facts without being able to state or comprehend them."[54]

As Nagel himself emphasizes, the heart of this argument against physicalism is an "objection to the reducibility of experience."[55] It is correspondingly obvious that a *non*reductive physicalism is not implicated. The nonreductive varieties can cheerfully admit—even insist—that there is something it is like to be a bat, that what it is like is inexpressible, and that even if it could be expressed, still it could not be expressed by or otherwise reduced to physical or any other objective discourse. It need only be determined, in the sense that the facts about what it is like are determined by facts at the level of mathematical physics. Expressibility, like reducibility, is beside the point. Contrary to Nagel, the physicalist need not "insist that everything real must be brought under an objective description."[56]

How and in what sense the purely objective phenomena thus determine the subjective phenomena, nonreductively, I explain elsewhere.[57] Here, it is enough to note that such determination is entirely compatible with the priority that the subjective often enjoys over the objective.[58] Consider our subjective experience of time. As many have argued, such experience seems especially resistant to physical reduction. Our experience of passage and becoming, and of the now or the present, seems utterly inexpressible in the objective temporal idiom of physics, which deals in spatiotemporal invariants, deliberately abstracting away from frame of reference, point of view, and what things are like for us here and now. But the irreducibility or ineliminability of our subjective temporal experience, and of our use of tenses, is irrelevant as regards whether the corresponding subjective phenomena are determined by the objective phenomena with which physics deals.

It might seem that the physical determination of the subjective phenomena entails that physical discourse enjoys some sort of deep, unconditional primacy over subjective discourse. It does not. Communication, for example, and other conversation, evidently require me to orient myself and my listener in time, by treating my utterance in effect as the origin on the time axis, relative to which things are spoken of as past, present, or future.[59] On such occasions, as on some others, tensed discourse takes priority over the tenseless discourse characteristic of objective physical description of how things are temporally related. Likewise, when practical action impends, typically we do better to construe temporal relations common-sensically. Our reflexes probably are keyed to some such perception. Thus, subjective expression of temporal relations rightly takes priority when we speak and act in our ordinary life-world. Furthermore, the ways of unifying the phenomena are hardly limited to physicalism or other objective accounts. Subjective ways must be included as well. A map of everything in polar coordinates centered on us is no less a map, and no less comprehensive, than a map that is coordinate-free.[60]

We see, then, how one can speak not only of intrinsic value in a scientific world, but also of the subjective point of view and its occasional primacy. But reenchantment also requires restoration of the familiar and often cheering ordinary properties of things that we call, tellingly, secondary qualities. There can be little enchantment in a world in which really there is no color, no sound, and no cheer.

On what grounds might one deny that there is any color in the world? A traditional approach begins by assuming that only mathematical physics can express the way things are, by way of expressing their primary qualities. Then it notices that the common-sense color vocabulary is irreducible to the appropriate mathematical-physical vocabulary, and concludes that we are merely projecting our idiosyncratic quality-spaces onto a world in which really there is no color. Here we encounter once more the themes of reduction and exclusive truth, both by now so thoroughly discredited that we hardly need pause over them. The secondary qualities of a thing, even though irreducible, nevertheless are determined by the mathematical-physical properties of the thing, *including* its relations with other things and with us.[61] Furthermore, grant that the commonsense color vocabulary does not express a primary (or objective) quality of the thing. It hardly follows that it does not express a truth about the thing, hence a way the thing is. All that is required for expression of such a truth is elimination of variable truth-value, so that it is true *period* that the thing has the color. And this is easily done by using the color predicates—such as "x is red"—to mean something like "x would be red to any normal human percipient in such-and-such appropriate conditions."[62] The same can be done for the predicates ordinarily used to express any other secondary qualities.

It is instructive to connect all this with what things are like for a bat. Suppose the bats say, "Things are like *P*," where *P* is a property of their auditory experience. Then they have treated their map of things, erroneously, as though it were coordinate-free. But suppose they say, "Things are like *P* for a bat." Then assuming this is true, they have expressed a way things are: Things are like *P* for a bat. Further, assuming they continue to say that things are like such-and-such for a bat, they can use their whole bat-specific vocabulary to express ways things are.

For these and other reasons, then, we cannot conclude that just because certain predicates express secondary qualities, in doing so they cannot express a way things are. Nor can we conclude that "if our philosophical task is, in part, to see the world *sub specie aeternitatis* . . . then we must eschew the concepts of color and other secondary qualities."[63] To view things under the aspect of eternity is *not* to view them filtered through a particular vocabulary, let along through some unconditionally privileged one. Rather, it is to view them so as to be able to use sentences about them that if true are true *period,* not true relative to some perspective of time, place, or species. Very many different irreducible vocabularies can be used to frame such sentences.

It is true that predicates for secondary qualities, even when time, place and state of the percipient are specified, retain an anthropic dimension, if not precisely an anthropocentric one. This means only that on analysis such predicates make reference to conditions of human percipients. It does not follow that such predicates cannot be used to express truths, or ways things are *sub specie aeternitatis*. It follows only that if our interest is in expressing truths having the kind of comprehensiveness and explanatory power characteristic of physics, then we are well advised to be wary of predicates for secondary qualities. Of course, we remain free to be interested in other things also under the aspect of eternity, as often we ought to be—an ought, as we've seen, that itself is determined by truths at the level of physics. Thus, it is irrelevant (and probably false) that beings on a distant planet would have little interest in anthropic predicates, or in what things are like for a human.[64] We may use our species-specific vocabulary to express ways things are; and even if distant physicists are not interested, distant psychobiologists presumably would be, much as we are interested on occasion in what it is like to be a bat.

What about cheer and all the various moods, emotions, desires, and passions generally? Words that express them can also be used to express ways things are, provided they are used to mean roughly "are like that for an appropriate human in appropriate conditions," rather than "are like that." Notice also that a thing to which we attribute cheer or somberness actually is a thing that has come to play a certain sort of role, however fleeting, in an individual's life, and sometimes in the life of a whole culture. It may play the role simply by virtue of an association, or constant conjunction, with the feeling. Typically, however, it plays the role by virtue of being an object of the emotion—of cheer, somberness, anger, love, joy, fear, greed, dread, anxiety, or whatever. Occasionally, the thing plays a role by virtue of representing or being a symbol for some emotion.

In whatever way the thing comes to play the role for us, and whatever the precise nature of its role, roles are mostly functional-intentional affairs. And clearly the functional-intentional role of a thing is irreducible not only to the structural-physical states of the thing, but also in all likelihood to any natural-science account of persons, and of the thing's role-playing relation to them. Whether the thing is an artifact or a product of chance, still, provided it is accorded an appropriate role, it is true that it is, say, somber, cheering, offensive, lovable, fearsome, awesome, nauseating, boring, sickening, inspiring, or whatever.[65] Furthermore, in certain appropriate contexts the correct answer to the question of what a thing is will be that it is a somber landscape, a cheery birdcall, an offensive remark, a loved one, a hated enemy. And in the circumstances this may be the most penetrating way of knowing what the thing is, meaning roughly that in the context the only pertinent way of classifying the thing is just this way, in terms of emotion.

Our passions probably are not just value judgments,[66] but obviously they involve them heavily. Our emotions, moods, and desires entail certain diverse valuings of things, where the values range from esthetic to prudential to moral, from hypothetical to categorical, from taste to matters of survival, and more. Now let us raise the old philosophical question whether our emotions have "any correspondence to Reality."[67] What Solomon means here by "Reality," or what he also calls "*the* world," is the totality of purely descriptive facts. He concludes, as have so many, that the emotions cannot correspond with anything in Reality, nor is it their business to do so. For subjectivity is a standpoint or perspective that is adopted in every emotion, according to Solomon, subjectivity being a matter of what things are like in *my* world not *the* world; and "what *my* world includes that *the* world does not is *value.*"[68]

In view of the arguments in the previous section, an emotion's valuational component, at least, *can* correspond with the facts, hence with something in Reality. Thanks to the determinacy of valuation, we are able to define what it means for a value judgment J to correspond with the facts. What J corresponds with is the class T_J of those natural facts that just suffice to determine J's truth-value as true. By the same token, what the valuational component of a passion corresponds with, if it is true, is the class of those natural facts that just suffice to determine, for all the value judgments entailed by the emotion, their truth-value as true. And if, as the physicalist claims, all natural fact is determined by physical fact, then there is likewise something in physical Reality with which the valuational components of emotions can correspond. Not only does *my* world include value, *the* world does too, in the sense that the phenomena admittedly in it determine the value phenomena. If Solomon is right after all that the emotions *are* just value judgments (or sets of them), then all this can be said of the emotions themselves, not merely of their valuational components.

Whether or not the emotions are just value judgments, we can still raise the question whether we ought to have a given emotion in a given situation, and which one we ought to have instead (assuming the emotions are controllable in that situation to some appropriate extent). Clearly, we ought not have a given emotion if the value judgments it entails fail to correspond with Reality in the sense just given. But suppose there is an ingredient in an emotion over and above its valuational component, perhaps some combination of inner feeling and disturbed state of the body. Then it could happen that the emotion's value judgments are true, and still we ought not have the emotion (again assuming it is controllable). For example, it could happen that all the value judgments involved in one's hatred of someone are true, yet the hatred is wrong. Thanks to the determinacy of valuation, the truth (or falsity) even of this value judgment—that the hatred is wrong—is determined by natural fact. "This world is but canvas to our imagination," as Thoreau says, in the sense that no emotional or other valuation of things in the world is derivable from or reducible to any description. Yet not only are there better and worse ways of spreading our emotions and desires on the canvas, some ways correspond with the facts and some do not. Contrary to Hume, we need not so thoroughly deplore the mind's "great tendency to spread itself on external objects."

These lessons also apply to nature as a whole, or the universe. Thus, the totality of natural fact might determine that certain value terms are true of the universe—say, that it is beautiful, terrible, awesome, eerie, intriguing, astonishing, and more. The universe then would have meaning at least in the sense that it objectively has certain value properties. But the universe could also have meaning in the sense that it is the appropriate object of certain emotions—not only, on occasion, of terror or awe, but of acceptance and even reverance. It would then be but a step to regarding it as "essentially good," even sacred, if not precisely sacramental. Even though the appropriateness of these and other attributions could not be read off from a mere description of the universe, scientific or otherwise, in the sense of being derived from or reduced to such a description, still the appropriateness could be nonreductively determined by the description, and thereby correspond with the facts.

PHYSICALISM AND DIVINE IMMANENCE

What, finally, of that element of enchantment we have been calling divine immanence? Nothing said so far enables us to speak of any such thing. So far we have seen that we may speak not only of intrinsic or objective values in a scientific world, but of the subjective point of view, secondary qualities, emotional valuations, and meanings—together with their occasional primacy.

It does not follow that we may speak of divine immanance. Worse, talk of divine immanence seems inconsistent with even a minimal physicalism. The minimal theses, once more, are that every entity whatever is a mathematical-physical entity, that there can be no difference without a mathematical-physical difference, and that all truth is determined by mathematical-physical truth. Where is God or any other divinity in this scheme? What, if anything, licenses talk of a theology of nature?

The crucial difficulty is that talk of divinity is typically talk of a particular being or entity, one that is nowhere to be found in a physicalist inventory of what there is (or in any other naturalist inventory). The inventory includes only the mathematical-physical entities (plus their spatiotemporal sums), and few believers have been inclined to identify their God with a spatiotemporal sum of basic physical or other natural entities. But if one's God is not among the natural entities, then it becomes extremely difficult—some would say impossible—to supply any rational justification for belief in this extra entity. Not only do the traditional arguments for the belief encounter well-known obstacles, one can give a satisfactory account of the world without positing an extra, supernatural entity.[69] Occam's injunction against multiplying entities beyond necessity thus comes into play, and we seem compelled to conclude that there is no God.

However, although a number of theologians insist, not always explicitly, that the question of God is not a question to which Occam's razor could apply, indeed not strictly a question of extra entities at all. The insistence does do justice to the theist's tendency to assert, "God is not this, not that, indeed not any*thing*—not any mere being, entity, or existent." It thereby amounts to a powerful bulwark against idolatry, or the identification of God with some limited being or aspect of existence. It thus emphasizes in perhaps the strongest possible way God's transcendence, as opposed to the status of mere beings, or even as opposed to the status of the Gods of the philosophers. And it helps account for what theists often see as a deep difference between science and religion, in virtue of which there really is no conflict between them: science asks questions to which Occam's principle is relevant; religion does not.

In addition, the denial that theism is in this way a matter of what there is enables theologians to steer clear of abstract metaphysical disputes, including the traditional arguments for and against the existence of God, and to concentrate instead on articulating and practicing the form of life to which they belong. This will involve, among other things, kerygmatic theology, or explaining the group's religious language-game, replete with its metaphors, myths, models, and paradigms, which not only express but give rise to certain ways of acting and of seeing-as.

Typically, the latter include seeing heaven and earth as made by God. But how could this seeing-as be correct, or based on fact, if it is not *true* that God made heaven and earth? And how can the latter be true if the existence of

God is not a matter of what there is, so that the noun "God" fails to refer? The price we pay for denying that Occam's razor has anything to do with ascertaining the truth of God-talk, hence for denying that theism is in this way a matter of what is in the physicalist or any other metaphysical inventory, is not merely to deprive "God" of any clear referent, but of any referent at all. It then seems impossible for assertions like "God is the maker of heaven and earth" to be true, since their subject-term fails to refer. Such would-be assertions appear to be in the same boat as "The present king of France is bald."

Is there some way a theologian might try to argue that God-talk *is* objectively true, even though "God" not only has no clear referent, but no referent at all? Indeed there is. To begin with, no law of logic or language requires an assertion's subject-term to refer even when the assertion is to be true (or false). Counter-examples abound.[70] There are no point-masses, frictionless surfaces, objects free of all perturbing influences, or other ideal objects. Yet many a truth in physics mentions such things, as do textbook paradigms like "A perfectly smooth elephant of negligible girth is rolling down an inclined plane. . . ." Nor need there be any entities called duties, rights, virtues, or the Good, over and above persons and their natural properties and relations. It can still be true that I have certain duties and rights, hence even in a sense that there are duties and rights, that the rights are inalienable and the duties sometimes painful, that the Good is unattainable, and so on. Hence God-talk could be true even if its subject-term fails to refer. Its surface grammar could be one thing, its depth grammar quite another.

In what could the truth of God-talk consist, if not in a subject's possession of a property? One answer is that, ultimately, its truth consists in or at least is based on the objective correctness of certain values and of a way of life. The God-talk, or much of it, could be a way of expressing the objectively correct values (as we see further below). Or it could be a way of expressing a vision of ourselves and the world which the values require us to preserve, a vision without which the way of life would disintegrate (roughly as morals disintegrate when we see each other always as an It, not a Thou). Thus, the God-talk could express a unified complex of seeings-as, whose objective correctness derives from the objective correctness of the values and of the way.

Likewise, predicates that express the holiness of certain places and events, or the blessedness of certain persons and acts, or bouyant confidence in the goodness of creaturely existence despite all suffering, or the redeeming power of *agape*—all these predicates and more, if construed in the manner proposed in the previous section for predicates for secondary qualities and for what things are like for a particular subject, could be true and could express a way things are, one which is perceived only by religious persons as a result of their training in these ways of seeing and feeling. Such predicates may be construed roughly as of the subjunctive form "would be that way (or would be like that) for an appropriately religious person in appropriate circumstances." Often, the things to which such predicates apply play a certain role in the life of a religious community. Even if the things are not literally made or created, but come to be only by chance (so far as any science is concerned), nevertheless they satisfy the predicates if accorded the appropriate role. Thus, even though everything is identical with some mathematical-physical entity or other, as the physicalist contends, nevertheless everything is describable by some subjunctive religious predicate, and in that sense is a religious entity.

Why use religious predicates, subjunctive or otherwise? That is, "Why drag in God?"[71] Evidently because there are purposes for which the predicates are wanted that other kinds of discourse do not adequately serve. We can get an idea of these purposes by listing some dimensions of meaning that religious discourse can have, occasionally perhaps all in one utterance. Such discourse, which includes parable, prayer, creeds, poetry, and more, may (i) suggest ways of interpreting certain experiences in light of a vision of meaningful existence; (ii) express ideas which, if lived up to, will save humankind; (iii) express answers to "Why am I here?"; (iv) provide patterns for human action—not just abstract ideals, but vivid, actual exemplars; (v) use compelling, unforgettable imagery; and (vi) arrest our attention by their strangeness, leaving us in sufficient doubt about their precise application to tease us into active thought, and also into active commitment and works; and so on. Particular religions tend to believe that their particular religious discourse, in their scripture or descended from it, serves these purposes better than any other.

The judgment that some particular religious discourse is the one called for on a given occasion clearly is in large part a value judgment. So long as the fact-value gap is held to be unbridgeable, the religious values and ways of life will seem in the last analysis to be arbitrary. But the gap is bridged, thanks to the determinacy of valuation. There is a fact of the matter as regards values and forms of life, and therefore a fact of the matter as regards the kinds of seeing-as entailed by them. Theologians need no longer be bullied into holding that the decision to participate in some favored religious language-game or form of life is a matter ultimately of subjective preference or "faith," on the ground, say, that the decision is neither derivable from nor reducible to any totality of natural fact. By so much would our theologian's task be made easier. Something else would make it nearly as hard as ever. *One would still have to construct a normative argument to the effect that the theistic values and form of life are indeed among the true ones, and that they require a theistic complex of experiencing and seeings-as.*

Suppose such an argument could indeed be constructed (despite the serious difficulties entertained below). Then the God-talk could be true even though "God" fails to refer. For the talk could express either these further correct values, or a correct vision of things required by the values and by the way of life based on them. In either case, the theologian would be engaged, not in covert metaphysics, inflating ontology to save the way, but in a variety of normative argument—complex and controversial, yet no less objective in principle for all that.

Still, what about the very assertion that God *exists?* Or that *there is* a God? How could such assertions be true if "God" fails to refer? Any theism worthy of the name must hold that God exists, that there is a God. Yet, to believe that God exists is surely to believe something about what there is. It is to believe that God is, hence, in effect, that God is in the complete, correct inventory of what there is.

Our theologian would have but one reply here. We must consistently treat "God exists" or "There is a God" as something other than an assertion to the effect that God is in the complete, correct inventory of what there is, hence that "God" refers. One possibility, probably the strongest, is to treat "God exists" ("There is a God," "God is," etc.) as a kind of *meta*-assertion, to the effect that the theist's God-talk *is true,* namely the God-talk that expresses the experiencing, seeings-as, and values required by the form of life to which the theist belongs.[72] As noted, provided the form of life and its values are correct, the God-talk is indeed true, and objectively so.

It follows that there is a sense in which a theologian could plausibly argue that in theistic experience we do not have *mere* projection. Rather, we have a projection matched by an objectively existing God. True, in all valuation and seeing-as we have projection, just as we do in emotion, if only in the sense that what the correct values are, and the correct seeings-as, cannot be reduced to or derived from natural fact, hence not read off from it. But thanks to the determinacy of valuation, some of the values and seeings-as (and emotions) are objectively correct, and some are *mere* projections. *If* the theologian can make good on the complex normative argument to the effect that the theistic values and seeings-as—the theistic experience—are indeed among the true ones, then they are not mere projections, but matched by an objectively existing God, in the sense that the meta-assertion that God exists is true, which is to say that the God-talk is true, and indeed objectively so, via the determinacy of valuation.

Unfortunately, some of the required seeings-as seem inconsistent with the lessons of an austere naturalism. For example, how is it possible to see the universe as created, when naturalism asserts that it is not? According to naturalism, there is nothing not part of the universe, and since a Creator would have to be something not part of the universe, the universe is not even the sort of thing that could have a Creator.[73] To deny that the universe is created, in this sense, however, is to deny that there is any being outside the universe who stands in the causal relation "Creator of" to the universe, on the ground that there is nothing outside. Hence, *this* idea of creation presupposes that a Creator must be in the inventory of what there is; but this is just what our imagined theologian denies. Therefore, the account of creation, whatever precisely it comes to, does not imply that the universe is created in the sense rejected by the naturalist. Thus, there is at least no inconsistency between the two. Our theologian's intended account of creation involves no extra entities, but is valuational through and through. Presumably, to see the universe as created *ex nihilo* is, among other things, to see what there is as essentially good, not as meaningless or absurd, and to see our lives as having a certain meaning and destiny dependent, not on our transient purposes, but on invariant and irreducible if sometimes mysterious imperatives about faith, hope, and love.[74] Or so our theologian may hope to make clear.

Reconstructions of religion in naturalistic terms are nothing new. Mostly, they do not pretend to be versions of theism. When they do, their strategy has been to identify God with nature or one of its aspects. They are therefore vulnerable to the charge that "God" is just another name for something with few or none of the properties of true divinity. Any such view is reductive; we would have to say that God is nothing but some aspect of nature. But the theology we have been imagining is open to no such charge. In it "God" is not just another name for some aspect of nature, or for anything else. For "God" does not refer, is not in that sense a name, and God, therefore, could not be nothing but such-and-such. By the same token, the theology is neither pantheist nor monist. For it does not identify God with anything, not even with the universe as a whole. The theology accords truth to "God is the maker of heaven and earth," which is incompatible with pantheism and with monism (where both are taken to entail it is never correct to value or see what there is as created, on the ground that doing so would imply a dualism). Because the theology assigns truth to the theist's characteristic creedal sentences, and falsity to the pantheist's, it is a version of theism, not pantheism.

This is so despite the fact that the theology is to be constructed within a naturalistic framework, and indeed within a physicalistic one. Nowhere do we need to multiply entities beyond the physical, or deny that all truth is determined by physical truth. On the contrary, we would be entitled to say that such truth determines that the theist's God-talk also is true *and frequently takes precedence.*[75] Or, rather, we would be entitled to say this *provided* the difficult normative argument mentioned above is sound—the argument to the effect that certain values and ways of life of a moral and religious sort are among the true ones, and that their pursuit requires a theistic complex of seeings-as, in which the universe is seen as created *ex nihilo* by a being at once personal yet transcendent, and in which certain events are experienced as revelatory, as miraculous, and so on.

Isn't there high tension between such God-talk and a purely naturalistic account of the world? Indeed there is, but no inconsistency. The tension derives mainly from two sources. One is the habit of supposing that a naturalistic metaphysics (or indeed any metaphysics), if true, must be monopolistically or exclusively true. But no discourse enjoys monopoly over any other.[76] So naturalistic metaphysics is not exclusively true, true though it is. Religious domains of truth not only can coexist with it, but can and frequently do take precedence. Entrenched habits die hard, however, especially the habit of supposing there is such a thing as *the* way things are; so we continue to feel a tension between naturalism and assertions about God. In due course the tension will disappear, with the disappearance of monopolistic metaphysics, or so our theologian may hope.

The second source of tension, and much the more intractable, is the habit of supposing God-talk can be true only if "God" refers, and indeed refers to a being beyond any naturalist's inventory of what there is. The habit is so strong that many may never be able to break it. It is rooted in the very grammar of much God-talk—in the surface grammar, subject-predicate in form, according to which to assert something about God is to ascribe a property to a subject. Construing God-talk in this subject-predicate manner may fairly be called a form of literalism. An analogue in morals would be to construe talk about virtues, duties, and rights as talk literally about entities, supernatural ones at that. An analogue in physics would be to search for a perfectly smooth elephant of negligible girth.

The advantages of outgrowing such subject-predicate literalism in theology are plain. To repeat, doing so would accord with the theist's tendency to resist identifying God with this or that, would thereby help thwart idolotry, would thus emphasize powerfully the divine transcendence, would help account for key differences between science and religion, would bypass abstract metaphysical disputes about what must be in the inventory of what there is, and would thereby pave the way for theologians to argue for the objective truth of God-talk, in the manner sketched above, all without violating the physicalist's account of what there is. The habit of subject-predicate literalism therefore seems well worth the sustained effort it would take to break it, via repeated exercises in self-conscious intellectual tact.[77]

Theologians and others have worried that the alternative to construing God-talk literally is vague abstraction, and, ultimately, emptiness. But at least as regards subject-predicate literalism, according to which "God" must refer, we need not worry. When the truth of the God-talk consists in expressing certain objectively correct values (including the value of certain seeings-as), then roughly speaking the content of such talk is the content of those values. Since the values in question are widely acknowledged to have implications that are specific and concrete, the content of the God-talk ultimately would be anything but abstract and vague. In some sense it would be at least as rich and detailed as the form of community it is meant both to reflect and to sustain.

Some other kinds of literalism depend on this one; if it goes, they go. For example, just as creation is commonly thought of as a causal relation between God and world, miracles are thought to be the result of God's causal intervention in the world. A certain event is seen as specially related to God's activity and plan, hidden though the latter may be. The believer may say of the event, "Here God acted to save a life (or the Israelites, or the true church, or . . .)," or "Here God acted to authenticate the Commandments," and so on. Construed literally, this implies that there is a being referred to by "God" who stands in a causal relation with the event in question. And the further presumption is that the laws of nature were thereby created and later momentarily broken, suspended, or bypassed. Who created and assures the regularity of events can also interrupt.

There is little doubt that the surface grammar of assertions about creation and divine miracles implies some such standard account of both. On any such account, belief in miracles must seem mere superstition from the point of view of naturalism and, naturalism aside, from the point of view of modern theories of rational evidence (as Hume in effect argued long ago). No wonder that "the chief problem that has plagued theistic analysis of the natural world is the apparent impossibility of any divine action in a completely causal order," so that "we now have to view God's action quite differently."[78] But if "God" does not refer, then it does not refer to a supernatural being who creates and overrides or bypasses natural laws and the causal order via some mysterious supercausal activity. The theologian is free to give a different account of the miraculous.

At this point it is customary to object that if miracles are not literally violations or suspensions of the natural causal order, then to call something a miracle is merely to report one's response to it as astounding, wondrous, or a sign, and perhaps to urge others so to respond as well. Since this is a subjective matter, the objection continues, we cannot say that a miracle is a miracle regardless of whatever anyone happens to believe about it, nor can we say of the miraculous event that it somehow transcends nature. So much for the "demythologizing" of miracle-talk.

Once more the determinacy of valuation is strategic. Here it allows us to deny that subjectivism is the only alternative to an account of miracles as violations of the natural causal order. We could argue that calling an event a miracle is to engage in a certain kind of seeing-as required by the theist's form of life, and that seeing the event this way is objectively correct, determined by natural fact. Thus, a miracle would be a miracle regardless of what anyone happens to believe about it, since there would be a fact of the matter as regards the value judgments involved when the believer says, "Here the living God of faith acted in the world." Because calling something a miracle would be a matter of values and seeings-as, then whether the miraculous event could be explained by the sciences, as perhaps always it eventually can be, would be irrelevant. Miracle-talk would not be a kind of inverse physics, not even metaphysics, but valuational through and through.

The miraculous event would "transcend nature," on this account, at least in the twofold sense that (i) its property of miraculousness would not be expressible by, reducible to, or derivable from any scientific description; and

(ii) no discoveries in the sciences would tell us whether or not it is a miracle. Instead, we would have to engage in a kind of religous normative inquiry, complex and controversial, but objective in principle nonetheless, thanks to the determinacy of valuation. Hume's doubts about miracles would thus have been met, not as one might have expected, but by overcoming his seemingly unrelated doubts about determining ought from is.[79]

The main problem for the present account is to make good on the difficult, controversial, normative argument to the effect that the theistic values and seeings-as are among the true ones, and that they frequently take precedence over others. There are at least three major potential objections to any such argument.

The first is that any normative justification for a theistic complex of seeings-as is heavily outweighed by various side effects of such seeings-as. The God-talk involved, some say, implies an authoritarian, patriarchal morality, fit at best for the early stages of childrearing; implied also are an archaic sexism, tribal arrogance, species chauvinism, and obdurate, hostile intolerance toward all who differ. Even if the God-talk can be shown, after all, to imply no such things, the habit of subject-predicate literalism is too ingrained to break, even by the utmost self-conscious intellectual tact, which the ordinary believer cannot achieve anyway. Hence, continued use of God-talk must inevitably encourage the wrong sort of supernaturalism, in talk of miracles, creation, power, and more. Since such supernaturalism not only has no evidence for it, but has the bulk of evidence against it, it seduces the believer into irrationalism and superstition. The evils of such side effects outweigh whatever normative support there might be for the God-talk at issue, and show that the theistic values cannot be among the true ones.

The second sort of objection is that *other* religious varieties of seeing-as might well be normatively justified too, or instead. What, if anything, is normatively superior about western theism (Jewish, Christian, Islamic)? Why not some Far Eastern variety of theism? Why not some nontheistic variety of a Far Eastern religion? All these alternatives represent forms of life and complexes of seeings-as that rival the best of ours, and indeed seem superior in some respects, as for example in the attitudes they encourage toward animals, plants, and the environment as a whole; if we are to have an adequate theology of nature, western theism, at least, is out.

The third is simply that the normative argument will lead away from any traditional variety of religious seeing-as, including oriental, perhaps because bad side effects of any such religous discourse, laden as it is with supernaturalism, must always outweigh whatever normative evidence there might be for the truth of such discourse. Thus, there can properly speaking be no theology of nature at all.

These objections and others may or may not succeed. They merely indicate that our theologian has work to do, either by way of arguing that the foregoing implications and side effects are not so bad, or that they really do not follow from theism properly understood or properly revised. The point here is that the work would be work in value theory, or axiology, not in metaphysics, or ontology. As seen, the axiological work can go on entirely within a physicalist metaphysics. The crucial normative assumption is perfectly consistent with the minimal physicalist theses, and when conjoined with them forms a synthesis of physicalism and enchantment in which each enriches the other while correcting the other's occasional extremes. The way is open to regard the world as far from "disgodded,"[80] but as an enchanted place of belonging, wondrous and alive.

NOTES

1. Barbour (1972), p. 3.
2. Compton (1972), p. 33.
3. Berman (1981), p. 23.
4. See Post (1987), especially Chs. 5-8. I am indebted to Cornell University Press for allowing the use here of parts of this book.
5. Berman (1981), p. 132.
6. Santayana (1896), p. 52.
7. Cf. Nagel (1979), Chs. 12 and 14; Nagel (1986); and Post (1987), §5.4.
8. Nagel (1986), p. 3.
9. Nagel (1986), pp. 208-223.
10. Smart (1963), p. 71.
11. Post (1987), §8.0.
12. As explained and extended in Post (1987), especially Chs. 3-7.
13. Compton (1986), p. 46.
14. Borgman (1984), p. 309.
15. See Post (1987), §1.1, for an account of this realism as regards truth. What that account mainly lacks, namely a naturalistic theory of meaning adequate to its purposes, I have subsequently realized may be found in the remarkable Millikan (1984).
16. Contrary to Berman (1981), p. 194.
17. Contrary to Alderman (1978), p. 37.
18. For analytical surveys of the major problems with reductionism, see Block (1980); Boyd (1980); Margolis (1984), Chs. 2 and 4.
19. Cf. Hellman and Thompson (1975, 1977); Haugeland (1982); Horgan (1982); Kim (1978, 1979, 1982); Lewis (1983); Teller (1984).
20. Post (1987), §§4.0-4.6. 5.1, 8.1.
21. Post (1987), Ch. 4. Closely related views appear in Hellman and Thompson (1975); Haugeland (1982); Horgan (1982); Lewis (1983).
22. Detailed argument for the claims in this and the next four paragraphs appears in Post (1987), Chs. 4-7.
23. Cf. Nagel (1979), Ch. 12.
24. Findlay (1970), p. 81.
25. Again, for details see Post (1987), Chs. 4-7.
26. Smith (1972), p. 73.
27. Mackie (1977), p. 41.

28.   Hare (1972), p. 47, who uses the phrase only to deny that it expresses a genuine issue. Cf. Hare (1985), p. 42; Mackie (1977), p. 21.

29.   Mackie (1977), p. 41. Cf. Mackie (1982), p. 115. On resultance, see Dancy (1981).

30.   Nozick (1981), p. 17.

31.   This possibility was first suggested by Hellman and Thompson (1977), subsequently explored in detail by Post (1984), and developed further in "Fact and Value," Ch. 6 of Post (1987).

32.   Contrary to Smith (1972), p. 73.

33.   Contrary to Berman (1981), pp. 139-140.

34.   For further details about determination, see Post (1987), and Post (1990), Ch. 5.

35.   Contrary for example to Blackburn (1985), p. 11, where realism about moral values is likened to realism about mathematical entities; and to Rorty (1982), pp. xv-xvi.

36.   As explained in Post (1987), pp. 177-180. See also Kincaid (1987); Post (1990), Ch. 5.

37.   Hare (1952), p. 145.

38.   Harman (1978), p. 159. Cf. Hare (1963); Lycan (1969).

39.   See further Post (1987), pp. 259-261, 269-271.

40.   Cf. Sayre-McCord (1988), who articulates the view in order to reject it.

41.   Here I rely heavily on Sturgeon (1985, 1986); Sayre-McCord (1988); McDowell (1985); Boyd (1988), §§3.1-3.3, 4.2-4.5. See also Rolston (1986), Chs. 5-7. In addition, one might well question the presumption that a principle is intelligible or acceptable only if it contributes to naturalistic or other explanation.

42.   Cf. Post (1987), §6.0; Brink (1984).

43.   As even Mackie agrees. Again see Sturgeon (1985, 1986); Sayre-McCord (1988); McDowell (1985); Boyd (1988).

44.   Contrary to Field (1982), p. 562

45.   Contrary to Berman (1981), p. 40.

46.   For technical reasons, if J is a necessary truth, we say that J corresponds with any facts whatever. But few if any value judgments are true in every physically possible world. Cf. Post (1987), pp. 36, 267-269, 275-276.

47.   Cf. Nielsen (1979) for a review of such questioning.

48.   Contrary to Nielsen (1979), p. 514.

49.   On the epistemic problem of how to tell which of our value judgments are true, cf. Post (1987), pp. 277-281.

50.   Sartre (1956), p. 625.

51.   Barbour (1972), p. 149. See further §5, below.

52.   Nagel (1979), p. 167. Cf. Post (1987), §5.4.

53.   Nagel (1979), p. 175.

54.   Nagel (1979), p. 171.

55.   Nagel (1979), p. 175.

56.   Nagel (1979), p. 210.

57.   Post (1987), §5.4.

58.   Post (1987), §§3.4.1, 5.4, 7.1-7.4.

59.   As Polakow (1981) argues in Ch. 5, especially pp. 102-104.

60.   On coordinate-free physical geometry, see Misner, Thorne, and Wheeler (1973), pp. 5-8.

61.   Post (1987), §7.5.

62.   See, further, Post (1987), §7.5; and Chisholm (1982) on "converse intentional properties."

63.   Smart (1963), p. 84.

64.   Contrary to Smart (1963), p. 150.

65.   Again, see Chisholm (1982) on "converse intentional properties."

66.   Contrary to Solomon (1976). Cf. Bergmann (1978).

67.   Solomon (1976), p. 61.

68.   Solomon (1976), pp. 75, 67.

69. Post (1987), Chs. 3-7, §8.0.
70. Mackie (1982), pp. 226-227, overlooks these.
71. Schilling (1972), p. 120.
72. Mackie (1982), pp. 216-229, overlooks this sort of possibility.
73. Cf. Post (1987), §3.2.
74. Cf. Gilkey (1965), pp. 23, 35, 72, 77-78, 150, 190, 204; Barbour (1972), p. 147.
75. Post (1987), §8.1.
76. Post (1987), §§4.0, 4.6, 7.2-7.4.
77. For an approach in which "God" does refer in certain uses, see Post (1987), §8.3.
78. Compton (1972), pp. 39, 35.
79. This reverses the verdict of Mackie (1982), p. 118.
80. Berman (1981), p. 70.

BIBLIOGRAPHY

Alderman, Harold. "Heidegger's Critique of Science and Technology." In *Heidegger and Modern Philosophy: Critical Essays,* Michael Murray, ed., (New Haven: Yale University Press, 1978), pp. 203-221.

Barbour, Ian, ed. *Earth Might Be Fair: Reflections on Ethics, Religion, and Ecology.* (Englewood Cliffs, NJ: Prentice-Hall, 1972).

Bergmann, Frithjof. "Review of R. Solomon's *The Passions.*" *Journal of Philosophy,* 75:200-208 (1978).

Berman, Morris. *The Reenchantment of the World* (Ithaca: Cornell University Press, 1981).

Blackburn, Simon. "Errors and the Phenomenology of Value." In *Morality and Objectivity,* T. Honderich, ed. (London: Routledge and Kegan Paul, 1985), pp. 1-22.

Block, Ned. "What is Functionalism?" In *Readings in the Philosophy of Psychology,* Vol. 1, Ned Block, ed. (Cambridge: Harvard University Press, 1980), pp. 67-106.

Borgmann, Albert. "Prospects for the Theology of Technology." In *Technology and Theology: Essays in Christian Analysis and Exegesis,* Carl Mitcham and Jim Grote, eds. (Lanham, MD: University Press of America, 1984), pp. 305-322.

Boyd, Richard. "Materialism without Reductionism: What Physcialism Does Not Entail." In *Readings in the Philosophy of Psychology,* Vol. 1, Ned Block, ed. (Cambridge: Harvard University Press, 1980), pp. 67-106.

Boyd, Richard. "How to be a Moral Realist." In *Moral Realism,* G. Sayre-McCord, ed. (Ithaca: Cornell University Press, 1988), pp. 181-228.

Brink, David. "Moral Realism and Skeptical Arguments from Disagreement and Queerness." *Australasian Journal of Philosophy,* 62:111-125 (1984).

Chisholm, Roderick. "Converse Intentional Properties." *Journal of Philosophy,* 79:537-545 (1982).

Compton, John J. "Science and God's Action in Nature." In *Earth Might Be Fair: Reflections on Ethics, Religion, and Ecology,* Ian Barbour, ed. (Englewood Cliffs, NJ: Prentice-Hall, 1972), pp. 33-47.

Compton, John J. "On There Being a Moral Sense of Nature." *Personalist Forum,* 2:38-55 (1986).

Dancy, Jonathan. "On Moral Principles." *Mind,* 90:367-385 (1981).

Field, Hartry. "Realism and Relativism." *Journal of Philosophy,* 79:553-567 (1982).

Findlay, John N. *Axiological Ethics* (London: Macmillan, 1970).

Gilkey, Langdon. *Maker of Heaven and Earth: A Study of the Christian Doctrine of Creation* (Garden City: Doubleday, 1965).

Hare, R.M. *The Language of Morals* (Oxford: The Clarendon Press, 1952).

Hare, R.M. *Freedom and Reason* (Oxford: The Clarendon Press, 1963).

Hare, R.M. "Nothing Matters." Reprinted in his *Applications of Moral Philosophy* (Berkeley: University of California Press, 1972), pp. 32-47.

Hare, R.M. "Ontology in Ethics." In *Morality and Objectivity*, T. Honderich, ed. (London: Routledge and Kegan Paul, 1985), pp. 39-53.

Harman, Gilbert. "What Is Moral Relativism?" In *Values and Morals*, A.J. Goldman and J. Kim, eds. (Dordrecht: Reidel, 1978), pp. 143-161.

Haugeland, John. "Weak Supervenience." *American Philosophical Quarterly*, 19:93-103 (1982).

Hellman, Geoffrey, and Thompson, F.W. "Physicalism: Ontology, Determination, Reduction." *Journal of Philosophy*, 72:551-564 (1975).

Hellman, Geoffrey, and Thompson, F.W. "Physicalist Materialism." *Nous*, 11:309-345 (1977).

Horgan, Terence. "Supervenience and Microphysics." *Pacific Philosophical Quarterly*, 63:29-43 (1982).

Kim, Jaegwon. "Supervenience and Nomological Incommensurables." *American Philosophical Quarterly*, 15:149-158 (1978).

Kim, Jaegwon. "Causality, Identity and Supervenience in the Mind-Body Problem." *Midwest Studies in Philosophy*, 4:31-49 (1979).

Kim, Jaegwon. "Psychophysical Supervenience." *Philosophical Studies*, 41:51-70 (1982).

Kincaid, Harold. "Supervenience Doesn't Entail Reducibility." *Southern Journal of Philosophy*, 25:343-356 (1987).

Lewis, David. "New Work for a Theory of Universals." *Australasian Journal of Philosophy*, 61:343-377 (1983).

Lycan, William G. (1969). "Hare, Singer and Gewirth on Universalizability." *Philosophical Quarterly*, 19:135-144 (1969).

Mackie, J.L. *Ethics: Inventing Right and Wrong* (New York: Penguin Books, 1977).

Mackie, J.L. *The Miracle of Theism: Arguments for and against the Existence of God* (Oxford: The Clarendon Press, 1982).

Margolis, Joseph. *Philosophy of Psychology* (Englewood Cliffs, NJ: Prentice-Hall, 1984).

McDowell, John. "Values and Secondary Qualities." In *Morality and Objectivity*, T. Honderich, ed. (London: Routledge and Kegan Paul, 1985), pp. 110-129.

Millikan, Ruth Garrett. *Language, Thought, and Other Biological Categories* (Cambridge: MIT Press, 1984).

Misner, C., Thorne, K., and Wheeler, J.A. *Gravitation* (San Francisco: W.H. Freeman, 1973).

Nagel, Thomas. *Mortal Questions* (Cambridge: Cambridge University Press, 1979).

Nagel, Thomas. *The View from Nowhere* (New York: Oxford University Press, 1986).

Nielsen, Kai. "On Deriving an Ought from an Is: A Retrospective Look." *Review of Metaphysics*, 32:487-514 (1979).

Nozick, Robert. *Philosophical Explanations* (Cambridge, MA: Harvard University Press, 1981).

Polakow, Avron. *Tense and Performance* (Amsterdam: Rodopi, 1981).

Post, John F. "On the Determinacy of Valuation." *Philosophical Studies*, 45:315-333 (1984).

Post, John F. *The Faces of Existence: An Essay in Nonreductive Metaphysics* (Ithaca: Cornell University Press, 1987).

Post, John F. *Metaphysics: A Contemporary Introduction* (New York: Paragon House, 1990).

Rolston, Holmes III. *Philosophy Gone Wild* (Buffalo, NY: Prometheus Books, 1986).

Rorty, Richard. *The Consequences of Pragmatism* (Minneapolis: University of Minnesota Press, 1982).

Santayana, George. *The Sense of Beauty* (New York: Scribner, 1896).

Sartre, Jean Paul. *Being and Nothingness* (New York: Philosophical Library, 1956). Translated by Hazel Barnes.

Sayre-McCord, Geoffrey. "Moral Theory and Explanatory Impotence." In *Moral Realism*, G. Sayre-McCord, ed. (Ithaca: Cornell University Press, 1988), pp. 256-281.

Schilling, Harold K. "The Whole Earth is the Lord's." In *Earth Might Be Fair: Reflections on Ethics, Religion, and Ecology,* Ian Barbour, ed. (Englewood Cliffs, NJ: Prentice-Hall, 1972), pp. 100-122.

Smart, J.J.C. *Philosophy and Scientific Realism* (London: Routledge and Kegan Paul, 1963).

Smith, Huston. "Tao Now." In *Earth Might Be Fair: Reflections on Ethics, Religion, and Ecology,* Ian Barbour, ed. (Englewood Cliffs, NJ: Prentice-Hall, 1972), pp. 62-81.

Solomon, Robert. *The Passions* (Garden City: Anchor Books, 1976).

Sturgeon, Nicholas. "Moral Explanations." In *Morality, Reason and Truth,* D. Copp and D. Zimmerman, eds. (Totowa: Rowman and Allanheld, 1985), pp. 49-78.

Sturgeon, Nicholas. "Harman on Moral Explanations of Natural Facts." *Southern Journal of Philosophy,* 24:69-78 (Supplement, 1986).

Teller, Paul. "A Poor Man's Guide to Supervenience and Determination." *Southern Journal of Philosophy,* 22:137-162 (Supplement, 1984).

TECHNOLOGY, NATURE, AND MIRACLE

Frederick Ferré

The otherwise diverse papers by John Post and Jane Mary Trau make contact at the nodal point where our modern technological and scientific capacities require Christian philosophers to clarify—from practical as well as theoretical needs—our concepts of nature and miracle. My aim is to focus discussion on this point of common concern.

Professor Trau freshly illustrates an old issue in Christian thinking—most typically but not exclusively Roman Catholic—concerning technological interventions in natural processes. In her clear defense of the permissibility of in vitro fertilization techniques, when used on behalf of loving spouses who would otherwise be unable to conceive their own children, she exposes a profoundly important case of question-begging that often arises in arguments containing the concept "natural":

1. In vitro fertilization is a technological intervention deliberately used to circumvent some natural disability.

Research in Philosophy and Technology, Volume 10, pages 281-286.
Copyright © 1990 by JAI Press Inc.
All rights of reproduction in any form reserved.
ISBN: 1-55938-062-4

2. Therefore it is artificial, and thus "unnatural."
3. Therefore it is illicit.

Trau rightly complains that such a swift passage from "unnatural" to "illicit," ignoring the provision of any bad-making characteristics that might justify the inference, is fallacious. As she writes, "this is precisely the question: when nature fails or must be limited, is the use of artificial technology licit? If one answers that it is not licit precisely because it is artificial, one simply begs the question" (p. 235).

Trau is understandably reluctant to conclude that the Roman Catholic Church, whose arguments she is opposing, would make "so simple an error." I agree. The argument does simply beg the question, but it is not quite so "simple" as that. What motivates this petitio principii, I sumbit, is what John Post has termed the "enchanted view of nature." Here is the root of what Trau calls the "prejudice in favor of nature over technology" (p. 236). Nature is taken by many Christians, with indebtedness to Artistotle but also to deep prephilosophical intutions, as containing intrinsic value, ends, and meaning. Nature is also taken by Christians, with no less indebtedness to our authoritative biblical imagery, as a domain for the mysterious activity of God and for the occurrence of miracles.

In the present example, the Church petitio is incurred on behalf of retaining the miraculous, intrinsically meaningful, character of human conception. Which, after all, is a more suitable setting for the mystery of life's beginnings: the warm and secret recesses of a woman's body during the celebration of love between persons, or a doctor's office and a Petrie dish? To choose the former is to affirm the enchantment of dusk over flourescent laboratory lighting. But more. Dusk makes room for agencies which act . . . just out of sight. Events allowed to occur in nature are not quite predictable, not exclusively and prosaically the result of our own human doing.

The artificial, by contrast, is the product, at least in significant part, of familiar human intelligence. As the character of that intelligence changes from grounding practical, rule-of-thumb technologies to inspiring artifacts and techniques based on demonstrable theoretical understanding, the growing realm of artificial light becomes an ever-greater threat to the dusk, and thus to all the mysterious agencies embraced by the dusk's welcome obscurity.

Trau's argument, that there should not be any absolute prohibition against any artificial means of conception, is victorious on her terms, but at a price. Her sensible view concludes that since the unitive values of sexual intercourse have been uncoupled from the procreative, as was clearly done in *Humanae Vitae*, then the procreative can be licitly—and lovingly—sought by other means than through natural sexual intercourse, since in vitro technology now makes this possible. The mere character of the means—natural or unnatural—ought not to be the issue, she argues. The surrounding good-making and bad-making considerations for some infertile couple's having a child under specific circumstances are what should be decisive. Put in these terms, Trau's position clearly wins our ethical assent.

What, on the other hand, does her successful argument cost? The price, I believe, is her acceptance of the fundamental modern conception of nature as neutral, neither intrinsically good or bad, wise or foolish, just "what is." Once nature is no longer taken as a normative, the further consequence follows that all norms are related instead to explicit human purposes, standards (including, of course, religious standards), and consequences. Trau, that is, gains her victory over the murky question-begging of the Church's "Instruction on the Origins of Human Life" by adopting the clear, austere conception of nature as a neutral realm, properly and fully open to ever-increasing human understanding and control. As we manipulate germ cells and amino acids under the bright lights of the laboratory, however, and thereby constantly increase our understanding of the processes involved, eliminating everything unexpected, what shred of mystery is left in human conception? What logical space is open for the miracle of God's action in creating each precious, personal life? Trau's victorious argument thus raises, in a vivid particular way, the general problem of the "disenchanted view of nature," which is the primary concern of John Post's paper.

Post's quest is to combine what he calls "austere" scientific naturalism, a minimalist ontology wholly expressible in terms of mathematical physics and wholly penetrable in principle by technological controls, with the "enchantment" of potentially true assertions about objective values, acts of God, and miracles. It is a bold quest, but in the context of Trau's strong moral case for neutralizing the natural and releasing the artificial from dim, premodern constraints, it is urgent.

Post's strategy, though subtle in its argument, is sweepingly simple in its outline: First, he must show that it makes sense to speak of objective values, not as somehow subsisting entities, but as genuine values that persons should really affirm, values determined uniquely for any possible world by the facts, no matter how austerely and unmysteriously these facts are described. Then, second, he must interpret theological assertions, even though their surface grammar seems to be making claims about mysterious events like acts of God or miracles, as wholly axiological in depth-grammar, grounded (if they are grounded) in objective values, and not referring to dusk-dwelling facts at all.

Post's bold suggestion would have the effect of releasing both theoretical and practical intelligence from any hesitation to turn up the lights to full intensity. It would free both science and technology to penetrate and control the universe of entities at will, under the constraints only of rationally held, explicitly uncovered, and unwarranted values and norms. The purely axiological reading of theological talk about miracles and acts of God would even have the virtue, if adopted, of allowing (in principle) some well understood and wholly controlled biochemical process in a Petrie dish—if that should be the germination of an objectively valuable human life—to be acknowledged as "miraculous," a gracious "act of God" in the fullest possible sense. These locations, if Post is followed, will not be taken as describing processes and events in vitro any more than they would, in "natural" contexts, be describing processes or events in utero. Events are not being *described* at all; they are being *evaluated* in terms of an ultimate religious value-scheme whose truth, if it is true, rests on the secure determination of these values by unenchanted facts. Post's proposal could thus give Trau the "both" she clearly wants: *both* religious tradition, clear of question-begging prejudices favoring a mysteriously normative concept of nature, *and* licit, rationally considered technological intervention on behalf of human good.

There is much to be praised in Post's proposal, then, but can Christian philosophers agree to allow axiology to bear the full weight of Christian discourse? Is Post's suggestion actually the revealing of a depth-grammar, as he hopes, or is it instead an axiological reduction of the richness of religious speech to one—though perhaps the most important one—of its dimensions? Can any set of values, however central to religion, continue to be intensely affirmed as comprehensively relevant once religion is logically prevented from making its own claims about the way things are?

To this set of questions we must add a second. Post makes much use of the presumptive force of ordinary langauge when he argues for the intelligibility of objective values. What happens to this respect for first-order usage, however, when the issue is religious language? If ordinary usage is a powerful argument for objective values, despite skeptical meta-ethicists, should not ordinary usage be a powerful argument against Post's driving so deep a wedge between "surface grammar" and "depth grammar" in religion? Ordinary users of language about God and miracles naively think they are referring to special entities or describing special events. Doubtless they are also evaluating as they speak— that does not need to be denied—but are they to be held wholly mistaken in supposing that somehow facts are simultaneously at issue?

My own view is that we have traditionally tended to overemphasize the fact-describing and to underemphasize the value-ascribing functions of theological discourse; against this tendency Post's proposal is a healthy antidote, but I doubt that the religious can remain whole and earnest when all factual-referential functions are excised from the language of faith. The metaphysical dimension of religious discourse is, I think, essential, both when religious thinkers are obliged to serve as critics of inadequate theoretical abstractions, and also when such thinkers attempt to construct alternative theories more adequate to fundamental human experiences and the puzzling universe in which we live. If we do a thoughtful job in criticizing and constructing our theories of reality, recognizing both the complexity of human experience and the fragmentary, far-from-final progress reports of the sciences for what they

are, we might even find—without dimming the lights of responsible inquiry—
that we are not forced to adopt quite such an "austere" model of nature as
Post supposes.

Whatever our chosen metaphysics, we may finally ask both Post and Trau
whether, on their views of nature, there is any use left for the ecologist's adage,
"Nature knows best"? Both their papers stress the virtues of clear, explicit
norms and values. On Post's theory, only by such explicitness could the
objective determination of values by the facts in every possible world be
demonstrable, or even discussable. And for Trau, explicit examination of
discernible "good- and bad-making characteristics" should take the place of
what she rejects as question-begging prejudice favoring "the natural" over
technology. Do we dare to place such utter trust in our human skills at
discernment, especialy when long-range, frequently irreversible technological
decisions are being made? According to Barry Commoner (who takes "Nature
knows best" as one of the four fundamental laws of ecology), our clearest, most
explicit human standards and norms are exactly the ones that tend to be most
guilty of "tunnel vision." Human intelligence is short-range and project-
oriented. We tend to see quickly the probable good effects of some possible
intervention, but only slowly—and often too late—to see the "side effects" of
our impatient technological hubris. The complex system of nature, having
evolved over vast lengths of time, contains in its gradually developed repertoire,
ways of coping with an enormous array of threats. Reminding one of the
immune system of an organism, nature has built up resistances and healing
strategies for virtually all normal problems. But human intelligence, intervening
too rashly in the balances of nature, poses radically new threats with artificially
developed materials and processes that the system is not prepared for, and poses
threats at such a pace and in such profusion that the antigens of nature's
immunological system are in danger of being overwhelmed.

Every technological intervention is meant to serve some human good, of
course, at least within the context of someone's explicit goals and values.
Without such goods in view, no technology would be invented or introduced.
Needs, or even minor wants, tend to feel urgent, while cautious reflections on
the infinitely complex fabric of nature's networks, and what some technological
penetration of the fabric might mean, tend to feel uncomfortably negative and
time-consuming. Thus, it is all too easy to decide that nature has "failed" and
that it is the human intellect, not nature, that "knows best."

Perhaps we humans do know best. But often we do not. Who would have
dreamed, a short time ago, that the chloroflurocarbons of our innocent spray
cans, refrigerants, and styrofoam cups would some day turn out to be a
potentially lethal nemesis, eating away at the protective ozone layers above
our heads, and threatening us—and other species—with a pandemic of skin
cancers? On the other hand, Trau confidently reminds us (and she might be
right) that there are many circumstances, as in the case of eye (or other organ?)

transplants, in which we may properly rejoice in new technological possibilities. In those circumstances, she argues, nature has "failed." But how do we know, in time to act or refrain from acting, which type of case is which? Are we often too quick in drawing the conclusion that *we* know best, and in reaching for the technological fix?

My point is not to urge Christian philosophers to return to simple question-begging or to antitechnological nature mysticism. The reenchantment of nature I hope for, with John Post, is one that can stand the highest intensity of illumination that we can bring to our inquiries. But it may be one of the duties of Christian philosophers to remind ourselves, and our secular colleagues, how feeble are the smoky lamps we carry. We cannot do without our clearest ideas or our most advanced techniques. They are our rightful pride and our necessity. We, however, tend to be tempted to place too much faith in our current abstractions, to be too much dominated by our immediate needs, to be too proud of the potent handiwork of our intelligence. Christian philosophers are not immune to any of these temptations, of course, but there is in our tradition a strong note calling for radical humility toward all things human. This note, though hard for humans to hear, may by grace prove salubrious not only for our desiccated souls but also for our threatened planet.

A REPLY TO FERRÉ, AND
A COMMENT ON TRAU

John F. Post

One does not often receive comments as thoughtful as Frederick Ferré's, and I am the more grateful for them. That even so sympathetic a reader may occasionally misconstrue is a measure of how very hard it can be for a couple of philosophers to understand one another. In the interest of mutual understanding, then, let me begin by remarking that I do not argue that the values determined by the facts are values that obtain in every possible world, but (only) that the facts about the actual world determine the values in the actual world.

Nor is it my intent to let "axiology bear the full weight of Christian discourse" via some kind of "axiological reduction," as Ferré puts it, so that "religion is logically prevented from making its own claims about the way things are." As I use the terms, to make a claim about the way things are is to make a truth-claim about them, and I have argued that religious truth-claims can be objectively, solidly true—true in a realist sense—via the determinacy of valuation. Indeed definition CD toward the end of §3 yields a notion of truth-

Research in Philosophy and Technology, Volume 10, pages 287-290.
ISBN: 1-55938-062-4

as-correspondence for value judgments. Thus, a truth about the religious value or significance of a thing or event is one of the truths about the way it is, and indeed often takes priority over other kinds of truth about it, scientific and other descriptive truth included.

Moreover, I spent a paragraph (the ninth of §5) listing various dimensions of meaning that religious discourse can have. Some of these dimensions clearly are not reducible to talk of values. Such discourse often refers to actual experiences or to historical events, or to concrete exemplars, and even though it typically does so in order to ascribe certain values to them by interpreting them in light of a vision of meaningful existence, still the reference to the experiences, events, and exemplars is not eliminatable in favor of talk only about values. When true, such discourse is factual, even referential, in at least the twofold sense that the things it refers to did occur, and that they indeed have the value or significance the discourse ascribes to them, and have it objectively. The "metaphysical dimension," as Ferré calls it, is hardly neglected. For instance, one can speak truly of events that are objectively miracles or acts of God, which surely is to make a truth-claim about the way things are.

Nor is my treatment of first-order usage asymmetric as between objective values and religious language. Just as ordinary users of language about God and miracles suppose (or tend to suppose) that they are referring to special entities, so also do ordinary users of language about values. No doubt this tendency to reify is in part what led Plato to posit the Form of the Good, and the others to posit similar extra entities, for the terms of our value judgments to denote. Even today, so sophisticated a philosopher and user of language about values as Simon Blackburn succumbs to the same temptation, when he likens moral realism to realism about mathematical entities. Richard Rorty likewise succumbs, when he supposes that moral realism requires that there be some shadowy, Platonic realm "out there," perhaps beyond space and time. That is why I piled up counter-examples to the assumption that a claim can be true only if all its terms refer. To reject the assumption is to drive a wedge between surface and depth grammar for *all* language, including language about values, just as much as for language about God.

Indeed I accorded language about God a respect I did not accord language about values. Whereas I took it quite for granted that value judgments can be true even though their characteristic terms do not refer to special entities, I pointed out that subject-predicate literalism about God-talk, according to which the term "God" must refer, may be too ingrained to break, along with the unacceptable kind of supernaturalism that goes with it. Thus if the truth-conditions of God-talk must after all include the existence of some such special entity, then of course the present approach would fail. It was partly for this reason that I inserted footnote 77 about having elsewhere developed an alternative approach in which the term "God" does refer in certain uses (although not to anything unacceptably supernatural, and not in contexts of positive predication about God).

Finally, it is not true that only if the norms and values are clear and explicit could the objective determination of values by the facts be demonstrable or even discussable. This is not, however, a point I make in the paper, but only in the book (§§4.3, 4.4, 5.3); readers of the paper may be excused the opposite impression. In any case, nothing in my argument encourages the tunnel vision Ferré so rightly condemns. On the contrary, the relation of nonreductive determination was deployed in large part precisely in order to accommodate the holistic, diachronic, ecological thinking that reductive approaches so often ignore or deny [§§4.3, 4.5; see also §1.5(v)]. In this and other senses, there is indeed room in my view for the addage "Nature knows best." Likewise, I endorse the call for radical humility toward all things human, but again this appears more in the book than in the paper. It is neither my intent nor a consequence of my approach that science and technology would be free "to penetrate and control the universe of entities at will," even under certain constraints, for this suggests that the presumption should always be in favor of such penetration and control, and hence that the burden of proof should always be on those who would impose constraints. Instead, I believe (with Ferré) that both the presumption and the burden should often be reversed, in this age of witless knowledge-explosion and mindless intervention in nature. I believe, further, that the correctness of this needed shift in our values is objectively determined by natural fact, although just how it is thus determined would have to be argued on another occasion.

With regard to Professor Trau's interesting paper, I'm afraid I cannot quite agree with Ferré that what motivates the Church's alleged *petitio* is what I call "the enchanted view of nature." There is no such thing as *the* enchanted view, but many, even among Christians. One kind of enchanted view evidently entails condemning *in vitro* fertilization; many more do not. To hold a view of nature as enchanted is simply to believe that nature contains intrinsic value, ends, and meaning; among Christians, it is to see nature as also "a domain for the mysterious activity of God and for the occurrence of miracles," as Ferré puts it. It is a further question as to what the intrinsic values, ends, and meanings are, and whether they allow *in vitro* fertilization.

Basically, the argument of my paper is, first, that one cannot reject enchanted views out of hand on the ground merely that such talk of value, meaning, and the like is irreducible to natural or other science; and, second, that one can form a synthesis of enchantment and physicalism in which each enriches the other, while correcting the other's occasional extremes. Again, it is a further question as to which of the several enchanted views that could possibly figure in such a synthesis is true and whether it allows *in vitro* fertilization. Some such enchanted view might endorse the Church's "prejudice in favor of nature over technology"; others would not (or not at all to the same degree). Indeed, it is even possible (although I think not the case) that the correct enchanted view favors technology over nature, for it is possible that the values intrinsically contained in nature (in the sense of being determined by natural—that is, descriptive—fact) entail a presumption in favor of the technological option (as at some earlier stage or stages of our evolution they probably did).

Nor, for related reasons, can I agree that the price Trau pays for her argument is "acceptance of the fundamental modern conception of nature as neutral." So far from being committed to a "disenchanted view of nature," her argument can be construed as an argument from within the pale about *which* enchanted view of the world is correct, and whether it entails condemnation of *in vitro* fertilization. Nature is taken as normative; the question then is what exactly nature's norms are.

At the same time, I am puzzled by some aspects of Trau's discussion. To take just one, consider her argument that the Church's condemnation of *in vitro* fertilization "actually contradicts" the Church's position in *Humanae Vitae* on conjugal acts. *Humanae Vitae* tells us that not every particular conjugal act requires the intention of procreation. And this does amount to a precedent for justifiable separation of the unitive and the procreative aspects of the act. Equally clearly, however, is that this is not to say the separation is justifiable regardless of the circumstances.

Now what does *Origins* tell us? Essentially, that every generation (conception) of a human person must have its "proper perfection" of "being the result of and fruit of a conjugal act in which the spouses become "cooperators with God for giving life to a new person." In effect, this is to tell us that one crucial circumstance in which the separation of the unitive and the procreative aspects of the act is *not* justifiable is when such separation would deprive the generation of a person of its proper perfection of being the result of an appropriate conjugal act. In practice, of course, this means that the spouses would have to anticipate the (likely) outcome of the act. If the outcome is (or could well be) conception, then the two aspects must not be separated. If not, then they may justifiably be separated. The rhythm method is compatible with this requirement, as evidently it is designed to be.

Thus, the Church requires neither that every conjugal act intend conception, nor merely that each act be open to the possibility of conception. Rather, the Church holds that some conjugal acts need not intend conception, that some need not even be open to the possibility of conception, but that none may both result in conception and not intend it, since otherwise the human person thus conceived would be deprived of the perfection of being the result of an appropriate act. I see plenty to disagree with here, but no inconsistency.

GOD-TALK, PHYSICALISM, AND TECHNOLOGY:
A MUTUAL ENDEAVOR

Jane Mary Trau

John Post's paper supports a position which many Christian philosophers wish to take concerning the intrinsic value of nature. The objective value that is justified by God's creative activity, or by Post's "God-talk," may be a "given" for many Christian philosophers. Post's attempt to defeat an important and respected challenge to the existence of objective values, however, is a valuable success which transcends the concern of Christian absolutists.

Physicalists, theist and nontheist alike, ultimately wrestle with the question of valuation. The identification of characteristics, and their relationship to normative values, is at the very heart of much work in that field. The move from physicalist metaphysics to the elimination of values, or their reduction to mere preferences, is a pivotal point of discussion in contemporary philosophy. The implications for ethical methodologies are far-reaching. By showing that physicalism, a system which appeals to twentieth century scientific

Research in Philosophy and Technology, Volume 10, pages 291-295.
Copyright © 1990 by JAI Press Inc.
All rights of reproduction in any form reserved.
ISBN: 1-55938-062-4

inclinations, is compatible with objective values, Post makes an important move forward in the debate.

Post's endeavor to demonstrate the compatibility between physicalism and objective values is an important step in undermining Mackie's "argument from queerness." Mackie has long been regarded as one of theism's most capable critics. It is also of vital interest, however, for *Christians* who find difficulty positing objective values in light of modern scientific inquiry. The reduction of values to mere subjective preferences is not a reduction which excludes the critical concern of Christian theologians and philosophers.

Much of contemporary moral theology rests on this point: the ontology of values and moral norms.[1] The camps are divided precisely along these lines. The struggle of theists to "modernize" their doxastic systems in light of science has led them to the same questions raised by the physicalist philosophers about the ontology of value. If Post makes any serious contribution to the discussion, which I believe he does, Christian philosophers and theologians must certainly take an interest in what he has to say.

Although Post does have much to add to this controversy, I do not accept the ontology of his "God-talk." He argues that God-talk can be meaningful, and compatible with physicalism, even if it does not refer to an indicable entity. Perhaps he is right, but I, as a matter of pure faith, do intend to refer to an entity within the classical Roman Catholic tradition.[2] I do, however, believe that a classical ontology is compatible with, and aided by, Post's claim about physicalism and objective value. Our point of departure would probably be the epistemology of religious beliefs.

From my ontological belief, I derive anything but a neutral value of the natural. Indeed, the universe as the creation of a loving and wise Father-Mother God is holy (both "tremens" and "fasciens") and delightful. Although Ferré is correct that a neutral position may be compatible with my argumentation, it is not implied. Rather, I wish to argue that the universe is intrinsically good, that nature is the source of intrinsic value. The question I wish to consider is, "What are the norms for the development and application of human technology?"[3]

I accept, as Ferré puts it in his response to my paper, a "radical humility toward all things human." Assuming that human nature as designed by God is rational and creative, we must rejoice in the creative abilities and products of human beings. A long-standing complaint ("If he wanted us to fly, he would have given us wings!"), is that human beings intrude upon, frustrate, and destroy the natural order. What is needed, then, is the development of guidelines for development and application.

My objection to the Vatican instruction on artificial reproductive technologies is that it provides no such norms or guidelines. Rather, it merely reiterates the artificiality of the technique and alleges that use of the technique is *contrary* to the natural order. The good-making and bad-making characteristics I request do not imply that *nature* is value neutral. Rather, I request some description of the *technology* which will demonstrate its licitness or illicitness. The document begs the question precisely because it does not move off the artificiality of the technology in the rejection of its use.

Perhaps a list of good-making and bad-making characteristics could be drawn up. For example, we might say that the permanent destruction of any part of the environment is a bad-making characteristic. Conversely, the preservation of the ecological system is a good-making characteristic. Further good-making characteristics might be: the restoration of damaged areas or organs, the increasing of crops or water supplies, the improvement of psychological well-being of individuals and groups. Some other bad-making characteristics might be: long-lasting and debilitating side-effects to persons or the environment, destruction of personal autonomy, psychological or mental impairment. (The lists could be much longer.) Also, each technology will have its own set of both good-making and bad-making characteristics. In each question concerning use of a given technology, certain intrinsic and extrinsic characteristics will have to be counted up and weighed. When the good-making characteristics outweigh the bad, the technology may be advocated; when the bad-making characteristics outweigh the good, the technology may be prohibited.

Under this system, nature is not neutralized. Rather, the prejudice is always in favor of nature; but where technology can improve the distribution of natural goods to persons and groups (e.g., irrigation, and crops to drought-stricken areas), or restore what nature has impoverished (e.g, draining flooded areas), or restore what nature or human beings have destroyed (e.g, replacing vital organs), technology is the instrument of human good. Thus, we may have at least one fundamental norm from which to proceed: Human beings have a natural good, and technology should enhance and never frustrate that good. This norm is justified by the belief in a divine and natural order, and thus is not neutral.

A further problem with the instruction is that it makes a questionable assumption about the natural order, i.e., the nature of human sexuality. In fact, the lack of explicit discussion about human sexuality is the critical error made in this document, and in *Humanae Vitae*. Both documents seem to proceed from an implicit, and sadly never explicit, understanding about human sexuality which is utterly physicalist. The correctness of this position is too large for this paper, but it does point to a vital concern of this entire discussion. One's understanding of the natural order affects the establishment of norms for the use of technology.

The Church's understanding of sexuality is inseparable from its conclusions concerning the use of artificial contraception and reproductive technologies. In fact, I believe that Post's "puzzlement" with parts of my discussion is actually his share in the confusion the document has generated.

He is right that the Church's position in *Humanae Vitae* "does amount to a precedent for justifiable separation of the unitive and procreative aspects of the act" (Post's comment). However, this separation is precisely what the Church denies in the instruction on artificial reproductive technologies. Some analysts, including Post, apparently, have denied that *Humanae Vitae* is problematic since the document does stipulate conditions for justifiable separation of the procreative and unitive aspects of the conjugal act. The granted exception is itself problematic, however, for it begs the question against artificial contraception, as I believe I have shown in the first two sections of my paper. Beyond the problem of *Humanae Vitae* itself, the later instruction flatly rejects the separation of the unitive and procreative aspects and insists that this rejection must be preserved.

> Contraception deliberately deprives the conjugal act of its openness to procreation and in this way brings about a voluntary dissociation of the ends of marriage. Homologous artificial fertilization, in seeking a procreation which is not the fruit of a specific act of conjugal union, objectively effects an analogous separation between the goods and the meanings of marriage.[4]

Post also refers to conception as the "proper perfection" of the conjugal act. The question of whether conception can be the result of the totality of conjugal love, rather than the perfection of one specific act has been raised against *Humanae Vitae* and the current instruction. The pronounced position begs the question against technology and stems from a questionable understanding of human sexuality.

The creation of norms for the development and application of technology ultimately reflects a theologian's or philosopher's understanding of the divine or natural order of the universe. That understanding will be historically and culturally nuanced; it cannot be value-free. Post's paper provides the justification for the coexistence of religious values with scientific descriptions. The task that remains is to harmonize religious values with scientific descriptions. This does not mean that religious values are not objective; we must scrutinize our values in light of scientific knowledge and "weed out" values that are nothing more than societal conventions in the first place.

Nowhere is historical context more blatantly influential than in the area of religious norms concerning human sexuality. The understanding of heterosexual relations, homosexual relations, and autosexual relations is greatly enhanced by modern sciences. What inferences can we draw from scientific knowledge for religious morality? To what degree is religious morality scripturally based? To what degree is it culturally, rather than scripturally, justified? The epistemology of religious ethics is another topic which transcends the scope of this paper. My point is to emphasize the constant reexamination of religious morality in light of scientific progress. I do not suggest rejecting religious morality, rather, I suggest rethinking religious morality in terms of *both* scientific and theological exegesis.

Just as scriptural exegesis is influenced by cultural and historical context, so too is religious morality. I differ from Post on the point of divine ontology, but agree with him that physicalism does not threaten to eliminate religious values. In fact, the responsible modernization of religious values may be a positive result of the physicalist impetus in our culture.

The harmony of religious beliefs and technological progress is not only important, but essential. It may be precisely the "re-enchantment of nature" that will save it from the blasphemous and reckless intrusion of human beings. The religious life of the faithful, or the God-talk of Post's theists, may serve as the foundations from which practical and workable norms are established for human cooperation with the natural order of creation. For the Christian, the ethical question, "What would Jesus do?" is as relevant to in vitro fertilization as it is to stoning the adulteress.

If we assume that a specific modern technology is illicit precisely because it is technology, or because it is artificial (nonnatural), we simply beg the question. If, however, we assume that a specific modern technology is illicit because our world view is archaic or obsolete, we rob ourselves of the opportunity for active transportation of eternal values into the contemporary era. The "God-talk" of the Christian and the values it discerns in nature is vital to the world described in modern physicalist terms, and may be our only hope of preserving the universe from our destructive and rapacious tendencies.

NOTES

1.   Compare, for example, the work of Germain Griesez and Charles Curran. These are but two among many who epitomize the controversy about absolute value and absolute norms.

2.   Although I do embrace this theology, there are certain problems of language (its exclusively male character), imagery (its poverty of female imagery), and ritual (its male supremacy) which I perceive. However, the ontology of God, as described by this tradition, underlies my work.

3.   I offer a brief sketch of some guidelines in my *Humanae Vitae* paper in this volume.

4.   "Instruction on Respect for Human Life in Its Origin and on the Dignity of Procreation," II, B 4.a.

CONTEMPORARY DISCUSSION SECTION

THE MYTHS OF THOMAS SZASZ

Michael J. Carella

For more than a quarter century, Thomas Szasz has carried on a crusade against institutional psychiatry, in particular, against involuntary psychiatric treatment[1] and the use of the insanity plea to avoid criminal liability.[2] This crusade has been noteworthy in at least two respects. The first is that Szasz himself is a professor of psychiatry at the Upstate Medical Center of the State University of New York at Syracuse; the second is that his crusade is based on the claim that there is no such thing as mental illness, that the concept is a myth.[3] Szasz also contends that drug addiction is a fiction,[4] that prohibitions against suicide abridge basic human freedoms,[5] that psychotherapy is conversation rather than treatment,[6] and that the use of sexual surrogates in psychotherapy is a form of prostitution.[7]

Szasz believes that adults should be free to do as they please, provided that they do not abridge the rights of others and that they accept financial responsibility for their own conduct. In the absence of physical coercion or the threat of violence, human conduct, no matter how far it deviates from acceptable social norms, how repugnant it is to our sensibilities, or how self-destructive, should be presumed to be free.[8] Szasz's main thesis is that mental

Research in Philosophy and Technology, Volume 10, pages 299-313.
ISBN: 1-55938-062-4

illness is not a medical category at all but a moral and political label.[9] It is, however, not some innocent or harmless label but one which permits psychiatrists to punish or imprison nonconformists under the guise of treatment (what Szasz calls "psychiatric slavery")[10] and enables "patients" to evade responsibility for their actions by claiming to be mentally ill (what he calls "moral bootlegging").[11]

Szasz's positions have gained him a loyal following among various anti-authoritarians who see him as the chief defender of autonomy and responsibility in a society increasingly prone to coercion and control. Yet, understandably, not all reactions to his crusade have been favorable. Within a year of the publication of Szasz's original manifesto, *The Myth of Mental Illness,* the Commissioner of the New York State Department of Mental Health tried to have him removed from his teaching position. The mental health establishment as a whole, however, has generally preferred to ignore him or to dismiss his work as quackery. With few exceptions, philosophers and other academics notoriously fond of polemic for its own sake, have made no serious attempts to assess his claims.[12]

This is unfortunate, for beyond his obvious talents as a thought-provoking writer and aphorist, Szasz has brought to public attention one very disturbing aspect of contemporary society: the medicalization of modern life. In a society where there is little or no consensus on fundamental political and moral values, there is a strong tendency to treat moral and political deviation as illness. One result of this tendency to medicalize morality is to treat subjective value-judgments of physicians not as personal opinions but as scientific facts.[13] In the case of the physician, whose experience lies in the understanding and treatment of physical illness, this misplaced confidence can be dangerous. In the case of the psychiatrist, who, according to Szasz, has no such medical expertise, the result can be catastrophic.

The problem with this line of criticism is not that what it alleges about the practice of psychiatry is untrue. Much of it, unfortunately, is all too accurate. Rather, it is that Szasz's particular account of psychiatry's shortcomings is based on a philosophical point of view that is every bit as naive as the one he criticizes. The tragedy is that, having built his critique of psychiatry on the oversimplified view of science and reality, Szasz has left his target relatively unscathed.

In this essay I wish to discuss four of the myths on which Szasz's critique is based: (1) the epistemological myth, the view that, while psychiatric theories are metaphors, medical theories are literally true; (2) the ontological myth, the view that disease is a purely physical entity; (3) the psychological myth, the view that human conduct is neither unconscious nor irrational; and (4) the ethical myth, the view that the mentally ill are malingering and that psychiatric theories are moral judgments in a medical disguise.

My purpose in this essay is twofold. First, I want to show that the problem of human conduct does not reduce itself to a choice between the brave new world of psychiatric domination and the simple-minded world of self-actualization. Second, I want to demonstrate that the problem of deviant behavior is far more complex than either Szasz or his critics have been willing to admit.

THE EPISTEMOLOGICAL MYTH

Since the publication of *The Myth of Mental Illness* in 1961, Szasz has consistently held that the concept of "mental illness" is a metaphor. Minds are "sick" only in the sense that jokes are "sick" or that economies are "sick."[14] This assertion rests on the premise that language which describes spatiotemporal events is literal; language which describes feelings and emotions is metaphorical. "Mental illness," he insists, belongs to the latter category.

Such a view, though straightforward and self-consistent, is utterly inadequate, given what we know of the history and philosophy of science. Why? Science, as a body of knowledge, is undoubtedly the most reliable knowledge we have about the world. But it is much more than that. The child who says that there are nine planets in our solar system is enunciating a "scientific" fact. But he is not a scientist because of the way in which he "knows" this fact. More important than the content of scientific knowledge are the methods by which that content is generated. Science is essentially a way of knowing whose content is constantly being refined and redefined.

The scientific way of knowing originated in ancient Greece when Thales tried to find a nonmythical answer to the question: What is the fundamental structure of the universe? Implicit in the very way Thales posed his question is the distinction—absolutely crucial to science—between *phenomena* (the appearance or perceptions which need to be explained) and *nature* (the "reality" which lies beyond the appearances). It is this distinction which historically has driven the dialectic of scientific inquiry. The world as we experience it with our senses is a riddle to be solved. The answer to that riddle lies in the hypotheses which science tests by means of structured experience.

What has characterized science from Thales to the present has been the attempt to account for the observable world, the phenomena, by postulating entities that are not directly observable. Consider, for example, Galileo's distinction between primary and secondary qualities. Color-as-seen, odor-as-smelled, texture-as-felt, flavors-as-tasted are all, according to Galileo, secondary qualities: they are the effects of nature upon our senses. Nature itself, he insisted, has only primary (i.e., mathematical) qualities: extention, motion, and their ideal derivatives, the knowledge of which requires an abstraction from sensation. The point of Galileo's distinction is that a scientific explanation of the world we observe with our senses requires the postulation of entities that are not observed by the senses but which, nevertheless, are understood by the mind.

The formulation of quantum mechanics in the twentieth century shed new light on the distinction between nature and phenomena. Quantum mechanics forces us to treat position, momentum, energy, time, spin, angular momentum—all of which, Galileo would have maintained, are primary and hence constitutive of nature—as secondary properties. Like color, shape, sound, taste, smell, and texture, they are the effects of nature on the observer. They are artifacts defined in part by the act of measurement.

What, then, is left of nature? What is the fundamental structure of the universe? The only properties we can ascribe to nature, that is, the only properties which do not depend on methods of observation and experimentation are certain abstract mathematical symmetries. These mathematical properties do not correspond to anything we can observe in nature, nor to anything we can imagine. In brief, the basic building blocks of matter are not found in nature.

What does all this have to do with Szasz's assertion that "mental illness" is a metaphor not to be taken literally? Simply this. All science involves the use of metaphor. It does so not because of some intrinsic limitation on what science can know, but by virtue of the kind of explanation science gives. If one wishes to "explain" the phenomena we experience, one must go beyond experiential categories, yet one must explain the unfamiliar in terms of the familiar. It is precisely the extension of the familiar to designate the unfamiliar which constitutes the scientific metaphor.[15]

"Mental illness" is indeed metaphorical; but so, too, is physical illness. One cannot explain scientifically the phenomenon of physical illness without recourse to psychological entities which ultimately are not themselves observable, but which explain what is observed. The link between the unobservable that is postulated and the data which is observable involves a metaphor. Indeed, without metaphor there can be no science.

Does this mean that there is no distinction between literal and figurative (metaphorical) discourse? Not at all! There are situations in which we intend our words to have a literal meaning and others in which we intend a figurative one. This distinction between literal and figurative or metaphorical meaning, however, is context-dependent. Whether a statement is to be taken as literally true depends entirely on the linguistic context in which the statement is made. If I say "The cat is on the mat," I am most probably using ordinary language to make a statement intended to be taken literally. Yet there are theoretical contexts where statements in ordinary language are no longer literally true but merely useful metaphors. When a physicist speaks of light as a particle or as a wave, he uses those terms as convenient metaphors because, while light appears to act at times as a wave and at other times as a particle, it is in reality neither wave nor particle.

Szasz is perfectly correct in characterizing "mental illness" as metaphorical and completely wrong about its significance. If there is a science of disease which even pretends to explain phenomena, it must include theoretical entities as part of its repertoire. "Mental illness" may not be an appropriate scientific metaphor for explaining the phenomena which it is supposed to explain, but it cannot be dismissed as unscientific simply by virtue of its being metaphorical.

THE ONTOLOGICAL MYTH

The fact that science is inevitably metaphorical does not guarantee that what "mental illness" denotes actually exists or even that the concept is a scientific one. Its fate, however, must be decided not by legislation or definition, but rather by accepted canons of scientific inquiry. According to Szasz, there is no such thing as mental illness because disease or illness can only affect the body.[17] Furthermore, he insists that "nonphysical illness" is a social construction, based on a category mistake, the kind people make when they take metaphors like "cruel fate" literally. Szasz is absolutely correct in asserting that mental illness is a socially constructed reality. His mistake is in assuming that social constructions cannot correspond to reality, or that physical illness is not a social construction but a self-evident reality. Let's deal with the latter assumption first.

Health and disease are complex not only as phenomena but also as ideas, for they involve the relationship of organisms to their environments. René Dubos once defined health as the ability of an organism to adapt successfully to its environment.[17] Illness or disease is whatever compromises that adaptive ability. Human health, he claimed, involves the interplay of three factors: environment, constitution, and language. The environment to which humans must adapt includes not only the physical, chemical, and biological determinants of adaptation but also such cultural factors as economic, political, esthetic and religious values. Human beings often risk life and limb in pursuit of cultural ideals without which living would not seem to them worthwhile.

The human constitution consists of the full range of capacities for adaptation that a human organism possesses. These include genetic endowment, early physical and emotional development, personal history, skill, lifestyle, habits, character, and ideals. All of these, insisted Dubos, are intrinsic to the concepts of health and disease because all can have a profound effect on one's ability to adapt successfully.

The third factor in defining human health is language, Dubos said. Language enables humans to adapt their environment to their own needs and thus to redefine the rules of adaptation. Language is the basis of human culture, and it is by virtue of language that human health and illness become, in large measure, cultural products. Much of our health depends not simply on the way our body functions but on the ideas that motivate and inspire us. So long as health is related to adaptation, human health implies cultural adaptation.

The view that disease is purely physical reality, Dubos claimed, is a conceit of the nineteenth century made plausible by certain spectacular gains in epidemiology and surgery. The discovery of anesthesia, asepsis, and antisepsis made it safe to do all kinds of sophisticated surgery. With the formulation of the doctrine of specific etiology and of the germ theory of disease came the view that medicine was the key to health. Yet the spectacular successes attributed to modern medicine are not all the result of medical science and technology. The passing of the great epidemics, the gains in health as measured by rates of mortality and morbidity were due, in the main, to better diet, better sanitation, and changes in lifestyle—in short, to human cultural adaptation.[18] The notion that disease is exclusively physical requires that we overlook the role of culture in human adaptation.

What of Szasz's assertion that the very idea of "mental illness" is a category mistake? This is a claim borrowed from Gilbert Ryle, the philosopher, who argued that Cartesian dualism was based on a similar category mistake.[19] Descartes had asserted that the private, conscious states of the mind, a thinking substance, are isomorphic with the publicly observable, physical states of the body, an extended substance.[20] In postulating the existence of a mind as the ultimate subject of sensations, feelings, and beliefs, Descartes had made— according to Ryle—a fatal category mistake. A mind cannot be a substance. Ryle's critique showed that Descartes' concept of the mind as a substance separate and distinct from the body leads the insoluble problem of their mutual interaction. How can a thinking substance affect an extended substance, and vice versa?

Despite the embarrassment of this problem, Cartesian dualism survived chiefly because of the enormous power of the concept of isomorphism. So long as one assumed that the mental and physical states of an organism are isomorphic, it did not matter whether one was a materialist, an idealist, or a dualist. One could do science without having to resolve the ontological question: what is mind and how does it relate to matter?

Until the twentieth century, the mind-body problem seemed susceptible only to antinomian solutions, none of which were satisfactory. The reduction of mind to matter seemed to succeed only by endowing matter with the properties of mind. The advent of the computer, however, while it has certainly not resolved the problem, has provided some valuable insights into the nature of symbols, and perhaps into the nature of mind. If a machine can be programmed so that its behavior is determined not by the *physical* properties of its casual antecedents but by their *logical* or symbolic properties, then the notion of physical objects as inert substances whose behavior is governed completely by physical laws is no longer adequate. My purpose here is not to make a brief for artificial intelligence, which I beleive is wrong in its epistemological claims, but simply to point out that structure or form is an intrinsic feature of physical objects. Without structure, physical objects can neither exist nor function.

It is in virtue of its structure or form that a physical object becomes a symbol, and herein lies the clue that may point the way to a solution of the mind-body problem. Symbols can interact with other objects to produce physical effects that depend not on the physical properties of the symbols but on their formal or representational properties. Even at the infraconscious level, symbols produce physical effects. I am not referring to dogs salivating at the sight of food or to the tropism of plants growing toward a source of light. What I have in mind is something far more basic, the idea that information is a constitutive of matter, a point that Norbert Wiener has made in a far more dramatic fashion.[21] While there is much to disagree with in Weiner's concept of cybernetics, his insight about the constitutive nature of information is right on the mark. So long as one conceives of information as something superadded to the concept of matter, one will always need a ghost in the machine to interpret the information provided by the world. If, however, information is a formal property of matter itself, then objects can interact with one another in complex ways that require an understanding of their formal structure over and above an account of the physical, chemical, or biological forces acting upon them.

In organisms that possess consciousness, behavior is mediated by the awareness of symbols. Thus, the behavior of an animal will depend on how it perceives its environment as well as on physical and biological causes. In organisms endowed with self-consciousness, behavior is also mediated by the comprehension of symbols. Thus, the behavior of a human being will also depend on how he understands his environment. Perhaps there is no object that corresponds to the noun "mind," but there certainly is a function which corresponds to the adjective "mental." That function is the perception, awareness, and comprehension of symbols. "Mind" is not some mysterious or esoteric entity but simply a shorthand way of referring to those activities involving symbols which seem to be characteristic of *human* existence.

What does all this have to do with Szasz's contention that illness is by definition physical? That contention involves a misunderstanding of mind as a substance rather than as a function, of disease as an entity rather than as a relationship, and of science as a description rather than as a theoretical reconstruction of phenomena. The real issue is whether the concept of mental illness provides an account of behavioral anomalies that meets the canons of scientific inquiry.

THE PSYCHOLOGICAL MYTH

In addition to mistaking the role of metaphor in science and of the relationship of theoretical entities to reality, Szasz subscribes to the myth that human

behavior is neither unconscious nor irrational. In *The Myth of Mental Illness,*
he argues against the psychoanalytic axiom that all action, including
unconscious action, is goal-directed. Such a position, he claims, makes it
impossible for human beings to make indifferent mistakes, that is, mistakes
based on a lack of knowledge or a lack of skill in the game of life. The symptoms
of mental illness are either mistakes (misinformation based on ignorance), or
lies (misinformation that is deliberate). "I believe it is cognitively more accurate,
and morally more dignified," says Szasz, "to regard it [hysteria] as a lie rather
than as a mistake."[22]

There are two separate issues here. The first is one of responsibility, and,
on this particular issue, there is no dispute between Szasz and orthodox
psychoanalysts. Both accept the common sense notion that no one can be held
responsible for what he or she is unaware of. The dispute arises over the precise
nature of human awareness.

Long before psychoanalysis, poets, playwrights, and philosophers assumed
that human beings were often unaware of the deepest motives for their own
conduct. From this insight Freud developed a theory that all human behavior,
even that which seems to be the result of mistakes or inadvertence, or without
apparent or even conscious motive, is purposive. This is precisely what Szasz
denies. For him, an action is either conscious and purposive, or it is unconscious
and random. In the latter case, the unconsciousness of the act implies a mistake
which is neither goal-directed nor rule-following, and thus the one who is
unconscious is not held responsible for his mistakes. In the former case, the
purposiveness of one's action implies consciousness which is either goal-
directed or rule-following; hence, the one who acts purposively must be held
responsible for his actions. In attacking the Freudian notion of unconscious
purpose, Szasz seems to have retreated to a position indistinguishable from
that of Descartes, who identified mind with consciousness. But such a position
is untenable in the face of overwhelming empirical evidence to the contrary.

In *The Manufacture of Madness,* Szasz makes it clear that he is not a
Cartesian but rather one who believes that "insane behavior no less than sane,
is goal-directed and motivated; or, as we might say today, that it is tactical
and strategic." He concludes that we should consider "the behavior of the
madman as perfectly rational from the point of view of the actor."[23] This
assertion signals a shift in Szasz's argument. Consciousness is no longer an
essential factor in determining responsibility. The crucial notion is rationality,
and, on that score, both the actions of normal persons and those of so called
madmen are equally rational because both are goal-directed or rule-following.

This particular argument exploits an ambiguity inherent in the concept of
rationality. We sometimes speak of objects, even inanimate or infrahuman
objects, as rational because their behavior corresponds to our expectation that
events have natural causes and can, in principle, be explained rationally.
Objects are irrational to the extent that, in principle, they defy our ability to

give a rational account of their behavior, either because of some putative supernatural cause (miracles) or some infrarational aspect of nature (randomness). This "theoretical" rationality is a function of the way we explain the world.

There is, however, another kind of rationality, a "moral" rationality, which is attributable not to the behavior of objects but to the activity of subjects who pursue moral ideals. In this latter case, we are not concerned with giving an account of a person's behavior—for such an account can be given even of inanimate objects—but rather of the relationship between the values which a person seeks to achieve or enhance and the norms which guide his or her actions toward such values. People are irrational when the norms which determine their actions are inconsistent with or destructive of the values to which they aspire.

Szasz's argument that the actions of madmen are rational because they are purposive is correct if by that he means that such actions are intelligible and, hence, can be explained rationally. He is quite wrong, however, if he means—which he evidently does—that the ability to give an explanation of a madman's actions means that norms which guide those same actions must be morally consistent with the values the madman seeks to attain. To the extent that they are not, it makes perfectly good sense to speak to actions as morally irrational.

THE ETHICAL MYTH

Szasz has consistently maintained that mental illness is not illness at all and that those who claim to suffer from this condition are in fact malingering. Those who brand others as menatally ill are trying to control their behavior through the dishonest use of medical labels. Mental illness is, in sum, an exercise in moral duplicity.

It must be emphasized, however, that Szasz has never denied that there are people who exhibit all the symptoms which psychiatry associates with mental illness. He has never questioned the fact that some people are disturbed, that they report hearing voices, that they claim to be in the grip of irresistible impulses, that they experience great anguish, that they feel morbidly depressed, utterly worthless, or even suicidal. He does not dispute the fact that psychiatrists can identify certain people as psychologically or socially dysfunctional. He does, however, claim that such persons have moral, not medical, problems. Their "symptoms" are indicators of unresolved "problems of life," not of diseases that require treatment.

Still, calling some dysfunctions "problems of life" rather than "mental illness" might be construed as a semantic quibble. The net result, at least from the point of view of the sufferer, may very well be the same. But Szasz sees the issue as political. Where he and his more orthodox psychiatric peers part company is over the strategy for dealing with these "psycho-ethical" problems.

Szasz claims that those who exhibit symptoms of "mental illness" have, in fact, opted for a certain style of life. The "symptoms" which they display are coping strategies, in effect, solutions which they have worked out to problems in their own lives. To treat such persons against their will, even under the guise of helping, says Szasz, is morally condescending, even tyrannical. To permit such people the kind of considerations we give the truly ill, simply because they have such problems, is irresponsible, perhaps self-defeating. In either case, treating such sufferers according to a medical model compromises their integrity as autonomous persons. The so-called mentally ill, according to Szasz, merit no special stigma nor any special consideration because of their chosen style of life.

What of those who exhibit the symptoms of "mental illness" but who profess dissatisfaction with their lives? What about those who want to be "cured?" Have they no recourse in Szasz's world of total responsibility and self-actualization? Are they to be told they are not ill, or that they should stop malingering? Are psychiatrists to be forbidden or, at least, urged not to treat these nonexistent mental illnesses? Not at all!

Szasz believes in consensual and contractual psychiatry. For those who are able and willing to pay, the contractual psychiatrist is there; not to treat in the medical sense, but to aid the patient gain an understanding of his "symptoms," of the self-defeating games they represent, and of the strategies he needs in order to modify his behavior and alleviate his suffering.[24]

By the time one gets through describing consensual or contractual therapy, one finds it hard to distinguish it from what most psychotherapists in private practice actually do. There are, of course, some differences. Szasz will not treat persons who are not his clients, that is, persons with whom he does not have a fiduicary relationship, and I think he is absolutely correct on this point. Psychiatrists who serve interests other than or antithetical to those of their patients should not be considered disinterested experts but as adversaries, subject to all the challenges of adversarial proceedings.

Neither would Szasz, I presume, accept government third-party payment for his services on the grounds that this both indicates and fosters irresponsibility on the part of the clinet. The one who suffers from ailments which the medical profession can verify as physically real is entitled to the normal remissions which society accords the ill. Those who suffer from ailments which are the result of moral problems (problems of life) are entitled to no such remission— at least not unless they have the wherewithal to pay for it.

Despite his rhetoric, Szasz turns out on closer examination to be an old-fashioned advocate of the free market in medicine. This view may have some merit to it, especially in these times when the increasing medicalization of life continues unabated. But Szasz's views are hardly radical, and their theoretical basis is woefully inadequate to perform the absolutely necessary task of disestablishing medicine as our national religion.

CONCLUSIONS

There is a lesson to be learned from the myths of Thomas Szasz about how best to fight against technocracy and its tendency to reduce moral and political issues to questions of efficiency or technique that are best decided by experts. That lesson is essentially that one must beat the expert on his own turf with his own weapons. To do anything less is to leave the technocratic myth of expertise intact. Like a weed which has been cut down but its roots not pulled out, the myth eventually grows back stronger and more resilient. One can only overcome the pretensions of the technocrat by demonstrating that, even on its own terms, technocracy is self-defeating. Szasz once appeared to have all the weapons needed to expose the myth of psychiatric expertise and to mount an effective counterattack against it. Yet his efforts to do so have failed, not because of the way he presents his arguments—as some of his own critics have contended—but rather because his attack on psychiatric expertise contains a seriously flawed view of technology and its relationship to moral and political values.

The myths of Thomas Szasz all presume a fundamental dichotomy of facts and values. In a manner reminiscent of Max Weber,[25] Szasz distinguishes between judgments of fact, which are rational, objective, and publicly verifiable, and judgments of value, which are subjective, nonrational, and only personally valid. The former are the proper domain of science and technology; the latter belong to the domain of religion, aesthetics, morality, and politics. On this view, science and technology achieve their objectivity by avoiding such issues as moral right and wrong, the nature of beauty, or the meaning of life. Politics, morality, and religion decide these issues, but only at the expense of having no truly objective criteria.

Weber's dichotomy of fact and value does afford Szasz a way to combat the technocratic myth of expertise. If questions of value are subjective, irrational, and utterly personal, then experts have no advantage whatsoever in matters of aesthetics, religion, morality, or politics. No amount of expertise can render value judgments objective. Indeed, this is the heart of Szasz's critique: that psychiatrists are in fact theologians, moralists, or politicians engaged in a self-defeating masquerade as scientists or engineers.

The price, however, that Szasz must pay for this particular way of circumscribing expertise is to render ethical and political discourse vacuous. Without rational canons of morality, the view that political problems are not susceptible to expert solutions soon gives way to the position that political issues are purely subjective. This position, in turn, inevitably yields to the practical policy that certain political viewpoints cannot be tolerated. As Weber himself was eventually forced to conclude, a stable society requires a consensus of values, even if it is only a subjective consensus. Where no such consensus is possible, the majority must ultimately resort to the threat of force as the only effective political arbiter. Szasz echoes this aspect of Weber's views when he asserts that societies, though they have no objective basis for deciding that certain actions are immoral, still have every political right to make laws enforcing morality.

Like the technocrats he criticizes, Szasz misunderstands the relationship between practical wisdom and expertise. Aristotle long ago recognized that human rationality is characterized by three different types of ability: theory (theoria), action (praxis), and skill (techné). Theory, according to Aristotle, is the capacity to understand an object by abstracting its intelligible form from its observable properties. Action is the capacity to choose between alternative strategies or means for attaining a desired end. Skill is the capacity to construct artifacts by imposing a design on natural objects. All three capacities are manifestations of one and the same human rationality. Though later philosophers have certainly refined Aristotle's analysis, its basic framework remains intact. Knowledge is the theoretical use of reason; action is its practical use; and skill, its technical use.

The technocratic myth of expertise attempts to reduce moral and political issues to questions of efficiency and technique by assuming that action (praxis) is a species of skill (techné). Thus, deciding whether it is moral to perform medical experiments on human beings is, in principle, no different from deciding how best to build a bridge. The content of the decision may be different, but the procedure for deciding is essentially the same. In adopting a dichotomy of facts and values, Szasz has effectively denied the ultimate rationality of human action. While this is certainly a direct assault on the technocratic myth, it does leave Szasz without a rational basis for criticizing expertise. Indeed, it deprives him of the strongest of all the arguments against the technocratic myth.

The chief flaw of technocracy lies in the intrinsically limited nature of expertise. To be an expert is to have some special knowledge or special skill which enables one to do more or comprehend more than the layman. But what the expert alone knows or what he alone can do does not imply that he has comprehensive or generalized knowledge, that he understands basic principles, or that he is wiser than the layman. Expertise is, by its very nature, goal-directed, socially-defined, and context-dependent.

Expertise cannot be understood apart from the particular goals which define it. It is, first and foremost, knowledge with a purpose. For example, the professional expertise of the physician is directed toward the successful diagnosis and treatment of illness; the expertise of an attorney, toward the successful defense of a client's interest; the expertise of the artist or artisan, toward the production of suitable artifacts. There are as many different kinds of expertise as there are different kinds of goals. Apart from those goals or purposes, expert knowledge is an empty concept. Even the expertise of the theoretical scientist—that most impractical of creatures—is directed toward the construction of successful theories.

Besides being goal-directed, an essential element of expertise is its social meaning. To be an expert requires the acknowledgement of one's expertise on the part of a community. This is especially evident in the case of the ethical professions, such as medicine and law, where the exercise of one's expertise requires the certification of one's status in the form of a license to practice. Such certification is an acknowledgement in law by the community of the expert status of the licensee. Without it, one cannot legally act as a professional nor even claim professional status, no matter what one's knowledge or one's skill. What is true legally and formally of professional expertise is also true in an informal but real sense of nonprofessional expertise. Without some kind of acknowledgement—albeit casual and informal—on the part of a community, one may possess a high degree of skill, but one is no expert.

In addition to being goal-directed and socially-defined, expertise is essentially knowledge or skill that is highly context-dependent. Granted that there are some experts who are less specialized than others, there is no such thing as expertise in general; there is only expertise in particular fields. Becoming an expert (say as an accountant or a computer scientist) entails, among other things, learning to think a certain way. It means learning to ignore whatever is immaterial or irrelevant to one's goals, and to concentrate on what is truly significant. It is only through a deliberate constriction of one's intellectual vision that one can acquire that quality which characterizes expertise: the ability to recognize easily and routinely what is important and relevant to the task at hand. Indeed, the more expert one becomes, the more narrow becomes the focus of one's expert vision. The specialist is more expert than the generalist to the extent that he knows more about less. Expertise is a form of cultivated myopia.

This point is made quite effectively by Thomas Kuhn in *The Structure of Scientific Revolutions.*[26] There he argues that normal science makes progress because each mature scientific discipline has a paradigm that defines which problems are worthwhile puzzles and which methods are canonical. The mark of a mature scientific community is that its members play the same game by the same set of rules. What is important is that the very same paradigm which coerces the members of a scientific community into playing the game of normal science a certain way also generates the unambigious criteria by which the community measures scientific success. If the normal scientist is, as Kuhn suggests, essentially a puzzle-solver, then his puzzle-solving interest is best served by playing a stylized game defined by the paradigm.

Kuhn's analysis is a vivid reminder that the greatest strength of expertise (the ability to recognize instinctively what is important to the performance of a specific task) is inextricably tied to its greatest weakness (the deliberate constriction of one's vision to what is immediately relevant). Thus, in matters of ethics and politics, which require a broad understanding of history, culture, literature and the arts, the expert is at a positive disadvantage—and not because he is ignorant. Rather, it is because his own knowledge or skill makes it difficult, if not impossible, for him to weigh the factors that are crucial to the pursuit of moral and political ideals. The last person to entrust with the task of deciding public policy is the one who by training and inclination tends to think of the world and its problems as a series of well-defined puzzles.

NOTES AND REFERENCES

1. Thomas Szasz, *Ideology and Insanity: Essays on the Psychiatric Dehumanization of Man* (Garden City, NY: Doubleday, 1970), Ch. 9: Involuntary Mental Hospitalization.

2. Ibid., Chapter 8: The Insanity Plea and The Insanity Verdict.

3. Thomas Szasz, *The Myth of Mental Illness: Foundations of a Personal Theory of Conduct,* revised edition (New York: Harper and Row, 1974).

4. Thomas Szasz, *Ceremonial Chemistry: The Ritual Persecution of Drugs, Addicts, and Pushers* (Garden City, NY: Doubleday, 1975).

5. Thomas Szasz, *The Theology of Medicine: The Poilitical-Philosophical Foundations of Medical Ethics* (New York: Harper and Row, 1977).

6. Thomas Szasz, *The Myth of Psychotherapy: Mental Healing as Religion, Rhetoric, and Repression* (Garden City: Doubleday, 1978).

7. Thomas Szasz, *Sex by Perscription* (Harmondsworth: Penguin Books, 1980).

8. Szasz subtitled his major work "Foundations of a Theory of Personal Conduct."

9. *Ideology and Insanity,* Ch. 5: Mental Illness as Ideology.

10. Thomas Szasz, *Psychiatric Slavery* (London: Macmillan, 1977).

11. *Ideology and Insanity,* Ch. 7: Bootlegging Humanistic Values Through Psychiatry.

12. Here is a sample of the critical literature on Szasz: D. Ausubel, "Personality Disorder *Is* Disease," *Mental Illness and Social Processes,* Thomas Scheff, ed. (New York: Harper & Row, 1967). Ruth Macklin, "Mental Health and Mental Illness," *Philosophy of Science,* 39:341-365; (September 1972). "The Medical Model in Psychoanalysis and Psychiatry," *Comprehensive Psychiatry* 14:49-69; (Jan.-Feb. 1973). Michael Moore, "Some Myths about Mental Illness," *Inquiry,* 18:233-265; *Law and Psychiatry: Rethinking the Relationship.* Ch. 4, "Does Madness Exist" (Cambridge: Cambridge University Press, 1984). Jonas Robitscher, "The Impact of New Legal Standards on Psychiatry or Who are David Bazelon and Thomas Szasz and Why are They Saying Such Terrible Things about Us," *Journal of Psychiatry and Law,* 3:151-174; (Summer 1975). Peter Sedgwick, *Psycho Politics,* Ch. 6, "Psychiatry and Politics in Thomas Szasz" (New York: Harper & Row, 1982), pp. 149-184. Alan A. Stone, "Psychiatry Kills," *Journal of Psychiatry and Law* (Spring 1973). E. Fuller Torrey, *The Mind Game: Witchdoctors and Psychiatrists* (New York: Bantam, 1972).

13. Ivan Illich, *Medical Nemesis* (New York: Oantheon, 1976).

14. *The Myth of Mental Illness,* p. 267.

15. When I assert that science is inevitably metaphorical, I am not at all agreeing with the claim that science is based on the "myth of reality as external to the human mind." [Roger S. Jones in *Physics as Metaphor,* University of Minnesota Press, 1982]. I think such a position is silly. My assertion amounts to the claim that all language, including that of science, has a surplus meaning. Scientific models derive their heuristic power by extending our intuitions beyond

ordinary common sense experience. In doing so, they must bridge the gap between the familiar and the unfamiliar, the known and the anticipated. That bridge is metaphor, the use of the familiar category to describe the unfamiliar reality.

16. Ibid.

17. René Dubos, *Man Adapting* (New Haven: Yale University, 1965).

18. René Dubos, *Mirage of Health,* (Garden City, NY: Doubleday, 1959).

19. Gilbert Ryle, *The Concept of Mind* (New York: Barnes & Noble, 1949).

20. René Descartes, *Meditations on First Philosophy,* (Cambridge: Cambridge University, 1967).

21. Norbert Wiener, *Cybernetics, or Control and Communication in the Animal and the Machine* (Cambridge, MA: MIT Press, 1961).

22. *The Myth of Mental Illness,* p. 133.

23. Thomas Szasz, *The Manufacture of Madness: A Comparative Study of the Inquisition and the Mental Health Movement* (New York: Harper & Row, 1970), p. 123.

24. Thomas Szasz, *The Ethics of Psychoanalysis: The Theory and Method of Autonomous Psychotherapy* (New York: Basic Books, 1965).

25. Max Weber, "Politics as a Vocation," and "Science as a Vocation," in *From Max Weber,* Gerth and Mills, eds. (New York: Oxford University Press, 1946).

26. Thomas Kuhn, *The Structure of Scientific Revolutions,* 2nd ed. (Chicago: University of Chicago Press, 1970).

COMMUNITIES OF CELEBRATION:
TECHNOLOGY AND PUBLIC LIFE

Albert Borgmann

INTRODUCTION

We live in a period of indecision and searching. In politics, the liberals had to yield their dominant position to the conservatives, but the latter have been unable to enact a distinctive and coherent program. In the arts, the relentlessly innovative vigor of modernism is spent, yet postmodernism has failed to do more than readmit superficially traditional elements. In social theory, the promise of rigorous analysis and effective solutions has faded. There has been a welcome dissolution of sterile disciplinary divisions and pretensions, but the newly fertile climate has yet to produce a vision of the common order that would inspire widespread and enduring enthusiasm. The only social force of undiminished vigor and self-confidence is technology. Sustained by scientific advances and fueled by magic prospects in electronics and computing, technology continues to hold out the promise of millenial liberty and prosperity.

Research in Philosophy and Technology, Volume 10, pages 315-345.
Copyright © 1990 by JAI Press Inc.
All rights of reproduction in any form reserved.
ISBN: 1-55938-062-4

If we are ready to grant social theory the privilege of being society's bellwether, we can perhaps discern a new and hopeful movement. It springs from the endeavor to join the liberals' inclusive sense of social responsibility with the conservatives' regard for moral excellence and rootedness, and to do so in a forward looking way. The old vocable "communitarianism" has been most widely used to name this new endeavor, and it is most often associated with the work of Robert Bellah, Alasdair MacIntyre, Michael Sandel, and Michael Walzer.[1]

This sort of evidence for the possibility of a radical transformation of the common order may be weak, but the urgency for a communitarian turn of events is strong. At any rate, I accept the need for such a turn wholeheartedly. At the same time, I fear that the new movement may get arrested quickly by a combination of wistfulness and terror. Few people altogether reject the communitarian ideals, the spirit of selflessness, the sense of belonging, and the warmth of cooperation; but many believe that these ideals are either irretrievable or inseparable from pernicious complements, from paternalistic moralizing, suffocating provincialism, and totalitarian oppression. Terrified by these apprehensions, the critics of communitarianism have been stressing the virtues of the present liberal order; they have attacked the vagueness of their opponents and challenged them to demonstrate that communitarianism can be both carefully articulated and benign. No one so far has risen to this challenge.

What has been left out in this debate and needs to be introduced is a consideration of the dailiness of life. But have not the liberal critics already called for concreteness and specificity on the part of the communitarians? And are not the liberals able to point to a well articulated, if imperfectly realized, conception of the common order? They have and they are, but it is the genius of the present order that it conceals for its part the sort of moral issue that the communitarians are forced to confront as soon as they begin to work out their conception of the common order concretely. Hence, communitarianism seems to be burdened with a profoundly troubling problem of which liberalism appears to be entirely free. This is semblance only, however, and as long as it remains unchallenged, the common order of daily life will seem easily superior to communitarianism and remain dominant by default.

What really matters, of course, is not which of two schools of social theory will win, but that the concealed moral quality of the present order and its concrete circumstances is debilitating and needs to be exposed. Only after that has been done will communitarianism have the openness and space to propose a persuasive alternative. Communitarianism cannot be constructive without being critical. Accordingly, my essay has two major parts. In the first I attempt to uncover the morally charged character of our concrete common order. I begin with a familiar aspect of the latter, namely, the public-private distinction, and try to show that it overlies a deeper and more consequential form of life, one whose vigor is rarely challenged or exposed—technology.

I concentrate my moral assessment of technology on the issue of public life and celebration, and use the latter as an example to illustrate the moral liabilities of the technological way of life. Celebration is a helpful topic because celebration, if anything, constitutes the concrete and hopeful center of communal life. To clarify the difference between the technological and the communal versions of public celebration is to join the critical and the constructive tasks before us.

The second part of this essay, then, is devoted to a description of communal celebration, of the celebrations that already exist in tentative and marginal ways, and of the measures we must take to give them a vigorous and central position in public life. It is not enough, however, to clear a space for communal celebration through criticism and then to fill it with reminders and suggestions of practices of celebration. Such proposals will seem so foreign to the body politic as presently constituted that they will be greeted, even by sympathetic readers, as transplants likely to be rejected. In a third part, therefore, I show that communities and practices of celebration, properly understood and supported, should be agreeable with the liberals' deeper and genuine concerns.

TECHNOLOGY AND CELEBRATION

The possibilities of celebration in an advanced industrial society are delimited by technology. The shape that technology assumes in this case is the public-private distinction. The latter exists in two dominant versions. Both have become so entrenched that they seem second nature to us. Accordingly, it seems obvious to us that the form of public celebration, favored by the public-private distinctions, is natural and legitimate and all other forms are not.

The philosophical task, therefore, is to expose the pecularity of the prevailing public-private distinctions and to show that they are inimical to a vigorous public life. All this becomes visible when we learn to recognize that the public-private distinctions are characteristic concealments of technology, the latter taken as our distinctive form of life. Further, we must show just how technology through the public-private distinctions transforms and really eviscerates public celebration.

The two public-private distinctions are the economic and the social. The latter has the more direct ancestry in the depth of human history, and its power and pecularity come into relief best when seen as they emerge from the premodern period. In a broad sense, the public-private distinction is nearly as universal as human culture. This is so because something like the family is found in most cultures, and the family normally constitutes a relatively closed and intimate (i.e., private) environment, set off in some way from the common or public order that embraces all members of a tribe, village, or people.[2] In the common recollection of European culture, the typical ferial setting of public life is the village community.[3] The prominent festal settings of our premodern European past were dominated by the church and nobility.[4] Our public aspirations are haunted to this day by the surveyable and personal life in the village community, and by the focused and festive splendor of religious and feudal celebrations. We have, of course, similar remembrances of Athens and of the early Roman republic.

At no point did public life of medieval character cease abruptly and entirely. Strands of it have survived to the present. But it did unravel gradually in the fire of the cultural and political conflagrations of the early modern period. Capitalism began to destroy the substance of the village community, and secularism began to supersede the cultural authority of religion and the feudal order. A distinctly modern successor arose in the London and Paris of the eighteenth century. The chief actor of this new public life was the newly prosperous and confident bourgeoisie. For a while, there was an artful celebration of public life, marked by stylized dress and speech, enacted in parks and streets, in theaters and coffeehouses.[5] For this achievement, the bourgeoisie borrowed heavily from the cultural treasures of the ancien régime. The challenge never met was the construction of a vigorous public life that would be both democratic and modern.

In the nineteenth century, the decay of public life began. It was a subtle sort of atrophy that was initially accompanied by an outward expansion of public facilities. This was the time when railway stations, department stores, libraries, and opera houses were erected as magnificent settings for the public to gather and enjoy itself. But the people who filled these spaces had become silent, passive, and distracted. No longer actors and connoisseurs of public spectacles, they had begun to turn into recipients and consumers of commodities, produced for them by experts.[6]

This largely negative picture of the fate of public life fails to disclose the reasons why these developments were so generally thought to be attractive and beneficial. There were two principal reasons: First, the apparent impoverishment of public culture was more than counterbalanced by a general sentiment of growing affluence. The nineteenth century was after all the time when the Industrial Revolution was beginning to make good the promise of prosperity that had inaugurated the modern era. More important, however, industrialization seductively specified the modern notion of prosperity that had been vague and implicit at first. It was prosperity based on the power of scientific insight and yielding freedom from the duress of nature and the demands of culture.[7]

I agree with Richard Sennett that public culture has been declining in the nineteenth and twentieth centuries. Still, a trenchant view of this development must include the gains that were taken to outweigh the losses. Fixed prices in the new department stores rendered transactions impersonal, but they also relieved the buyer of having to challenge the seller. Advertising, to be sure, was often fanciful to the point of fraudulence, but it did heighten and sanction the customers' acquisitive desires.[8] Paganini's and Liszt's pyrotechnics tended to reduce compositions to a mere means, but they disburdened the listeners from having to know or judge the merits of a composition as well. And the silence of the newly passive audience liberated one from the irritations and impositions of rude or vociferous listeners.[9]

The other reason for the attractiveness of the nineteenth century developments that must be kept in view is this. The leisure side of public life was declining, to be sure. But the labor side was growing enormously and diverted attention from the loss of public leisure. As labor moved out of the family, it became a public affair, something that was done out in the open, requiring cooperation with strangers and conformity with impersonal rules. These changes in the habits of work went hand in hand with the rise of imposing public structures: bridges, roads, harbors, mines, factories, and many more. Many of these public structures belong, of course, to the private sector. This inconsistency of usage concerns us below.

In the twentieth century, a yet more radical transformation of the public realm took place. The most obvious and typical manifestation was the construction of highways and highrises. The highways reshaped space in its horizontal dimension, the skyscrapers in the vertical dimension. In all of human history there has never been so massive a reordering of public space. Remarkably, both of these new kinds of public structure have an avowedly subservient or instrumental position in our culture; they are means to an end. Expressways are meant to get the commuter from home to work and goods from one place to another. Highrise buildings for the most part contain offices where people do work that is not usually considered ennobling or rewarding apart from the money to which it is a means.

Naturally, we feel a desire to center our culture in its most prominent tangible expressions. We are moved to celebrate the highways as the distinctive way in which we appropriate this country and to see in the skyline of a metropolis the embodiment of modern power and sophistication. But these sentiments are belied by the grim or sullen moods that we exhibit when we drive on the expressways or work in our offices.

Thus, the public sphere of the twentieth century has become both hypertrophied and atrophied, both excessively developed in its sheer physical presence and devoid of intrinsic or final dignity, bereft of celebration and festivity.[10] This unhappy condition of the public sphere is aggravated by the absence of a counterbalancing sphere of finality or celebration. As public space has been taken over by instrumentality (i.e., production and administration), finality (i.e., consumption) has passed into the private realm. The latter must remain inconspicuous because of the nature of privacy.

Privacy, unlike the private realm, is a uniquely contemporary social phenomenon and is best understood when seen in its legal setting. We think of privacy today as both eminently desirable and frequently threatened. This tension has naturally led to litigation and to the United States Supreme Court; but privacy has no explicit mention in the Constitution. Hence, to protect privacy, the Court had to search the penumbra of the Bill of Rights for grounds to do so.[11]

There is not only a problem of saying why privacy should be protected, there is the prior difficulty of saying what privacy is and what constitutes a violation of it. Privacy is something different from autonomy or personal liberty, for it is possible to grant someone freedom in all personal regards, and still to invade his or her privacy through snooping or eavesdropping. Nor is just any intrusion of the personal realm a violation of privacy. Some, such as unwanted noises or odors, are merely nuisances.[12]

Reasoning along these lines, Thomas Huff has helpfully isolated the notion of privacy as freedom from intrusions that can lead to an unwarranted judgment on the person whose sphere of intimacy has been invaded. Of course, our next of kin, who are naturally members of our personal circle, and our friends, whom we have invited into it, are entitled to judge whatever we do. No one else may without our permission.[13]

Such a notion of privacy would have remained sharply limited and largely uninteresting in a pretechnological (premodern) setting, where the highly contextual nature of work and celebration was mirrored in a greater continuity of family and community. Families identified themselves with and through the moral standards and judgments of the community, and they depended on communal cooperation for entertainment and celebration. With the rise and progressive articulation of modern prosperity and liberty, these communal ties came to be seen as burdens. Consumption is the imperious and unencumbered enjoyment of goods or commodities. What Huff calls the privacy norm is in large part the collective affirmation of consumption as an exercise of freedom that would be encumbered by judgmental intrusion. Intrusion by whom? Huff speaks of the private realm as "that part of our lives conducted with families and friends,"[14] but we increasingly withdraw from the judgments of our friends, parents, and spouses, too. Ultimately, the realm of privacy is in each case occupied by one consumer.

If consumption is located in millions of separate compartments, finality and celebration are accordingly scattered and inconspicuous. It is possible, of course, to aggregate a thousand condominiums into a soaring and gleaming tower, but such a structure no more bespeaks a spirit of festive engagement and public celebration than does an office highrise building from which it is outwardly indistinguishable.

Consideration of the *social* public-private distinction reveals the emergence of a division between public machineries of production and administration, and a realm of private compartments for the consumption of commodities. Revealed in this division is the pattern of modern technology, the shape on which the application of science, the ingenuity of engineering, and the energy of industry have been converging. The emergence of this pattern is not caused by scientific necessity, by engineering convictions, or by industrial aspirations. It is simply the configuration that the several parts of modern culture are assuming. Technology, I believe, is a helpful vocable for this emergent structure, although surely not the only possible one.[15]

In spite of the entrenchment and power of technology, we are reluctant to recognize it, and inclined to confuse and conceal our implication in it. The significance of the *economic* public-private distinction is that it provides us with an arrangement and a rhetoric that enable us to avoid explicit responsibility for the common order and to ignore the impoverishment of public life. To show how responsibility and impoverishment are intertwined and joint concealed, I discuss side by side, more or less, the economic public-private distinction and two affairs that were as public and celebratory as technology would permit.

The economic distinction between the public and private gets its semantic flavor form the noun it qualifies, namely, "sector." Talk of the public and the private sectors is common in political and economic discourse, and at first it seems as though this distinction had nothing in common with the social distinction just considered. It is obvious that the two distinctions are not parallel.[16] Both the private and the public sectors fall within the public realm in the social sense. Both are sectors of the public machinery of production and administration. Both are distinct from the areas of leisure, consumption, and strictly personal discretion.

To see how the economic public-private distinction hides our implication in the common order, let us begin by defining the public sector in the conventional way. It is thought to consist of three parts. First, there is the government with its machinery, the bureaucracy, and the personnel that immediately serve the three branches of government as they design and enact public policy. Second, there are certain means of producing goods and services that belong to the state, such as timber and grazing lands, the educational system, the national weather service, and so on. Finally, there is the share of the total social resources that is collected and spent by the government for the public good through private enterprise, e.g., the tax funds given to private construction firms to build or maintain highways, to produce weapons, or to reforest public lands. The rest of the economy constitutes the private sector.

In party politics the distinction between the private and the public sector looms large. Liberals generally favor the first and conservatives the second. From the standpoint of what social structure and its technological pattern require, the economic distinction is superficial and misleading,[17] but it helps us to cope with our unsettled attitudes toward the technological society. To see this, consider the organization of the 1984 Olympics and the restoration of the Statue of Liberty. These were clearly public tasks and, under a liberal administration, would have been supported with public revenue. Instead, they were turned over to inspired leaders from the private sector, Peter Ueberroth and Lee Iacocca, who raised hundreds of millions of dollars from private corporations.

Conservatives find this approach appealing because it promises to avoid the coercive and inefficient hand of the government, and to engage instead the initiative and self-reliance of the individual. Closer inspection of these two enterprises shows, however, that they were more public than private, not only in the social but in the economic sense as well. The government had in effect given Ueberroth and Iacocca a well-defined taxing authority by entrusting them exclusively with a prominent national task, and with the use of valued symbols. Both Ueberroth and Iacocca were quick to invoke the force of the law when they saw encroachments on their exclusive authority. Given such power, it was relatively easy to force the hand of large corporate givers who came forward with gifts of several million dollars at a stroke. The government supported these supposedly private enterprises in other ways as well. It put the U.S. Treasury and Mint at their disposal to raise tens of millions, and it contributed, in effect, the tax revenue, again in the tens of millions, that was lost because the corporate gifts were tax-deductible.

Even the large remainder of funds that in one sense came undeniably from economically private sources did not do so in another. The corporations did not collect their millions through contributions from their members. The corporate gifts did not represent sacrifices as one would expect of private contributions. Rather, the money came from advertising budgets that in turn are supported from earnings which, finally, come from the consumers. In effect, every buyer of MacDonald's hamburgers or Kodak film was assessed a few cents to support the Olympics or the Statue of Liberty, and in this sense the consumer came to be a taxpayer. To be sure, not everyone did pay up unwillingly; but many, certainly, did so unknowingly. Even then, the assessments were not coercive, but the cost in time and energy of avoiding corporate sponsors would have exceeded the benefit, if any, of avoiding the assessments.[18]

These are particularly clear examples of how socially public celebrations, supposedly based on economically private endeavors, are enmeshed with the public sector. There are equally clear examples of public-spirited endeavors that hardly at all rely on the government or on assessments to the consumer-taxpayer, e.g., cases where people in a local setting collect money from individual persons to support a charity or a sport. There is a continuum between the truly and the nominally private institutions that promote public causes, a continuum on which at various places one would locate the United Way, symphony societies, private universities, and many other institutions.

All of these examples merely illustrate a broader thesis, put forward by Galbraith in 1967 to the effect that, in the new industrial state, government, business, the unions, the educational and scientific estates form but one coherent system beyond the public-private distinction.[19] This, of course, is not to say that the new industrial system fails to have functionally distinct parts and that it is unimportant to keep those parts distinct. It is just to point out that from the economic and technological point of view, the economic public-private distinction draws a peculiarly confusing line of distinction.

But there is method to our confusion. It allows us to avoid the burden of explicit responsibility for the decisive cast of our lives, namely, technology. One can only avoid, however, what in some sense one recognizes. The character of technology, at a deep and implicit level, is well understood by the citizens of this country.[20] There is a common and tacit agreement to shape the world and conduct one's life according to the technological pattern. This agreement has given our society its stability and resilience, and since we are basically in agreement, we have the license of expressing our misgivings and discontents about the common order at the surface of politics.

Thus, entrusting public celebrations to the private sector allows us to pretend that we do not have to pay for them. When *Time* and *Newsweek* as much as tell us that we have to after all, we are not disturbed. We knew all along, at least at the deeper and more implicit level, that nothing comes from nothing. What is troubling, however, to anyone who values the dignity of politics is the ease and radicality with which people have surrendered the determination of public life to the machinery of technology. People appear to have no desire to claim, through their elected representatives, the authority and responsibility for the staging of public celebrations.

This of course leads us to the point, reached above from another angle, that in any substantive sense there is hardly a public life any more. Politics has become technology of last resort, the governor that regulates the machinery of production and administration. Far from desiring or enjoying government, people seem to be annoyed by it. They want to be disburdened of it and are reluctant to support it directly and consciously through taxes, but again their resentment does not threaten or revoke their basic acceptance of technology. In some way, so they realize, the machinery of society must be supported. Thus, while the federal tax reform of 1986 lightens the tax burden for most individuals, it increases corporate taxes. And the latter make their way to the individual via higher prices just the same. This is rarely emphasized in the political debates, but neither is it a closely guarded secret. It is enveloped by the same twilight that shrouds people's pact with technology.

Although the technological society is stable and resilient, it is shallow, too, having lost dimensions of life that we used to value. The loss of vigorous politics, i.e., the loss of an active, shared, and ennobling determination of the common order, is a diminishment of public life. An analogous loss is visible not just in the organization but also in the quality of the public celebrations that we have been considering. Two matters that received wide publicity shed light on this privation, the commercialization of these events, and the important role of David Wolper.[21] What we see here is an extension and aggravation of the malady that Sennett first found in the nineteenth century. Commercialization, as Fred Hirsch has pointed out, is the conversion of a genuinely common or public good into one that can be bought by the individual and privately consumed.[22] Even when people are out in the open and in the public realm, one prominent way in which they celebrate the public event is to buy something that they can possess individually and take home.

We must also remember that, if thousands witnessed the Olympic games in the stadium, millions did so through television in the privacy of their homes. And as we all know, the television picture is more sophisticated, more embroidered and privileged than any that can be had from the grandstand, which brings us to the role that David Wolper played at these two celebrations.[23] He was the impresario who fabricated the crowning events at the Olympics and the celebration of the Statue of Liberty. In his hands, the common and cultural achievements of this country became raw material that Wolper molded and arranged for the greatest possible impact on the viewers. People no longer had to work to gather and grasp the meaning of the many things they witnessed. Wolper at once disburdened and overwhelmed them.

Here again I have concentrated on the tendency of technology to dissolve the depth of a genuinely public and celebratory life into a sophisticated machinery that yields an easily and safely consumable commodity.[24] To be sure, in the interstices of machinery and commodity, groups of people did celebrate publicly and vigorously.[25] And, moving now to a more general level, the economic public-private distinction not only serves to conceal our implication in technology and to express our discontents with this arrangement, it also bespeaks, in a frustrated way, people's desire for a kind of moral excellence and sanction that the technological system in its undisguised form cannot provide.

In general, we refuse to accept explicitly the integral complexity of the new technological state and continue to insist on splitting it into two sectors. That split is evidently inimical to the welfare and productivity of technology. The progress of technology today requires a high degree of coordination between government and industry, yet the American conservatives, unlike their Japanese and West German counterparts, adamantly insist on dividing them, and in doing so they are starving the goose that lays their golden eggs. Why? The reason for the conservative attitude lies in the fact that the conservatives are the principal holders and beneficiaries of the power that the technological machinery constitutes, and of the affluence it has generated. In attempting to place as much of this machinery as possible into a private sector, the conservatives in this country are concerned to maintain and extend their control over power and affluence.

At the same time, the conservatives, to their credit, continue to feel the appeal of the traditional virtues, and they desire to hold their privileges with the sanction of the traditional morality. The notion of the private provides it admirably. It draws from the concept of the private in the social sense the force of personal freedom and initiative, and so engenders the illusion that whatever is part of the private sector has been earned in free competition, and merited by personal initiative.

The conservative attitude is not the idiosyncrasy of an elite but reflects a widely shared, if usually unrealized and universally unrealizable, aspiration. The liberals mistakenly believe that people largely desire an equal distribution of affluence. It appears, however, that above a floor of universally assured welfare, people find the blessings of technology most alluring in an arrangement of inequality. Most people look upon the favored position of the conservatives not with reproach, but with envy. And as long as a minimum standard of living is assured for all, most people would rather aspire to a privileged position of luxury than actually share a lesser position with everyone else.[26] Like the conservatives, we would like our privileges to be the manifestation of moral excellence, and so we lend a willing ear to the conservative rhetoric of traditional values.

To sum up the argument of this section, if we are concerned to promote a more communal common order, and if we agree that public celebration is at the heart of community, then we must recognize and take issue with modern technology and the public-private distinctions that both articulate and conceal it. The social distinction makes genuine public celebration impossible. The public realm is for production, not celebration. The private realm, to be sure, is for leisure. But leisure is now commodious consumption, not festive engagement. And if it were the latter, it would still be subject to the confinement of privacy.

The economic distinction allows us to act as though we could avoid responsibility for this impoverishment of our common life. The public sector is the realm of explicitly responsible citizenship, but we are reluctant to embrace it as the forum to shape and support the common order, or as the place for common celebrations. Instead, we shift these tasks in large part to the private sector. This works well enough since technology undergirds and interconnects the two sectors, and it does so with our implicit approval. The price of our indirection is the evisceration of politics and the replacement of genuine celebration with the counterfeit of spectacles produced for consumption.

From the consideration of the social distinction between the public and private realms we should draw the lesson that we must challenge modern technology if we are to make room for communal celebration. The examination of the economic distinction should teach us that we are implicated in the determination of the common order, like it or not, and that we better assume our responsibility openly and constructively. This entails particularly that we should permit ourselves neither to be frightened by, nor to seek cover behind, the current definition of the public and the private sectors. Such frankness, moreover, will prevent our traditional moral aspirations from being deflected into private and acquisitive diffidence.

COMMUNAL CELEBRATION AND PUBLIC AFFIRMATION

Our time may be more favorable to communal celebration than it has been for many generations. The public-private divisions have come into question, and communitarian writers have broken up the social ground to make it more fertile to communal aspirations. I begin this section by examining these openings, and then proceed to consider community and celebration directly.

Both the social and the economic distinctions between the public and the private realms have become centers of political controversy. The division of moral concerns between the private and the public sphere seemed more or less settled in the late 1970s, but in the recent debates about the moral and intellectual quality of American education there is a widely expressed need to give privately held values more public recognition, and to revive a sense of public commitment in the private realm.[27] The economic distinction between the public and the private sectors has come into question due to the decline of our economic standing in the world order.[28] Are these debates likely to foster a renewal of public life?

There are two possible resolutions of the present social and economic crisis. They may be understood as a disjunctive prediction: This or that is bound to happen. Yet the path of the future may lie somewhere between these clearcut alternatives. More important, in outlining two sharply distinct resolutions, I am not concerned to predict the future, but to clarify the currently confused and ambiguous situation, and to do my part in urging that we take the second, less traveled road.

The first resolution is the technological. Its proponents urge a reconsideration of the social public-private distinction because they fear that the stability and vigor of the present system require an infusion of traditional values. The licentiousness of the private realm has exacted unacceptable costs of social disruption, mental breakdown, and criminal behavior. These costly inefficiencies have infected the realm of production and administration, and slowed if not arrested the growth of affluence. The solution is a return to the discipline of a God-fearing citizenry.

Proponents of a technological renewal will also come to reconsider the economic division between the private and the public sector. This reconsideration will be slower and more painful since it requires the abandonment of fondly held prejudices about heroic individualism and the rewards of moral excellence. But empiricism and a devotion to economic affluence will prevail. The superiority of eocnomic systems such as Japan's or

West Germany's, where the line between the two sectors is blurred and increasingly erased, is so starkly evident that the American elite will increasingly listen and learn.

Although there is much groaning and puzzlement about the challenge of the technological resolution, it is trite and predictable from the standpoint of trenchant social analysis, and it would only give us shallowness at a higher level. The alternative resolution is the communitarian one. As remarked at the beginning, it is moved by the insight that the presently prevailing social division into a public and a private sphere has diminished the vigor and grandeur of human life on both sides of the divide. Robert Bellah and his associates, Jean Bethke Elshtain, and Hannah Arendt, have given penetrating and helpful examinations of this decline and its consequent malaise, but when one turns to these authors for proposals of reform, one finds little, less, or nothing.[29]

Arendt's book ends with an almost gleeful indictment of the present cultural bankruptcy. Elshtain's book concludes with a chapter "Toward a Critical Theory of Women and Politics: Reconstructing the Public and Private."[30] She stresses that the "political thinker, as witness, must imagine a livable future, must proffer coherent proposals for reordering our public and private worlds if he or she is to make a claim on the attention of others."[31] No such proposals are forthcoming, however. The discussion of her last chapter sets out to propose again and again, only to end up recalling the past, criticizing social critics, and clearing the ground for proposals. To be sure, Elshtain does champion the family in the private realm and plead for a more egalitarian and compassionate complexion of the public sphere. But given the detail and urgency of her analyses, her proposals are disturbingly sketchy and tentative.

Bellah and his co-workers, after many pages of investigation, offer a fairly brief chapter on "Transforming American Culture."[32] In this instance, the authors throughout the book uncover strata of public and moral life that encourage and instruct one how to move further ahead in outlining proposals of reform; something similar holds for the work of Arendt and Elshtain. Still, the task of moving from historical sensibility and theoretical circumspection to definite and detailed proposals is daunting. The difficulty of the task seems to support the liberal theoreticians' claim that the communitarians' vagueness is but a reflection of the inconsistency or latent perniciousness of their position.

To move matters off dead center, let us ask how, to start with, one may bring about a reform of culture. The development of any culture is so deep and massive a phenomenon that it is beyond anyone's final comprehension and design. One may intervene, propose, plead, and even try to compel. In the end, the culture as a whole comes to pass and embraces us all.[33] As the work of Benedict or of Marx tells us, the endeavors of an individual can have great catalytic power. Still, culture is never wholly or even predominantly of an individual's design.

There is, in addition, a specific contemporary reason why one should avoid thinking of reform as design. Modern technology, thought of as a culture, owes its most dubious aspects to the specter of conscious and radical design. Not that design was able to overwhelm culture, but it did contribute to unique cultural concealments and imbalances. Hence, to allow cultural change to occur, to let things be, is to take a new and salutary stance, I believe. Obviously, if there is a need for reform, there is a need to do something. Seeing alone is not enough. What is needed is not the design of a technological machinery but the nurture of things in their own right. Such things like all earthly things are vulnerable to corruption. To nurture them is to change them if the presently prevailing conditions are unfavorable. To nurture them is to grant them their proper strength and radiance.

These remarks are ambiguous, of course, and need to be clarified in what follows. The idea is not to think up and impose designs, but to be alert to the liabilities of present technology, and to be mindful of counterforces that are growing even now. My proposals, therefore, have nothing novel or spectacular about them. They are more like reminders. I call attention to athletic, artistic, and religious celebrations that everyone knows. In particular, I talk about tennis, street corner music, and St. John's Cathedral in New York as examples.

I sketch the cultural reform in three steps. First, I discuss the notions of community and celebration in an abstract way. Second, I sketch different types of communities of celebration. And third, I talk about the three specific communities of celebration mentioned above. In the most general terms, the point I urge is this: A vigorous public life needs communities of celebration; genuine communities of celebration need public affirmation.

Community, to begin with, is generally used to designate a number of people with a common bond of some sort, a common interest or habit. In this sense, the gun owners, the joggers, or the viewers of a television program form a community. I want to use community in a stronger sense, one that is close to Robert Bellah's notion of a community of memory and of practices of commitment, and refers to a group of people who are in one another's bodily presence and engaged in a common enterprise.[34]

Although stronger, this notion of community is weaker than the one used by sociologists in distinction from that of a society. I refer to this concept above to characterize the prevailing common order prior to the rise of modern technology. A community in this sense shares not just one thing but nearly everything, not just a sort of celebration but also work, residence, religion, and ancestry. Communities in this sense are rare and precarious today; for good reason, their establishment and promotion in this country must be rejected as the goal of public policy. (I return to the implications of this issue, in the next section.)

Turning to celebration, we can think of it broadly as the public performance of a solemn or entertaining enterprise. In this case we can come closer to the sense that concerns me by distinguishing it from three that anthropologists have explicated. The first two are correlative, play and ritual. Play is a celebration that mimics, mocks, and criticizes the prevailing power relations in a society. Ritual is a celebration that sanctions and solemnizes an existing social establishment.[35] Third, one might think of celebration as a text that, properly interpreted, tells us how a community interprets itself.[36]

I do not deny that celebrations may have these functions, but what a technological society needs are celebrations in a different, namely, real and focal sense. The three anthropological senses of celebration dematerialize the things that are at their center. Those things do not really matter. Thus, Clifford Geertz says of the Balinese cockfight: "For it is only apparently that cocks are fighting there. Actually it is men."[37] I am in no position to dispute this view of the Balinese case, but I want to point out that the dematerialization of central things is congenial to technology; a celebration wherein concrete things are really secondary is susceptible to technological subversion. If it is men who actually fight and not cocks, could not the men use video games, financial instruments, or cars as proxies? In a certain sense they could, of course, but under the aegis of that sense, the difference between a premodern and a technological society evaporates, and, most important, the peculiar liabilities of the latter remain concealed.

A celebration, then, in the sense that I want to use here, is centered on some concrete thing. It is a joyful engagement with the physical presence and radiance of that thing. The latter, within narrow limits, is central and indispensable to the celebration. In calling this the real and focal sense of celebration, I want to draw on the old meaning of "real," namely, *thinglike,* and on the centering and radiating force that is conveyed by "focal."

In some instances, the physical reality required by a community of celebration, can be austere indeed. Gymnastics requires only a level, hard, and springy floor. Folk or square dancing in addition needs a fiddle or piano. But space, reduced to utter simplicity, rarely comes to life as vividly as it does in tumbling or dancing. It is seldom as spacious and rich as when it is so artfully filled and appropriated by humans.

When we think of a gymnastics club housed in an abandoned store, or of square dancing taking place in the basement of a housing project, we are alerted to the connection between the real and the focal aspects of a celebration. Although in the cases just suggested, tumbling and dancing have the minimal space they need, the indifference or hostility of the wider physical context in effect dampens and denies the festivity and radiance of these practices. Communal celebrations will be salutary and central for our lives only if the material things and settings that ground and nourish them are granted public and prominent locations.

We must next try to gain a tentative overview of what kinds of communal celebration are actual and possible today. To obtain that survey, we should turn to the typical setting of contemporary life and cast our net wide. The typical setting is the megalopolis. It is of course an urban setting, but it is typical in a way that transcends the traditional contrast of urban and rural, as Lawrence Haworth has pointed out:

> City and country once signified two distinct styles of life, and the nation was two nations side by side. This is no longer true: the two styles are coalescing into one, in the same way that all classes are moving into the middle class. The truer image is that of a nation becoming urban, not merely in the sense that cities are growing outward, but in the deeper social sense that styles of life are becoming uniform, and uniformly urban. Megalopolis is a vanguard.[38]

Clearly, if we are unable to find or imagine communities of celebration in a megalopolitan setting, the prospects of a vigorous contemporary public life are doomed, but we should not settle for just any sort of communal celebration. They must be possible in the open, generally accessible spaces of the megalopolis; they must be public.

We should take a wide and generous view of communal celebrations to practice the kind of sensitivity and receptivity needed to recognize and advance genuine reform. At the same time, we must avoid aimlessness. I suggest we center our view on clear and eminent cases where a community is actively engaged in a celebration, and centered on a definite public thing.

A softball league, playing throughout the summer in a city park, is a case in point. The participants are players, not spectators. They delight in their skills and team work. It is the open and verdant center of the city that they appropriate in their playing. It is the easy living of summer that they enjoy. We may abbreviate the human excellence of the communal celebration in calling it active; we can capture the celebrants' intimacy with a great and prominent thing in calling the celebration focused. Active and focused communities of celebration shade over into more passive and diffuse ones. People who go to a concert attend a focused celebration but do so more passively. People who enjoy walking or running through a city are actively engaged; but their engagement has a more diffuse setting.

It is helpful to mark off the boundaries of communal celebration by considering the limits of diffuseness and passivity. The extreme and degenerate case of a diffuse public setting is indifference. A physical setting is indifferent when location and integration in the larger environment are accidental or contingent on efficiency. Shopping centers and malls are indifferent in this sense. Their indifference often clashes with the designers' attempts to give malls and shopping centers a striking spatial or historical appearance, but this overlay of culture is immaterial. One can readily imagine the mall's disappearance and its replacement by computerized video shopping from the comfort of one's home. It must be this dissonance between spatial pretensions and functional indifference that induces mall nausea.

Passivity of communal celebration has its limit and decay in disengagement, the human counterpart to environmental indifference. Shoppers are disengaged from the fullness of their capacities and their environment. The same is true of drivers who in a superficial sense are active and form a community, but who fail to be deeply in touch with their surroundings.

Indifference and disengagement are the ways in which technology has invaded and subverted public life and left us with a semblance of the public. For that reason, active and focused celebrations constitute the powerful and hopeful center for a public renewal. This point is overlooked by social philosophers who take the ideal, if vaguely conceived, setting for public life to be an open space that accommodates a rich mixture of institutions and activities.[39]

Michael Walzer calls such public spaces open-minded to distinguish them from the single-minded spaces that are devoted to just one purpose.[40] To be sure, the latter term captures indifferent and disengaging technological structures such as shopping centers and highways. But as Michael Rustin has replied, bird sanctuaries, music festivals, and yachting marinas are single-minded institutions and yet conducive to communal celebration.[41] Conversely, as Marshall Berman points out, Disney Worlds-by-the-sea can be open-minded in Walzer's sense and yet "absent-minded," i.e., indifferent in their larger setting and distracting to their visitors.[42]

Berman himself, however, is not sufficiently attentive to the power and depth of focused engagement in public life. What he admires and would like to promote in public spaces is a kind of free-floating theatricality that is reminiscent of the bourgeois public life, extolled by Sennett.[43] Surely, we should welcome and encourage this sort of public celebration, particularly because it provides an opening for the kind of spontaneous cultural growth we should nurture and cherish, as said before.

At the same time, we should look closely and in a more focused way at present communal celebrations where people do not just play at something, but in playing are definite persons, where they do not just take up some role on some stage, but are fully engaged in this, their own place, and where they do not just send and receive messages in some fashionable code, but encounter one another in the depths of their being.

This brings me to the third step in the explanation of communities of celebration where I invite the reader to look at particular cases. Everything and nothing depends on the following illustrations. Everything depends on their reality and intrinsic vigor, but nothing depends on any one of these instances. The public support of communities of celebration is essentially a pluralist affair. If other and brighter instances come to the reader's mind, so much the better.

Let me begin with street corner music and illustrate, first of all, the point that communal celebrations will not arise from abstract designs. Modern classical music has suffered from an excess of abstract design and has, therefore, in spite of substantial institutional support, failed to inspire popular communities of celebration. Street corner music, on the other hand, in all its classical, jazz, and popular varieties, has sprung up and spontaneously attracted communities of listeners.

Granted, only the musicians constitute a community in the active and focused sense. The audience is usually anonymous, sporadic, and passive. But a community is not an all-or-nothing affair. The bodily presence, the skill, the engagement, and the good will of the musicians radiate into the listeners and transform them to some degree. It becomes obvious here that theatricality is not enough. The performers cannot just pretend to be musicians. Struggling amateurs will not for long be able to engage their listeners. The musicians must be competent in their own right.

Another way of highlighting the significance of engagement for the vigor of communal celebrations is to consider someone sitting at a street corner, "making" music with a tape recorder. The music as mere sound may be greatly superior to what street musicians would accomplish, but the sound would not be rooted in the presence of things and persons, in instruments and performers here and now. The music would be shallow and at best serve as a means of calling attention to a beggar.

Music as a celebration that is real all the way down will also sink its roots into the reality of the public space where it takes place. Celebration and place will inform one another. Thus, although street corner music is not and should never be the result of a design thought up by public officials, surely much can and ought to be done to make the physical environment of the city more generous to such music. It is a matter of providing space, shelter, and a little quiet in the midst of the urban commotion, and comfortable seating for the audience. These settings should be sufficiently thoughtful and beautiful to express our admiration for the music and the musicians. There is also a need for coordination. Not all possible groups can be accommodated at the favorite places. There needs to be some selecting, spacing, and scheduling. Finally, there has to be a more or less formal common understanding of the economic rights and obligations of the musicians and the listeners.

Surely these tasks can only be solved publicly, i.e., with the help of those persons who alone are empowered and enabled by all of us to act effectively. And surely how those tasks are solved will have a large bearing on just how prosperous, festive, and communal street corner music will become. It is crucial to prevent public arrogance and design from overtaking the spontaneity of celebration. Public support must be extended in a spirit of service, experiment, and fairness. The musicians and their experiences must retain a guiding role, and whatever setting and organization street corner music settles into with public help, these arrangements must remain open to further development.

Next, let me turn more directly to the issue of realism, i.e., to the importance of having a concrete thing as the focus of our celebration. I have touched on this issue just now and once before when I introduced the notion of focused celebration. More light falls on this point when we turn to the unlikely case of tennis. Clearly, the real side of tennis, the court, has in its normal contemporary version suffered impoverishment compared with the stately late medieval courts and the verdant lawns of English gardens. Such real richness cannot be recovered for today, but we can enhance the focal power of tennis courts by situating them out of doors in central and aesthetically favored locations, surrounded by facilities where people can sit, watch, talk, and refresh themselves. To be sure, in the heat of a match, the larger physical surrounding, no matter how magnificent, evaporates into an implicit and immaterial periphery. But there is more to tennis than the intensity of the game. It is being with friends, exposing our competence to public view, glorying in our skills, learning from our betters. It should also be a way in which we physically appropriate a central space in our city and bodily experience its moods in the passage of the seasons. Such appropriate inhabitation is in marked contrast to the fleeting and furtive ways in which we normally pass through our public spaces.

Here again it appears obvious to me that only society as a whole has the means and authority to establish and maintain such tennis courts. And here, too, the practitioners themselves, the tennis players, should have the lead in determining the lay-out of the courts, the assignment of playing time, the staging of tournaments, etc. Here, too, we can see how communal celebration and public space are reciprocal. Conventional tennis courts are single-minded in Walzer's sense, and therefore adequate for competition but adverse to celebration. If they are set in an environment favorable to walking about and sharing a drink, public space has become more open-minded.

I come to the most difficult and important case of communal celebrations, those of religious character. My point has been that public life requires communal celebrations, and that communities of celebration need public support. But since Jefferson there has been a strongly held position that church and state be separated by a wall. This position draws strength and legitimacy from an undeniable history of religious intolerance and persecution. I return to these concerns in the next section of this essay. Here, I want to consider the reasons why we should publicly support religious communities of celebration, and then call attention to one that deserves such support.

There are formal and substantive considerations why a vigorous public life needs publicly supported religious celebrations. The formal ones come into view when we distinguish between engaging and reflective celebrations. This is a distinction of fact, not a disjunction of conceptual necessity. Let me explain.

Tennis is an engaging celebration in that it calls forth our participation forcefully and in many ways. Tennis can draw us into the excitement of a game to the point where the wider context of time and place recedes into an indistinct and no longer noticed background. The game engages our speed, coordination, strength, cunning, gallantry, and cooperation; but tennis is not reflective. It does not explicitly gather in and reflect the larger and largest contexts of life. We now have several adjectives to name the various dimensions and frameworks of reality, the traditional, cultural, political, ecological, and cosmological. All of them used to be simultaneously collected and reflected in religious celebrations.[44] These aspects and realms exist in a scattered way to this day. Clearly, public life is poorer the less these dimensions are united and reflected in one celebration.

Our national celebrations are attempts at reflective and festive gatherings, but they are often painfully flat and unengaging, since by design and under the stern countenance of the First Amendment, as it were, they exclude what in fact provides the deepest reflective occasion for most citizens, that is, religious celebration. This is the substantive consideration in favor of public support for religious celebrations. It is simply the case that most people in this country find their deepest orientation in religion.[45] As members of the national community we ought to affirm this devotion explicitly. As long as we officially ignore it, our public life will remain empty.

The reflective power of religious celebration has astonishing appeal. No political or cultural institution draws people so regularly and in such great numbers out of their homes and into a community. Whatever charges one might bring against the national culture, it certainly does not pressure or seduce people into attending religious worship. The faithful today come from an authentic need.

It must be the need for *reflective* religious celebration since religious service has become rather unengaging. With few exceptions, most churches have failed for several generations now to inspire or incorporate great art.[46] Hence, one might say that the public needs religious communities of celebration; religion, in turn, needs the inspiration of real and focal celebration. I believe that the churches can hope again to become vital forces in our culture only if they learn to be genuine communities of celebration in the sense described above. That means that they have to give up on abstract designs handed down by a hierarchy. Instead, they must listen to the holy spirit that animates people in unforethinkable ways. Religion must also recover a sense of realism that asserts the sacramental dignity of things and practices against their conversions into commodities for consumption.

Openness to the holy spirit and a sense of sacramental realism are practiced, I believe, in the work and celebrations that are going on in the Cathedral of St. John the Divine in New York.[47] There is an ecumenical acceptance of Christian, Jewish, Islamic, and East Asian worship, a generous hospitality toward the arts and crafts, and a reaching out to the poor and the powerless. There is no problem of intolerance here. Atheists are welcome and feel at home in St. John's. St. John's is public in its generosity, and so deserves and would benefit from public support.

I realize that strong liberal reservations remain. I answer these below. If those reservations can be met positively, then it will also have been shown that the communitarian aspirations can be worked out positively and concretely.

COMMUNAL TOLERANCE AND COMMUNAL POLITICS

Let me first place the notion of communities of celebration in a wider scholarly context. To urge communities of celebration is to press for a reform of technology, the latter taken as the predominant way in which we take up with reality today. Technology, I said above, has a distinctive pattern whose prime feature is a division and correlation of means and ends, of machinery and commodity, production and consumption, labor and leisure, the public and the private. To urge the public affirmation of communities of celebration is to cut across the dominant divisions; it is to recommend the reinvigoration of public leisureliness.[48] Such a proposal implicitly challenges the normal relations of labor and leisure, and of the public and the private. An explicit discussion of how communities of celebration would promote and benefit from the reform of work and of personal leisure would be helpful. Here, I merely point up these contexts for broader orientation,[49] but I do say something more about the import of the present proposal for the relation of the family to the public realm.

The particular topics of this last part of the essay are two, the problem of tolerance and the politics of community. Liberals generally assume that a devotion to community inevitably leads to intolerance. But this follows only, as Christopher Lasch has noted, if we cling to an organic and sentimental notion of community. "Social solidarity," Lasch holds to the contrary, "does not rest on shared values or ideological consensus, let alone on an identity of interests; it rests on a public conversation."[50]

With Michael Sandel, we can go further and argue that a public conversation, inspired by communitarian responsibility, is more likely to assure tolerance than a liberal society of individuals who refuse to share and affirm their deepest convictions publicly. This is the force of Sandel's remarks that

intolerance flourishes most where forms of life are dislocated, roots unsettled, traditions undone. In our day, the totalitarian impulse has sprung less from the convictions of confidently situated selves than from the confusions of atomized, dislocated, frustrated selves, at sea in a world where common meanings have lost their force.[51]

However tolerant one may agree to be in the communitarian spirit, does not the First Amendment strictly exclude religion as a positive concern of public conversation? To be sure, the amendment has almost universally come to be taken this way, but neither the wording nor the origin of the First Amendment prohibit more than the establishment of one national religion.[52] Granted that, the issue must be reopened in what Lasch calls

> a conversational relationship with the past, one that seeks neither to deny the past or to achieve an imaginative restoration of the past but to enter into a dialogue with the traditions that still shape our view of the world, open in ways in which we are not even aware.[53]

The crucial point is to open and sustain this conversation. At length, I would hope, it will lead to the political affirmation of communities of celebration. But it would certainly violate the spirit of community if one would make public support of religion the sine qua non of one's commitment to public celebration.

Disagreement, then, is not just tolerable but natural in communal politics. It is crucial, however, to urge that the disagreements be substantial. Liberals tend to reduce the political agenda to the question of civic membership, spelled out in terms of rights.[54] This, they remind the communitarians, is the burning and unsolved problem, one that the communitarians, so the liberals continue, are more likely to aggravate then alleviate. Walzer has well shown, I believe, that the question of membership is primary and distinct in the pursuit of justice, but that it certainly does not exhaust the proper domain of politics.[55] In liberal theory the stress on rights and membership leads to a debilitating one-sidedness. It suppresses the question of what sort of common order it is that we want to give everyone admission to. Consequently, liberalism ends up protecting technology as a way of life from critical scrutiny. Nor would criticism alone be sufficient. It tends to become aimless and dispiriting unless guided by a substantive concern. Communitarianism provides it generally, and communal celebration constitutes it concretely.

I am not disavowing the liberal concern for full or equal membership in the nation. I favor using the force of the law to support the poor and the powerless, women, the minorities, the disabled, and the aliens. But the popular appeal of these measures has miserably flagged for close to a generation now, so the substance of the common order should concern us not just in its own right, but as a way to equal membership in it as well.

Indeed, there is a principled tie between communal celebration and justice. To begin with a less than burning and yet deeply distressing issue of injustice that can only be solved through public support of celebration, consider Richard Sennett's remarks:

> It is estimated that there are eight hundred classical pianists in New York City trying to have full concert careers; there are five concert halls in the city which "count"; in a given

year, from thirty to thirty-five of the eight hundred will appear solo in these halls. Of the thirty, at least half are so well known that they appear year after year. Around fifteen new pianists get a hearing in New York each year.... These new pianists get a paragraph in the *Times* which describes them as "promising" or "accomplished," and then they sink back into obscurity.[56]

Obviously, this system inflicts a terrible injustice on our best young musicians and on the vast American hinterland that has little resident excellence in music, no highly focused communities of musical celebration, no practices of commitment to art. As Sennett points out clearly, if implicitly, it is the force of technology that concentrates, or rather, constricts, the exercise of music to a few centers and at the same time procures performance as a commodity.[57] Only public conversation and action can remedy this prostitution and injustice.

The more urgent and pervasive aspect of the connection between justice and celebration comes to the fore when we remember that the rich can always buy memberships in communities of celebration, in country clubs, health spas, symphony societies, and, indirectly, in Lake Forest's Episcopalian parish. But as Robert Bellah and his coauthors have well pointed out, the reproach of exclusiveness and idleness rests on such "lifestyle enclaves."[58] Being exclusive, they are not deeply communal; being marginal to the public centers of power and excellence, they are not really celebratory.

It follows that communities of celebration deserve public support only if they have open membership, that is, anyone must be able to join as long as he or she is devoted to the cause the community has been established to celebrate. Practical circumstances such as overcrowding may require modifications, but the principle of open membership must remain the norm.[59]

Open membership will also be conducive to the kind of interpersonal relationship needed to invigorate public life. We often and individiously contrast communal warmth and intimacy with the cold anonymity of modern society. Richard Sennett has tried to expose intimacy as an altogether uncivilizing and enervating force, a pernicious and irredeemable tyranny.[60] I think this is an extreme and extravagant, though provocative, argument. Even those who favor intimacy in the family and oppose anonymity at large recognize that genuine public life requires a certain impersonality.[61] This seems an unfortunate term to me although I accept what it intends: a friendly openness on definite terms. Intimacy requires an unconditional closeness that becomes strained when extended to greater numbers of people, and fraudulent when offered to the public.[62] But how are we to define the terms of public openness and engagement?

One way, mentioned above, is theatricality, the spectacular enactment of conventions of dress, movement, and speech. Again, such public interaction should be welcomed. Still, communities of celebration, I believe, allow us to encounter one another on deeper and yet well-defined terms. In a tennis game, persons reveal their timidity or gallantry, their awkwardness or grace, their acrimony or good humor. They generally do so in a way that avoids the artless narcissism Sennett finds objectionable in intimacy.

To be sure, theatricality and celebratory self-disclosure are not disjoint. Conventions of politeness and courtesy help us to participate enjoyably in celebrations. At any rate, it appears that communities of celebration can sponsor a social condition that is well placed between the intimacy of the family and the anonymity of mass society. That condition and attitude is properly called community. The spirit of community fosters both the pleasure of acquaintance among people who regularly meet one another in celebration, and the friendly openness that invites newcomers to join in.

I have pleaded for a realist view of celebrations. When the latter are centered on concrete things and practices, celebrants tend to be secure and serene in the devotion to their cause. Tennis players love their game. They teach their children and invite their friends to play it, but they will not insist, nor will they crusade against musicians. In fact, they may be musicians also, or have friends and relatives who are. Communities of celebration overlap and interconnect; we are apt to take pleasure in such diversity, and enjoy in the talents and practices of others what for one reason or another is denied to us.[63]

I do not want to belittle the need for continued vigilance against communal intolerance. Broadly based historical communities as well as contemporary communities centered on a narrow issue of self-interest have inflicted terrible misery on outsiders.[64] It is surely conceivable that communities of celebration will remain, or come to be stuck, in intolerance. In any case, it is worth pointing out that the modern temperament is attuned to the discovery and exposure of communal intolerance.

It is quite insensitive, however, to its own intolerance. Inasmuch as the modern spirit has been embodied in the liberal and technological society, it strongly favors a particular style of life and tends to suffocate alternative ways. In particular, it all but enforces a life divided between public production and private consumption, and it clearly discourages communities of celebration. This is simply to restate earlier points under the heading of intolerance.

Communal intolerance tends to be acute and visibly destructive, while technological intolerance is more implicit, diffused, and insidiously detrimental. The Constitution allows for the vigorous national advancement of technological intolerance through the Interstate Commerce Clause, but shows no other reflection of it. If the Constitution contained an explicit provision, enjoining maximum growth of the GNP by every available means, we might be more conscious and critical of our characteristic contemporary intolerance. Still, we should be on our guard against both communal and technological intolerance. This task, among others, must find its place in communal politics, and it leads me to the last major point of this essay.

Without public support, genuine communities of celebration will be impossible, and to secure such support appropriately is the task of communal politics.[65] Public support is needed, for without it communal celebrations will founder on the shoals of marginality, injustice, and instability.

I have discussed the first two perils. Consideration of the third brings us to the center of communal politics. Instability is the fate of communities of celebration when they are entrusted to truly voluntary associations. Liberals favor the latter as vehicles of the good life because they seem both to serve our higher aspirations and to preserve the moral neutrality of the government unsullied. But even if we were to assume that voluntary associations could avoid the straits of marginality and injustice, they would suffer shipwreck on the problem of instability.

As we have seen in the discussion of the Olympics and the restoration of the Statue of Liberty, what seems private and voluntary may well be public and mandatory. Symphony societies with paid staffs and regular corporate contributors are not actually voluntary associations. In a democracy, there are few things of social importance that we can disclaim public responsibility for. An association is voluntary in the liberals' sense only when its members work without or against the implicit support of the government, the support that is given above all through education and the tax laws. Hence, the measure of an association's voluntariness is its dependence on volunteer work. But genuine volunteer work, effort we take out of our own hide, is exhausting. Unless there are ever new groups of volunteers to fill the breach, a truly voluntary association will sooner or later collapse.

Government, to be sure, should not arrogate or preempt the place of genuine voluntary associations. Rather, the task of communal politics is to accept and support explicitly the communities of celebration that already exist or are struggling to be born, so that they can assume a central and stable position in the public realm. Public support is not a matter of everything or nothing. There must be a balance between public officials and the officers of voluntary associations. The latter possess a skill of community building that is indispensable.

Some community builders disdain or resent government and take pride in keeping public support and authority at bay. Again, such people deserve respect and liberty, but we should remind them that to give up on government is to give up on an inclusively communal and explicitly responsible common order. Just as government must embrace communal celebration, community building must claim government.

Public support through the government, then, can provide the stability communal celebration requires. But just as community is set between intimacy and anonymity, so stability should be set off against inertia as well as precariousness. Public funding of communities of celebration must remain contestable. It should be stable enough to allow practices of celebration to grow, prosper, and evolve gradually, but each community of celebration should have to explain and prove itself periodically in public hearings or plebiscites.

In exercising the vigilance that stable communities require, communal politics is some third thing between technological and theocratic politics. According to the prevailing pattern of technology, politics is the machinery of last appeal, the governor, as said above, that regulates the vast industrial machinery. Politics today cannot disavow this task, but neither should it be confined to it. Politics needs to serve and represent the deeper aspirations of the people, but it hardly needs saying that people do not worship one divine power whose vicar the government could presume to be. Our time is essentially pluralist, yet we should not allow its pluralism to degenerate into a mere variety of degrees of affluence and styles of consumption. A profound pluralism is realized in a plurality of communal celebrations. It should, moreover, leave room for those who find fulfillment in consumption.

Communal politics cannot constitute or stage national celebrations in the properly communal sense, but it is the forum for the public affirmation of communal celebration. To affirm, in this instance, is to embrace, to foster, and to order. Communal politics must, in analogy to Walzer's view, establish and guard the boundaries of the various communities of celebration.[66] This task will be no less contentious than that of current politics, but the contention will be deeper and more fruitful, and it can certainly lead to nationally shared moments of reflection or days of celebration.[67] Regarding the latter, one might hope not only for a more substantial enactment of our national holidays, but for a sympathetic national sharing of, say, the commemoration of the Passover and Exodus.[68]

Communal politics, at any rate, will lead to a significant physical and moral restructuring of the common order. Let me begin with the physical and conclude this essay with the moral. There is a widely felt need for the reordering of our built environment.[69] The technological spirit of our times has made any significant attempt in this direction inconceivable apart from a master plan or overall design; this approach typically fails in the face of political inertia or resistance, and where it succeeds, under limited and favorable circumstances, the result is often cold and arid.

There is now a growing public awareness that the Cartesian approach of radical razing and reconstruction is destructive, and that urban renewal requires a contextual sensitivity.[70] But there is a danger that renewal gets arrested in simply giving the vast machinery of technology a more pleasant and livable appearance, and that we fail to challenge the dissolution of the truly public spaces into the public instrumentalities of labor, transportation, and shopping, and the private enclaves where, as the chair of a marketing consulting firm tells us, "people are interested in 'cocooning' in comfortable dens."[71]

To recover or establish a public site for communal celebration is to restore public space from instrumentality to finality, from a transportation link to a dwelling place. This may seem to be a rather bland prescription. The reply is that to translate the suggestion into the construction or rehabilitation of parks, plazas, and pedestrian zones; of playing fields, golf courses, and running trails; of amphitheaters, concert halls, and museums; of churches, synagogues, and mosques; all this and more should be entrusted to professional people.[72] It seems clear, at any rate, that if we were to follow this suggestion, there would be a radical change of our economic and public lives.

I come to the moral conclusion. Communities of celebration will breach the wall that technology has erected by dividing the world into public production and private consumption. They would not tear the wall down. Although I share some of the concerns of the radical thinkers who would erase the public-private division, I agree with Jean Bethke Elshtain that our welfare and that of our children require the private realm of the family.[73]

Elsewhere I have argued that we can begin to reform the personal and private sphere of our lives if we center it on focal things and practices.[74] The latter are communal celebrations writ small, celebrations in the smallest communal circle of the family. I think the observation remains valid, but it has been clear from the start that focal concerns which remain confined to the personal realm will remain precarious as well.[75] As long as society at large is centrally and finally technological, it contravenes personal focal practices morally and tangibly; morally by disavowing them in public, tangibly by constantly reducing or eliminating the things and settings a family needs for its focal practice.

Without communities of celebration, familial focal practices furthermore become precarious at the point where the family must let the children venture into the world at large. At that moment, youngsters pass from private focal practices, if this is what we have given them, into a public realm where their communal aspirations now clash with the distracting and solipsistic character of the one "activity" that our culture procures for them, consumption.

Communal consumption is an oxymoron and leads to the peculiarly unstable and perilous leisure of young people, an unhappy mix of cars, drugs, and sex, of videos and junk food.[76] We surrender our children to communal consumption by default and by design. We fail to take responsibility for the decay of vigorous public life. At the same time, we expend energy and ingenuity on the design of consumption goods to make them as alluring and gratifying as possible.

Of course, it is not physically or socially impossible for a girl or a boy of fourteen to continue with a sport, an art, or a religious commitment in a wider and more public setting, and some in fact do. But young people have a fine sense of where the cultural center of gravity lies, what finally carries the society's approval and authority and what does not. Communities of celebration in their presently stunted or marginal states do not usually hold a teenager's interest and loyalty.

They do so in the hybrid cases where a community of celebration can serve as a feeder for the professional entertainment industry. Parental ambition and unrealistic expectations inspire intense work and competition to groom football heroes or pop stars.[77] This subversion of community reminds us that the communal spirit needs nurture and protection. In this endeavor, society needs to follow the instruction of the kind of feminism that has rightly pointed out that women, for whatever reason, are the bearers of the better part of our culture, of a spirit of nurture, care, and connectedness.[78]

I suggest that feminism and celebration require one another. Careful feminism needs a way of extending its heritage and concern into a real and public setting. Celebration needs compassion and sharing if it is to be sustainable and avoid the intoxication of imperious and invidious competitiveness. If we are able to establish and sustain truly public and communal celebrations, we will enable our children to pass in a more secure and salutary way from the family into the wider world.

NOTES AND REFERENCES

1. See Amy Gutmann, "Communitarian Critics of Liberalism," *Philosophy and Public Affairs*, 14:308-322 (1985); Don Herzog, "Some Questions for Republicans," *Political Theory*, 14:473-493 (1986); H.N. Hirsch, "The Threnody of Liberalism: Constitutional Liberty and the Renewal of Community," *Political Theory*, 14:423-449 (1986); Christopher Lasch, "The Communitarian Critique of Liberalism," *Soundings*, 69:60-76 (1986); Michael Sandel, "The State and the Soul," *New Republic* (June 10, 1985), pp. 37-41; Philip Selznick, "The Idea of a Communitarian Morality," *California Law Review*, 75:445-463 (1987).

Here is a list of further communitarians, identified by one or more of the foregoing authors (in parenthesis). Jerold Auerbach (Hirsch), Benjamin Barber (Gutmann, Selznick), Richard John Neuhaus (Sandel), Quentin Skinner (Herzog), Thomas Spragen (Lasch), Jeffrey Stout (Lasch), William M. Sullivan (Selznick), Charles Taylor (Gutmann, Selznick), Laurence Tribe (Hirsch), Roberto Mangabeira Unger (Gutmann, Selznick), Robert Paul Wolff (Selznick). I would add Christopher Lasch and George F. Will.

2. Hannah Arendt, *The Human Condition* (Chicago: University of Chicago Press, 1958), pp. 50-67; Jean Bethke Elshtain, *Public Man, Private Woman* (Princeton: Princeton University Press, 1981), pp. 3-16.

3. Peter Laslett, *The World We Have Lost*, 3rd ed. (New York: Scribner, 1984).

4. For the description and discussion of such a festal occasion, see Erwin Panofsky, *Abbot Suger on the Abbey Church of St. Denis*, 2nd ed., Gerda Panofsky-Soergel, ed. (Princeton: Princeton University Press, 1979); and Otto von Simson, *The Gothic Cathedral*, 2nd ed. (Princeton: Princeton University Press, 1962), pp. 129-141.

5. See Richard Sennett, *The Fall of Public Man* (New York: Knopf, 1977), pp. 45-122.

6. Ibid., pp. 123-255.

7. See my *Technology and the Character of Contemporary Life* (Chicago: University of Chicago Press, 1984), pp. 33-113.

8. Sennett, pp. 141-149.

9. Ibid., pp. 197-218.

10. Ada Louise Huxtable indicts this hypertrophy in "Creeping Gigantism in Manhattan," *New York Times* (March 22, 1987), section 2: pp. 1 and 36. In the *New York Times Magazine* of that same day, on p. 52, James F. Clarity, in "Softball Immortality," tells of communities of celebration that continue to lead a marginal life in the shadow of these gigantic structures.

11. See Thomas Huff, "Thinking Clearly About Privacy," *Washington Law Review,* 80:785-786, and Judith W. Decew, "Defending the 'Private' in Constitutional Privacy," *Journal of Value Inquiry,* 21:171-184 (1987).

12. Huff, pp. 779, 786, and passim.

13. Ibid., pp. 777-794.

14. Ibid., p. 780.

15. In my *Technology* ..., I have called this pattern "the device paradigm." See pp. 40-48.

16. Parker Palmer has noted this curious inconsistency in "The Nature and Nurture of Public Life," *Kettering Review,* 47 (Fall 1986).

17. As Lasch emphasizes, pp. 73-74.

18. See "Going for the Green," *Time* (June 18, 1984), pp. 60-61; "In Olympics, Business Also Goes for the Gold," *U.S. News and World Report* (June 23, 1984), pp. 73-74; Jacob Weisberg, "Gross National Production," *New Republic* (June 23, 1986), pp. 19-23.

19. John Kenneth Galbraith, *The New Industrial State* (Boston: Houghton, 1967).

20. See my "Reply to Professor Carpenter and to Professor Stanley," in *Philosophy and Technology,* 4:29-43 (1988).

21. Regarding commercialization, see the references in Note 18 and "The Lady's Party," *Time* (July 14, 1986), p. 10.

22. Fred Hirsch, *Social Limits to Growth* (Cambridge, MA: Harvard University Press, 1976), pp. 71-114.

23. See "Going for the Goose Bumps," *Newsweek* (March 26, 1984), p. 78; "Wolper: Impresario of the Big Event," *Newsweek* (July 7, 1986), p. 19; and Weisberg, pp. 19-20.

24. For a study of the contrast between a genuine communal celebration and one that is technologically procured, see Herman W. Konrad, "Barren Bulls and Charging Cows: Cowboy Celebrations in Copal and Calgary," in *The Celebration of Society,* Frank E. Manning, ed. (Bowling Green, OH: Bowling Green University Popular Press, 1983), pp. 145-164.

25. See Robert D. McFadden, "Miss Liberty Reopens Amid Gaiety in the Harbor," *New York Times* (July 6, 1986), pp. 1 and 16; Samuel G. Freedman, "A Cheerful Celebration of the Good-Hearted American Idyll," ibid., p. 17.

26. See my *Technology* ..., pp. 107-113 and my "Reply ...," Notes 7 and 20, respectively.

27. See e.g., Allan Bloom, *The Closing of the American Mind* (New York: Simon, 1987).

28. Robert B. Reich, "Toward a New Public Philosophy," *Atlantic Monthly,* 255:68-79 (May 1985).

29. The same is true of Sennett's *The Fall* ... (Note 5) and of Alasdaire MacIntyre's *After Virtue,* 2nd ed. (Notre Dame, IN: University of Notre Dame Press, 1984). For comment on this predicament, see Jeffrey Stout, "Liberal Society and the Languages of Morals," *Soundings,* 69:44-46 (1986).

30. Elshtain, pp. 298-353.

31. Ibid., p. 298.

32. Robert N. Bellah et al., *Habits of the Heart* (Berkeley, CA: University of California Press, 1984), pp. 275-296.

33. Cf. Ann Swidler, "Culture in Action: Symbols and Strategies," *American Sociological Review,* 51:273-286 (1986).

34. See Bellah et al., pp. 333, 335, and passim.

35. See Don Handelman, "Play and Ritual: Complementary Frames of Meta-Communication," in *It's a Funny Thing, Humour,* Antony J. Chapman and Hugh C. Foot, eds. (Oxford: Pergamon, 1977), pp. 185-192.

36. Clifford Geertz, "Deep Play: Notes on the Balinese Cockfight," *Daedalus,* 101:1-37 (1972).

37. Ibid., p. 5.

38. Lawrence Haworth, *The Good City* (Bloomington, IN: Indiana University Press, 1963), p. 145.

39. See Palmer, p. 51 (Note 16), and Marshall Berman, "Take It to the Streets: Conflict and Community in Public Space," *Dissent* (Fall 1986), pp. 484-485.

40. Michael Walzer, "Pleasures and Costs of Urbanity," *Dissent* (Fall 1986), pp. 470-471.

41. Michael Rustin, "The Fall and Rise of Public Space: A Postcapitalist Prospect," *Dissent* (Fall 1986), p. 493.

42. Berman, p. 483.

43. Ibid., pp. 478, 480, 483-484.

44. See the references in Note 4.

45. See William A. Galston, "Public Morality and Religion in the Liberal State," *PS*, 19:807-824 (1986).

46. For an account of the misgivings that divide artists and the Catholic Church, see Tim McCarthy, "'The Church and the Artist': Salvaging a Stormy Love Affair from the Rocks," *National Catholic Reporter* (September 18, 1987), pp. 9-15.

47. See "The Awakening of a Cathedral," *Newsweek* (June 16, 1986), pp. 59-60; and Ari L. Goldman, "More Than a Cathedral: St. John the Divine," *New York Times Magazine*, part 2 (November 15, 1987), pp. 22-25, 74-76..

48. For an explication of leisureliness, see Lawrence Haworth, *Decadence and Objectivity* (Toronto: University of Toronto Press, 1977), pp. 144-146.

49. On the reform of technology, see my *Technology ...*, pp. 155-249.

50. Lasch, p. 67; see also Bellah, "A Response: The Idea of Practices in *Habits*," *Soundings*, 69:183 (Spring/Summer, 1986).

51. Michael J. Sandel, "Morality and the Liberal State," *New Republic* (May 7, 1984), p. 17.

52. See Galston, "Public Morality ...," pp. 810-812, 819, 822, and Walter B. Mead, "How Strict Was 'Separation' of Church and State?" *Cross Currents*, 26:244-247 (1986).

53. Lasch, p. 66.

54. See Elshtain, pp. 342-348; Hirsch, "Threnody"; Ronald Dworkin, "To Each His Own," *New York Review of Books* (April 14, 1983), pp. 4-6.

55. Michael Walzer, *Spheres of Justice* (New York: Basic, 1983), pp. 3-63.

56. Sennett, p. 288.

57. Ibid., pp. 289-293.

58. Bellah et al., pp. 71-75.

59. Cf. Berman's concern in "Take It ...," pp. 480-483.

60. Sennett, pp. 257-340.

61. Palmer, pp. 52-53; Haworth, *The Good City*, pp. 105, 158 (Note 38); Walzer, *Spheres*, p. 470.

62. See Arendt, pp. 38-39.

63. Here is a contact with liberal theory. Cf. John Rawls's notion of social union in *A Theory of Justice* (Cambridge, MA: Harvard University Press, 1971), pp. 520-529.

64. For a contemporary case see Sennett, pp. 294-312.

65. This point is approximately made by Walzer, "The Pleasures and Costs," p. 474, and by Rustin, p. 493.

66. Walzer, *Spheres*, pp. 281-282.

67. Cf. Galston's defense of a moment of silence in public schools in "Public Morality ...," p. 822.

68. See Michael Walzer, *Exodus and Revolution* (New York: Basic, 1985), for the power that the Exodus story commands in our culture. In *Spheres*, pp. 243-248, Walzer supports the wall between church and state, and in *Exodus* he emphasizes the secular significance of the Exodus story. But the force of *Exodus and Revolution* is to the effect, as far as I am concerned, that the wall needlessly intimidates and impoverishes us, and that significant secular matters shade over into religious ones. We must not impose our religious traditions; we can learn to share them.

69. Cf. Haworth, *The Good City*, pp. 53-62, 102-128.

70.   René Descartes, *Discourse on Method,* tr. Laurence J. Lafleur (Indianpolis: Bobbs, 1950), pp. 7-11. "Urban Planning: What Went Wrong?" *U.S. News and World Report* (March 30, 1987), pp. 76-77.

71.   William Glaberson, "A Sense of Limits Grips Consumers," *New York Times* (March 15, 1987), section 3:14.

72.   Hope and help can be found in Kent C. Bloomer and Charles W. Moore, *Body, Memory, and Architecture* (New Haven: Yale University Press, 1977).

73.   See Wolfgang Schirmacher, "Privacy as an Ethical Problem in the Computer Society," *Philosophy and Technology,* vol. II, Carl Mitcham and Alois Huning, eds. (Dordrecht, Holland: Reidel, 1986), pp. 257-268; see also the feminists, discussed by Elshtain, pp. 204-228. For Elshtain's support of the family see pp. 322-337.

74.   See my *Technology ...* , pp. 196-210.

75.   Ibid., pp. 226-227.

76.   See Peter Uhlenberg and David Eggenbeen, "The Declining Well-Being of American Adolescents," *Public Interest,* 82:25-38 (1986).

77.   On the conflict of practice vs. ambition and competition, see MacIntyre, pp. 195-196 (Note 29).

78.   See Carol Gilligan, *In a Different Voice* (Cambridge, MA: Harvard Uniersity Press, 1982).

REVIEW SECTION

BOOK REVIEWS

Theology and Technology: Essays in Christian Analysis and Exegesis, Carl Mitcham and Jim Grote, eds. Lanham, MD: University Press of America, 1984. Pp. ix, 523.

TECHNOLOGY AND RELIGION

This is an important book that gives a perfect survey of the variety of positions in contemporary theological interpretations of technology. The book comprises four parts: (1) Two intelligent and judicious introductory essays by the editors; (2) five articles dealing with basic approaches in the interaction between Christianity and technology; (3) twelve articles dedicated to the theological reassessment of the Christian heritage vis-à-vis modern technology; (4) a comprehensive critical, annotated bibliography of about 850 mainly English titles—this bibliography to a large extent building on bibliographies that have previously been published in *Technology and Culture,* 14 (1973), and in *Research in Philosophy and Technology,* 1 (1978); 4 (1981); and 6 (1983).

Naturally, the work under review is of greatest interest to the (Christian) believer who wants to arrive at an attitude about modern technology founded on the Bible. Since theology aims at ultimate meaning, and thus is to some degree a concentrated form of philosophy, the book is also of considerable interest to every "secularized" person mindful of and concerned about the problems of our technological world. The relationship between theology and

Research in Philosophy and Technology, Volume 10, pages 349-376.
Copyright © 1990 by JAI Press Inc.
All rights of reproduction in any form reserved.
ISBN: 1-55938-062-4

philosophy is not entirely harmonious, however. There is also a traditional competition, and even contradiction, between the two fields, since they rely on different sources, namely on divine revelation and on faith versus mundane understanding and rationality. Thus, with respect to ultimate meaning and rationality, although the basic idea of the editors to "present philosophical issues as the outgrowth of theological understandings" (p. vi) may be partly true, it does not hold up completely. After all, a good deal of enlightenment philosophy was directed against theological orthodoxy.

Is there a specific theology of technology? The articles combined here give witness to a broad range of approaches (systematic and exegetic, the mystical tradition and cultural orientations, opposition to and acceptance of modern technology). Overall, a critical attitude dominates, at least as far as actual problems (medical ethics, pollution, arms race) are concerned. Since technology is an inherent element of civilization, it is consistent only that, with some of the authors, the opposition toward modern technology is a part of a much more far-reaching rejection of the modern world. This is justified insofar as concern for the innermost nature of man and his spiritual life are in question, as opposed to an extroverted drive for transforming the physical world.

With regard to the variety of results, there is a striking similarity with nontheological philosophical approaches. From a pragmatic perspective one might even consider the theology of technology as just a more concerned philosophy of technology which relies on a specific form of justification for its normative judgments. In this interpretation, however, theology would be tacitly absorbed by philosophy and crucial categories (God, the sacred, faith, revelation) ignored. Bearing in mind this qualification we can say that in an important respect theology is indeed in the same boat as philosophy, since both aim (in their specific ways) at "timeless," eternal truth, and yet both are actually performed as an intellectual activity under always contingent cultural and social conditions, which are in their turn the outgrowth of a specific historical heritage. So it is not astonishing that in both fields a similar variety of opinions can be observed. Being bound to the historical dynamics of culture is an uneliminatable element of the human condition, as is the liberating and useful, and at the same time alienating and detrimental, character of (modern) technology.

The well-composed, rich material collected in this volume, and the abundant information yielded by the annotated bibliography, should draw attention to central issues of modern technology as seen from a theological perspective. Modern technology and the secularized world are closely related to each other. In the last analysis many of the problems with which we are faced (i.e., that we have produced) can be linked to the loss of the sacred dimension, to generally accepted or unquestioned normative standards. If anything goes, and if technology makes all things possible, then anything can happen, including the production of half-human monsters, destroying the ecological environment, and waging an atomic war. Clearly, in a pluralistic, secularized society no theological school of thought can claim to be in the possession of absolute truth; but, due to its very subject-matter, theology has the legitimate task to maintain higher values, so it can indeed contribute a good deal to handling the urgent normative issues of the dynamics of modern technology.

—FRIEDRICH RAPP
Philosophie und Technologie
University of Dortmund

THEOLOGY IN A TECHNOLOGICAL WORLD

"What has Athens to do with Jerusalem?" The question perplexed the philosophers of the early Christian era. Contemporary American Christians may think of the ancient centers only as stopovers on "Ancient Wonders" tour packages, not as sources of competing worldviews. In a technological age of microsurgery and microcircuits, an age that has learned to disassemble the atom and the gene, we face new questions: "What has Rome to do with Chernobyl? Is Silicone Valley the proper concern of 475 Riverside Drive?"

Carl Mitcham and Jim Grote assist us in answering these questions by gathering twenty thoughtful essays on the relationship between Christian theology and modern technology. Most were written for this volume or for a symposium which was its germ, the remainder culled from a variety of sources. The editors contribute two introductory essays, and Albert Borgmann adds a closing roundup.

Following Borgmann's concluding essay is an extensively annotated bibliography, nearly 200 pages long, of books and articles on technology and theology. Each of the entries, more than 800 in all, is accompanied by a descriptive paragraph, often containing references to several more works. The bibliography alone makes the anthology an important scholarly resource.

In an introductory essay Mitcham invokes H. Richard Niebuhr's typology of five fundamental stances toward culture to distinguish the essays in the opening section of the anthology defending various "Basic Approaches." The Niebuhrian types do not seem to me quite so clearly in evidence as Mitcham suggests, but the essays do exemplify diverse starting points for theological reflection on technology. "Technique is anti-Christian," insists George Blair, because it "is trying to pretend that it is God, who can create out of nothing" (p. 46). Wilhelm Fudpucker asserts, in contrast, that contemporary spirituality requires creative assimilation of, even submission to, technology, and he quotes with approval the suggestion that "man can opt to submit himself to technological organisms as their junior partner in a symbiosis that will transform him and them" (p. 65). Egbert Schuurman rejects both of these approaches and argues forcefully for the transformation of technology in service to Christianity.

The second part of the anthology, headed "Exegeses of the Christian Traditions," traces the origins of Christian attitudes toward technology in Scripture and tradition. Prominent here are two essays (translated from the French for this collection) by Jacques Ellul, surely the most tenacious theological critic of the pretensions of technique. Rejecting the view that humankind is a co-creator with God—"a simple absurdity that is not considered anywhere in the Bible"—Ellul argues that in using technology we are not imitating God but simply doing our own work as creatures and caretakers of creation. Technology entered only when sin had disrupted the order that God made: it is not part of "the order of creation," but rather part of "the order of the fall" (p. 131). From this theological stance Ellul derives an extreme caution toward contemporary technology. "We cannot glorify God through the splitting of the atom, nor through manufacture of new chemical products," he insists (pp. 142-143).

While Ellul's harsh conclusions are not endorsed by other contributors, neither do any of them undertake an explicit response or refutation. Ernest Fortin's discussion of Augustine and George Shields' of Hartshorne are largely expository. George Grant and Douglas John Hall, in contrast, offer the beginnings of an original theology for a technological world. Reproaching American thinkers for holding to well-trodden European patterns of thought, Hall proposes instead "an indigenous theology in North America" that would focus on "raising and meeting the question of limits," and on equipping "a Christian community which is prepared to suffer" (pp. 263, 265).

P. Hans Sun seeks to answer the question, "What kind of technology is most compatible with prayer?" Escaping the formulaic and predictable tendencies that weaken several other contributions, Sun's wide-ranging essay is a highlight of the collection. Equally provocative, albeit informal and unfinished, is Paul Durbin's exploration of "Natural Law Theory and the Problems of a Technological Society." Durbin ends his essay by outlining the divergence between natural law and "eclectic pragmatism" on problems of urbanization, the role of women, worker safety, war and technology, and a half-dozen more issues. Briefly stated and scarcely defended, his suggestions nevertheless serve to bring many of the other contributions to the volume into clearer focus.

Few of the other contributors state as clearly as do Sun and Durbin just what questions they are addressing. Several, taking a cue from Heidegger or Ellul, grapple with something large and amorphous called "Technique," which is perhaps a self-disclosure of some sort of Hegelian world-spirit. Other contributors comment on current issues such as extra-uterine reproductive technology, atomspheric pollution, and nuclear weapons. Philosophy and theology confront technology at every level, from the most practical to the most abstruse, and it is appropriate to address both in a collection such as this one. Its value would be enhanced, however, if the various essays fit more clearly into some unifying framework relating the abstract to the particular.

The invitation to review this collection arrived as I was finishing John Updike's recent best-seller, *Roger's Version* (Ballantine Books, 1986), one of whose central themes is precisely the challenge of a technological society to religious faith. The novel sinks quickly into dreary predictability, theological digressions alternating with "dirty bits" to rouse the reader who has nodded off. Still, Updike's choice of topic confirms the timeliness of Mitcham and Grote's collection. Another popular novelist, Chaim Potok, addressed some of the same themes in his far livelier and more engaging novel, *The Book of Lights* (Ballantine Books, 1981), whose characters are caught between the nightmares of the atomic age and the pure visions of mysticism. Potok's sympathies, unlike Updike's, are unambiguously with those who choose commitment and faith over despair and anomie.

The novelist's imagination can help us experience the gravity of the choice to make technology our servant or permit it to become our master. Theologians and philosophers stand at a greater distance, from which the field of vision is wider but the necessity of choice less urgently evident. The reader of Updike or Potok, and the religious believer who struggles to hold to religious moorings against the incursions of a technological society, will find helpful guidance in the Mitcham and Grote anthology, despite its shortcomings. Containing several first-rate essays and an invaluable guide to further reading, it deserves to be read and consulted widely.

—David A. Hoekema
American Philosophical Association
University of Delaware

THEOLOGY AND TECHNOLOGY

Just forty years ago, H. Richard Niebuhr presented the series of lectures that were published as his classic study, *Christ and Culture*. For Niebuhr the theologian, the relation of Christianity to culture has been "the enduring problem" about which "bewilderment and uncertainty has beset many Christians." His analysis of theological tradition concluded that no one can say, "This is the Christian answer." For any finite person with limited measure of faith, to upsurp the Lordship of Christ would not only do violence to the Christian liberty of others, but to the unconcluded history of the Church in culture.

Five typical answers analyzed by Niebuhr about the relation of these two complex realities—Christ and culture—form an ideal structure for Mitcham and Grote. Theologians have treated Christ and culture as opponents, e.g., John I. Kierkegaard. On the other hand, theologians have also stressed Christ and culture in harmony, e.g., early Gnostics, Ritschl. In between, Niebuhr explains three intermediate attitudes: synthetic attitudes, e.g., Clement of Alexandria, Aquinas; dualist attitudes, e.g., Paul, Luther; transformers of culture, e.g., John's Gospel, Augustine. These same five answers form Mitcham and Grote's spectrum of possible attitudes for theologians towards technology.

After two introductory essays by the editors, Part I contains five essays, each one representative of one of the five answers. Part II offers an exegesis of attitudes within the Christian tradition—in four essays on the biblical and monastic traditions, five essays on classical theology (Augustine, Aquinas, Luther) and three contemporary individual theological viewpoints on technological history.

The introductory essays by the editors are a fine overall introduction to the book. Hermeneutics is discussed at a level which permits theologian and nontheologian readers alike to begin on common ground.

Most students in Catholic colleges these days take an introductory course in religious studies/theology and one in philosophy before moving to one or two electives in these areas. This book would be a fine selection for an elective course in theology. Like Niebuhr's *Christ and Culture,* it offers an opportunity for students to wrestle with the profound meaning of Christian tradition in the most appropriate context for our time, theological reflection on the meaning of technology. Average students could not interpret the writing with much profit, however, without a strong lecture support system to explain the philosophical background required by some of the essays. There is no question that the students would grow in their understanding of theology and the Christian tradition by interaction and reflection with the authors in this book.

The editors make it clear at the onset that they favor a Christian answer regarding technology, on the side of opposition-dualist attitudes in Niebuhr's categories. In other words, they are wary of technology and emphasize the protection of the integrity and uniqueness of the Judaeo-Christian revelation. If this perspective is emphasized, then theology and culture (or technology) can be viewed as antagonists. Hence, other contemporary Christian theologians favor an attitude which emphasizes openness to conversion of technology (culture in Niebuhr's book) by Christ and His grace. Although there might seem to be little difference between conversionist and dualist attitudes toward technology (and culture), the theological underpinnings for these differences are profound. Discussion of these differences could be most attractive for use of the book in courses involving advanced undergraduate and graduate students in religious studies/theology programs.

Christ and Culture would be good background reading for someone adapting *Theology and Technology* for classroom use. It is not absolutely necessary for understanding; rather, the classical-historical perspective of Niebuhr toward culture in general is invaluable background for interpreting the essays in *Theology and Technology*. It would also offer nonprofessional theologians who teach such courses a broader perspective of Christian tradition from which to judge the value of the various attitudes towards technology. My impression is that Mitcham and Grote are less gentle with contrasting attitudes than was Niebuhr. The fact that two of the three essays on biblical exegesis are from the writings of Jacques Ellul makes manifest the opposition-dualist preference of the editors. It would have been interesting if one of these essays contained the development of the theme of the image of God in man, an important biblical theme found in Cyril of Alexandria and other Greek Fathers. This approach opens up a concept of humanism for an age of technology that provides a more synthetic or transforming role for Christianity than does an approach of opposition.

Part III contain 177 pages of a selected bibliography of theology and technology. This invaluable study is divided into eight sections which reflect areas of current writing about technology from a theological perspective. The editors' selective comments in the bibliography are sensitive and most helpful. The contributions in this section of the book are "a must" for someone who wishes to see what has been going on in theology and technology studies.

In the introduction to Part III, Mitcham and Grote explain their understanding of the divisions of theology. I could not find them offering similar divisions of technology. It is a question raised by general discussions of technology such as those in *Theology and Technology*. Historians of technology often divide it into various phases, e.g., inventions, entrepreneurships, production, marketing, etc. These historical studies are helpful because they can clarify the meaning of technology and the human element involved in technological development. Just as the careful study of the history of science (promoted by Duhem, Polanyi, and others) radically changed the common understanding of science and, ultimately, the thinking of the philosophers of science, it would be helpful if teachers using theology and technology were familiar with the growing amount of information relating to technological history. Such historical data undoubtedly will help shape the answers of future theologians regarding technology, just as our understanding of science has changed over the past 30 years. In the meantime, the book by Mitcham and Grote is the best book on theology and technology that I have read.

—James F. Salmon
Society of Jesus
(*Maryland Province*)

A RESPONSE

The reviews by Friedrich Rapp, David A. Hoekema, and James Salmon each provide insightful comments on *Theology and Technology*. It is thus a pleasure to acknowledge them and to comment further on some of the issues raised.

Rapp introduces the fundamental question of the relation between philosophy and theology by defining theology (in an implicitly Aristotelian manner) as a "concerned form of philosophy." At the same time, Rapp identifies a tension between theology and philosophy insofar as the former is based "on divine revelation and on faith versus mundane understanding and rationality."

These two observations rest, however, on conflicting notions of theology. On the one hand, Aristotle's theology, the tradition of natural theology, does not postulate any need for revelation or faith. Indeed, in the text under review there is actually a tension between two kinds of theology—natural and revealed—as represented by the divergent views of the assimilationists (Fudpucker and Lonergan) and the oppositionalists (Blair and Malet). On the other hand, philosophy itself depends at some level on its own faith, that is, a faith in reason. Rapp's allusion to "enlightenment philosophy" and its animadversions against theology certainly point toward a kind of belief in rational revelation.

Consider that the life of reason has not dislodged the possibility of biblical revelation because reason has failed to provide an airtight explanatory framework for all natural phenomena. To quote the mentor of P. Hans Sun and Willis Dunlap, Leo Strauss:

> If this is so, philosophy must admit the possibility of revelation. Now that means that philosophy itself is possibly not the right way of life. It is not necessarily the right way of life, not evidently the right way of life, because this possibility of revelation exists. But what then does the choice of philosophy mean under these conditions? In this case, the choice of philosophy is based on faith. In other words, the quest for evident knowledge rests itself on an unevident premise.

Finally, Rapp's objection to the thesis that present philosophical issues related to technology are the outgrowth of theological understandings would seem to be at odds with his own admission that "in the last analysis many of the problems with which we are faced . . . can be linked to the loss of the sacred dimension." And it is certainly arguable whether any theology—even one found in a pluralistic, secularized society—can offer any sustenance for "higher values" without making some claims to "the possession of absolute truth."

Hoekema, likewise, introduces the quarrel between Athens and Jerusalem. The standard philosophic position in this quarrel has been that Jerusalem at best cloaks the truth of reason in an imaginative or mythological garb most attractive to the many—as is sometimes necessary for public communication and application, but dangerous insofar as it can corrupt the mind of the few with what might be called "soulful" pleasures. The typically theological response, by contrast, is that Athens at best presents the truths of revelation in a desiccated conceptual form useful for certain limited argumentative purposes—but in ways that tempt the soul to neglect its proper care in favor of mental gymnastics like those illustrated in Tom Stoppard's *Jumpers.*

In the world of technology there exist ready adaptations of both positions. Partisans of Athens are not adverse to viewing technology as ministering primarily to the diversions and the imaginations of the many, diversions that might be prone to debased manifestations. Television is O.K. in itself, but the yuppie psychology of "thirtysomething" must not be allowed to crowd out "Masterpiece Theater" and Carl Sagan's "Cosmos." Partisans of Jerusalem can readily be found who describe technology as a useful but sometimes debased ministration to the personal. The worldwide satellite transmission of the Pope's Christmas Eve Mass and the 700 Club can too easily substitute Nielsen ratings for true confession and conversion. The former rhetorical strategies suggest that technology may indeed function as a kind of religion; the latter that philosophy exhibits some of the characteristics of impersonal technique.

Hoekema indicates affinities with the former position at two points. The first is his suggestion that the essays in the collection fail in "relating the abstract to the particular;" the second in his appeal to "the novelist's imagination" to "help us experience the gravity of choice to make technology our servant or permit it to become our master." The mythologies of art have, in the age of modern technology, largely replaced the mythologies of religion as philosophically acceptable imaginations.

Perhaps reflecting their philosophical commitments, Rapp and Hoekema emphasize certain theoretical issues. By contrast, Salmon, a theologian, includes a quite practical one—namely, how the text might be taught. Although his comments along this line can be read as elaborating Hoekema's regarding application and imagination, the tone of Salmon's remarks indicates more concern for care of the soul over clarification of the mind. He specifically mentions, for instance, the problem of students at a Catholic college.

Salmon also raises two theoretical points that warrant brief, albeit inadequate, consideration. First, he points out the absence of any discussion of "the theme of the image of God in the human"—a discussion that would open up "to a humanism for an age of technology more congruent with a synthetic or transforming role for Christianity than one of opposition." It should at least be noted, however, that the traditional theology of the imago Dei implied a human action quite at odds with technology. To act in harmony with our createdness in God's image entailed for the prophets, for Talmudic commentators, and for Christian theologians before the Renaissance, prayer, fasting, and almsgiving. The idea that the imago Dei doctrine could be the foundation for a theology of technology as co-creation with God outside of "procreation" and the spiritual life is something that has its origins in heterodox mysticisms of the Renaissance. The contemporary willingness to utilize such ideas by way of theological apologia for technology is, to say the least, quite remarkable.

Salmon's second point is that the indicated divisions of theology are not complemented by an equally sensitive presentation of distinctions in technology. In "Types of Technology," *Research in Philosophy and Technology,* volume 1 (1978), Mitcham has attempted to develop a comprehensive analysis that could perhaps be used to fill in this gap, but this is something that was not attempted in the present instance.

To conclude, with reference to the annotated bibliography of 800-plus items that all three reviewers commented on with approval, it might be well to mention that somewhat sporadic and impressionistic updates can be found in the *ITEST Bulletin* available from the Institute for the Theological Encounter with Science and Technology, 221 N. Grand Blvd., St. Louis, Missouri 63103.

—CARL MITCHAM
Philosophy and Technology Studies Center
Polytechnic University

—JIM GROTE
St. Vincent de Paul Society

Philosophy of Technology, Frederick Ferré. Englewood Cliffs, NJ: Foundations of Philosophy Series, Prentice-Hall, 1988. Pp. x, 147.

PHILOSOPHY OF TECHNOLOGY

Frederick Ferré's addition to the Prentice-Hall Foundations of Philosophy series is an approachable and balanced contribution to increased general understanding of the field. Addressed both to students of philosophy and to other readers interested in technology (e.g., engineers, engineering students, other informed readers, etc.), it should be engaging and informative for all. That is, although he has planted his treatment "solidly on the relative permanences of philosophy," rather than let it be "too absorbed in gadgets," it treats philsophical issues of technology in a comprehensible and not too abstract fashion. Given the introductory purpose of the series my primary focus is its value for students. In this context, I found the first, second, third, and sixth chapters most interesting.

Chapter two, characterizing "technology," is a nice exercise in explication drawing those not familiar with philosophic methodology into the work and the subject. Ferré motivates the meaning of technology as "practical implementations of intelligence" (p. 26). He acknowledges some jeopardy possible with his definition of technology, but shows its fruitfulness in the rest of the book. Moreover, the introductory chapter, "What Is Philosophy of Science?" motivates and integrates this emerging subfield by assimilating it to other parts of philosophy, for Ferré asserts, "My main thesis is that philosophy of technology is *simply philosophy* focusing on a tremendously pervasive topic of great importance" (p. ix). He demonstrates his thesis by fleshing it out convincingly through the book, engaging nonphilosophers and neophytes in philosophy in the process. His framework and taxonomy of problems, issues, etc., recommends itself to students of philosophy, and his approach has already won some praise among interested philosophers for making the "new" field approachable, rather than just loosely connected writings, claims, arguments concerning various topics, etc.

"Technology and Practical Intelligence," chapter three, treats epistemological issues fundamental to technology. It is a nice survey and treatment of practical knowledge and reasoning, the distinctive knowledge and know-how aspects of technology. To shift to "intelligence" from "reason" relieves his epistemological discussions of many problems of traditional philosophical development; typical, for instance, of philosophy of science. In particular, his approach also provides a context for appreciating the cultural and historical development and importance of technology, and its social impact and transmission. Contemporary students are often unaware that technology was important long before science played an important role, before the common sense of our time defining technology as applied science. Ferré brings out the unlikelihood, the uniqueness, of present day connections between science and technology in the context of the epistemological discussions along with the commonalites, conflicts, complimentary corrective aspects, etc., between practical and theoretical intelligence; he sketches the actual development of several technologies to amplify his discussion of issues. Philosophy of science is properly complemented by studying the history of science, and the same should be true for technology; the philosophy of technology should allow for and properly be informed by the history of technology, and Ferré opens the door. Moreover, Ferré's treatment *supplements* discussions of theoretical intelligence or reason—usually theoretical science—which dominate contemporary epistemological discussions as the philosopher's preferred paradigm of knowledge. His refocus is instructive, for it points on the one hand to profound connections between technology and science, but also to important differences. For instance, this way helps the reader to understand the important interactions of technology and science unique to the present era of scientific technology where there is strong and creative stimulus *between* science and technology, a point ignored, for instance, in contemporary philosophy of science. I assume that the placement of practical *before* theoretical intelligence is intentional to bring attention to the practical, and to show what the philosophic tradition has to offer to philosophers and nonphilosophers alike.

Furthermore, his shift to epistemological discussion of practical intelligence also gives a role for discussion of goals or intentions in technology, which is characteristic of the language and discussion of technology as opposed to science. This introduction could be especially constructive as a propaedeutic for engineering students to consider—to bring explicitly to mind—what they are about professionally, and what will be expected of them. Engineers can be considered agents in the development and application of technology, but in the face of a curriculum dominated by science and scientific technology the discussion of purposes they will be asked to service, for instance, is primitive and is a hidden agenda which gets left out in their course of studies as somethings(?) that fall between specific technical courses but which, nevertheless, engineers are supposed to be aware of, to "know." Humanities courses are often the only opportunity where engineering and other professional students are encouraged to consider such matters and help them prepare for this, the heart of their professional work.

I am particularly interested in chapter six, and I think it has strengths, but at the same time could have been easily extended. I will use it as an introduction to ethical issues in my Humanities class for engineering students, for I think he does a nice job of what I have come to do over the years, introduce the ethical tradition to nonhumanities students. It is crisp and clear, and gets to the point without dwelling on the philosophical niceties of theories. Moreover, in his ethical critique of Technology Assessment he has made an interesting contribution. Likewise, in his treatment of a variety of contemporary—but persistent—dilemmas from particular important technologies he engages his reader in the fruits of the philosophical heritage applied to our world.

Ferré makes a remark in chapter one which is very pregnant, tying the philosophical topics of his book together: "If the principal source for our most reliable factual knowledge is science, and if the basic values of any society constitute its actual functioning religion, then the technosphere we inhabit is nothing less than the incarnation in social life of science and religion" (p. 11). This is very tantalizing, and he seems to be on to something important, but it is a related point that he might have elaborated further in chapter six, concerning the professional responsibilities of technical professionals, e.g., engineering or professional ethics. This is an area that I find engages students in consideration of the issues which the philosophical traditions bring to them, and which is just beyond the reach of chapter six. His claims stated above could provide motivation for engineering students to take their responsibilities seriously, and they have to draw that conclusion by putting things together. Chapter six does go well together with chapters five and seven, which deal with social philosophy and religion, and together show what the field can be concerning axiology and other topics of philosophy.

Ferré's book is not a piece of research, but a general introductory survey—it covers the topics in the field following major categories of philosophy. There are topics which he could have elaborated, but any intelligent and informed reader should be able to draw from his book what philosophy of technology is, or could be, and what interest he or she might have in it. Ferré does not make his work obscure or difficult, or assume and depend on previous special knowledge to demonstrate its, or his, profundity; quite the opposite: it is very readable, and there is a disarming simplicity to his style. Moreover, it is not tenditiously or tediously argued; nevertheless, one can draw the ingredients for debate or dispute in the field from this text. I do think he could have referred readers to more of the literature of the field, but he does mention or treat contributors all members of the field recognize, and they would recognize the field in what he says about it. I recommend this book to my students and colleagues, and use parts or all of it in my classes. I think his approach and simple style will recommend the work and philosophy generally—by example—to other interested readers outside philosophy, and it will bring philosophy of technology to the attention of a wider circle of interested readers and potential contributors.

—Thomas Rogers
Department of Philosophy
California Polytechnic State University

ATTENTION, SHOPPERS!

The Supermarket of Silly Ideas is proud to announce the grand opening of a *Technology* section. In the applied philosophy aisle, right next to our very successful business and professional ethics section, you can now find, for your shopping pleasure, a full line of precooked merchandise. Delicately hermeneutered Marx chunks; Marcuse McNuggets; Heavenly Heidegger Hash; Rawlsian Rhetorical Rolls (repackaged specially for the consumer of technology); Pope tarts; smoked Whitehead; all sterilized, placed in tamperproof pouches, and ready to pop into the mental microwave.

As implied criticism is this unjust? Hyperbolic? Irresponsibly unresponsive to the issues and their learned treatment? No, none of the above, especially since the implied criticisms are not of the book, but of the feckless discursive practice into which it has to fit. Indeed, once you accept the practice, the book is amazingly good. It's well written and a pleasant read. The range of material is laudably far broader (more ecumenical) than we're used to. But why accept the practice? It's a conspicuous manifestation of the problem, not the road to a solution.

Ferré has no choice but to stock the shelves with as full a display of prepackaged goods as he can produce. He also has no choice but to accept (and refine) the rules of consumer behavior already well entrenched in the simulacrum of an ethos we call Western Liberal Democracy. His role of purveyor of "thoughtful reflections" to a nearly totally commodified "culture" is well delimited. What are the rules? Well, at some level "values" and "way of life" must be submitted to the marginal preferences of the sovereign consumer of "ideas." "Ethical theories . . . can push our perferences back to our fundamental convictions about what is real and worthwhile . . . but it is not designed to guarantee moral behavior or even to guarantee unanimity on exactly what moral behavior requires" (p. 75). Of course not. The alternatives to this "ethical theory" are all illiberal, potentially undermining the autonomy of the wise shopper. In line with what has come to be called the trickle-down theory of culture production, Ferré has to refrain from human engagement with others in a search for a coherent life-world, and confine himself to hawking intellectual wares from a point of view of platonic isolation. Truth in advertising. All Trojan horses must be labeled: Caution, contains Achaeans; may be hazardous to your health.

The Trojans do drag in the horse, nonetheless, and Ulysses wins again. The totalization of technology proceeds apace since *its* purveyors are unaffected by the scruples of the intellectual game self-sterilized philosophers must play. The technology manufacturers' representatives needn't truck with illusions and self-deceptions about "autonomy." They know their market, and what the traffic will bear. *They* get to define what autonomy means: entry into the warehouse outlet. The sovereign consumer won't spend much time in the ideas section. That's guaranteed, since none of the goods in the ideas section come with a guarantee. There is, in short, nothing to prefer among them. Better to move to sections containing more tangible consumer products. A whole life can be led there; and maybe if we leave the technologists free to compound their technology the life can be a long one.

The Supermarket of Silly Ideas would simply be the site of harmless buffoonery if it were not for its assigned role in the reproduction of the world it pretends to scrutinize with "the Reason of Plato" (passim.) as "gadfly." But a requirement of the smooth perpetuation of commodified technology in our culture with its history and pretensions is that the illusion of sober, detached *critical* intelligence must be maintained. This critical intelligence must be domesticated and institutionalized in such a way that it has no effect—a stream of hermeneutrinos going right on through without leaving a trace. No serious analysis of the interpenetration of technology and economy. No inquiry about the way in which our habituation to cold war mentality disciplines us to the generation (after generation) of military technology. All in all, the required omissions and evasions must be handled deftly by the critical intelligence.

Some omissions are really intriguing. In the expansive spirit of universal tolerances a page or so on the relationship of Buddhism, Taoism, and Hinduism to technology is put up on the shelves (in the gourmet section). Wonderful. We're led to think of Taoists behind the veil of ignorance, or whatever. But what about Islam? They're sitting on top of lots of oil, you know, and they've got several megatons of our top technology tied up in the Persian Gulf at the moment. But not a word about them. What place does technology find within Islam? The answer is easy. Islam can actually think of technology as a mere means. They have no doubt about what life is all about, and have no trouble subordinating something as adventitiously instrumental as technology to their ends. They're serious people.

Nor, of course, do they have to reject the three helpful ethical maxims we're offered by Ferré for our guidance: "Do not destroy good. Try to create good. Be fair" (p. 80). Now what the hell do you suppose the Ayotollah is trying to do, if not fulfill those three maxims? Be fair? What could be fairer than giving the infidel precisely what he deserves? But of course the Ayotollah doesn't subscribe to the *real* maxim at the root of Ferré's project: Assume that everyone is willing [or can be forced(?)] to play the floundering liberal.

Many of the people Ferré discusses would reject that maxim, although you would never know it from their appearance on the display rack. Heidegger, Marcuse, Marx, and Norris Clarke, among others, refuse to play the liberal intellectual game. Each of them knows that the game is intertwined with technology both as product and as producer. Each of them would be (or have been) embarrassed to lead a student on a mall crawl for ethos and identity picked up off the shelf.

Ferré's book isn't bad; it's impotent. Its impotence is the result of scrupulous obedience to the rules of marginalization and self-sterilization hidden in the noble sounding canons of free liberal inquiry. It demeans serious, intelligent life in favor of a fey elitist fantasy of reason. What the intellectual sees as his stewardship of a long tradition of detached inquiry, everyone else recognizes as the voluntary renunciation of meaningful involvement in a difficult world. Students, for example, see it that way. If the best that Western intellectual culture can offer nowadays is the blind production of technology on the one hand, and impotent finger flapping on the other, then there doesn't seem to be much point in bothering ourselves about it. It's just talk.

—CHARLES DYKE
Department of Philosophy
Temple University

COMMENTS ON FERRÉ'S
PHILOSOPHY OF TECHNOLOGY

In *Philosophy of Technology,* a new title in Prentice-Hall's Foundations of Philosophy Series, Frederick Ferré has provided a discussion of this subject that is of use both to the philosophy student and to the general student enrolled in a philosophy course devoted in whole or in part to the topic of technology. There is a helpful exposition, accessible to the general student, of the nature of philosophy and a careful discussion of the definition of technology. The book is well organized within the framework of the philosophical distinctions offered in the first chapter. In addition to its role as an introductory text, this volume also contains some interesting philosophical arguments on the nature of technology. In these brief remarks, I focus on two places in the text where, I believe, Ferré's presentation falls into some philosophical confusion.

First, in discussing, in chapters three and four, the epistemological issues raised by technology, Ferré focuses on the kind of intelligence (or reason) that is involved in technology, specifically on the relation between practical and theoretical intelligence. His central idea is that modern technology is a blend of both practical and theoretical intelligence, as is modern science itself. Modern technology could not exist without science. Nor could modern science exist without technology, in the form of the sophisticated instruments of measurement and cognitive extension with which science is currently practiced. This close working relation between technology and science leads him to introduce the notion of "techno-scientific thinking," and this notion leads him astray. Ferré seems to ignore that the close working relationship between science and technology does not obviate the need to keep these activities distinct, at least for the sake of a philosophical critique of them.

Ferré speaks of the "epistemological authority of techno-scientific thinking" (p. 49). Certainly, modern science has epistemological authority, based on the extent to which it has succeeded in explaining natural phenomena. But the success of modern technology is of a different sort, success in creating material abundance and in raising the "standard of living." Does this success impart to modern technology any epistemological authority? Ferré claims: "The proven capability of techno-scientific thought to create modern civilization is of profound epistemological importance" (p. 51). This seems wrong in both of the senses in which it might be taken. On the one hand, the epistemological importance of science does not reside in its contribution to the technologically sophisticated gadgets on which modern civilization is based, but rather directly in its ability to explain natural phenomena, that is, to predict correctly the outcomes of crucial experiments. The practical success of science is its experimental success, not the success of its technological spin-offs. On the other hand, technology itself is of limited epistemological importance, because practical intelligence is concerned with knowledge of the proper ends of action as well as of the means to those ends. Practical reason seeks to tell us both the ends for which to aim and the means with which to pursue those ends. Technology, however, is concerned with means alone, as Ferré emphasizes (p. 24).

In fact, technology can be said to be successful, to have *raised* our standard of living, only relative to a set of assumptions about the proper ends for human action. These assumptions are not themselves part of technology, and technology, while operating at their behest, has nothing to say about them. Strictly speaking, the practical success of technology depends on the truth or falsity of these assumptions. In this regard, it seems to me, a major shortcoming of Ferré's book is that he provides only scattered and underdeveloped remarks concerning the social and political critique of the technological society, which is the critique of these assumptions.

The second source of philosophical confusion is in Ferré's discussion of the ethical assessment of modern technology. He says something very important about this early on, remarking that some of the ethical questions raised by modern technology may be new in kind, since the immense quantitative changes that technology has made in our ability to manipulate the world may have brought about a qualitative change in our ethical situation (p. 11). But when he turns to discuss the ethical questions, the force of this point is missed. He proposes three principles to be used in the ethical assessment of technology: beneficence, nonmaleficence, and justice. There are two problems arising from these principles and the way he uses them in the ethical assessments.

First, the principle of justice is required, in effect, to do duty for all that is deontological. There is no direct discussion of *rights* and the ways in which some forms of modern technology may lead to their systematic violation. Ferré may believe that the principle of justice adequately covers the moral territory of rights. But injustice, as he presents it, is a specific kind of deontological wrong, unfairness in treatment or distribution, and does not adequately represent all deontological wrong. For example, citizens arguably have a moral right not to be lied to by officials, a right that can easily be violated when those officials believe that they must make decisions paternalistically for citizens about social policy involving complex technological matters which the officials believe are beyond the citizens' understanding. It is stretching Ferré's notion of injustice out of recognizable shape to claim that such lying is unjust. The notion of rights has different moral work to do than his notion of justice. Ferré does understand the other two principles to be concerned with human individuality and agency, notions closely connected, through the Kantian notion of autonomy, with respect for rights. But these principles cannot do the job of ensuring respect for autonomy, because they are explicitly aggregative.

The second problem arises from Ferré's discussions of the way in which the three principles conflict in the assessment of particular technologies. He seems not to recognize that there are two very different sorts of conflict involved. The conflict between the principles of beneficence and nonmaleficence is basically a matter of weighing benefits against harm within a comprehensive consequentialist framework. The conflict between these principles and the principle of justice is very different. Here, there is no metric which would allow us straightforwardly to weigh, for example, a certain injustice against a certain harm avoidance. We must rely on a scheme for the ranking of duties or on moral intuition. Conflicts between justice and the other principles are, from a moral point of view, more intractable than conflicts between the principles of beneficence and nonmaleficence, and often they lead to genuine moral dilemmas. Only by recognizing the difference between these two kinds of conflict can we appreciate the full extent of the moral problems technology poses. Ferré fails, in practice, to recognize his own point that modern technology may lead to moral problems that are new in kind.

The moral dilemmas to which modern technology leads are often greater in scope than those that otherwise arise. They are often more tragic. Modern technology creates possibilities both for vastly improving the human lot and for the systematic violation of rights on a grand scale. Respecting the rights may mean foregoing the great benefits, while accepting the great benefits may mean ignoring the rights. In some cases, because of the size of the moral stakes involved, the application of modern technology may pose a moral dilemma of uniquely tragic proportions. Consider, for example, Ferré's discussion of nuclear energy. When he assesses nuclear weapons from the perspective of the principle of justice, he talks of the risks of nuclear war, but, unfortunately, not about the policy of nuclear deterrence. Whether the great benefits nuclear deterrence is said to provide outweigh the risks of nuclear annihilation (that is, how we assess nuclear deterrence in terms of the principles of beneficence and nonmaleficence) is mainly a matter of coming up with an adequate risk assessment. While this is, of course, a matter of great difficulty, the problem is more empirical than moral. When we consider the conflict between the principles of beneficence and nonmaleficence and deontological principles, such as that of justice, things are quite different. If the benefits of nuclear deterrence do greatly outweigh its risks, as most people believe, then the main moral problem created by nuclear technology is the tragic dilemma of having to choose between leaving ourselves open to aggression and systematically violating the rights of millions of innocent persons by creating a significant risk of their dying if we launch a nuclear attack. By not attending to the nature of the conflicts between his principles, Ferré misses the most serious moral problem posed by nuclear energy.

The problems with Ferré's text that I have outlined do, I believe, seriously undercut the overall philosophical strength of his work, but there is much of philosophical interest there nonetheless, and the book serves well its primary purpose of providing to students a stimulating introduction to this fascinating topic.

Acknowledgment

I discussed some of these issues with Scott Brophy, and I would like to thank him for helping me to think more clearly about them.

—STEVEN LEE
Department of Philosophy
Hobart and William Smith Colleges

REPLY TO REVIEWERS

It is a rare treat for the author of a new book to be allowed to respond to a whole gripe of reviewers. I wish to thank Leonard Waks, the Book Review Editor, for cooking up such a delicious idea: namely, this symposium of reviews for *Philosophy of Technology* with the chance for me to respond.

I am given no provocation to anything but the sweetest of tempers by Thomas Rogers, who has honored my book with a careful, sympathetic reading, and has seen just what I was trying to accomplish. I hope the book is as useful to him and his students as he anticipates. His main wish—for more of an explicit discussion of engineering ethics and the professional responsibilities of technical experts—is one with which I readily sympathize. My experiences of teaching young engineers, while on the faculties of two quite different schools of engineering, alerted me vividly to the needs and possibilities of such a discussion. My only excuse for keeping it just offstage is that I was writing to a tight word-limit, and my hope was that if those limited words could "merely" lay an adequate foundation for such a discussion, many different superstructures could be custom-built on my foundation in many engineering classrooms by concerned faculty like himself.

The most acute pain in writing this book, which was in the main a pleasure, lay in the constant need to cut things out. I am sure that my readers are all aware of how much more difficult it is to write a short assignment than a long one. The Prentice-Hall Foundations of Philosophy series is properly valued for what it provides, but the rigorous brevity of these slim volumes comes at a cost. Rogers's legitimate wish for "more"—both more topics that lie "just beyond reach," as he puts it, and more discussions of other literature—is the main price the book pays for belonging to a series that is deliberately designed to be usable together with other readings.

My funny bone was tickled by Charles Dyke's satirical review. Even at its most outrageous, it still makes one smile, although perhaps it fails to sustain its sparkle quite all the way to the end. Still, it is based on one perfectly correct point: *Philosophy of Technology* operates, for better or for worse, in the atmosphere of thoughts, arguments, and conceptual alternatives. It is premised on the conviction that ideas have consequences, and that gaining altitude for the sake of finding ampler horizons expands not only individual minds but also long-run possibilities for social reality. Dyke objects to my "liberal" approach and questions its potency. In the short run, I admit, fanaticism makes more fireworks. But I believe that critical intelligence, although seemingly powerless in the short run, works away at fundamental beliefs and attitudes and can be enormously influential over time—if given enough of it. That is just what I said to my readers at the opening of the Preface of this book, and that confession of belief in the quiet power of philosophy remains personally important to me.

This does not mean that I believe philosophy can do the whole needed job. We must have short-term strategies, too, which can effectively defend the possibility of there being a decent long-term in which the "weakest of human passions," reason, can do its salubrious work. Even (especially) those short-term strategies themselves need deeply thoughtful consideration if we are to avoid the panicky adoption of temporary means that will undermine the very ends for which they are ostensibly employed.

Dyke's main opponents, as he reveals in his final paragraph, are the "noble sounding canons of free liberal inquiry." I am glad he considers my book "amazingly good" within the genre of discursive practice, but I think the canons do not simply sound noble; they *are* noble. In the end, like quiet flowing water, they are capable of wearing even a stony status quo to sand.

Steven Lee, finally, raises the most detailed philosophical objections to positions I develop in the book. He takes me to task on issues in (1) epistemological and (2) ethical theory.

His epistemological objection concerns my treatment of "techno-scientific thinking" as a significant topic in its own right. He would prefer that I stick with the more traditional custom of talking about scientific thinking and technological practice, but that I not "confuse" the two. There is much virtue in such a custom, as I hope my fairly extended treatment of the deep contrasts between practical and theoretical intelligence will help to interpret. Indeed, later in the very passage Lee cites, I allow myself some rare italics when I warn that *"practical success is no guarantee of truth"* (pp. 51-52). This warning rests on the important logical point that Affirming the Consequent is a deductive fallacy even though, in inductive scientific confirmation-theory, it seems difficult to avoid. When scientific theories successfully predict, this (as Popper reminds us) is no logical guarantee of truth. The more they yield anticipated results, and the more they tie together in mutually supporting networks of theories and applications and coherent new extensions of range, the more epistemologically impressive they become.

The same point, but on a larger scale, can be made about the successes of the characteristic style of thinking in our modern age, which I call "techno-scientific." My reasons for this coinage are (a) to encourage readers to remember that modern scientific thought would be literally impossible without the technological instrumentation that makes scientific thought what it is today, and (b) to remind readers of the extent that technological objectives shape the direction—the interests, organization, and funding—and the very content of modern science itself. Describing this unique blending of practical purpose and high theory is, as Lee points out, one of the primary themes of my book.

Even when such thinking is capable of finding confirmations not only in specific experimental settings but also, even more impressively, in suggesting and supporting the great institutions of a civilization—economic, political, educational, etc.—we would logically still fall into the fallacy of Affirming the

Consequent, were we to say that any of this successful applying, networking, predicting, and extending shows that the fundamental notions of techno-scientific thinking are true. That was the point of the warning I italicized: that we should not be misled even by the impressive consequences of a mode of thought into supposing that such powers of application prove the truth of its categories.

To insist on this, however, as I do (with Lee), is not at all the same as to deny (as he does) my other view that "the proven capability of techno-scientific thought to create modern civilization is of profound epistemological importance." The epistemological importance of that capability is analogous to the epistemological importance of a scientific theory's capability of generating successful predictions. Inductively, such capabilities are of the utmost epistemic interest. What is it about these thoughts functioning in this world that makes them fruitful? What level of confidence dare we place in them?

Therefore, I remain unrepentant in having associated myself with Whitehead's observation that "the supreme verification of the speculative flight is that it issues in the establishment of a practical technique for well-attested ends, and that the speculative system maintains itself as the elucidation of that technique" (*Function of Reason,* p. 80). The need to keep the activities of science and technology, ends and means, distinct for the sake of philosophical analysis is one important phase in the process of philosophical understanding. But after that phase, we need to see how they mutually influence one another and how, combined, they shape a world of thought and practices.

Lee's other objection was to my ethical theory-sketch, in which he thinks I let the concept of Justice carry the entire deontological weight of ethical obligation in the theory proposed. The "goods" needing just distribution, on the other hand, he assumes I put into an exclusively consequentialist category. One of Lee's concerns is that too much, especially the rich language of "rights," is left out of ethical theory on my sketch. I am not quite convinced. True, it is only a sketch, but I shall not again plead the necessity of leaving things out. In this case, I deliberately tried to get away from the language of "rights," which I find often overemphasized and sometimes misleading in recent ethical literature. In its place I prefer to think about our duties to respect the valuable wherever found. This covers respect for other people (who can and often do demand that we obey our duties toward them, and such demanding is what I mean by "claiming rights"); but it also covers extended cases, e.g., animals (who have value for themselves and deserve our moral consideration, but who cannot themselves claim rights or be held responsible for obeying reciprocal duties toward us or one another). Such a set of obligations for enhancing good and not doing harm falls under the principles of Benevolence and Non-maleficence. Thus, if "rights" turn out to be analyzable as a certain subclass of obligations, i.e., obligations toward the sort of intrinsic goods who can speak up in their own defense, then the supposed need to make Justice carry the whole deontological weight disappears. Further, rights can be recognized as important but second-order ethical concepts. My theory, though bipolar, is not so binary as Lee thinks, then, since both duties and concern for good will be found within both poles.

Another of Lee's concerns—that conflicts within the consequentialist pole are more tractable than conflicts between what he takes to be the poles themselves—is therefore somewhat recast. It still is true, as he says, that "there is no metric" for the solution of moral conflicts, but this in my view is universally the case, not simply when Justice may clash with (say) Benevolence.

I hope that these rebuttals to Lee in no way suggest lack of appreciation for his challenging comments, and especially for his final plea that we appreciate the magnitude of the dilemmas posed by the historically novel powers of technology in our era. I do find it disappointing that, after all his thoughtful work on of my text, he premises his final criticism on what can only be a lapse of attention. He takes my discussion of nuclear weapons to task for allegedly omitting the goods of deterrence as against the injustice of putting millions of lives at risk. That is just what my discussion was about. I earlier identified "survival" as a basic good. Then I wrote: "Now 'survival' is sought through mutual deterrence in which, it is argued, unilateral abandonment of nuclear weapons would open the way to self-destruction" (p. 91). A little later, this is followed by: "The mind-numbing implications of atomic war for ecological and intergenerational justice are horrendous. Decisions made by members of our generation could irreversibly damage the biota on this precious planet for all time to come" (p. 92). I think the "tragic dilemmas" Lee was looking for, but somehow missed, are there. Indeed, my treatment extends the moral arena wider than his, to include not just the "millions of innocent persons" that he mentions but also the biosphere and future generations. It is a pity that Lee, whose views are closely allied with mine in many important respects, seemingly based his rather negative final assessment of my book at least in part on faulty reading.

—FREDERICK FERRÉ

Science, Technology, and Policy Decisions, Anne L. and Richard P. Hiskes. Boulder, CO: Westview Press, 1986. Pp. 198.

Despite the fact (or maybe because of it) that problems facing public policy making in the areas of science and technology are enormous, sustained philosophical reflection on these issues has been slow in developing. Philosophers have long thought about the *nature* of science and technology, but questions concerning what policies we should establish in the development and regulation of technological research and implementation have been neglected. Furthermore, books on these questions suitable for classroom use are even rarer. Thus, the volume from Anne Hiskes, a philosopher of science, and Richard Hiskes, a political theorist, is welcome.

The book has many strengths. It shows a commendable acquaintance with recent developments, not just in philosophy, but in many areas of technology. It treats a number of these areas but seeks to bring them together under a single general approach to decision making. It is quite readable, always an important consideration in a text, and it uses examples judiciously.

Moreover, the organization of the book is excellent. Chapter one discusses the relationship between science and technology, describing two views and arguing for one of them. Chapters two through eight consider seven different problem areas for policy making, including the relationship between science and government, energy, nuclear power, hazardous waste, telecommunications, recombinant DNA research, and biomedical technology. Chapter nine concludes with considerations designed to promote the development of coherent and comprehensive principles for policy formation. The authors clearly are troubled with the piecemeal casuistry that plagues current practice.

Despite these strengths, however, the book is also beset with puzzling difficulties. In my view these difficulties outweigh the book's strengths. I comment on three such problems: (1) the authors' view of science and technology, (2) the lack of coherent ethical considerations, and (3) disturbing oversimplifications of issues and views.

Science and Technology

According to the authors, there are two competing views concerning the nature of science and its relationship to technology. The first, which they call "logical empiricism," is characterized by the ideas that data obtained through careful observation and experimentation are objective, there is one universal logic for science, and through application of logic to data science makes gradual progress toward more complete and accurate theories. Science aims to discover laws and principles. Technology, on the other hand, aims not at understanding nature but at "manipulating and controlling nature for some practical purpose through the creation of a physical tool or device." (p. 10). Furthermore, according to the authors' description, logical empiricists construe the relationship between science and technology as an "assembly line" in which science (knowledge) is always logically prior to technology (application). On this view technology is always merely the application of principles already discovered and understood by science. Technology never comes prior to science.

The authors contrast the logical empiricist view with what they call "the new synthesis." By this they seem to mean some sort of relativistic instrumentalism. On the basis of this more "recent work by historically oriented philosophers of science and technology" (p. 21), they contend, we must discard logical empiricist views of science for an approach in which "scientific truth may then be viewed as equivalent to utility in a broad sense of the word: Scientific truth is what at the time is most useful in achieving the goals set for science" (p. 27). This new view has implications for our understanding of the relationship between science and society.

> Consequently, one would expect changing norms and values of the scientific community to bear some correlation to changing religious, political, and economic values of the surrounding community. Furthermore, if transcendent, objective knowledge in science is just a delusion—because in the final analysis such knowledge can be reduced to some form of utility—then it is no longer imperative to isolate science from the influence of society at all costs (p. 27).

Now there are several disturbing features of all this. First, this is an amazingly simplistic account of how things stand in current philosophy of science. For one thing, scientific realism is not quite so out of philosophical fashion as the authors would lead us to believe. Indeed, some philosophers of science contend that realism is the dominant view. But even if that claim is exaggerated, surely realism is not merely the quaint relic of our overly optimistic past views of scientific practice. Indeed, lumping all realistic views of science under the name of logical empiricism belies the authors' misunderstanding of the current forms of the view.

This leads us to a second point. Undoubtedly the authors have presented us with a transparent false dilemma. According to them, if we accept scientific realism, then we are committed to the view that science proceeds gradually and smoothly by discovering objective facts and applying universal principles, that technology is simply an application of scientific knowledge, and that external features of how science is pursued—funding decisions, moral accountability for how the results of research are used, and the like—ought to be separated from social considerations as much as possible. After all, according to this view, no one knows what practical applications science will have. Therefore we ought to allow research to go on basically unfettered by social constraints. If, on the other hand, we accept an instrumentalist view in which science aims not at knowledge but at some sort of utility, we can avoid the objectionable conclusions concerning the relationship of science to both technology and society.

Surely a scientific realist need not accept the view that science is always logically prior to technology, nor need she concede that science and society ought to be kept separate (in the sense described above) as much as possible.

In fact, she need not claim that science always proceeds gradually and smoothly. Many realists have accepted these views, of course, but my point is that they *need* not accept them. In other words, the authors provide an account of our options here that is oversimplified to the point of serious distortion. I could overlook this problem, however, if it were unrelated to the discussion of the remainder of the book. But it is not unrelated. According to the authors, how one proceeds on policy matters will be greatly influenced, perhaps even determined, by one's view of science and technology. If we've got a hopelessly confused picture of our options on what science is, and if policy decisions are dependent on this picture, it is hard to see how the authors' discussion of policy matters is going to be helpful. Actually, their subsequent discussion is better than this first chapter portends; this suggests that perhaps the relationship between one's philosophy of science and one's policy views are not quite so close as the authors contend.

One additional matter deserves comment here. One of the virtues of a realist understanding of science is that it permits a rather plausible understanding of the difference between the goals of science and the goals of technology. Hiskes and Hiskes themselves note that a realist is likely to see technology as a practical activity that aims to control or manipulate nature through creating some tool or device. Then, the distinction between science and technology is apparent in theory if not always in practice: science aims at understanding, technology aims at control and production.

A scientific instrumentlaist, however, sees science, too, as aiming at control and production because on that view knowledge is reduced to utility. Thus, on the authors' view of science, one plausible way to distinguish between the respective goals of science and technology is lost. Now if the authors provided us with some other way to draw the distinction, this would not be a problem. But they provide nothing of the sort. Consequently, either they deny the distinction, or they think it not worthy of explanation, or they have no explanation. In any case their understanding of just what technology is, and its relationship to science, is left thoroughly murky. Somehow, for a book on science and technology I find that troublesome.

To be fair, Hiskes and Hiskes may have a response here. Perhaps they would say that science does aim at knowledge and technology at application, but that knowledge must be seen as sort of utility and not as mere understanding of an independent reality. Whether this works remains to be seen. In any case, we get no explanation of this sort (or any other sort) in the book.

Ethical Considerations

In most of the book the discussion is long on empirical matters pertaining to the problems at issue and short on ethical considerations needed to address the problems adequately. This need not be troublesome in a text; after all, the instructor needs *something* to do. However, the failure runs deeper, for an apparent inconsistency arises between the final chapter, in which ethical considerations are emphasized, and chapter four, in which ethical considerations are minimized. Perhaps this inconsistency is inevitable in a jointly authored book, but I think it does display a deep ambivalence (or disagreement?) on the role of morality and public participation in the relationship between science and society. Let me explain.

In the final chapter the authors argue for the importance of ethical and political considerations in science and technology policy making. In explanation and defense of the risk-cost-benefit analysis method of decision making, the authors claim that values enter into decision making at several places. Indeed, they assert, risk-cost-benefit analysis can and must include considerations of value and not just "objective knowledge that is value-neutral" (p. 170). Furthermore, "the modern policy maker can resolve the problems that he or she faces only by taking a stand on some of the most fundamental issues of ethics or political theory (p. 164).

However, Hiskes and Hiskes themselves take no such stance. After a brief and unsatisfactory consideration of utilitarianism and what they call "absolutism," they politely decline to become involved in the debate.

> Obviously the debate between utilitarians and absolutists cannot be resolved here; in the context of public policy, each side has some merit. According to a middle position, policy makers should be sure that their approach incorporates ethical concerns and does not equate ethics with mere practicality (p. 181).

Even this wishy-washy "position" is too strong; the authors quickly proceed to qualify it.

Now, if ethical and political values are essential to arrive at equitable policy, then one would think that citizens from a wide spectrum of society ought to participate in the policy making process. After all, that seems to be the only way for the interests of each to be given adequate voice. Even though scientists are the alleged "experts" here, their views should not be given undue weight, although the fact that their views are presumably well informed will lend some authority to their opinions. This is the authors' real concern in this chapter.

> In a democratic society, the interests of each member deserve consideration on matters of public importance: This is a "given." The job of democratic institutions is to ensure that the interests of all people are justly considered. For these reasons, U.S. citizens have a right to be heard on matters of science and technology policy, and the professional interests of government policy makers should be to listen carefully (p. 183).

This seems to suggest that public opinion, say, against nuclear power is not merely a nuisance that grudgingly must be considered, but rather is an essential part of a fair decision procedure. Scientific opinion is not the only opinion that counts. Even if all physicists agree that nuclear power is safe (which of course they don't), if the public is opposed to the construction of new nuclear power plants, Hiskes and Hiskes seem to suggest, it may be that we ought not build new nuclear facilities. The message of this chapter is that public opinion ought to be taken seriously as a necessary aspect of good policy making, and that to see it as interfering with the progress of science and technology it to misunderstand how a democratic society does and ought to work.

Chapter four, however, takes quite a different view of the matter. Although we get no direct pronouncements, the message of this chapter seems to be that public misinformation and irrational fear often gets in the way of technological progress and otherwise good policy. For example, although "many policy questions may appear to rely largely on scientific or technical factors, the public often does not view them that way" (p. 71). In the Midland (Michigan) nuclear power plant case, the authors tell us that the initial court judgment against building the plant was a result of the District of Columbia Circuit Court of Appeals' "historic sympathy toward antinuclear intervenors" (p. 73), despite the fact that popular opinion in Michigan at the time was solidly against construction. The 1971 Calvert Cliffs decision "*imposed* on the industry the responsibility of providing expensive environmental impact statements with every licensing application to the AEC" (p. 79, emphasis mine). The use of the word *imposed* here is not accidental; it is used again in discussing the same decision on page 83.

Furthermore, the authors reluctantly admit that public opposition to nuclear plants has been successful. But "a negative aspect of this success has been the decline of the nuclear industry," and advocacy groups have "damaged the nuclear industry and therefore threatened long-term policy" (p. 87). The authors' pronuclear bias shows most strongly in their account of the atom bombs the United States used in World War II. According to them, the Manhattan project "won the war" (p. 75).

Now even though I do *not* share the authors' view that the decline of the nuclear industry is regrettable, there is a more important issue here. In this chapter Hiskes and Hiskes build a case (albeit a weak one) for the view that, on nuclear policy at least, the success of public opinion has resulted in poor policy! They seem to be saying that if we had just allowed the scientists to decide the issue instead of permitting ignorant average citizens to have their say, we would now have abundant and cheap nuclear energy, and our energy future would be secure. This obviously contradicts the view of chapter nine, in which citizen participation is seen as good even if it results in abandoning a technology.

Oversimplifications

The third major weakness of the book is its abundance of oversimplifications. By themselves none of these is a major defect, but the cumulative effect causes a great deal of irritation for the careful reader. If I used the book in the classroom, I would feel obligated to spend too much time correcting these mistakes.

For example, the authors display an incredibly naive view of Medieval philosophy. "During the Middle Ages all scholars, of whom Thomas Aquinas is a representative example, organized their world according to the ancient Greek philosophy of Aristotle" (p. 22). In addition, on the same page we are treated to this description of the "Scientific Revolution": "Authority and dogma were being challenged on all fronts as people came to see freedom of belief as an important value."

Intellectual history is not the only thing that gets dealt with in such a cavalier fashion. The authors describe Utilitarianism as the recommendation to "maximize the expected utility" and seek "the greatest good for the greatest number" (p. 180). Even Rawls receives his fair share of over-simplification; the authors describe his maximin rule as advocating that "the best policy option is the one associated with the least possible harm" (p. 182).

I could list more examples, but I won't. To put it simply, there are just too many minor slip-ups, and such sloppiness only encourages similar sloppiness in students. Undergraduates do not need such encouragement.

Conclusion

Even though I would like to recommend this book, and although as I've noted it is not without its strengths, in my view the book has more vices than virtues, and some of the vices constitute serious problems. Since some of these problems are significant misrepresentations of issues and positions, and since these are the sorts of mistakes I wouldn't want my students to make, I would have serious reservations about using it in the classroom.

—David C. Snyder
Department of Philosophy
Calvin College

ERRATA FOR VOLUME 9

COSMOS HELPS THOSE WHO HELP THEMSELVES: HISTORICAL PATTERNS OF
TECHNOLOGICAL FULFILLMENT, AND THEIR APPLICABILITY TO THE HUMAN
DEVELOPMENT OF SPACE
By Paul Levinson

Page 92, third paragraph, second sentence should read: "Contrary to recent critiques of technology
that warn of their autonomy and domination of us, technologies need to be constantly
reworked and revitalized if they are to achieve our designs.[1]"

Page 92, third paragraph, third and fourth sentences should read: "Technological designs are
vulnerable throughout their development and implementation to human decisions—or lack
of decisions—that may scotch or misdirect their application. Thus, the history of human
technology on Earth is by no means a clear, uninterrupted vector of continuing progress:

Page 95, last paragraph, first line: "look" should be "loom."

Page 96, last paragraph, second line: "stimulates" should be "simulate."

Page 99, fifth paragraph, first line: "conforming" should be "comforting."

Research in Philosophy and Technology

Edited by **Frederick Ferre,** *Department of Philosophy, University of Georgia.* European Editor: **Walter Ch. Zimmerli,** *Technische Universitat Braunschweig.* Review Editor: **Leonard J. Waks,** *Pennsylvania State University*

Volume 1, 1978, 390 pp. $63.50
ISBN 0-89232-022-2

REVIEWS: "...Reflecting a sudden burst of interest in this subject over the past decade, the essays attempt to answer the question 'What would constitute an adequate philosophy of technology?'...the collection offers an introduction to the subject that will be useful to specialists and nonspecialists alike."

—Science

"...a series which has been overdue and is bound to be a significant factor in the development of this field".

—Dialogue

Volume 2, 1979, 403 pp. $63.50
ISBN 0-89232-101-6

REVIEW: "All serious readers of *Technology* and *Culture* will find this volume of Research in Philosophy and Technology, like its predecessor, useful reading and resource material. In sum, this is a sort of reference book rather than the sort of work one might expect to read straight through. It is meant for chewing, bit by bit, rather than swallowing in a gulp. It's readers, I am sure, will find it meaty and nourishing."

—Technology and Culture

Determinism in a Technological Setting, *Albert Borgmann, University of Montana.* The Normative Side of Technology: Philosophy and the Public Interest, *Edmund Byrne, Indiana University—Indianapolis.* Art in a Technological Society, *Phillip R. Fandozzi, University of Montana.* Marx, Machinery, and Alienation, *Bernard Gendron, University of Wisconsin— Milwaukee, and Nancy Holmstrom, University of Wisconsin—Madison.* Technological Culture and the End of Philosophy, *Michael Zimmerman, Tulane University.* Comment of Zimmerman's "Technological Culture and the End of Philosophy", *Robert E. McGinn, Stanford University.* Reply to McGinn, *Michael Zimmerman, Tulane University.* Part III: Historico Philisophical Studies. The Concepts of Nature and Technique According to the Greeks, *Wolfgang Schwadewaldt, University of Tuebingen.* On the Nature of Nature, *Jacob Klein, St. John's College—Annapolis.* Documentation: Analyses of Machines in the French Intellectual Tradition (Espinas, Lafitte, Weil), *Edited by Carl Mitcham, St. Catherine College.* On the Antagonism Between Philosophy and Technology in Germany and Austria, *Werner Koenne, Austrian Elektrizitat Wirtschafts-Aktiengellschaft, Vienna.* Heldegger and Marcuse: Technology as Ideology, *Michael Zimmerman, Tulane University.* Part IV: Review and Bibliography. Philosophy of Technology and the Verein Deutcher Ingenieure, *Alios Huning, Wulfrath, Germany.* Philosophy of Technology in France in the Twentieth Century: Overview and Current Bibliography, *Jean-Claude Beaune, University of Clermont.* Symposium: Hendrik van Relssen and Dutch Neo-Clavinist Philosophy of Technology, *Edited and Translated by Donald Morton, Free University, Amsterdam.* Technology Assessment: A New Type of Science?, *Frederick A. Rossini, Georgia Institute of Technology.* Technology Assessment: Supplementary Bibliography, *Carl Mitcham and Jim Grote, St. Catherine College.* Kenneth Sayre on Information Theoric Models of Mind, *K.S. Schrader-Frechette, University of Louisville.* Appendix: Author Index to Current Bibliography in the Philosophy of Technology: 1973-1974. Research in Philosophy and Technology, Volume One, *Carl Mitcham and Jim Grote, St. Catherine College.*

Volume 3, 1980, 412 pp. $63.50
ISBN 0-89232-102-4

CONTENTS: Introduction, *Paul T. Durbin.* Part I: Selected Symposia from Second University of Delaware Philosophy and Technology Conference, June 1977. Symposium on the Citizen and Technological Decision Making: Public Interest: Rights for What? Responsibilities to Whom?, *Thomas Conry, Center for Science in the Public Interest.* Which Interest are Public Interests?, *Sandra Harding, University of Delaware.* A Reconsideration of the Idea of a Science Court, *Alex C. Michalos, University of Guelph.* Against Feyerabend: The Meaning of Progess in Science, *Michale Goldman, Miami University, Ohio.* Symposium on Ethics and Biomedical Research, Policy, and Philosophy, *George J. Agich, Southern Illinois School of Medicine.* Technological Innovation and Health Planning Policy, *Ronald E. Benson, Ohio Northern University.* Cultural Issues in Medical Research, *David C. Thomasma, University of Tennessee Center for the Health Sciences.* Symposium: Reviews of Recent Books in Philosophy of Technology and Medicine, With Authors' Replies: Review of Technology and the Human Condition, *Bernard Gendron, Paul T. Durbin, University of Delaware and Michael Goldman, Miami University, Ohio.* Reply: Growth, Power, and the Imperatives of Technology, *Bernard Gendron, University of Wisconsin—Milwaukee.* Review of Autonomous Technology, *by Langdon Winner, Stanley R. Carpenter, Georgia Institute of Technology.* A Response to Stanley Carpenter's Review, *Langdon Winner, Massachusetts Institute of Technology.* Philosophy and Medicine: Some Reflections on a Critical Assessment by Caroline Whitbeck, *H. Tristram Engelahrdt, Jr., Georgetown University.* Part II: Other Conference Papers, 1978-1979. The Metaphysics of Paolo Soleri, *Henryk Skolimowski, University of Michigan.* Skolimowski on Soleri, *Willis H. Turitt, University of South Florida.* Part III: Symposium on Jacques Ellul. The Sociology of Jacques Ellul, *Katherine Temple, Catholic Worker, N.Y.* The Absolute Dialects of Jacques Ellul, *John Boli-Bennett, Stanford University.* Technology as the Sacred Order, *David Lovekin, Sauk Valley College, Illinois.* From the Technical Phenomenon to the Technical System, *Daniel Cerezuelle, Universityi of Grrenoble.* Nature, Technique, and Artificiality, *Jacques Ellul,*

University of Bordeaux. **Part IV: Symposium, on Crises in Technological Praxis. Should Montana Share Its Coal? Technology and Public Policy,** Albert Borgmann, University of Montana. **Technology, Public Policy, and the Price-Anderson Act,** K.S. Shradder-Frechette, University of Louisville. **Adams, Inhaber, and Risk Benefit Analysis: Ethical and Methodological Problems wtih Two Recent Assessments of Nuclear Safety,** K.S. Shrader-Frechette, University of Louisville. **The Relation of Moral and Strategic Arguments in the Defense Debate,** J. Byran Hehir, Office of International Justice and Peace, U.S. Catholic Conference. **Appropriate Technology: Fact and Values, J. Van Brakel, Delft University.**

Volume 4, 1981, 305 pp. $63.50
ISBN 0-89232-181-4

CONTENTS: Preface. Current Bibliography in the Philosophy of Technology: 1975-1976, Carl Mitcham with the assistance of Jim Grote. **Introduction. Analytic Table of Contents, I. Primary Sources, II. Selected Supplementary Sources. Author Index. Appendix: Author Index for Bibliography of the Philosophy of Technology. 1973.**

Volume 5, 1982, 339 pp. $63.50
ISBN 0-89232-322-1

CONTENTS: Part I: Miscellaneous Papers: Art in a Technological Setting, Phillip Fandozzi, University of Montana. **The Idea of Progress and the Politics of Technology,** Andrew Feenberg, Western Behavioral Sciences Institute. **Technology, Democracyy, and the Work Place,** Bernard Gendron, University of Wisconsin-Milwaukee. **Comment:** John P. Burke, University of Washington. **Language, Politics, and Technology,** Hwa Yol Jung, Moravian College. **Artifacts, Politics, and Imagination,** David Lovekin, Sauk Valley College. **Concern About Responsibility in Applying Science,** Egbert Schuurman, Amsterdam and Delft, Holland. **The Relationship of Technology to Engineering,** George Sinclair and W.V. Tilston, Sinclair Radio Labs and Til-Tek, Canada. **Part II: Symposis: Critiques of Technology Assessment, Law as Technology Assessment,** Edmund Byrne, Indiana University at Indianapolis. **Environmental Impact Analysis, Technology Assessment, and the Problem of Geographical Equity,** Kristin Shrader-Frechette, University of California at Santa Barbara. **A New Social Philosophy as Technology Assessment,** Henryk Skolimowski, University of Michigan. **Comments on the Philosophy of Technology of Hans Jonas. Comments on Hans Jonas: Philosophical Aspects of Technology,** Marx W. Wartofsky, Boston University. **Commentary on Hans Jonas, Technology, and Ethnics,** Ronald Bruzina, University of Kentucky. **Part III: Historico-Philosophical Studies. Art and Architecture, Ancient and Modern,** Ronald Bruzina, University of Kentucky. **Dewey and Technology,** Webster F. Hood, Central Washington U. **Ernst Casier's Theory of Technology,** John M. Krois, University of Trier, Germany. **The Frankfurt School Critique of Technology,** Patrick Murray, Creighton University. **Marx, The Primacy Thesis, and Technological Determinism,** Kai Nielsen, Calgary, Canada. **Dialects and the Primacy of Human Labor Power,** Willis Truitt, University of South Florida. **Friedrich Dessauer as Philosopher of Technology: Notes on His Dialogue with Jaspers and Heldegger,** Klaus Tuchel, late of University of Tubingen. **Technology and the Ship of Fools,** Donald P. Verene, Pennsylvania State University. **Part IV: Bibliography: Anotated Bibliography on Professional Ethics of Scientists,** Albert Flores and Denise Taber, RPI. **Technology as a Subject of Research in Poland; Selected Bibliography,** Lech Zacher, Polish Academy of Sciences.

Volume 6, 1983, 282 pp. $63.50
ISBN 0-89232-352-3

CONTENTS: Part I: Symposium on Appropriate Technology, Introduction: What Makes a Technology Appropriate? C. Thomas Rogers and Robert Taylor, Montana College of Mineral Science and Technology. **The Good Life and Appropriate Technology,** Albert Borgmann,

University of Montana. **A Positive Case for Appropriate Technology,** *Stanley R. Carpenter, Georgia Tech.* **Appropriate? Inappropriate?-What's the Difference?,** *Phillip R. Fandozzi, University of Montana.* **Decentralization: It's Meaning in Politics and Material Culture,** *Langdon Winner, California at Santa Cruz.* **Part II: Miscellaneous Papers. Technology as Both Art and Science,** *Joseph Agassi, York University and Tel Aviv.* **Alternative Technology and the Norm of Efficiency,** *Stanley R. Carpenter, Georgia Tech.* **Art and Imagination in Technological Society,** *Alan R. Drengson, University of Victoria.* **Tedeusz Kotarbinski's Methodology of the Practical Sciences and Its Influence,** *Wojciech Gasparski, Polish Academy of Science.* **Technology, Utopia and Dystopia,** *Don Ihde, SUNY, Stony Brook.* **The Iron Cage, Single Vision, and Newton's Sleep,** *George B. Kleindorfer and James E. Martin, Pennsylvania State.* **Values and Technology: How to Introduce Ethical and Human Values into Public Policy Decisions,** *Earl R. MacCormac, Davidson.* **Humanism, Ontology, and the Nuclear Arms Race,** *Michael E. Zimmerman, Newcomb/Tulane.* **Part III: Historico-Philosophical Studies. Symposium on Religion and the Rise of Technology: Concerning the Religious Origins of Technological Civilization,** *Daniel Cerezuelle, Bordeaux.* **Doubts Concerning the Religious Origins of Technological Civilization,** *Katherine Temple, Catholic Worker, New York City.* **A Jewish Commentary on the Religious Origins of Technological Civilization,** *Mark Swetiliz, Jewish Theological Seminary, New York City.* **A Philosophical-Anthropological Perspective on Technology,** *Arnold Gehlen, late of Technischen Hochschule, Aachen.* **Leibniz and Technology,** *Frederick C. Kreiling, Polytechnic Institute of New York.* **Part IV: Review and Bibliography. Technological and Humanism: A Review Essay on Edward G. Ballard's Man and Technology (1978),** *Ian H. Angus, Simon Fraser University.* **Current Bibliography in the Philosophy of Technology, 1977-1978,** *Carl Mitcham, Polytechnic Institute of New York, with assistance of Jim Grote.* **Appendix: Author Index.**

Supplement 1 - Jacques Ellul: A Comprehensive Bibliography
1984, 301 pp. $63.50
ISBN 0-89232-478-3

Edited by **Joyce Main Hanks,** *University of Costa Rica* and **Rolf Asai,** *University of Freiburgh.*

CONTENTS: Introduction and Acknowledgements. Jacques Ellul: A Comprehensive Bibliography. PART I. WORKS BY ELLUL; Published Books, Articles, Reviews, Letters and Interviews. Title Index. Select Subject Index. PART II: WORKS ON ELLUL; Reviews of Ellul's Books. Interviews with Ellul. Dissertation. Books, Articles, and Notices. Author Index. Select Subject Index.

Volume 7, 1984, 304 pp. $63.50
ISBN 0-89232-505-4

CONTENTS: List of Contributors. Preface and Acknowledgements. Introduction: Conflicting Interpretations of Technology and Society, *Paul T. Durbin.* **PART I: TECHNOLOGY PRO AND CON. Section A. Pro-Technology Views. Plumbers, Technologists and Scientists,** *Jose Felix Tobar Arbulu, McGill University.* **Can Science and Technology Be Held Responsible for our Current Social Ills?,** *Mario Bunge, McGill University.* **Toward a Pragmatic Social Philosophy of Technology and the Technological Intelligentsia,** *Hans Lenk, University of Karisruhe.* **Technology as Evil; Fear of Lamentation?,** *Emmanuel G. Mesthene, Rutgers University.* **Section B. Antitechnology Views. The Latest Develolpments in Technology and the Philosophy of the Absurd,** *Jacques Ellul, University of Bordeaux.* **Technological Desire,** *Donald Phillip Verene, Emery University.* **PART II: MEDICATING THE DISPUTE. The Techne of Philosophy and the Philosophy of Technology,** *Steven L. Goldman, Lehigh University.* **Three Conceptions of Technology: Satanic, Titanic, and Human,** *Joseph Margolis, Temple University.* **The Chances of Alternative Science and Technology,** *Friedrich Rapp, Technical University, Berlin.* **Good**

Science-Bad Science or Dr. Frankenstein's Dilemma, *Marx W. Wartofsky, Baruch College of the City University of New York.* **PART III: TECHNOLOGY AND POLITICS.** Political Philosophy and Its Implications for Technology, *Albert Borgmann, University of Montana.* Liberalisms Ambiguous Legacy: Individuality and Technological Constraints, *Morton Schoolman, State University of New York at Albany.* **PART IV. CONCRETE ISSUES: FEMINISM, THE THIRD WORLD, AND THE COMPUTER REVOLUTION.** Reproductive Technology and the Future of Women: A Feminist Perspective, *Azizah al-Hibri, University of Pennsylvania.* A Way Out in a No-Exit Situation? *Jacques Ellul on Technique and the Third World, Joyce M. Hanks, Universitiy of Costa Rica.* **Myth Information: Romantic Politics in the Computer Revolution,** *Langdon Winner, University of California at Santa Cruz.*

Volume 8, 1985, 280 pp. $63.50
ISBN 0-89232-593-3

CONTENTS: List of Contributors. Acknowledgement. PART I. PROCEEDINGS, SECOND INTERNATIONAL PHILOSOPHY AND TECHNOLOGY CONFERENCE (NEW YORK, 1983). Introduction, *Carl Mitcham and Alois Hunting, University of Dusseldorf, Polytechnic Institute of New York.* **SECTION A. Theoretical Issues. Homo Mensura: Human Beings are Their Technology-Technology is Human,** *Alois Hunting, University of Dusseldorf.* **Technology and Cultural Variations,** *Don Ihde, State University of New York at Stony Brook.* **SECTION B. Practical Issues. Democracy and Reindustrialization: The Politics of Technology in New York State,** *Michael Black and Richard Worthington, Rensselear Polytechnic Institute, State University of New York at Plattsburgh.* **Scale in Technology: A Critique of Design Assumptions,** *Stanley R. Carpenter, Georgia Institute of Technology.* **The Ethical End-Use Problem in Engineering,** *C. Thomas Rogers, Montana College of Mineral Science and Technology.* **Technology Assessment, Expert Disagreement, and Democratic Procedures,** *Kristin Shrader-Frechette, University of Florida.* **PART II. MISCELLANEOUS PAPERS. Utopia Without Work? Myth, Machines and Public Policy,** *Edmund E. Byrne, Indiana University, Indianapolis.* **The Effects of Traditional Eskimo Patterns of Cognition and on the Acceptance or Rejection of Technological Innovation,** *George M. Guilmet, University of Puget Sound.* **Technology as the Cutting Edge of Cosmic Evolution,** *Fairleigh Dickinson University.* **Hazardous Technologies: How are the Hazards Measured?,** *Helen Longino, Mills College.* **The Plutonium Economy: Technological Links and Epistemological Problems,** *Kristen Shrader-Frechette, University of Florida.* **PART III. REVIEWS. Review: Microelectronic Skepticism,** *J. Merrill Smith, Falmouth, Maine.* **Review Essay: "No Nukes" is Not Enough,** *Katherine Temple Catholic Worker, New York, New York.* **PART IV. A SURVEY AND BIBLIOGRAPHIES ON ETHICS IN ENGINEERING AND COMPUTER SCIENCE. Ethics in Engineering Curricula,** *Vivian Weil, Illinois Institute of Technology.* **Industrial and Engineering Ethics: Introductory Notes and Annotated Bibliography,** *Carl Mitcham, Polytechnic Institute of New York.* **Computer Ethos, Computer Ethics,** *Carl Mitcham, Polytechnic Institute of New York.*

Supplement 2 - Mind at Large: Knowing in the Technological Age
1988, 271 pp. $63.50
ISBN 0-892342-816-9

by **Paul Levinson,** *Fairleigh Dickinson University*

Contents: Series Editor's Introduction, *Frederick Ferre.* **Preface,** *Paul Levinson.* **Acknowledgments. Mind as a Product of Evolution. Rationality and Evolution. Fallibilism and Optimism. Technology as the Embodiment of Human Ideas and the Unnoticed Philosophic Revolution. Technology as an Agent of Cognitive Evolution. The Double Entrndre of Communications Media. Socratic Technology: Media as Mirrors of the Mind. Technology and Globalization of Intellectual Circles. Technology and the Evolution of the Cosmos. Bibliography. Biographical Sketch of the Author. Index.**

Approach, *Gabriel Vahanian, University of Strasbourg.* **Technology and the Richness of the World,** *Robert Cummings Neville, Boston University.* **Technology: Our Contemporary Snake,** *David E. Schrader, Austin College.* **Temptations of Design: A Meditation on Practices,** *Martin H. Krieger, University of Southern California.* **Colloquium Section. Humanae Vitae and the Current Instruction on the Origins of Human Life,** *Jane Mary Trau, Barry University.* **On Reenchanting the World,** *John F. Post, Vanderbuilt University.* **Technology, Nature, and Miracle,** *Frederick Ferre, University of Georgia.* **Reply to Ferre, Comment on Trau,** *John F. Post, Vanderbuilt University.* **God-Talk, Physicalism, and Technology: A Mutual Endeavor,** *Jane Mary Trau, Barry University.* **Contemporary Discussion Section. The Myths of Thomas Szzasz,** *Michael J. Carella, San Diego State University.* **Communities of Celebration -- Technology and Public Life,** *Albert Borgmann, University of Montana.* **Book Review Section. Theology and Technology: Essays in Christian Analysis and Exegesis,** *Carl Mitcham and Jim Grote, eds.* **Reviews by:** *Friedrich Rapp, University of Dortmund, David A. Hoekema, University of Delaware, and James F. Salmon, Society of Jesus.* **Response,** *Carl Mitcham, Polytechnic University and Jim Grote, St. Vincent de Paul Society.* **Philosophy of Technology, Frederick Ferre, University of Georgia.* **Reviews by:** *Thomas Rogers, California Polytechnic State University, Charles Dyke, Temple University, and Steven Lee, Hobart and William Smith Colleges.* **Reply to Reviewers,** *Frederick Ferre, University of Georgia.* **Science, Technology, and Policy Decisions,** *Anne L. and Richard P. Hiskes.* **Review by** *David C. Snyder, Calvin College.*

Volume 11, In preparation, Fall 1990
ISBN 1-55938-210-4

Approx. $63.50

JAI PRESS INC.
55 Old Post Road - No. 2
P.O. Box 1678
Greenwich, Connecticut 06836-1678
Tel: 203-661-7602